A
SHORT HISTORY OF
GREEK LITERATURE

A
SHORT HISTORY OF
GREEK LITERATURE

Jacqueline de Romilly

Translated by Lillian Doherty

THE UNIVERSITY OF CHICAGO PRESS
Chicago and London

JACQUELINE DE ROMILLY, professor at the Collège de France until her retirement in 1984, has published numerous works of classical scholarship. Two have already appeared in English: *Thucydides and Athenian Imperialism* (1963) and *The Rise and Fall of States According to Greek Authors* (1977).
The present work was first published in Paris under the title *Précis de littérature grecque,* © Presses Universitaires de France, 1980.

This translation was supported in
part by a generous grant from the
French Ministry of Cultural and Foreign Affairs.

THE UNIVERSITY OF CHICAGO PRESS, CHICAGO 60637
THE UNIVERSITY OF CHICAGO PRESS, LTD., LONDON
© 1985 by The University of Chicago
All rights reserved. Published 1985
Printed in the United States of America

94 93 92 91 90 89 88 87 86 85   5 4 3 2 1

LIBRARY OF CONGRESS CATALOGING IN PUBLICATION DATA
Romilly, Jacqueline de.
A short history of Greek literature.

Translation of: Précis de littérature grecque.
Bibliography: p.
Includes index.
1. Greek literature—History and criticism.
I. Title.
PA3055.R6513 1985   880'.9   84-16457
ISBN 0-226-14311-2
ISBN 0-226-14312-0 (pbk.)

Contents

Translator's Note

In a few places, this translation diverges considerably from the French text of 1980. This is due in most cases to the correction of *errata*, all of which have been checked by the author. In response to some queries of mine, Madame de Romilly has also suggested slight changes in wording, and at one point (p. 154 of the present edition) has expanded a passage for greater clarity.

In rendering translations from the Greek, I have tried to be faithful to Madame de Romilly's understanding of each passage, but have also consulted the original Greek. In a very few places (indicated in the notes) I have used existing English translations I did not think I could improve on. The bibliography has been completely revised with the needs of an English-speaking audience in mind.

I owe deep thanks to Madame de Romilly for her careful responses to my queries; to Mr. Arthur Adkins for many improvements in the translation; and to Mr. Richard Garner, Mr. Adkins, and Mr. Jeno Platthy (of the Center for Hellenic Studies) for important additions to the bibliography.

LILLIAN DOHERTY

Preface

To write about Greek literature in the hope of helping others know it better is a pleasant task indeed. To do so concisely, however, is a harsh assignment, demanding a series of difficult and even arbitrary choices.

First, with respect to chronology, I felt I ought to trace the whole history of Greek literature in order to give the reader a synoptic view of that extraordinary flowering in all its diversity, over the course of more than ten centuries (from the eighth century before Christ to the fourth century after, without touching on the Byzantine era). This could be done only by abridging the account of the final periods and making do with a brief overview of the Christian literature, which follows different canons and is rooted in different traditions. For the latter, the limited information offered will be just enough to let the reader see the various forms of Greek literature in their proper relations to one another.

Instead of giving each period equal consideration, then, I have put the greatest emphasis on the classical centuries and, within those centuries, on the authors destined to have the widest influence on the literatures of the future. I have done so in the expectation that these authors will continue to hold a place of honor in the curriculum, so that the information offered here will prove useful to students at various levels. In the same perspective, I deliberately abandoned the idea of including in my "short history" a summary of the issues outlined in Albin Lesky's excellent *History of Greek Literature*, which is available in German, English, and Italian and is frequently revised and updated.[1] I preferred to limit myself to the most firmly established facts, of which one cannot afford to be ignorant. By the same token, I avoided offering personal opinions, which might have been open to debate. A short history of this kind must aim at the greatest possible objectivity.

Naturally I have tried to give the work a historical direction. The historical spirit is that of our own age, distinguishing it from the age that produced, for example, the Croisets' fine *History of Greek Literature*, published in Par-

1. The first German edition dates from 1957–58, the first English edition from 1966; revisions are made in each successive edition.

is, in five volumes, at the end of the last century. Today any moral or aesthetic judgment would seem old-fashioned. This is not to say that I have systematically avoided assessments based on literary criticism. After all, whatever the importance of historical perspective, Greek literature is much more than a mere cultural phenomenon: both the beauty of the works and their meaning can speak forcefully to each one of us, as they have to others for centuries. I hope to have fostered this meeting of minds, which an understanding of the historical circumstances and the internal development of Greek literature can only enhance.

In trying to give the reader a sense of this internal development I encountered problems of organization. Although I resolved these as best I could, the flaws inherent in my solutions cannot be glossed over.

The overall organization was not a problem: the rhythm according to which Greek literature unfolds is that of history—a history that falls into well-marked phases. It begins with the Homeric epic, which preserves traditions reaching back to the Trojan War and the Mycenaean period, that is, to the twelfth century B.C. But in Homer's day the Greek world had already been transformed by the arrival of the Dorians and the recent migrations to Asia Minor. The archaic age of the seventh and sixth centuries is thus an age of new beginnings: lyric poetry unfolds and develops, and philosophy makes its appearance, along with the first prose works. Next, extending from the Greek victory (largely an Athenian victory) in the Persian Wars to the defeat of Athens, and of Greece as a whole, at the hands of Philip of Macedonia— from 480 to 338 B.C.—are the two great Athenian centuries. The century of glory, the "Periclean" age of the fifth century, is followed by the age of reflection—that of Plato—in the fourth. The fifth century saw Athens at the height of her power, but her defeat in 404 ruined and disillusioned her. Philip and Alexander completed her subjugation. With the death of Alexander an entirely new period opens, with new centers, new genres, and new tastes; Alexandria is its great capital. Finally, in the period of Roman supremacy, Greece and its literature entered the orbit of Rome. At the same time, the bursting through of old boundaries made possible the development of new centers of learning throughout Asia Minor and later around Byzantium. Nothing could be clearer than these major lines of development, imposed by shifts of political power. The reader will note, however, that following my decision to emphasize the classical period I have devoted three chapters each to the fifth and fourth centuries, while the other major periods are covered in single chapters.

Clear as the outlines were, problems arose over the division of material in the central chapters and the order of these chapters, not to mention the details of presentation. The chapters covering single centuries could not be organized in strict chronological order. Works follow one another thick and fast: tragedies, comedies, philosophical treatises, historical works take shape simultaneously. Parallel developments can be traced, from year to year, in different genres. Chronologically, the influence of the Sophists should fall between Sophocles and Euripides, as between Herodotus and Thucydides. But how are we to separate two poets so close and so comparable to one another? A logical order would permit us to follow the internal history of a genre. Yet the order I have adopted is neither chronological nor strictly "logical." It seemed more to the point to begin with a joint discussion of the two authors who were most clearly influenced by the Persian Wars, before examining separately the evolution of the genres they created. As a result, the sophists appear in my book after Euripides, who was influenced by them: the complexities of life escape and resist one's every attempt to simplify them. Similarly, for the fourth century, the authors I have divided among three chapters are in fact nearly all contemporaries: how could they be classified if not according to the genres in which they worked? I should add that I have always taken care to point out overlappings like these in my text; and a chronological table at the end of the book puts everything back in temporal order and indicates which authors were writing concurrently.

Even in the chapters covering the other periods, some overlapping seemed acceptable where it clarified the overall view. That is why I have put the Homeric hymns, which belong to the archaic period, at the end of the chapter on Homer; and that is why I have separated philosophers who were contemporaries of one another and have placed them with philosophers of the archaic age or of the fifth century, depending on the tenor of their philosophies. Likewise, the earliest historians are discussed along with Herodotus, for they were his forerunners, rather than with the earliest philosophers, who wrote at the same time but seemed to deserve separate treatment within the context of the archaic age.

These difficulties of organization may cause misgivings and even misunderstandings; but that in itself is worth thinking about. Why is it so difficult to arrange the Greek authors in a satisfactory order if not because Greek literature displays a more constant and complex evolution than any other? Here we touch on one aspect of what has been called "the Greek miracle," a phenomenon that hinges, I believe, on two factors.

The first of these is the extraordinary faculty of invention, discovery, and self-renewal that Greek literature has always shown. Among its inventions, for our Western world, are lyric, tragedy, comedy, history, philosophy, biology, the romance, the dialogue: all had their beginnings in that literature. The reason it is so difficult to trace tendencies from year to year is that everything is constantly changing. No one can write in the same way after the Sophists, after Socrates, after a particular military victory or defeat. Nothing could be less stable or less fixed than this literature, later styled "classical."

As for the second factor, the parallel evolution of diverse genres and the role played by public events in this evolution are enough to remind us that Greek literature—all ancient Greek literature, at least—is anchored in the life of the community: the author is first and always a citizen. Literary genres like drama are organized around civic festivals. Others, like history, take the city-state and its destiny as their theme. And philosophy itself, at least in the classical period, never ceases to be moral and political philosophy. This common concern explains the fact that the authors' lives share a common rhythm and that influences are felt from one genre to another. This civic focus—which, incidentally, is as characteristic of French as of Greek literature—makes a chronological organization particularly necessary and particularly impracticable.

In the long run, the imperfections of my account will not weigh too heavily if my readers are willing to correct their impressions by turning to the texts themselves. The present work aims merely to whet the appetite and to serve as a framework or guide. The only way to know a literature is to read it; this short history is intended as an invitation to that reading.

Map of Greece and Greek Asia Minor in Classical Times

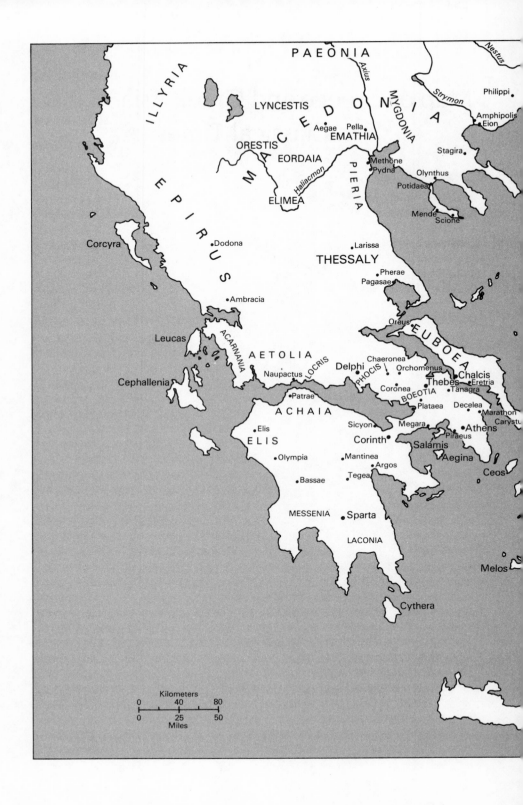

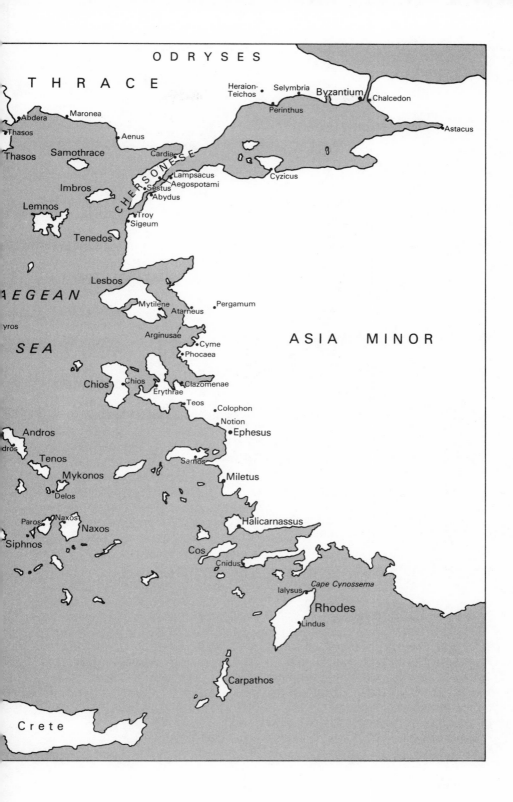

1

Homer

Greek literature as we know it begins with two great epics, handed down under the name of Homer—the *Iliad* and the *Odyssey*. The two works are written in dactylic hexameters; the first is about 15,000 lines in length, the other about 12,000. One tells of a part of the war the Achaeans waged against Troy, and includes the wrath of Achilles, his withdrawal from the fighting, and his return to battle to avenge his friend; it ends when he has killed the Trojan hero, Hector, and returned Hector's body to his own people. The other tells of the return of Odysseus to his home after the sack of Troy.

The ancients assumed that these two poems were the work of Homer, who lived in the eighth century B.C. (the Trojan War, of which he tells, having taken place about 1200 B.C.). All the rest is controversial. It was believed that Homer was blind, but this may have been a legend linked to the idea of inspiration: the prophet Teiresias was also said to be blind. Different cities are said to have contended for the honor of being called his birthplace; the probabilities are that he was from Asia Minor, and he seems to have lived for a time at least in Chios. Tradition has it that his poems were reedited at a later date, in Athens under Pisistratus, that is, in the sixth century B.C. The text thus established was to serve as a standard for the annual recitations that took place at the Panathenaea. Certainly it served as a benchmark for all poets who came after him, and the Greeks saw it, from then on, as the basis of their education and the starting point for all their speculations. As soon as we try to go beyond these "givens," so imprecise in themselves, the difficulties begin; for the interpretation of the Homeric poems offers many problems.

As a matter of fact, these poems can be read in two ways, which need to be combined. The first consists of an inquiry into the poems' formation, which we try to place in the context of the centuries separating each poem from its original material; we examine the poem for traces of its growth and elaboration. The second reading considers only the finished work, in its unity and its literary content, as the centuries to come were to know it.

I · THE EPIC AND ITS FORMATION

After the successive revelations of archaeology, no one can be unaware of the relationship between the epic and the historical period extending from the

1

Trojan War to Homer. Archaeologists have found Troy (at Hissarlik, in Asia Minor) and have identified, with considerable likelihood, the outline of the town sacked about the year 1200 (Troy VIIA). They have found Agamemnon's palace in his "Mycenae rich in gold." They have found carved vases and the frescoes of "Crete of the hundred towns." At Pylos they have found Nestor's palace and his very bathtub. Finally, and most important, they have discovered that the Mycenaean tablets found in Crete, Mycenae, and Pylos bear, in a script ill suited to them, Greek words. With this finding, the dim past of the rediscovered palaces became directly linked to the Greek poet, and to the origins of the civilization he describes.

All these discoveries connect Homer to a brilliant, living, and tangible past; yet they also connect him to a past of disruption and diversity—a succession, sometimes violent, of peoples and civilizations. When the first representatives of the Indo-European group who were to become "the Greeks" arrived from the north, they found a people who spoke a different language, from which they borrowed words—including the name for the sea. At that time a highly developed and powerful civilization was flowering in Crete. Its center was Knossos, which radiated its influence until about 1400 B.C. A closely related but cruder civilization flourished on the Greek mainland at Mycenae, Tiryns, and Pylos. This was the civilization of the "Achaeans" of whom Homer speaks. But it, in its turn, disappeared—as did the use of the script that had been used to record the Greek language. New Indo-European groups descended on Greece; this period saw the arrival of the Dorians, a primitive and warlike people. By virtue of these vicissitudes the period has been called the Greek Dark Age; at the same time, other movements of population were taking place in Asia Minor and parts of the Aegean. Not until the ninth century was there a Greek renaissance, with a renewal of prosperous trade and a revival of cultural exchanges between Asia Minor and Greece proper. Finally, in the eighth century, the age of Greek colonization began. The Greeks learned to write again, in a new script better adapted to their tongue and borrowed in most of its particulars from the Phoenicians.

So there was a vast span of time encompassing many changes between the period of Cretan influence reflected in Homer and the period when his epics were composed. We might expect, as a result, that the past he evokes will be manifold and various—especially if, as is probable a priori, this tale of centuries-old events is itself the product of long epic traditions built up in the course of those centuries; traditions whose harvest, so to speak, we may see in the two works that have come down to us. This probability can be confirmed by analogy and by the very nature of the two works.

A · Analogy

In the *Iliad* and, more prominently, in the *Odyssey* epic singers appear. The *Odyssey* devotes a good deal of space to two such singers, Phemius and Demodocus, one of whom lives in Ithaca and the other among the Phaeacians.

The poet portrays them as singing songs of two kinds at celebrations and feasts: legends about the gods, and the more recent exploits of the heroes of the Trojan War. The audience may request a particularly well-known episode; thus Odysseus asks Demodocus to sing the episode of the Wooden Horse, which brought about the fall of Troy (*Odyssey* 8.492). Details like these suggest that the Homeric poems themselves grew out of similar performances, in which improvisation as well as memory undoubtedly played a part.

This analogy tempted scholars to compare the Homeric epics with the evidence offered by oral poetry, as it has been preserved up to our own day among certain peoples. Such a comparison was made by Milman Parry and, later, by Albert Lord (among others), who for many years studied the works of Yugoslav bards. Their research revealed extraordinary resemblances of theme between the Yugoslav songs and those of Homer (the importance of the hero and of his honor, descriptions of beautiful objects); but, even more significant, it revealed similarities in certain formal qualities of the songs, similarities that are related to the conditions under which the songs were transmitted. Indeed, as soon as we see that the process is one of improvising on given themes with the aid of memory, we can understand why such poetry includes typical scenes, formulaic lines, and recurring epithets, or generic epithets. These are characteristic of the Homeric epics as well, in which a great number of lines or half-lines are repeated from one place to another and fill a variety of useful functions. This is also true of small blocks of lines describing a wound, a meal, a departure, a dawn, or simply serving as transitional passages. Likewise, Homer's characters, and the things that make up their everyday environment, are assigned special adjectives or epithets designed to resound in the memory and to furnish ready half-lines that seem to flow of themselves.

There is thus every reason to believe that if, in Homer's day, writing had made its reappearance, and even if he had recourse to it himself, the basis for his poems was an oral literature of this type, with a stock of heroes and *gestes*, or exploits, the treatment of which might vary in detail from one bard to the next, from one place to the next, from one century to the next. And what is true of the battle exploits may also be said of certain themes that appear in the *Odyssey*, bearing the traces of folktale and local legend, which make up a sort of "saga" and, like the battle themes, may be reworked and adapted as circumstances require.

With this insight we can infer that each of the two epics is made up of many different layers, not equally well integrated with one another. A reading of the two poems makes this clear.

B · The Composite Nature of the Language

The language Homer uses is itself a composite, revealing a combination of different times and places. It is a mixture of two Greek dialects, Ionic and

Aeolic. Forms from one or the other seem to be used indiscriminately. Sometimes, in a passage where the forms are Ionic, we find the Aeolic form of a word unknown in Ionic (like the word for goddess). Or we find Ionic and Aeolic endings in alternation, as the meter requires. And, while historically the Ionians supplanted the Aeolians, what we see are not *successive* layers. The dialects are mixed, forming a literary and artificial language in which the heritages of two different groups are melded. To this mixture are added Attic forms, probably introduced later, at the time of the recension of the poems in sixth-century Athens; if that is the case, the mixture of forms reflects the mixture of time periods as well.

This mixture occurs not only in later revisions: the Homeric language as a whole takes it for granted. We can offer two simple pieces of evidence, based on specific cases. The first is a lost consonant, the digamma (F) [pronounced like English *w*], which, when it faded from the language, was no longer written. The presence of a consonant, however, can be important in a line of verse, to help lengthen a preceding vowel or to prevent a hiatus. Thus, in certain cases, in order to scan a line we must take account of the influence of the lost digamma; in others, its influence is not felt. The oldest formulas, obviously, assume the presence of this letter, while the most recent disregard it; but in most cases the poet does as he pleases, mixing the usages of different periods as they prove useful to him. It is also possible that in some cases a later poet has modified an old formula to bring it into conformity with the new state of the language.

The second piece of evidence is that of the contract verbs in which an ō had replaced -ăō and thus counted metrically as a short vowel followed by a long; in these cases we sometimes find the arbitrary substitution of -ŏō for -ăō. This may simply be a question of spelling, but it demonstrates well enough that behind the text we have there was an older one, and that the language of the older version was not yet that of the era when our text assumed its present shape. All this abundantly demonstrates that the Homeric language, even without the transformations imposed by the later recension and then by the work of copyists, reflected a long history in itself; and that this language was grounded in the transmission of epic songs, lines, and formulas that antedate Homer by some centuries. The various strata of language juxtaposed in the text reveal the existence of earlier models, which the poet inherited in a more or less intact state.

C · A Composite Civilization

The objects, practices, and rituals described by Homer offer a mixed testimony that is no less diverse: different eras rub shoulders in the epic. Sometimes we find descriptions of objects that seem to come straight out of the Mycenaean past: Nestor's beautiful cup in the *Iliad* (11.632ff), with its doves, is almost identical to a cup found at Mycenae. Nor is this an isolated example. But as soon as we leave individual cases behind, complications and con-

flicting testimony come to light. Iron, for example, was practically unknown
to the Achaeans but was in common use in Homer's day. It is in fact portrayed as rare and precious in the *Iliad* (23.261, 834, 850); the common metal
is bronze. Yet iron comes up in isolated passages; it appears in similes; and
the heroes are sometimes described as having hearts "of iron." Side by side
with bronze, which the tradition calls for, iron conjures up the world to
which the poet was accustomed. In the same way, fishing and horseback riding are described only in exceptional cases or in similes.

Other juxtapositions are still more baffling. Shields are sometimes small
and round, sometimes "like a tower," sometimes large, shaped like a figure
eight; there seems to have been a series of different styles, yet the vases of the
Geometric age portray a mixture of styles similar to that found in the epic.
Other mixtures of the same type are evident in such details as the number of
swords a warrior carries (one or two); the material of which his helmet is
made (leather or metal); and the architecture of the palaces described, sometimes similar to that of the Cretan palaces (as in the case of the Phaeacians,
with their frieze of lapis lazuli, or Circe, with her second story and rooftop
veranda), and sometimes simpler, with a central *megaron*. In a few cases—
that of cremation, for example—the dominant practice may come as a surprise. The *Iliad* ends with two cremations (Patroclus's and Hector's), but the
practice of the Mycenaeans was profoundly different, as their great tombs attest.

Contrary to what we might have hoped, these divergences of detail offer
no help with dating. For example, a typically ancient object, the leather helmet reinforced with boars' tusks, figures prominently in a passage that seems
to be among the latest, the Doloneia (*Iliad* 10.260ff.). Scholarly hypotheses
abound but seem to lead nowhere. At the same time, the very divergences
prove that Homeric poetry has deep roots in ancient traditions, which were
slowly fused and modified over time. The same can be said for historical
facts as treated in the epics. As a general rule, Homer deliberately omits any
mention of the arrival of the Dorians; but he refers to Dorians once in the
Odyssey (19.177). On the other hand, he says a good deal about the Phoenicians, who only became prominent two or three centuries after the time of
Agamemnon. It is possible that in some cases historical circumstances had an
indirect influence on the poems: thus some scholars see a connection between
the Phaeacians and Cyclopes of the *Odyssey* and the role played by Chalcis
in the period of colonization as well as in the Lelantine War between Chalcis
and Eretria (see, for example, F. Robert's *Homer*, Presses Universitaires de
France, 1950). Undoubtedly, the process of "modernization" continued after
the composition of the poems, this time by means of interpolation. According to Plutarch, Solon based Athens's claim to Salamis on an interpolated
line (*Iliad* 2.558).

The *Iliad* and the *Odyssey* can thus be seen to reproduce, sometimes in
isolation and sometimes freely mixed, aspects of Greek history and life that

never coexisted outside the works themselves. We might be inclined to think—and often correctly—that what we have here is a free syncretism, purely literary in nature. But the fact is that the poems themselves can strike us as aggregates of pieces that do not always fit together.

D · Diversity within the Poetic Structure

Each of the two poems includes a central theme and others that are more or less closely linked to it. When the link is not an obvious or necessary one, it is only natural to conclude that we are encountering originally independent traditions that have been combined with varying degrees of success.

The *Iliad* begins in the ninth year of the Trojan War, and its theme links the wrath of Achilles to a decision of Zeus about the course the war is to take. Is it plausible that after the announcement of this decision we should find the Catalogue of Ships and the episode in which Helen tells Priam the names of the Achaean chiefs? These episodes would be more appropriate to the beginning of the war. Likewise, the single combat of Paris and Menelaus in book 3 and that of Hector and Ajax in book 7 cause puzzling interruptions to the action. There is equally little warrant for the Achaeans' building a rampart at the end of book 7; the later Trojan attack on the rampart is problematic for a variety of reasons.

Still clearer examples are to be found in the *Odyssey*, where the interweaving of passages centered on Odysseus with those centered on Telemachus can be disconcerting: one wonders whether these stories were originally independent. Odysseus's stay among the Phaeacians is drawn out to unexpected length, as if there were two different versions of the episode. The descent to the underworld in book 11 stands out strangely from the rest of the account. What is the purpose of the foot-bathing scene in book 19, which allows Eurycleia to recognize the hero while Penelope fails to do so? Might this be a remnant of another version? What is more, the scar that makes this first recognition possible is ignored in the previous book, when Odysseus tucks up his clothes for the wrestling match.

When we look closely at the poems in this way, we find doublets and slight contradictions. There is no reason to emphasize the contradictions—even a literate author who freely fashions a work that comes to him in one piece, and who can write and rewrite it at leisure, is liable to make minor errors. He may resurrect a character he has already killed (like Pylaimenes, killed in book 5 and still living in book 13 of the *Iliad*); he may forget some detail after a lapse of too many pages. The doublets, on the other hand, can put us on the track of artificial joinings or conflations. Scholars have suspected that such a conflation explains the two assemblies of gods in *Odyssey* 1 and 5, which are strangely alike (the first having had very little effect). We must allow too for the possibility of later interpolations. Some were already suspected in the second century B.C. by scholars like Aristarchus or Aristophanes of Byzantium. There is scarcely an ancient author whose writings were not subject to interpolation; the flexibility and diversity of the epic, as well as its great age, must[1] have made it still more tempting to interpolators.

Observations like these, taken together with the evidence gleaned from literary analogy, from the language, and from the cultural background, help to explain the existence of a question that both stimulates and handicaps every study of Homer. This is the famous "Homeric Question."

E · The Homeric Question

The first person to ask the Homeric Question was François Hédelin, abbé d'Aubignac, who wrote his *Academic Conjectures*, or *Dissertation on the Iliad* in 1664 (it was published in 1715). The second to ask—more loudly this time, and to greater effect—was the German F. A. Wolf, in his *Prolegomena to Homer* of 1795. Since that time it has been the focus of endless debates, which continue to divide scholars to this day.

This is not the place to enumerate the various hypotheses and supporting arguments. In simple terms, the question comes down to this: Do we have, in the work of Homer, two great poems, each of which is a literary whole conceived in the form we know today? This is the "unitarian" hypothesis. Or do we have a more or less successful assemblage of shorter poems conceived at various times, independently of one another, in some cases even as parts of larger wholes other than those we know? This is the theory of the "analysts," who seek in the existing text the traces of previous versions.

After the appearance of Wolf's book, the analysts' thesis grew steadily in popularity; then there was a reaction in favor of the unitarians. Around the time of the Second World War, new analytic theories appeared that were less absolute and less destructive; at the same time, the unitarians were forced to recognize that a whole tradition lay behind the two poems. Today the two theories have drawn closer together, making it possible to outline the problem more clearly and to identify the general principles that emerge from the debate.

In the first place, it is clear—for reasons I have discussed above—that the Homeric poems have their roots in a distant past; and it is reasonable to assume that certain episodes had been sung for a very long time. This assumption is reinforced by the fact that epic poems independent of the *Iliad* and the *Odyssey* did exist. It is true that they were later than Homer; but they too must have had their ancient sources, in the same tradition from which Homer drew his material. Thus for the *Iliad* it is possible to imagine an *Achilleid*, which could have inspired the cyclic poem designed as a sequel to the *Iliad*;[1] for the *Odyssey*, there must have been poems about the Argonauts. Even traditions preserved in very late sources can sometimes put us on the track of ancient versions.

---

1. The *Aethiopis*, which tells of Achilles' encounter with the Ethiopian prince Memnon, and of Achilles' death at the hands of Apollo and Paris.—Trans.

At all events, there came a time—a crucial time—when a particular poet (or group of poets) went ahead to compose literary wholes destined to become the epics we know. This poet (or group of poets) used the elements of which I have spoken, organizing them around a central idea. After this period of composition, various additions were made, some possibly quite late, as we have seen.

At this stage of the debate, the real problem remaining is to determine the extent of the versions put together at this crucial time. One proposed solution is that they were the cores, or nuclei, of the works we have, sizable but much shorter; a different poet or poets, according to this theory, then expanded them by inserting passages, some amounting to several books. This position, which is analytic, can be found in the work of Paul Mazon, among others (*Introduction to the Iliad*, Presses Universitaires de France, 1942). It does not insist on splitting each epic into a group of independent poems; on the contrary, it maintains that each book was composed for the place in which we find it but that the composition was a process of expansion, carried out in several stages. In the same spirit, contemporary "analysts" suggest that the adventures of Telemachus and Odysseus's recital of his wanderings were not always parts of a single poem, but that the version we have is a synthesis.

The other possible solution is that the versions put together at the "crucial time" were very close to those we have. Aside from a few interpolations, Homer remains, in this view, the sole architect of the epics—with the reservation that the *Odyssey* (which is by every indication later than the *Iliad*) may be the work of a successor.

It is impossible to choose with any certainty between these two solutions. At one time the length of the poems was raised as evidence, when it was thought that no oral poem could reach such dimensions; but comparative studies have shown that bards can retain works of comparable length. The existence of writing, which had reappeared in Homer's day, makes the length of the poems still less problematic. Detailed arguments are, of course, always open to discussion.

Whichever solution is finally adopted, two general principles for further study seem to emerge from the debate. The first is that no intelligent reading of a Homeric passage or line can afford to ignore the possible echoes of history or of previous poems, or the signs of reworking—in short, the evidence of a long evolution. Though we cannot trace the course of this evolution, we cannot deny that it took place. The second principle is that we are dealing with literary works, intended as such by their authors, presented as wholes and governed by a conscious art. If there were epics before those that have come down to us, and if they contributed to the elaboration of our *Iliad* and *Odyssey*, it is still self-evident that these two poems would not have prevailed—would not have been, in fact, the only ones to survive—if the artistry of their author had not been such as to insure their survival. So it is appropriate to turn from the problem of their formation to an appreciation of their finished form, whose perfection stands out all the more clearly against the uncertain course of this formation.

II · THE EPIC IN ITS FINISHED FORM

If we look at their overall composition, the two epics take the form of distinct wholes, each with its unity of action. A summary of their contents will make this clear.

A · The Structures of the Two Poems
1 · THE ILIAD

The action of the *Iliad* can be outlined book by book. There are twenty-four books in each epic; they are commonly referred to by numbers or by letters of the Greek alphabet (capitals for the *Iliad*, lowercase letters for the *Odyssey*). We must remember, though, that these divisions were made after Homer's day, possibly as late as the Alexandrian age.

Book 1 is devoted to the wrath of Achilles, its causes and its effects. The book opens in the camp of the Achaeans. To lift a plague sent by Apollo, the Achaeans must return Chryseis, the daughter of Apollo's priest, who has been taken captive and awarded to Agamemnon. Agamemnon returns the girl, but in her place seizes Achilles' captive, Briseis. Achilles is enraged and withdraws from the fighting. The scene then shifts to Olympus, home of the gods, where Thetis, Achilles' divine mother, elicits a promise from Zeus: the Achaeans will not be successful in battle until they have made good the wrong done to Achilles. Thus the situation that will determine the whole future course of the action is clearly set out; all the fighting in the first half of the poem must lead up to Achilles' return to battle and his victory over Hector.

Book 2 sets the stage for these early clashes of arms: it includes a dream sent to Agamemnon, urging him to open battle; an assembly of the Achaeans; and the Catalogue of Ships.

Book 3 describes a first isolated clash, a duel. Paris, Helen's abductor, is spurred by Hector's reproaches to face Menelaus in single combat. Helen goes up to the ramparts of the city and, at her father-in-law's request, names for him the chiefs of the Achaeans. Aphrodite rescues Paris and sets him down unhurt in Helen's chamber.

In *book 4*, battle is joined, and the battle continues through the next three books. First the chiefs spur one another on and the melee begins. It continues in *book 5*, as the gods join in; Ares, the god of war himself, is wounded by Diomedes. Hector then tries to marshal every advantage on the Trojan side: in *book 6* he returns to the city to arrange for special prayers to Athene. At the same time he takes leave of his wife Andromache and their infant son, whom he fears he will leave an orphan. In *book 7* the narrative returns, with Hector, to the battle, which is interrupted early in this book by a single combat between Hector and Ajax. Nightfall puts an end to the duel, and a truce is struck.

With *book 8* there begins a second battle, preceded by another assembly of the gods, whom Zeus forbids to interfere in the fighting. The Achaeans are repulsed, and their attempt at a counterattack fails. The coming of night halts the Trojans at the Greek rampart.

Faced with this danger, the Achaeans decide to appeal to Achilles; an embassy is sent (*book 9*) to offer him amends, but the offer is refused.

There follows a nocturnal episode, which has little connection with the plot as a whole and exhibits characteristics suggesting that it was a late addition: in *book 10*, the Achaeans Odysseus and Diomedes, sent out as spies, kill the Trojan Dolon (whence the name, "Doloneia," given to this passage); thanks to information pumped out of Dolon, they are able to surprise and kill men sent to Troy as reinforcements by the Thracian king Rhesus.

Next begins a third battle, occupying *books 11–15*, which brings the Trojans as far as the Greek camp, where they prepare to set fire to the ships. For a short while the gods on the Achaean side have some hope: Hera succeeds in luring Zeus to Ida, where he falls asleep (book 14); but he wakes in the following book, and the fate of the Achaeans hangs in the balance. At this critical moment begins the sequence of events that will lead to the "reversal" or turning point. Achilles, who was unmoved by the offer of gifts, will be driven back into action by his grief at the death of his friend Patroclus.

In *book 16*, Achilles, after resisting Patroclus's desire to fight, gives in when the first ship is set on fire. He lends Patroclus his own armor, and Patroclus goes into battle, where he is at first successful; then he dies, struck senseless by Apollo and dispatched by Hector. A battle for his body ensues in *book 17*; the Achaeans manage to carry it back to their camp. Achilles' grief in *book 18* is intense. His mother tries to console him and persuades Hephaestus to forge new arms of peerless beauty for him. There can be no doubt now: Achilles must avenge Patroclus.

Thus in *book 19* he solemnly unsays his wrath. Agamemnon offers reparations, and Achilles prepares for battle. His horse, inspired by Hera, predicts his impending death, but it makes no difference to him: he must go.

The exploits of Achilles fill *books 20* (which describes a fierce battle, in which the gods once more take part), *21* (where Achilles puts the Trojans to flight), and finally *22*, in which he kills Hector.

Hector has killed Patroclus; Achilles has avenged his friend. In both camps, mourning is the order of the day. *Book 23* describes the games held by the Achaeans in funerary homage to Patroclus; *book 24* tells of Priam's painful visit to Achilles to seek the return of Hector's body. He obtains the body and brings it back to Troy, where Hector is mourned and buried.

Thus the central plot line of the epic emerges with a clarity matched only by its tragic power. Though the war lasted ten years, the action takes up only a few days (fifty in all, if we count the days of inaction and waiting, before the wrath of Achilles or after the funeral of Patroclus). In these few days it depicts a whole series of battles in which first the Trojans and then the Achaeans have the upper hand—a kind of synopsis of the ten-year struggle. But the arrangement of these battles follows a pattern that is both tragic and simple. So that the fates of the protagonists may touch the audience more deeply, the battle scenes are interspersed with scenes between intimates—on the Trojan side (Helen and Paris, Andromache and Hector) as well as on the Achaean side (Achilles, Patroclus, and Briseis). Toward the end, this human element even eclipses the interest in warfare: the epic ends not in victory but in mourning. Finally, as if to elevate still further the meaning of these struggles and give them a more exalted scope, the *Iliad* mingles gods and men and deliberately juxtaposes the warriors' assemblies with those of the gods.

Where details are concerned, there may be some minor inconsistencies, and it is worth looking at these to get an idea of the work's evolution. Yet the architecture of the whole is not only unified and soundly built; it also reveals a consummate literary art and an artist conscious of his skill. Added to this there are the finer points of composition—the poet's ability, for example, to vary a theme, maintain the interest of his audience, or summon up, in the midst of a battle, the human compassion that is the warrior's due. Only a detailed study of the text can convey the mastery of its composition; and such a study is always fruitful if the principles I have outlined are kept in mind.

The *Odyssey* is a somewhat different case.

2 · THE ODYSSEY

Like the *Iliad*, the *Odyssey* deals with an episode in the life of one man, within a limited time span; only Odysseus, his family, and his followers are involved, and the action properly speaking takes only forty days. But with an art at least as sophisticated as that displayed in the *Iliad*, the poet has managed to fill out the action with stories, so that *all* the adventures of Odysseus on his way home are included—and so that diversity of focus is reconciled with unity of action. The action is spread, moreover, over two settings, which are farther apart and more independent of one another than were the two camps in the *Iliad*. Before Telemachus and his father join forces, the poet follows them on their separate paths. He opens his tale in Ithaca, at the palace where the dénouement of the epic will be set, and thus begins with Telemachus. Then he moves on to Odysseus, by way of an assembly of the gods: here Zeus decides to intervene and sends his messenger Hermes to Calypso, with the eventual result that Odysseus puts out to sea once more, on the last lap of his homeward journey. This sophisticated arrangement of material gives us four groups of books.

Books 1–4 are devoted to Telemachus. An opening assembly of gods results in Athene's visit to the young man, to encourage him in his struggle against the suitors who have been ensconced in the palace for years (1). He calls an assembly and prepares for a voyage (2), intending to seek news of his father. First he goes to Pylos to see Nestor (3), then to Sparta, home of Menelaus (4). Toward the end of book 4 he is preparing to return to Ithaca, while at the same time the suitors are planning to ambush him on the way home.

The danger Telemachus faces from this ambush provides a motive for Athene's renewed intercession at the council of the gods. Thanks to her action, *books 5–8* are devoted to Odysseus. Book 5 finds him with the nymph Calypso, who has kept him a virtual prisoner for years. She releases him and helps him build a raft. After a storm, he is washed up on the coast of the Phaeacians (5). Nausicaa, daughter of King Alcinous, has gone to do her washing at the beach; she finds Odysseus and leads him back to the palace (6). He is well received, but does not reveal his name (7). As the Phaeacians are preparing to escort him safely home, games are held in his honor, and the bard Demodocus sings the episode of the Trojan Horse (8). At this, Odysseus cannot hide his emotion, and at the end of the song Alcinous questions him more pointedly: who is he, and what adventures has he met with? This serves as prelude to the next group of books.

Books 9–12 comprise Odysseus's account of his wanderings. He tells of strange and marvelous adventures that belong to the realm of folktale. Chief among these are his visits to the Cyclops (9), to Aeolus, to the Laestrygonians, to Circe (10), and to the underworld (11), as well as his encounters with the Sirens and the cattle of the Sun (12). This series of adventures brings him at last, by the end of book 12, to Calypso—the point at which the poem itself had opened and at which he had begun his own briefer account to the Phaeacians in book 7. In this way the complete adventures of Odysseus since the fall of Troy have been fitted into the poem, and the action proper of the epic resumes. We move now from fabulous tales to the thoroughly human undertaking that will reestablish him as king in Ithaca.

First there is a period of preparation. *Books 13 and 14* tell of Odysseus's arrival at the hut of his swineherd, the old Eumaeus, whom he beguiles with false tales and questions about the situation at the palace. *Book 15* brings Telemachus in his turn to the hut; he has escaped the suitors' ambush (described in book 4). In *book 16*, father and son are reunited and begin to plan their revenge on the suitors.

The plan unfolds in *books 17–23*. In book 17, Odysseus, disguised as a beggar, is recognized only by his old dog; in book 18 he is drawn into a fight with another beggar. Book 19 finds him still in disguise; his old nurse, Eurycleia, recognizes him by a scar but keeps the secret. The suitors order a special feast (20), at which Odysseus wins the contest proposed by Penelope, who says she will marry the man who can wield her husband's bow (21). Penelope retires to her own room while Odysseus, armed with the bow, sheds his rags and kills the suitors (22). The homecoming is crowned by the reunion of Odysseus and Penelope (23).

A final book serves as epilogue: it describes the reunion of Odysseus and his old father, the descent of the suitors to Hades (the Second Nekuia), and the reaction of the Ithacans to Odysseus's revenge. This ending has often been rejected as spurious by critics, who cite Aristophanes of Byzantium and Aristarchus to the effect that the *Odyssey* ended at line 296 of book 23. The final episodes are certainly less polished and less necessary than the rest—and the Second Nekuia is especially suspect.

But with the exception of this last book, the inescapable impression is of a work that rivals the *Iliad* in sophistication and mastery. There is a difference in the principle of composition: the *Iliad* moves inevitably toward a crisis, to which everything else contributes, while the *Odyssey* has a more leisurely movement and is not averse to backtracking or storytelling for the sheer pleasure of it. This great fluidity has made the *Odyssey* fertile ground for the analysts. Yet the unitarians also draw encouragement from the skill with which the episodes are linked, and from the successful combination of diversity and continuity.

There are enough similarities in composition between the two epics to warrant the view that they were by the same author, who probably composed the *Odyssey* twenty or thirty years after the *Iliad*. But we can consider the *Odyssey* as a unity without necessarily accepting this conclusion. Indeed, we might well expect that a worthy successor should have appeared among the bards trained in the style and taste of Homer. The Homerids of Chios, who called themselves the disciples and descendants of Homer, belong to a later age; but their existence lends credibility to the hypothesis of a poet close to the master, who might have sought to rival him in a work of equal scope but using different themes. In any case, the two works imply a deliberate and mature art of composition, the fruit of long cultivation.

The civilization they reflect is no less refined.

B · The Homeric World

We see the Homeric world at war in the *Iliad* and at peace in the *Odyssey*. But a single conception of human life is reflected in both spheres. Perhaps the first characteristic of the Homeric world to strike the reader is the unique way it brings together men and gods.

1 · THE GODS IN THE EPIC

In the course of its development (which lies outside the scope of this book) Homeric religion had made room for a fusion of Hellenic and pre-Hellenic elements. It imagined the gods as living on Mount Olympus, or simply in the sky. Their king and father was Zeus; but each had his or her own distinct personality. The poet imagines their relations with one another as those that might exist in a small human kingdom. Hera, Zeus's wife, now challenges him, now dupes him; some of these scenes are almost comic. Other gods cajole him; some try to disobey him. The gods live as men do: if they have a king, they also have their assemblies. Book 1 of the *Iliad* closes with one of these assemblies; another opens book 1 of the *Odyssey*. Again like men, these gods have passions that are not always licit (in book 8 of the *Odyssey*, Demodocus sings of the adulterous love between Ares and Aphrodite— though it should be noted that this passage has been considered a late addition). Their passions often lead them to mingle with men, sometimes in their proper shapes, sometimes in disguise. They have their friends and their enemies. Indeed, Achilles is the offspring of a mortal and a goddess.

With all these characteristics, the Homeric gods are not merely anthropomorphic but "human" in the extreme, with all the failings the word implies. Yet they are also radically different from men, for they are immortal and enjoy superhuman powers. Zeus wields the thunderbolt and Poseidon raises tempests. The gods transform themselves freely; and they transform men as well, making them old or beautiful at will—not to mention the more drastic metamorphoses of which the *Odyssey* offers several examples (notably Circe's transformation of men into pigs). The gods move through space as they please, and can transport men in the same way; they can clothe a man in light or shadow; they can keep a weapon from hitting its mark. Homeric man is always afraid that a god may be present to thwart him. Sometimes he fears a particular god; sometimes (especially in the *Odyssey*) he speaks of divinity in the abstract—of the *daimon*. As a result, in the epic every human event takes place on two levels at once; the gods have a hand in everything.

Remarkably, the two camps in the *Iliad* pray to the same gods. The gods, however, have their individual preferences; some are for the Achaeans and some for the Trojans—in each case for personal and selfish reasons. Thus Hera, Athene, and Poseidon back the Achaeans wholeheartedly, while Apollo backs the Trojans. They bring such passion to these preferences that at times they confront each other in real battles (as at *Iliad* 20.67ff.). They intervene likewise in human battles, tricking their enemies and helping their friends with headstrong enthusiasm.

The close ties between gods and mortals can also lead to a kind of affectionate familiarity—at least in the *Odyssey*. If Odysseus is hounded by Poseidon's anger, he is just as constantly helped by Athene, who is always acting in his behalf, either among the gods, or in Ithaca, or wherever he is. There are few scenes as charming as that between Odysseus and Athene in book 13. Athene is disguised as "a young shepherd, a tender boy who might be a king's son"; Odysseus fails to recognize her and launches into a tall tale. Athene is delighted; she assumes her proper shape, laughing: "What rascal, what thief could outdo you—even if he were a god—in wiles of any kind!" (291ff.). And the scene ends with the two of them seated under a sacred olive tree, plotting together. Such intimacy is unique in Greek literature: this is as close as a god can be to a mortal, whose existence is ultimately indifferent to him or her.

But the partiality and variability of these divine interventions raises a serious problem—that of divine justice. To judge from the examples I have given thus far, such justice does not exist; but this is not the whole story. It is certain that the Homeric epics do not give divine justice the prominence it was to acquire later. Yet it is present to the extent that Zeus, as king of the gods, acts as an arbiter among them and prevents any of them from winning too decisively at the others' expense. It is true that Zeus himself feels considerable fondness and concern for specific mortals; but there are also passages in the *Iliad* reminding us that he is angered by mortals who spurn justice and fail to honor the gods (16.386–88). Not only does he protect guests and suppliants; he also insists on the keeping of oaths. It is in his name that kings administer justice (1.238–39). Men acknowledge that the violation of an agreement (as in book 4) is an act that Zeus will punish. As Agamemnon says, "The Olympian may not act at once; but he always acts, whatever the delay, and the guilty pay their debt—with interest . . . A day will come when sacred Ilion will perish, and Priam, and the people of Priam of the good ash-spear" (4.160ff.) Such statements are relatively rare in the *Iliad*; they are already more common in the *Odyssey*, where many passages anticipate the punishment of the wicked (the suitors, for example), or the happiness that will reward the just ruler (like Odysseus or Penelope). This justice required by the gods is mentioned, for example at *Odyssey* 1.262; 3.133; 17.484ff.; 19.109ff., etc. The gods of the *Odyssey* are more benevolent, generally speaking, than those of the *Iliad*; worship is also more prominent in the later epic—which ends happily to boot. There may well have been an evolution in Greek views of divine justice. But in both the *Iliad* and the *Odyssey* it comes down to a question of proportion. Conflicts among the gods do not exclude morality. The two perspectives coexist and blend; yet no coherent doctrine emerges.

The same imprecision surrounds another issue. In addition to the conflict between Zeus's will and the biased interventions of the other Olympians, there can be conflicts between Zeus and a fate that seems inescapably fixed—a fate that Zeus himself seems bound to obey. Even a sort of pressure exerted by the gods as a group can prevent him, in the name of fate, from acting as he wishes. Thus, although he loves his son Sarpedon tenderly and wants to save him, Hera protests: "What! A mere mortal, long since doomed to die, and you would release him from cruel death? Go ahead, then; but we other gods will not all approve" (16.441–43). In his grief, Zeus sends down a shower of blood; but he lets his son die. Nor is he the only god to act in this way. All the gods have mortal protégés who are dear to them, but it is not in their power to preserve these men from death (see, for example, *Iliad* 18.464ff; *Odyssey* 3.236ff.).

At times we even see Zeus consulting Fate and letting it take its course. This happens in the episode of the scales (*Iliad* book 8): Zeus holds up his golden scales to weigh "two goddesses of painful death"—one for the Achaeans and one for the Trojans—against each other; and "the fatal day of the Achaeans" tips the scale (72). Zeus then carries out this verdict. The same thing occurs when Zeus consults the scales to decide the contest between Achilles and Hector, "and Hector's death-day [is] heaviest" (22.212).

    In each of these various cases there is the sense of an ineluctable order—
always, I must add, with death as its focus. This order, called *moira*, binds
the gods themselves, who are its agents. Must we then see a contradiction in
the passages where Zeus himself seems responsible for each man's fate? Not
necessarily. In the first place, the epic is hardly a theological treatise; and
Homer is entitled to as much uncertainty on such questions as we allow ourselves. Second, the notion of a world order that even the gods must respect
does not really deprive the gods of power. It is possible to imagine various ac-
commodations between these powers; but Homer did not worry about such
technicalities, nor did he need to. For him and for his heroes, Zeus, the gods,
divinity, and fate are usually interchangeable: each of these powers, personal
or impersonal, is an expression of man's sense of his own weakness when
faced with the strokes of fortune, which he attributes to the gods, or with the
fact of death, which the human condition imposes. Men are by definition
"the mortal ones."

    The gods and fate thus preside over human destinies; but the gods have an
even more remarkable power. Repeatedly in Homer we see gods intervene to
inspire a man's thought, desire, or sudden response, to make him brave or
cowardly. In the midst of the quarrel in book 1 of the *Iliad*, Athene comes
down from the heavens to restrain Achilles; suddenly she is there, visible to
him alone, and at her word Achilles thrusts his sword back into the scab-
bard. It has sometimes been thought that such interventions sadly limited the
initiative of men. But, as Fernand Robert has shown in his *Homer*, this is a
way of describing the sudden irrational impulses that men feel within themselves. When a spear or arrow fails to hit its mark, the Homeric hero thinks a
god has deflected it; similarly, when a man responds in an unexpected way,
the hero thinks a god must have inspired him. Nor is this mere allegory. It is
the direct expression of what a man feels and believes in a world where gods
are seen as actively interfering: they are saddled with the inexplicable. Where
the emotions are concerned, this happens all the more easily as Homer's psychology is rudimentary by our standards and gives no clear account of the
inwardness of the soul; Bruno Snell has studied this aspect of the poems in his
book *The Discovery of the Mind* (Hamburg, 1948; trans. T. G. Rosenmeyer,
Harper & Row, 1960.) It is worth noting that the *Odyssey* tends to differenti-
ate more often than the *Iliad* between impulses inspired by gods and those
that are purely human.

    To conclude, it is obvious that we cannot talk about the world of the epics
without taking account of the gods, who are constantly involved in the action. From a literary point of view, it is they who give the epic its share of the
marvelous; indeed, scholars long dwelt exclusively on that quality. One reason for this emphasis was that the epic presentation of the gods does not seem
charged with true religious feeling as we understand it. But it is important to
realize that for the Homeric hero the existence of the gods makes a difference
to every aspect of life. It inspires fear; it also inspires confidence. In particu-

lar, it gives human life distinctive contours and reveals it in a distinctive light. The extraordinary closeness it establishes between gods and mortals has the effect of elevating man to an unusual eminence, rarely matched in later ages; while the cheerful familiarity with which the gods are mentioned reveals a human delight in, and love for, this life where the divine is everywhere. At the same time, the constant reminder that these superior powers exist inspires a kind of pity for man. The two perspectives are compatible because the hero himself accepts the limits of his existence. Hector's death appears the more tragic to us because we know of the divine verdict and the deception of Athene to which he succumbs; but this death takes on a new nobility from the fact that Hector accepts it, declaring, when he sees fate holding him fast: "So be it! But I do not intend to die without a fight, nor yet without glory" (22.304). In cases like this, the role played by the gods actually brings out the greatness of men.

2 · THE HUMAN IDEAL

The men who people the epic are heroes, and almost all are kings. Even in the *Odyssey*, where humbler people appear—the swineherd, the nurse, the beggar—these belong to the entourage of a prince. The epic thus reflects an aristocratic world, and the virtues it recognizes are aristocratic ones. The hero's merit, his *arete*, consists primarily of valor. The *Iliad* displays this valor in its natural setting, which is war. There exploits are accomplished—feats of force, of swiftness, of magnanimity. Above all the hero seeks to win glory and avoid shame, the stigma attached to cowardice. Next to the merit of the warrior there is of course the merit of sound decisions taken in council; but the council is above all a council of war. Because of the insecurity of the small patriarchal kingdoms described in the epics, the lord, or *anax*, is essentially a warlord.

Yet this aspect of the poems may have been overemphasized at the expense of others. It is the most obvious; but it is not the only aspect or, indeed, the most original in an epic work. The society depicted in Homer has two faces, that of war and that of peace. They are contrasted on Achilles' shield in book 18 of the *Iliad*; they are also contrasted from one epic to the other. The *Iliad* is about warriors, while the *Odyssey* is about Odysseus's return to the homeland where he had always ruled "like a gentle father." Nor must we forget that the epic heroes, even those of the *Iliad* when they are at war, display wonderfully humane virtues as well. The most remarkable of these is their hospitality. It is directly portrayed only in the *Odyssey*, in episodes like those of Telemachus's reception at Pylos and Sparta, or in the welcome Odysseus receives among the Phaeacians. Clearly such scenes are ritualistic, prescribed by a long tradition and involving much ceremony. But at the same time they call into play qualities of the heart and subtle forms of respect. A characteristic example is the way Alcinous honors Odysseus without prying into his identity. Nor is this all: once the host-guest relationship has been established between

two heroes, it becomes an indissoluble bond, which is passed down from father to son. Even in the midst of a battle, such ties can prevent two heroes
from fighting one another. Thus expressions of respect for others are hardly
unknown to the civilization described in the epics.

The same is true of courtesy in general. The Homeric heroes may be adept
at hurling insults (not only at enemies but at allies as well); in their rages they
may call each other "heart wrapped in insolence" or "dog's eyes." Once away
from the battlefield, however, they know how to observe the proprieties, address each other with complimentary epithets, and follow the protocol of a
meal or a sacrifice. Rather than mistreating their captive women, they actually try to console them. Courtesy even turns to tenderness and generosity
when the old Priam speaks gently to Helen and questions her about the
Greek chiefs: "Come here, my daughter, and sit beside me. You will see your
first husband, your friends, and your relatives by marriage. In my eyes you
are not to blame: the gods alone are responsible for all that has happened."

Clearly, tenderness is not at all alien to the epic. Sometimes it is familial
tenderness, as in the scene in book 6 of the *Iliad* where Hector bids his last
farewell to Andromache and his son. Andromache weeps and begs Hector
not to put himself in danger, reminding him that he is everything to her. Then
Hector holds out his arms to take the child, who shrinks back, crying in fear
of his father's helmet; the hero must take off his helmet before picking up his
son, whom he dandles and kisses while invoking the gods' blessings on him.
Finally he gives the boy back to his mother, who receives him "laughing in
tears," and Hector is moved to pity. There could not be a simpler or a more
intimate scene. In other places tenderness takes other forms, from the flirta-
tiousness of Calypso to the ingenuous grace of Nausicaa. Liaisons are formed
and broken without emotional scenes; possibilities are sketched, including
some that are only suggested beyond the poem—like that of a union between
the two young people, Telemachus and Nausicaa.

The world of the epic thus offers us the portrait of a civilization by no
means primitive, in which the sense of propriety and the ideal of human behavior are already at an apogee. This in itself suggests a love of life.

C · The Homeric Love of Life

Homer sees beauty in all he describes, beginning with physical objects. There
are beautiful cups, beautifully embossed armor, shining helmets, brilliant
fabrics; there are rich palaces with vast storehouses, perfumed by reserves of
oil; there are well-balanced ships that speed across the sea. The characters,
divine or human, are equally beautiful—at least those who belong to the first
ranks of the nobility. All the warriors are tall and strong. All the women
have white arms. It is not surprising, then, that Homer so often applies to human beings the characteristic formula that pronounces them "godlike." The
landscape in which these men live is equally worthy of praise. Ithaca is described as a good land for raising grain; it has inexhaustible supplies of wine,
woods in which all species thrive, fresh water . . . But then, the universe as a

whole is full of splendors. How often Homer describes the dawn with her "rosy fingers," her "saffron robe," and her "golden throne"! Night is no less beautiful, with its brilliant moon and shining stars—not to mention the sweet sleep that is night's gift to men. Even the wilderness has its own more fearful beauties: no one has surpassed Homer in describing the thunderous noise of a storm in the forest, or the leaping of wild animals in the mountains.

In such a world, every activity has something noble about it, something to gladden the heart—even battle, with its victorious strokes and the dull sound of bodies falling, a sound which, to the victor, means success and glory. By contrast, Eumaeus with his pigs and Nausicaa with her washing evoke a humbler way of life, which yet has its own pleasures. Wine too is good, poems cheer the heart, and sporting contests combine the glory of victory with the joys of peace.

This love of life is as powerful a reinforcement to the desire for survival in the *Odyssey*, and hence to the dramatic interest of the work, as it is to the horror of death in the *Iliad*, and to that poem's tragic force. The narrator's words of pity for those who fall, "forgetting their horsemanship forever," recall what it is they are leaving behind and increase the merit associated with courage. For all go out to meet death, even when they see that it is imminent, as Hector does, or when they are sure of encountering it, as is Achilles. Yet the same Achilles will say, in the *Odyssey*, when his days of heroic action are past, "I would rather live as a herdsman in the service of some small farmer with a meager living than rule over all the race of the dead" (*Odyssey* 11.489–91).

We can see, then, that heroism in no way excludes a fervent love of life. The fervor might be attributed to the fact that this poetry was composed for noblemen and thus designed to reflect their lives in a flattering light. But such an explanation ignores the fact that in Homer the love of life is shared by all, even the humblest, and never loses its human resonance.

An art that is both supple and direct makes this possible.

D · The Literary Art of Homer

We do violence to the very nature of the poems when we try to express their artistic motivation in abstract terms. For the two chief characteristics of Homer's art—which are well suited to express the love of life in its most diverse forms—are its concreteness and its variety.

Homer never analyzes; he shows us his characters in action, arming or fighting, feasting or sailing. He uses verbs more frequently than nouns. If at times we have trouble following his lines of thought, it is because they are embedded in action; instead of an explanation, we have Zeus holding up his scales, scolding or smiling. This concreteness in the description of actions makes for a certain technicality in the vocabulary, so that we are at a loss to render some of the terms precisely. Each piece of armor, each veil in a woman's headdress, each part that goes into the making of a raft has its name. In the *Odyssey*, the precision and concreteness with which household tasks are described has suggested to some scholars that the poet must have been a woman.

But Homer does not simply *show* us people in action; he gives them speech as well, the better to convey their living presence. Zeus holds up his scales, but he also debates questions with the other gods, and quarrels with them. The heroes strike boldly, but they speak as often as they strike, and Homer gives us all they say in direct discourse. Many passages in the epics can be set up typographically as plays are, with the characters' names in the margins; to judge from Plato's *Ion*, the art of reciting Homer was very much an actor's art.

Direct discourse in itself contributes to the diversity of the narrative. But there are many other ways in which Homer varies his tale. All of these bear the marks of a highly controlled art; and it is worth emphasizing them, particularly since features such as the formulas, generic epithets, recurring blocks of lines, and typical scenes might strike some readers as monotonous.

In the first place, there is a great diversity in the portrayal of characters and in what we would call their psychology. Given that all the heroes are admirable and their epithets always the same, we might expect them to resemble one another; but nothing could be farther from the truth. There is, indeed, a certain simplicity of characterization; but it tends to bring out the individuality of each figure: the passionate wrath of Achilles has nothing in common with the sense of responsibility that quickens Hector's valor; and Helen's grace is wholly unlike the conjugal ardor of Andromache. The characters themselves bring these contrasts to the foreground in their confrontations with one another, as when Patroclus reproaches Achilles for his hardness, or Hector blames Paris for his softness and indolence. A similar case is Athene's affectionate mockery, in the *Odyssey*, of Odysseus's skill in the art of lying. This last example also demonstrates that simplicity of characterization does not exclude an awareness of nuances; for Athene's words mingle reproach with tenderness, familiarity with mockery. Of course, Homer does not indulge in psychological analyses of these various emotions; but because he knows how to portray emotion truthfully in the words and acts of his characters, the nuances of feeling, in all their complexity, are there.

The action of the poems, and their narrative portions, are also varied—even in the *Iliad* and even in the scenes in both epics that seem to follow traditional patterns. So it is with the battle scenes in the *Iliad*. In the first place, Homer alternates between episodes involving men and those involving gods. In the former scenes, he moves from descriptions of the melee to those of individual exploits; in the latter, he moves from the word (exhortation, reproach, insult) to the deed. The act of hurling a weapon, and the warrior's success or failure, death or victory, are of course described in formulaic terms; but in each case the stroke is different, as is the wound that results in the clattering of armor as the warrior falls.

Finally, one distinctive feature of the Homeric style offers a perfect example of this taste for variety, this art of playing on a fixed model—the similes.

The Homeric simile may occupy no more than two lines but is frequently much longer. It opens with formulaic rigidity: "As when . . . even so . . ." But the "as when . . ." often introduces a secondary but fully drawn scene, presented in a series of juxtaposed clauses. Or several images may be grouped together. For example, when Patroclus kills Sarpedon, Sarpedon's fall is first compared to that of a tree that has been felled; then his groans are compared to those of a bull mortally wounded by a lion. Neither of these images is original, but the double simile helps to throw Sarpedon's death into relief. It calls attention to him, to the motion of his fall, and to the groans of the defeated warrior.

At the same time, the similes bring two different worlds into conjunction. Note that the first simile above is drawn from daily life; this is often the case in Homer. The second is taken from the world of animals, as are many motifs in the plastic arts contemporary to Homer (the very motif of the bull and the lion is preserved on later coins). To the same category belong all the images of natural violence: torrents, winds, fire. Thus the similes evoke two spheres—that of daily life and that of untamed nature and animals in the wild. Yet the two spheres border on one another in certain places (for example, in the hunt); and Homer juxtaposes similes drawn from each. Thus, in describing the advance of the Achaeans across the plain, he first compares the glare of their armor to that of a fire on a mountainside (2.455–59); then he compares the sound of their advance to the sound of flocks of birds ("geese or cranes or long-necked swans"), beating their wings and alighting with loud cries (460–68); finally he compares the masses of fighters to swarms of flies "hovering around a sheepfold on spring days, when milk is filling the pails" (469–73). Here we have three similes, taking up twenty lines; and all three summon up the country life of Homer's day—a life in which unusual and imposing scenes might be juxtaposed with the most familiar sights.

By means of this counterpoint that intermingles peace and war, a mythic time and the poet's own time, Homer avoids whatever tedium a purely narrative work might induce. The similes give the events of the epic a more tangible existence as well as a more broadly human resonance. Long after Homer, the use of similes was to remain a literary technique proper to the epic genre.

The Homeric epics mark the beginning of Greek literature; but they also represent the end of a civilization. What we call the archaic age came later, after a decided break in cultural continuity. There are only two groups of works that can be connected with Homer's as extensions or continuations of the epic tradition. I shall deal with these in the appendix that follows.

APPENDIX
THE EPIC CYCLE AND THE HOMERIC HYMNS

The epic cycle consisted of those poems that dealt, in a more or less Homeric style, with other aspects of the heroic legends and thus made up a sort of "cycle" of mythic materials. Their origins may have been very ancient, but they received their finished forms at various times between the eighth and sixth centuries B.C. All have been lost, and we know of their contents only through indirect and late sources (Proclus's *Chrestomathia*, the mythographers, the scholiasts). Grouped with the *Iliad* were several sequels: the *Aethiopis* and *Iliou Persis* ("The Sack of Troy") by Arctinus of Miletus (eighth century), and the *Little Iliad* by Lesches (seventh century). There was also an epic called the *Cypria*, which dealt with events preceding the action of the *Iliad*. Grouped with the *Odyssey* were the *Nostoi*, or "Homecomings" (of heroes other than Odysseus), and the *Telegonia*, a sequel to the *Odyssey* composed by Eugammon of Cyrene (sixth century).

One group of cyclic poems dealt with the Theban legends—the *Thebaid*, the *Oedipodea*, and the *Epigoni*. Others dealt with the battles of the Titans, with the life of Heracles (the *Oechalias Halosis*, or "Capture of Oechalia"), or with still other legends. If these poems were more fully known, we would be in a better position to appreciate the originality of the tragic poets, who dramatized many of the same legends.

The popularity of the Homeric poems can also be inferred from the existence of parodies, such as the *Batrachomuomachia* ("Battle of the Frogs and the Mice"), which has survived, and the *Margites*, whose hero was an anti-hero and could do nothing right. In antiquity these works were ascribed to Homer—a fact that ought to teach us caution. Also ascribed to Homer was the group of works called, for that reason, the Homeric hymns.

The collection bearing this name includes hymns to many different gods (Demeter, Apollo, Hermes, Aphrodite, Dionysus, and others). These were written over a considerable time span; the most important must date from the seventh and sixth centuries, though later pieces have been added to the corpus. They vary in length, from twenty lines to several hundred. We can generalize to the bare extent of suggesting that the hymns called Homeric were longer and more descriptive than the invocations ascribed to Orpheus. But whatever the diversity of the Homeric hymns, they deserve their name insofar as they do belong to the epic tradition. They do so, in the first place, by virtue of their meter, which is dactylic hexameter as in the epics; the lyric poets, by contrast, were to compose hymns in different meters, destined not for simple recitation but for musical accompaniment. In the second place— again like the epics—the Homeric hymns delight in narrative; they tell, for example, the story of the rape of Persephone and Demeter's search for her, or of Apollo's birth in Delos. We can even find in them descriptions of contemporary life, like that of the crowds of Ionians come to Delos for a festival of Apollo (in lines 146ff. of the Delian Hymn, which forms the opening of the *Hymn to Apollo*).

These various extensions or continuations of the Homeric epics testify to their immense influence—an influence that will recur in less tangible but no less important forms throughout the subsequent history of Greek literature.

2

The Archaic Age

After the eighth century B.C., Greece emerged from the period of disorder that had followed the disappearance of Mycenaean civilization. The new age was a kind of renaissance, marked by the rise of colonization and the growth of commerce. Such developments made people more aware of social inequalities, and bitter struggles followed. These struggles led to new forms of government, such as tyranny, and a greater participation in political life, with its confrontations and self-conscious taking of stands. The new political temper gained ground steadily up to the time of the Persian Wars.

In this period, a kind of poetry developed throughout Greece in which the role of the author and his personality was more strongly marked. At the same time, such poetry made room for questions about the nature of the universe; and from it, in the sixth century, philosophy emerged—a philosophy still couched for the most part in poetic form and still reflecting the religious framework of archaic thought. Not until the struggle with "the barbarian" and the resulting hegemony of Athens would there evolve, in the fifth century, a literature centered on the city-state, taking man as its measure.

Several of the authors included in the present chapter belong to the fifth century; they are not Athenians, however, and are discussed here because they mark the final stages of genres developed by earlier writers.

I · HESIOD

Hesiod was compared with Homer by the Greeks themselves; indeed, there existed a poetic *Contest of Homer and Hesiod*.[1] In meter and in language their works are closely comparable; yet it is hard to imagine two more different poetic worlds. Homer represented the spirit of the Greek aristocracy of Asia Minor; Hesiod was essentially a Boeotian peasant. His father had come from Aeolia to settle at Ascra, near Mount Helicon. There Hesiod spent his life. We know from his works that he had a disagreement with his brother, and that he farmed a small and infertile piece of land in a troubled age. It is

---

1. This contest was of course the work of a later poet or poets; it consisted of an imaginary dialogue between Homer and Hesiod, followed by famous passages from their works.—Trans.

generally thought (though we have no proof) that he lived around the middle of the seventh century.

Hesiod's work, as it has come down to us, consists of two poems, very different from one another: the *Theogony* and the *Works and Days*. The ancients ascribed others to him; one of these, *The Shield*, has survived. A work of about five hundred lines, it tells of Heracles' encounter with Cycnus, son of Ares, and gives a detailed description of the hero's shield. While it includes some Hesiodic elements, the poem as a whole is clearly later in date and mediocre in quality. Hesiod is more likely to have been the author of a *Catalogue of Women*, or *Ehoiae*, some lines of which are included in the *Shield*; and there is some likelihood in the attribution to him of other works we no longer have, such as the didactic poem called *The Precepts of Chiron* and the epic *Aegimius* (named after a Dorian king for whom Heracles fought). All of these have been lost; and the two surviving poems have themselves been disfigured by many later interpolations, often difficult to delimit.

Turning to these two major poems, we find in both a bewildering archaism and some remarkable innovations. The archaism appears in the choice of subjects and in the tone.

The *Theogony* describes the genealogy of the gods and the formation of the world, which they embody or personify. In Hesiod's account the gods arise from the primal Void (or Chaos), Earth, and Eros. Earth gives birth to Sky and Sea; the many offspring of these early generations include the Titans—Ocean[2] and Tethys, Cronus and Rhea, and their siblings. At last Zeus appears, to impose his law and triumph over the Titans. From time to time, mere lists of names occur, like those found in many religious traditions. Elsewhere we find descriptions of monsters half human and half animal, or creatures with a hundred arms. The pattern of the work as a whole is based on the divine succession, the passing of power from one god to another, marked by violence and leading up to the eventual triumph of Zeus, who establishes a new regime. All this implies a very archaic form of thought, and seems to draw on remote mythic traditions. The same is true of the violence with which one generation of gods succeeds another in Hesiod's account. Thus, for example, Uranus is mutilated by his son (as Earth and Sky are separated), and Aphrodite is born from the drops of fallen sperm (lines 173–206); thus Cronus swallows his children (459ff.). The ancient origins of such accounts have been confirmed by the discovery (around 1950) of Hittite and Ugaritic texts containing related tales that go back to the second millennium B.C. The *Theogony* may also owe something to a body of Orphic poems, which we know only through relatively late versions but which seem to have emphasized, as Hesiod does, the roles of the Void, Night and Eros.

The most original aspect of Hesiod's *Theogony* is probably his effort to introduce a moral order into this heritage of myth. He does so (in the later epi-

2. Hesiod's word for "Sea" suggests "the watery element," the expanse of salt water, rather than a particular body of it; to the Greeks, "*the* sea" was the Mediterranean. They thought of Ocean as a river encircling the limits of the earth. —Trans.

sodes, including the legend of Prometheus) by exalting the victory of Zeus, whose reign is to be different from those of the older gods. He does so likewise by offering genealogies for "divinities" that are in fact moral concepts. Thus Strife, or Eris, gives birth to "painful Sorrow, Oblivion, Hunger, tearful Griefs," etc. (see lines 226ff.). Where these ideas are introduced into the poem, we can detect a certain awkwardness of composition and a decided stiffness of tone. What makes the *Theogony* interesting is the remote past we can glimpse in it: it grips us because it surprises us.

The same is true to some extent of the other poem, which has a purely didactic tone. Here, Hesiod advises his brother Perses to devote his life to hard work and the careful management of his property. The poet lists a farmer's major tasks, adding some advice on navigation (which he distrusts) and a few religious prohibitions of a strictly material order. At first glance all this seems very archaic, impersonal and alien. Nor does it help that the opening of the *Works and Days* includes an excursus in the style of the *Theogony*, tracing the myth of Prometheus and Pandora and that of the races of man (races of gold, silver, bronze, heroes, and iron). The second myth, whose import is pessimistic—since Hesiod says he lives in the age of iron, an age of hardship, violence, and suffering—undoubtedly goes back to remote Oriental sources, which Hesiod has arranged and modified, sometimes awkwardly (thus the age of heroes oddly intrudes on the sequence of metals and alters its meaning).

Yet if on such counts the Hesiodic poems seem tied to a distant past, both also display traits that are amazingly fresh and personal. This is especially clear in the two preludes. To begin with, Hesiod is the first Greek poet to say "I," the first to speak of himself and his own life. To be sure, he claims the inspiration of the Muses; but his very account (at the beginning of the *Theogony*) of the way the Muses appeared to him on Mount Helicon is an account of a personal experience. In fact, he introduces himself by name: "It was [the Muses] who taught Hesiod a beautiful song, as he was pasturing his lambs at the foot of sacred Helicon. And these are the first words the goddesses spoke to me. . ." (lines 22ff.). The Muses even offered him a branch of laurel; then "they breathed into me divine speech, that I might sing of what was to be and what had been." Here we have the evocation of a specific place and of an individual man touched by inspiration. At the same time, the direct link between the poet and the Muse implies an exalted notion of poetry. The passage closes with a hymn to the Muses, describing the blessings of poetry and the way song has of dispelling cares while spreading wisdom. In fact, there is a kind of revelation in this meeting between the poet and the Muses, who tell him "what is, what will be, and what has been." The phrase is well suited to the breadth of Hesiod's subject and the gravity of his tone. It is no accident if Hesiod's work ignores the familiarity Homer saw in the relations between gods and men, or the weaknesses he was pleased to ascribe to the gods.

The same Hesiod who thus describes his relationship with the Muses has no hesitation, in his other poem, about describing his life and tribulations.

Everything we know about his origins, his differences with his brother, his poetic career, and the voyage to Chalcis that he undertook to further it comes from his own account in the *Works and Days* (lines 27–41, 631–40, 650–62). The life he describes is that of a man of humble status, with its work and leisure; he speaks of winter clothing, modest summer feasts, harvest time and vintage time. The magnificence imagined by Homer is replaced by everyday reality, which is explicitly that of a place and a milieu—the poet's own.

The poet, though present in these concrete details, is still more forcefully present (in both poems) in his ideal of morality; for Hesiod is a man who craves justice. This is evident from the beginning of the *Theogony*, where the gifts of the Muses are said to ensure that kings "administer justice with upright verdicts" (86). The theme recurs when Justice appears among Zeus's kin—whether in the form of Themis, a lover of Zeus, or of Dike, who (together with Order and Peace) is born of his union with Themis. But the full importance of justice emerges only in the *Works and Days*. The prelude opens with a warning against the "bad" Strife (Eris) who leads men to covet what does not belong to them.[3] Then, at line 202, the theme of justice comes to the foreground—and stays there for nearly one hundred lines. To instruct not only his brother but also the men of power who administer justice, Hesiod tells the fable of the hawk and the nightingale, which illustrates in the starkest of terms the conflict between force and justice. The hawk snatches up the nightingale in his claws and mocks him: "Wretch, why cry out? You are in the grip of one much stronger than you!" Next, Hesiod adds his own advice, no less clear and specific: "But as for you, Perses, listen to justice; don't let arrogance breed in you. Arrogance is a bad thing for poor folk; even the powerful have trouble bearing up under it, and its weight crushes them when they meet with disasters. Much better is the road that leads another way, toward just deeds" (213ff.). Hesiod goes on to describe the misfortunes that overtake false judges, and the prosperity of lands where justice prevails. Such prosperity touches everything, including nature itself. Conversely, a whole city may pay for a single man's offense; Zeus is vigilant. The poet sings the praises of "Justice, daughter of Zeus, whom the gods honor and revere"; he describes her as sitting at Zeus's feet to denounce the guilty. Justice, then, has Zeus as its guarantor; it is the most precious possession of mankind. Animals devour one another, but men know a better fate. Whether they are protected or punished by Zeus depends on their own action—on whether they are just or unjust.

Such a plea for justice, and such a profession of faith in *divine* justice, are nowhere to be found in Homer. The convictions expressed here with such force inaugurate an important strain in Greek thought whose best-known representatives (before the fourth-century philosophers) were to be Solon and Aeschylus.

---

3. According to Hesiod, there is also a "good" Strife, emulation.—Trans.

It should not be forgotten that this appeal to the notion of justice took shape in a world racked by hardship and struggle, or that it was put forward by a man of modest means, anxious to protect his property and troubled by the arbitrariness with which cases at law may be decided. Hesiod is also a spokesman for the farmer, who knows that his harvest or the increase of his flocks depends on forces beyond his control—forces that Zeus can be seen to personify. Such attitudes show how firmly this early doctrine of justice is rooted in a specific time and social milieu, from which it later becomes detached in the works of Solon and Aeschylus.

The link I have just traced between the two original features of Hesiod's poetry—his personal tone and his praise of justice—also accounts for the link Hesiod sees between justice and work (a much rarer notion in Greece). Here is his second piece of advice to his brother: "Come, then, always keep my charge in mind: work, Perses, worthy son, that famine may shun you and that you may earn the love of garlanded Demeter, who will fill your barn with life-giving grain. Hunger is the constant companion of the man who does nothing" (298ff.). The concern for work is closely related to the concern for justice: men must live by honest and upright means because, in Hesiod's view, ill-gotten gains profit no one. This is the sense in which he can claim work makes men dear to the gods: "There is no disgrace in working; the disgrace is to sit idle" (311). Since hard work is commonly contrasted with dishonesty, we find nothing surprising in such sayings. Yet in Greece they have an unfamiliar ring; work has never been a value in itself to the Greeks, nor a popular theme in their literature.

Thus, in the two brilliant prologues to his poems, Hesiod introduced a series of new and original themes—some that we might even call modern. Several of course were suggested by the age in which he lived; and these were destined for fuller development in the lyric poetry of the next century.

II · ARCHAIC POETRY: FROM HESIOD TO PINDAR

From the eighth to the fifth centuries there were many poets in Greece, known to us for the most part from quotations in later works. Unlike Homer and Hesiod they no longer wrote in hexameters but used a variety of meters, composing fairly short works that were meant to be sung. Because the instrument in most common use was the lyre, the poetry it accompanied came to be called "lyric"—a term that later outgrew this narrow and technical meaning. Alongside this poetry sung to the lyre, either by an individual or by a chorus, various other forms existed, including "elegy" (usually sung to the flute) and "iambic" poetry (so called from the name of the meter), which was recited to the accompaniment of special instruments. Such poems were not novelties at the time; already in the Homeric epics we find references to occasional poetry such as paeans, wedding songs, or dirges. In the archaic age, however, the genre struck a new vein of personal expression; and this phenomenon was not confined to any one region of Greece.

Indeed, the multiplicity of geographic centers was a major feature of the new poetry, already visible in Hesiod. It corresponds to the development of new city-states. Asia Minor was still a prolific region, producing Callinus, Mimnermus, Phocylides, and Anacreon. But the islands put forward their own favorite sons and daughters: Archilochus was born in Paros and emigrated to Thasos; Alcaeus and Sappho were natives of Mytilene. Soon the mainland cities were to be reckoned with as well: Solon was an Athenian, Theognis a Megarian, Pindar a Theban; and even before their time Sparta had adopted poets from abroad, such as Alcman. Where choral lyric was concerned, the influence of Greek Italy was far from negligible in the sixth century. Stesichorus was a Sicilian; Ibycus came from Rhegium (on the Italian coast opposite Sicily); Bacchylides and Pindar composed odes for Hieron, a tyrant of Syracuse. Corresponding to the plurality of centers was another feature new to Greek poetry: the plurality of dialects in which verse was written.

Remarkably, this poetry, which encompassed a variety of genres and developed in diverse cities, manages to reflect a number of common features of the period as a whole, in which political institutions throughout Greece were evolving in similar ways. Just as the centers of Greek cultural life were multiplying, the different strata of society were becoming more autonomous. The old hereditary monarchies had disappeared, and city-states in the fullest sense were coming into their own. Within the cities, wealth was no longer confined to the old aristocracies. New men rose to power, founding regimes in which rule was not hereditary (the tyrannies); still later, democratic regimes appeared. Whether or not it was associated with the political struggles, poetry became more personal, as in Hesiod's case. Henceforward all poets did as Hesiod had done, and still more emphatically: they spoke of themselves, of their loves or their adventures, or of what they hoped for their cities in war and in peace.

Yet in the midst of this renaissance age, a theme was found that reconciled the exaltation of the individual with that of the city, and the old aristocratic values with the growth of new states throughout Greece—praise of victorious athletes. The Olympic Games were established at the beginning of the eighth century, and the other major games at the beginning of the sixth. In its celebration of athletic victors, choral lyric—which marks the last stage of development of this kind of poetry—exalted at one and the same time a hero, a city, and an ideal conception of life.

Diverse as the lyric poets were, most had in common the sense that they were imparting a kind of wisdom. From the brief moralizing verses we find quoted here and there to the great visions of Pindar, we can see a distinctive moral thought emerging in the course of these three centuries of turmoil, liberation, and discovery. Beginning with Hesiod, the dominant strand in this thought is the idea that the gods will punish the excesses, or *hubris*, of men.

1 · IAMBIC POETRY

Iambic poetry is an exception to the general rule. The meter in itself has a somewhat sharp and pungent quality, which lends itself to satire. Iambic lines had been inserted among the hexameters of the *Margites* (see appendix to chapter 1 above); and Aristotle observes (in the *Poetics*, 1448b) that this meter was commonly used for satiric or comic exchanges. His description perfectly fits the best-known of the iambic poets (who also composed "elegiac" verse), Archilochus. Since Archilochus is one of the earliest Greek poets (he seems to have lived in the first half of the seventh century), and since practically no other iambic poets are known to us, I have placed iambic verse earlier in this account than would otherwise be warranted.

Archilochus was born in Paros; but his father Telesicles had led a group of Parian settlers to the richer island of Thasos. Archilochus was the son of Telesicles and a slave woman. In his turn, he too left for Thasos, where his life was spent in combat, fighting the Thracians and Naxians (he was finally killed by a Naxian). But his was the life of an adventurer rather than that of a warrior in the heroic mold. Indeed, his originality lay in his rejection of the Homeric tradition, both social and poetic, in order to embrace its opposite. Speaking in the first person, he idealizes nothing; he is a realist who refuses to glamorize war and makes a boast of rejecting the heroic code. He tells, for example, of abandoning his shield near a bush: "But I saved my life. Let the old shield rot! I'll buy another just as good" (frag. 6 Diehl).

In the same way Archilochus refuses to glamorize love—to say the least. When the man who had promised him his daughter Neobule in marriage changed his mind, Archilochus attacked the whole family in verse, including his former betrothed, whom he branded an "old courtesan." Pindar called Archilochus "the insulter"; a few fragments of his epodes, in very bad condition, suggest that his verses could be quite obscene. This did not prevent Archilochus from having his own brand of morality ("I know how to love those who love me, and hate my enemies"), as well as a crude popular wisdom, with a tone sometimes reminiscent of fable.

Semonides was another iambic poet who, like Archilochus, moved from one island to another (Samos to Amorgos); he too must have lived in the seventh century, but his work was not as well known. His major surviving poem is an attack on women, whom he divides into categories corresponding to different animals. Hipponax of Ephesus was another poet in this tradition; his work, dating from the sixth century, consists of realistic complaints interspersed with personal insults. After Archilochus, however, the genre as a whole quickly lost its luster; and even its greatest successes stand apart from the mainstream.

2 · ELEGY

In meter, Greek elegy is closest to Homer and Hesiod, since it consists of alternating lines of epic (dactylic) hexameter and dactylic pentameter. We should not judge its content by the modern meaning of the term "elegiac," which stems from the Latin elegists. The first Greek elegies, in fact, were war poems.

The earliest poets in this tradition are Callinus, Tyrtaeus, and Mimnermus. Callinus seems to belong to the first half of the seventh century; his apparent source of inspiration was the heroic tradition. Tyrtaeus, who lived at Sparta in the seventh century, is likewise known to us for several elegies combining an exhortation to warlike courage and a glorification of death in battle. Mimnermus, by contrast, is known for poems that have nothing warlike about them. An Ionian who lived about the year 600 or a little before, Mimnermus sang of the shortness of life and enjoyed retelling episodes from the myths.

Unlike iambic poetry, elegy continued into the classical period. Toward the end of the archaic age, two poets whose work is better known to us used the elegiac form—Solon and Theognis. The contrast between their work and that of their predecessors is revealing: instead of a warlike zeal still close to the epic model, we have in Solon and Theognis the testimony of two men who took part in, and pondered, the political struggles of their time.

Theognis probably lived about the middle or the second half of the sixth century, though some scholars date the beginning of his career as early as 630. He was from Megara (probably the mainland city of that name). A collection of over 1200 lines of his elegiac poetry has survived, along with 200 lines of love poetry (making up book 2), much of which is clearly apocryphal. Even book 1 is made up of heterogeneous elements, probably by several different authors. Yet there remains a substantial core, marked by a distinctive point of view. It consists of admonitions addressed to a young man named Cyrnus. All are morally impeccable ("Be prudent, and seek neither honors, prestige, nor fortune by base or unjust actions," 1.29ff.); but they take on a highly personal coloring as soon as politics is mentioned. Theognis thinks his city is on the road to ruin because "wicked men are corrupting the people, and sanctioning injustice for the sake of their own profit and power" (45ff.). Apparently he himself was ruined as a result of political upheaval; so he bewails the evils of the age, especially the fact that "those who once were gentlemen have become nobodies" and cannot even hold their own. The only refuge is in friendship—when it is constant—and in a wisdom difficult to attain. Theognis is a fierce and rousing witness to the bitterness of aristocrats who saw themselves being dispossessed in favor of people for whom they had nothing but scorn.

Solon was involved in the same struggles but was able to rise above them, and his poems radiate an earnest attachment to the common good. We know of his career from these poems and from such later works as Aristotle's *Constitution of Athens* and Plutarch's *Life of Solon*. An Athenian, born about 640, Solon was appointed archon in 594. He took courageous measures to stem social upheaval (among others, the abolition of enslavement for debt), and many Athenian laws are attributed to him; he was seen by many as one of the fathers of Athenian democracy. Having finished his work as peacemaker and lawgiver, he left for a long trip abroad. On his return, he took a stand against the tyranny of Pisistratus. He died about 560. His poems (of which we have only fragments, some iambic and some elegiac) reflect both his political and his moral ideals, which were inseparable.

The moral standard he proposes is close to that of Hesiod. Solon wants no riches unless the gods give them, for he knows what damage hubris can cause (frag. 1 Diehl, lines 9ff.); he also knows that Zeus will punish this offense sooner or later. The idea of divine will is ever-present in Solon. In contrast to Hesiod, however, he deals mainly with the application of this standard to the city-state. He trusts that Zeus and Athene will preserve his city (frag. 3 Diehl); but only if it is not ruined by the folly of its own citizens, who are ready to opt for hubris and injustice if they think they can turn a profit. To ward off these evils he proposes the ideal of *eunomia*, the order of good laws, which will put an end to harmful desires (ibid., line 32). To help others achieve this ideal, Solon describes his own attitude during the time of crisis when he was in power: "To the people I gave just as much power as was necessary, without reducing or overextending their privileges. As for the powerful, whose wealth was a source of envy, I took care that they too should be shielded from indignity. I stood firm, covering both factions with a sturdy shield, and I let neither seize an unjust victory over the other" (frag. 5 Diehl). And again: "As if between two armies, I held firm, like a boundary stone" (frag. 25 Diehl). He says repeatedly that he succeeded in restraining both the common people and their enemies; this politics of compromise is based on the conviction that the good of the *polis*, or city, comes before every other consideration. The word *polis* thus recurs with a peculiar insistence in certain of Solon's elegies.

Even before his archonship, Solon had written an elegy that put heart into the Athenians and persuaded them to retake Salamis. This episode confirms his patriotism but leaves a disagreeably narrow impression of it. For his patriotism was chiefly a concern for good citizenship, and his politics had an important ethical coloring. It was for this reason that the first great Athenian statesman, who wrote about himself, his work, and his struggles, was also numbered among the Seven Sages of Greece. He provides the link between the ethical thought of the archaic age and the fight for democracy.

3 · PERSONAL LYRIC

Throughout ancient times, the island of Lesbos produced lyric poets of exceptional ability. The island had been home to the early poets Terpander and Arion, of whom we know very little. Toward the end of the seventh century and the beginning of the sixth (i.e., roughly during Solon's lifetime), Lesbos produced two great poets, whose fame and literary influence were substantial. The two were contemporaries, one a woman and one a man—Sappho and Alcaeus. Both were members of the local aristocracy and may well have known one another. Living in a troubled age, each experienced exile; but Sappho, unlike Alcaeus, took no part in politics. Both also enjoyed a highly civilized and pleasure-filled way of life, which may have been influenced by that of nearby Lydia. Finally, both wrote in a direct, concrete, and spontaneous style that cannot leave the reader indifferent.

Sappho represents the feminine side of this poetry, not only because she was herself a woman but because she lived among women (young girls to whom she taught her art) and it was women that she loved. Love is never far to seek in her poems. Among her works are wedding songs (or *Epithalamia*) and a *Prayer to Aphrodite*. There are fleeting glimpses of the graceful girls in whose midst she lived; there are also burning descriptions of erotic feeling. On this subject Sappho was quoted and emulated for centuries—and with good reason, for the emotional intensity of some of her lines is remarkable. A famous example reads: "My tongue is severed; a subtle fire steals suddenly under my skin; . . . my ears are filled with sound; sweat pours down my body; trembling seizes me; I turn paler than the grass" (frag. 2 Diehl).

In the history of versification, Sappho has given her name to the Sapphic stanza (also used by Latin poets). It is because of her that women who love women are called "lesbians." But, most important, we owe to her the creation of "lyric" poetry as we still understand that term; and the Latin lyrists, in their love poetry, all echo her. Sadly, only meager fragments of her work have survived (augmented from time to time by the discovery of new papyri).

The poems of Alcaeus survive in much the same state. But his subject matter contrasts with Sappho's, for he tended to celebrate the pleasures of life *not* inspired by love. He wrote hymns to the gods, similar in inspiration to the Homeric hymns (see appendix to chapter 1 above) and incorporating mythic elements. In particular, we have fragments of his hymns to Apollo, to the Dioscuri,[4] to Hermes, and perhaps to Artemis, if the attribution is correct. Along with this religious vein, however, we find two major themes in Alcaeus that seem more characteristic, more revealing of his personality. First, there are the drinking songs, in which the joys of wine are associated with all occasions and all seasons. Wine suggests feasts and festivals—and the pleasures of the aristocrat; thus one of the longer fragments describes the glittering weapons lining the walls of the poet's house. Then there are the political poems. In conjuction with Pittacus, Alcaeus had opposed the tyrant Myrsilus. Pittacus then came to power and, like Solon in Athens, took the double role of sage and statesman charged with restoring order. At this point Alcaeus broke with him, calling him a tyrant and otherwise vilifying him. Late versions of the story assure us that Pittacus pardoned him. But in his poems we see Alcaeus in the thick of these struggles, deploring the sentence of exile

---

4. The twin brothers Castor and Polydeuces, sons of Zeus and brothers of Helen.—Trans.

that excludes him from the assembly, exulting over his enemy's death—in short, giving a passionate commentary on current events.

The Alcaic stanza, like the Sapphic, was destined to remain in the poetic repertoire of the Greeks and Romans. Yet between these two poets, who offer such striking parallels and were, moreover, contemporaries and compatriots, lies the gulf that even in Mytilene divided the concerns of men from those of women.

With Anacreon, an Ionian from the small town of Teos who lived in the mid-sixth century, we move closer to the Greek mainland. Anacreon's patrons were tyrants: after spending some time in Abdera, on the Thracian border, he lived first at the court of Polycrates of Samos and then with Hipparchus, tyrant of Athens. Thus he called no one city his home. His genius was that of the court poet, amiable, sophisticated, fond of banquets and beautiful boys and girls—in a word, fond of love, though the love he celebrates lacks the personal and passionate note struck by Sappho. Anacreon composed light odes and epigrams; we possess many fragments, though all are quite short. The Romans are well known to have imitated him, and collections of "Anacreontic" poems assembled in later antiquity were to have a considerable influence on later European poetry.

Personal lyric inevitably ran the risk of becoming insipid; this was not the case with choral lyric, however.

4 · CHORAL LYRIC BEFORE PINDAR

Choral poetry appeared first in Sparta, where Terpander, a native of Lesbos, had gone to found a school of choral lyric. We know that one other such school existed. It was in Sparta too that Alcman (who apparently came from Sardis) distinguished himself as a choral poet in the seventh century. He wrote songs for girls (*Partheneia*), which engaged the young singers in spirited exchanges but were not lacking in moral advice and denunciations of hubris. Alcman wrote in the Laconian dialect; indeed, the genre of choral lyric was never to lose its Doric accent: the choruses of Attic tragedy continued to be written in Doric.

At the end of the seventh century, with Stesichorus (whose name means "director of choruses"), we follow choral lyric to Sicily (Himera). Stesichorus wrote hymns to various heroes of the epic cycle. His poem about Helen, and a sequel called the *Palinode*,[5] inspired Euripides' *Helen*. No less influential were his treatments of other myths; we know, for example, that he composed an *Oresteia*. Unfortunately, only a few brief fragments of Stesichorus survive. The same is true of Ibycus, a choral poet from Greek Italy who lived shortly after Stesichorus.

In the second half of the sixth century, choral lyric seems to have found a new strain with Simonides of Ceos. Born near Athens, he lived in that city at

---

5. In which he took back the criticisms of her expressed in the first poem. —Trans.

the court of the tyrant Hippias; later he moved to Syracuse, where he was a guest of the tyrant Hieron. His life was long and his literary output extensive, including dithyrambs, songs of praise, dirges, epigrams, and "epinicia," or odes for victorious athletes, a genre he seems to have pioneered. His tone is generally lofty and he does not hesitate to moralize, somewhat in the vein of Solon; he also sings of the shortness of life and the caprices of fortune. This is not to say that he avoids political themes, but he does not treat them in a partisan spirit; he was still living during the Persian Wars and drew from the climate of the time a spirit of Panhellenic patriotism. In competition with Aeschylus, he produced an epitaph praising those who died at Marathon; he also composed several epitaphs for the heroes of Thermopylae. Simonides gave choral lyric the same breadth that Pindar, forty years his junior, would later achieve. At the same time, we can see in Simonides' case, as in that of Solon, the definitive placing of the poet within the city-state that was to characterize the whole of the fifth century.

III · PINDAR AND BACCHYLIDES

Pindar's work is better preserved than that of any of the poets I have discussed since Hesiod. His poems fill not just a few pages, but a volume or more in modern editions. Even so, we have an incomplete and one-sided view of his work, for only his epinician odes have survived, though he also wrote hymns to the gods, processional hymns, choral songs for young girls, threnodies, and songs of praise (panegyrics). Of his work in these genres we have only a few fragments. On the other hand, the epinicia have been well preserved. They are grouped, according to the contests involved, into Olympian, Pythian, Nemean, and Isthmian odes. From this corpus we can form an idea of his life, his thought, and his talents.

Like Hesiod, Pindar was a Boeotian; he was born near Thebes, apparently in 518, and was clearly of noble birth. He was probably still quite young when he left for Athens; there he seems to have made connections with the powerful Alcmaeonid family, for whom he wrote several poems. But he did not share the Athenians' fervor at the time of the Persian Wars (Thebes was among those cities that sided with the Persians). As early as 498, his victory odes had earned him public notice (the *Tenth Pythian*, honoring a Thessalian, was composed in that year). His fame soon spread throughout Greece. He wrote many odes for victors from Aegina, and composed a paean to the island itself. Shortly after 476 he moved to Sicily, where he frequented the courts of two famous rulers, Theron (tyrant of Acragas) and Hieron (tyrant of Gela and Syracuse); many of the odes are in honor of Sicilian victors. Still later, he returned to the Greek mainland. He found appropriate words of praise for Athens (the famous lines beginning, "You of the violet-crowned brow . . ."); he also received commissions from Corinth, Rhodes, and Cyrene (Libya). He had, in fact, written an ode for a Cyrenian victor as early as 474, and later wrote two Pythians for King Arcesilas, in which he did not hesitate to offer political advice. He died in 438 at the age of eighty.

Pindar's poems thus allow us to reconstruct the story of his life, including his quarrels with powerful men, his hopes, and his beliefs. Most striking to us, perhaps, is the very considerable place Pindar occupied in the Greek world of his day, even though that world was engaged in life-and-death struggles. To understand Pindar, we must first of all realize that his poetry, though written in celebration of athletic feats, was anything but purely "occasional" verse. Pindar never *describes* the feats he praises, nor does he tell us anything about the victors' lives. He aims at once for the highest meaning of the victory, its universal and symbolic implications for the whole of human life. He reaches this higher plane by associating the individual victory with a myth and with a moral teaching.

The openings of his poems are, in the truest sense of the word, brilliant. Often they invoke glory, divinity, gold—and these three are one, for glory is a gift of the gods and shines like gold. Sometimes the next phrase or two recall the victor's earlier successes or those of his relatives. But then, gathering all his forces, Pindar leaps without transition into the world of myth. He offers no explanation for his choice of myths. He may take his cue from the victor's place of origin; for a Cyrenian, for example, he tells of the maiden Cyrene and her liaison with Apollo (*Pythian* 9), or speaks of the Argonauts, whose quest led to the foundation of Cyrene (*Pythian* 4). It may be the site of the victory that sets off his train of thought: Hieron's Olympic victory summons up the legend of Tantalus and of Pelops, who had a cult at Olympia (*Olympian* 1). Occasionally an incident in the victor's life is the source of inspiration. For Hieron, founder of the new city of Aetna, Pindar recalls Zeus's crushing defeat of Typhon, and Typhon's imprisonment in Tartarus, where his rages, far below the earth, cause the eruptions of Mount Aetna (*Pythian* 1).

Such extrinsic connections, however, are never the sole reason for Pindar's choice. It is clear, for one thing, that he sees instructional value in the myths. Unlike the epic poets, he does not *tell* the stories but merely evokes them by means of a few dazzling images; nor does he adhere to precise chronological order. Such evocations always yield either a reflection on the meaning of the world or a piece of advice. Thus Typhon's imprisonment in *Pythian* 1 fits into a passage praising the power of music—and the power of Zeus. After focusing on music in the opening lines, Pindar continues: "But all that Zeus does not love trembles on hearing the cry of the Pierides—whether on earth or on the wide sea; and he too trembles who lies in awful Tartarus, the enemy of the gods, Typhon of the hundred heads" (13ff.). After describing Typhon's fate, Pindar concludes: "Let us hope, O Zeus, let us hope to please you" (29). Similarly, the Argonauts' quest, in *Pythian* 4, has Cyrene as its point of departure; but its import—at least a part of its import—is to highlight the luminous figure of Jason with his resplendent blond curls, as he agrees to end the old feud with his uncle and embark on his quest: for "the Fates stand aloof when there is hatred between those who share one blood" (145). Pindar means on this occasion to recommend moderation and reconciliation to the king of Cyrene.

It must be admitted that in some cases the connections between myth, praise, and exhortation are not so clear. Since Pindar's style is always concise and taut, suggestive rather than explicit and lacking obvious conclusions and transitions, scholars have often been at a loss to reconstruct the unity of intention behind a given ode. It is important to recognize that the unity of Pindar's poetry is not in its linear development. The poet moves freely and sometimes abruptly from one theme to another; as he himself observes, his songs are "like the bee" and "flit from one subject to the next" (*Pythian* 10.54). Only at the level of the entire poem, beyond individual allusions and occasions, can a convergence of the different themes be discerned.

On top of this, Pindar is self-conscious about the importance of his art. His asides on the subject are not confined to the power of music but extend to the making of a good poet and the role he should take in society. We even find references to Pindar's disputes with rival poets. All such observations confirm and contribute to the untrammeled quality of his poems. Yet this freedom he allows himself is justified insofar as the nature of poetry and the poet's responsibilities are proper concerns of ethics in general. Pindar's comments about poetry are related to the other moral judgments he expresses in his odes.

To reduce his work to a series of moral judgments, however, would be to distort it seriously. It consists, in the first place, of images—examples of all that is most beautiful and brilliant in human life. It celebrates the aristocrat's enjoyment of festivals and feasts. Yet these beauties and pleasures are always bathed, as it were, in a religious light; the gods grant them and preside over them. This is the source of sublimity in Pindar's lyrics, even when his images are most concrete. For example, at the beginning of *Pythian* 1, as he celebrates the power of music, he ascends in one sustained movement from the human to the divine sphere: "Golden lyre, common possession of Apollo and the dark-haired Muses, at your voice the rhythmic steps of dancers open the festival; and singers obey your signal when, vibrant with music, you cause to ring out the first notes of the preludes that lead choruses. You know too how to extinguish the eternal fire at the tip of the thunderbolt; and Zeus's eagle sleeps, perched on the scepter of the god." The thought that the gods exist is ever present in Pindar, expressed with a respect that leads him to emend the less edifying of the myths or to pass over certain of their details in silence. At the same time he *adds* to the myths a sense of divine omnipotence and mystery: "God, who overtakes the eagle in midflight, outstrips the dolphin on the sea, curbs arrogant mortals, and sees to it that glory, which is imperishable, passes to others . . ." (*Pythian* 2.50ff.). The corollary to such beliefs is that everything depends on the attributes God gives to men; an aristocratic ethic is thus fully compatible with Pindar's religion. One is born brave, or born a poet (*Olympian* 9.100); in each case the natural talent, *phua*, is paramount. "Nature causes to shine, in children, the magnanimous spirit they inherit from their fathers" (*Pythian* 8.44); "Best by nature is best"[6] (*Olympian* 9.100); "The wise man is he who owes to nature his fund of wisdom; those who know only for having learned are like crows in their endless chatter—let them croak in vain against the divine bird of Zeus" (*Olympian* 2.86ff.).

At the same time, this perpetual confrontation between man and the gods dominates Pindar's philosophy and his ethics. He shares with the other poets of the archaic age a vivid sense of man's vulnerability; but, unlike them, he also has a sense of what man can become by the gods' grace. He makes this point repeatedly (e.g., in *Nemean* 6.1-7), but most brilliantly at the end of *Pythian* 8: "Creatures of a day! What is each of us? What is he not? Man is the dream of a shadow. But when the gods cast a ray of light on him, a great brightness surrounds him, and his life is sweet." Men are blind without the help of the Muses but may be led by them to the truth. Pindar's continual references to the gods make for the grandeur of his odes, giving each victory song a hymnlike quality.

In such a world there can obviously be no greater fault than to desire more than one's portion, i.e., to be guilty of hubris (as is Ixion, in *Pythian* 2): those whom Pindar praises are like the Rhodian of whom he says, "He goes straight ahead on the path inimical to hubris" (*Olympian* 7.90). But Pindar is not satisfied with this purely negative teaching. We find in his odes the incarnation of many virtues: friendship, courage, hospitality, moderation. We also find a civic ideal of peace and understanding. The opening of *Pythian* 8, addressed to Tranquility, is especially evocative of this ideal: "Kindly Tranquility, daughter of Justice, you who make cities great . . ." This resembles Hesiod's ideal of justice, adapted to the world of the city-states—the world of Solon. Yet in the realm of politics, as elsewhere, Pindar's thought is frankly conservative; where Solon struggles against inequity, Pindar asks only for harmony and peace. The same note is struck, for example, at the opening of *Olympian* 13: "There dwells Eunomia (good order), with her sisters: the prop of cities, unshakable Justice, and Peace, dispenser of wealth."

By respecting such virtues, man can hope to win the goodwill of the gods and a measure of prosperity. But there is also a way for him to earn an immortality of his own—glory—endorsed and generated by the work of the poet. So the poet's responsibility is great; he must never stray from the truth, for it is up to him to save from oblivion those who deserve to be remem-

---

6. Translated by Richmond Lattimore, in *Odes of Pindar* (Chicago: University of Chicago Press, 1976), p. 30. Although the other translations from Pindar are my own, following De Romilly, all line references are to the Greek texts used by Lattimore (Bowra's Oxford Classical Text edition) and are correct for Lattimore's version as well.—Trans.

bered. Exploits can only survive if, "by the grace of bright-crowned Mnemo-sune [Memory], they win glorious songs in recompense for harsh toils" *(Nemean* 7.15ff). The task is shared by the Muses and the Graces, who inspire the poet and use him as their mouthpiece. In this way the gift he receives from the gods permits him in turn to confer on others a form of immortality.

This conviction of Pindar's accounts for the majestic quality of his poems. Almost always composed in triads (consisting of strophe, antistrophe, and epode),[7] the odes combine breadth of form and internal tension. Sentences are compressed to the point of obscurity; rare and compound words and periphrases give the language an esoteric cast, as if it were meant for initiates only; metaphors allow the poet to work on several levels simultaneously; meaning is deliberately hidden, as in oracular responses. Yet if the movement of each ode seems erratic, even jerky, the images burst forth one by one with all their symbolic force: gold and purple, the chariot, the time of flowering . . . Sometimes the sentence leaps like a torrent into long, thundering word pictures; sometimes, by contrast, a gesture is described with such sobriety that the emphasis falls on what is suggested but not spelled out. These characteristics of Pindar's style have baffled readers whose first love is rationality; but they give his work an incomparable vividness. We shall find some of the same traits a few years later in the most religious of the tragedians, Aeschylus.

Pindar found a rival in a man ten years his junior, Bacchylides. Bacchylides was a nephew of Simonides and, like him, a native of Ceos. It must have been his uncle who introduced him to Hieron; we know that the tyrant extended his patronage to both Pindar and Bacchylides. The younger poet's work was little known until the last years of the nineteenth century, when newly discovered papyri yielded fifteen of his epinician odes, along with some paeans and dithyrambs. His art, as revealed by these works, is much simpler than Pindar's: his panegyrics are truly poems of praise, his thought is clearly expressed, and Homer's influence is palpable. In a way, the fragments of Bacchylides seem to signal the transition from early lyric to tragedy; some of his dithyrambs include dialogues (e.g., between Theseus and Minos), and some were written entirely in dialogue form (the return of Theseus).

Indeed, with Bacchylides we are nearing the end of the line of lyric poets. A few more names could be cited, including that of a woman, Corinna (not to mention Timocreon, who attacked Themistocles); but the great age of lyricism is past. One reason, undoubtedly, was that triumphs in sport occupied a lesser place in an age when the outstanding developments were intellectual; a more important reason was the growth of democracy, causing aristocratic festivals to be eclipsed by an art form whose audience and judges were to be the body of assembled citizens.

---

7. The strophe and antistrophe are two stanzas of identical meter and length; the epode, which follows, is somewhat different in form. —Trans.

IV · PRESOCRATIC PHILOSOPHY

As lyric poetry was reaching its full flower, the first works in prose were written; once again Asia Minor was the source of the innovation. I shall trace these beginnings in chapter 3, when I turn to the early historians. Prose was also used for folk genres such as the fable; Aesop, who is thought to have been a Phrygian slave, lived in the sixth century and was quoted by Herodotus. Finally, prose was the medium chosen by the Milesian philosophers— though other philosophers frequently wrote in verse, which was considered more imposing and somehow more akin to the sacred.

For all practical purposes, Greek philosophy can be said to have been born in the sixth century. It developed simultaneously in two regions, at opposite ends of the Greek world: Asia Minor to the east, and southern Italy and Sicily to the west. The early works fall into two periods, roughly corresponding to the two halves of the century.

A · The Beginnings of Philosophy

Two distinct strains were present in Greek philosophy from the beginning. On the one hand there were movements of a mystical or esoteric cast, organized around personalities who were at least partly legendary; these movements were to enjoy a vast influence. On the other, there were philosophers in the modern sense of the word; the first group of these was centered at Miletus.

1 · ORPHISM AND PYTHAGOREANISM

Orpheus was a frankly mythic figure. He was said to have been born in Thrace, before Homer; the son of a Muse, he was unequaled as a musician. He took part in the quest of the Argonauts, and descended to the underworld in search of his wife Eurydice. The tradition that grew up around this figure depicted him as a kind of prophet, even something of a magician, and deeply religious. A theogony was attributed to him (echoes of it may be found in Aristophanes' *Birds*, 693 ff.). Even more important, belief in an afterlife was ascribed to him, as were a body of rites, ascetic exercises, and initiations designed to help his devotees in this future life. Gold leaves have even been found engraved with sacred texts, meant to accompany the faithful to the next world and guide them through it; central to such texts, it appears, is the theme of successive purifications. Here we have an important aspect of Greek religion that neither Homer nor Hesiod gave any inkling of; it was to have a great influence throughout later Greek history (though some scholars have overestimated its influence). Most of the surviving Orphic texts are late, but the doctrines must have been established in the period under discussion, that is, the sixth century.

The same concern for immortality and for purification was attributed to a figure scarcely better known than Orpheus—namely, Pythagoras. At least we know that Pythagoras actually lived. Born in Samos, he left the island—

probably when the tyrant Polycrates came to power, about 530—to settle in southern Italy, at Croton. No writings of his were known, but miraculous stories were told about him in which he exercised unheard-of powers. His disciples kept a very rich oral tradition alive. Like the Orphic sects, the Pythagoreans believed that the soul survived the body; more specifically, they believed in the transmigration of souls, and offered many practical rules designed to purify the soul for its future reincarnations. Some of the rules were dietary and can be understood from the perspective of possible reincarnations in animal form. In other respects, however, Pythagoreanism differed from Orphism. In the first place, it included a political strain that occasionally produced concrete results in southern Italy; in this it may seem to pave the way for Plato. But the chief characteristic of Pythagoreanism (and this too has a bearing on Plato) is its founder's interest in mathematics, and his doctrine that everything depends on numbers and the harmony of numbers. He was undoubtedly influenced by Near Eastern and Ionian mathematics; but he developed it further and made number the principle by which the entire cosmos may be explained. The philosopher Archytas, whom Plato visited in Tarentum, taught Pythagorean philosophy; it is worth noting that he was both a statesman and a mathematician.

In their mystical content, Pythagoreanism and Orphism probably reflect Oriental and Egyptian influences, which were to have a long history in Greece. With the Milesian school, we can see how a spirituality still closely tied to myth moved toward a more rational and objective consciousness, bearing a more clearly Greek stamp.

2 · THE MILESIAN PHILOSOPHERS

Like the Orphics, the philosophers of the Ionian city of Miletus speculated about the origins of the universe; but they used a different vocabulary. Orphism offered a theogonic account of the creation of the world (beginning with Time, followed by the Aether and the divine egg from which Phanes-Eros emerged). Other theogonies of this kind were elaborated. In the mid-sixth century, Pherecydes of Syros wrote one in prose (whose central figures were Zas, Cronus, and Chthonia); and the Cretan Epimenides, famous for his purification of Athens, composed a *Theogony* in verse. The Milesian philosophers also investigated the origins of the world; but their originality lay in their attempt to find a properly scientific solution to this problem: they sought to identify the elements involved in the world's formation (its *phusis*).

The Milesians, who wrote in prose, were Thales, Anaximander, and Anaximenes. They lived in the first half of the sixth century. Thales, the oldest, was a contemporary of Solon; Anaximander was a little younger and seems to have been born just before the turn of the century; Anaximenes must have been about twenty years younger still. We have only brief fragments of their works. Though theological tendencies can still be detected, the entities these men describe belong to the physical order. Oriental influences are also recognizable, but the thought is no longer cast in mythic form. The Milesians are thus transitional figures between the poetic theology of the previous age and the scholarly investigations of reality that were to come. We have no reason to doubt that their basic orientation was scientific. If we can believe Herodotus (1.74), Thales was able to predict an eclipse of the sun; his successors, equally well versed in astronomy, proposed geometric models for the universe. Anaximander is said to have been the first Greek to draw a map of the world.

The three Milesians resembled one another in the objects of their curiosity and the spirit in which they approached them. They differed chiefly in their choice of the element from which they thought all else had emerged: for Thales it was water; for Anaximander it was the *apeiron*, or boundless undifferentiated matter; for Anaximenes it was air. Each offered theories—partly conceived in the imagination, partly based on physical observation—to explain how the various parts of the universe were formed from its original element. Thus a knowledge of physics was made to serve the ambitious project of explaining all things—a project inherited from the authors of the theogonies.

From my brief summary it should be possible to perceive just how expansive and creative the sixth century was. It is worth noting that this was the era of the so-called Seven Sages of Greece. The list of their names may vary from place to place, but two are always included: Solon and Thales, the great representatives of moral and scientific thought. These early thinkers opened a path of investigation that was to lead to further discoveries. From the second half of the sixth century to the end of the fifth, there followed an unbroken series of great names—men who produced true philosophic systems and whose work is better known to us.

B · Philosophic Systems at the Close of the Archaic Age

In my account of the preceding period, one name was omitted. Xenophanes of Colophon was born a little after 600, and Colophon is not far from Miletus. But, like Pythagoras, Xenophanes left Asia Minor for political reasons (the Persian conquest of Ionia); and from then on he was connected with other currents of thought. What is more, Xenophanes was not only, and perhaps not even primarily, a philosopher. He wrote in verse—epic verse (as in his *Foundation of Colophon* and his poem on the Ionian settlement at Elea in southern Italy), or elegiac verse dealing with ideas and moral values. His pioneering contribution—his audacity, we might say—was to criticize severely the anthropomorphic representation of the gods, whose weaknesses, he claimed, were sheer inventions of men. The godhead, Xenophanes maintained, was one and immutable (frag. 26 Diels-Kranz). Other innovations of Xenophanes were the distinction between "being" and "seeming," and the idea of progress in human affairs over time (frag. 18). His interest in the city of Elea and his insistence on the immutable oneness of the deity (which in a sense is identified with the universe) suggest a link—tenuous perhaps, but real—between this solitary thinker and Parmenides, the founder of the Eleatic school.

The three great names in philosophy at this period are Heraclitus of Ephesus, Parmenides of Elea, and Empedocles of Acragas (Agrigentum).

1 · HERACLITUS

It is hard to say who was born first, Heraclitus or Parmenides; in any case they were quite close in age. Heraclitus was born around 540. He belonged to one of the first families of Ephesus, and this may have been the source of the contempt he always expressed for the masses or for anything common. We do not know whether he wrote a unified treatise or whether his work consisted of self-contained reflections like those that have been preserved in chance citations. All of the latter are couched in difficult terms, condensed, and designed to take the reader by surprise. Already in antiquity Heraclitus was called "the obscure"; indeed, it was not his intention to make himself understandable to most people. He expresses himself like a man who, aloof from all others, plumbs the secrets of the world. Sometimes he even takes a prophetic tone. Such an attitude is characteristic of all three authors I shall be discussing here; it indicates that they saw themselves not as philosophers in an open, scientific society but as sages or "masters of truth"[8] in an archaic and fundamentally religious society.

This stance of the philosopher helps to explain, at least in part, why in Heraclitus's view so few men are "awake"; almost all are sleepers, hearing like deaf men and absent when they are present (frag. 34 Diels-Kranz). According to Heraclitus, even poets can know many things without profiting from their "polymathy" (Greek *polumathia*): Hesiod and Pythagoras, Xenophanes and Hecataeus, Homer and Archilochus wrote only foolishness (frags. 40, 42, 57). Heraclitus, by contrast, in seeking to understand his own nature (frag. 101), arrives at the truth.

Truth for Heraclitus can be summed up in two complementary propositions. The first is that there exists a *Logos*, a unitary and sovereign Thought, which is at once human thought and the governing principle of the universe. The second is that the universe is perpetually in flux, its existence assured only by the conflict between opposites. A corollary to the first of these principles is the idea of the importance of fire, which in the material order is the element most akin to the *Logos*. Such views are not unrelated to the vision of the world later developed by the Stoics.

The second proposition is more characteristic of Heraclitus, who saw change reigning everywhere. In his view, change operates in a kind of cycle, whereby the disappearance of one element leads to the birth of another. This endless flux is illustrated by the famous saying (frag. 91) that one cannot step twice into the same river (since the water is constantly replaced). The ex-

---

8. For the phrase "master of truth," see the influential work of Marcel Detienne, *Les Maîtres de vérité dans la Grèce archaïque* (Paris, 1967).—Trans.

changes between elements are described in sayings like that of fragment 36: "The death of souls is to become water, that of water to become earth; from earth is formed water, and from water, soul." Even in individual bodies, so long as they exist, there is tension between opposing elements; thus Heraclitus can claim that conflict is "the father of all things," making each what it is (frag. 53). This is also the source of his claim that there is a unity resulting from opposite thrusts; the harmony of the lyre, and that of the bow, is produced by pulling in opposite directions (frag. 51, discussed by Plato in the *Symposium*).

But there is still another way in which opposites may be reconciled in Heraclitus's world—not merely equilibrated this time but canceled out. For qualities are only in opposition because they are limited to the observer and to his point of view. A road is the same going up and going down; writing is both straight and curved; sea water is both pure and unhealthy: excellent for fish, but harmful for man (frags. 60, 59, 61). If one considers the whole of the universe, from the perspective of God or of the *Logos*, many opposites are merged in a unity that human faculties cannot grasp; hence, Heraclitus can affirm that day and night are one (frag. 57) or that some "live the death of others" (frag. 62). In other words, experience has a double meaning; and that which accounts for the diversity and perpetual flux of reality can also, finally, be seen to account for its underlying unity.

This brief review should give some idea of the baffling quality of Heraclitus's thought—which is intentional on his part: his sayings shock and surprise the reader, offer explanations that are not explanations, and present everything in a different light from what most people are accustomed to. This is partly because his doctrine is an unusually bold attempt to reconcile unity and change. But such an explanation is insufficient; for the philosophies of Parmenides and Empedocles are no less difficult, yet the former emphasizes the unity of all things, while the latter emphasizes change or fluctuation.

2 · PARMENIDES

Parmenides was born at Elea, in southern Italy, and became the founder of what was called the Eleatic school. His place of birth accounts for probable contacts with Xenophanes, who spent time at Elea; similar connections have been made between him and the Pythagoreans, whose seat was nearby.[9] It is harder to be specific about his dates, because of a meeting with the young Socrates described by Plato in the *Parmenides*, 127b, which does not square with other sources; but the discrepancy is minimal, and Parmenides can be said to have lived from the end of the sixth century into the first half of the fifth. He is known to have been a legislator as well as a philosopher, though his philosophy was paramount. He expounded his ideas in a long hexameter

9. The Pythagorean "order," or religious society, had its center at Croton, also in southern Italy.—Trans.

poem, *On Nature*, of which some sizable fragments have survived (the longest is 61 lines).

The choice of poetic form is well suited to the sense of awesome revelation pervading Parmenides' thought. In the prologue of his poem he gives an account—in the first person, like Hesiod's—of his initiation into truth; and the initiation has all the sublimity of myth. Parmenides describes a kind of journey toward the truth: he is riding in a chariot, on his way to the goddess, while the daughters of the sun show him which direction leads to the light (frag. 1.1–10 Diels-Kranz). In this way he arrives at a gate where the paths of night and day diverge; Justice (Dike) guards the keys. Parmenides is allowed to go through the gate, and the goddess welcomes him with a promise to teach him everything: "From me you are to learn all things—both the unshakable heart of Truth, whose circle is perfect, and the opinions of mortals, which do not admit of true belief" (frag. 1.7–9). This imposing introduction, which seems to symbolize a religious initiation, portrays the author as another "master of truth" and sets him apart as its sole possessor.

The above revelation portrays Truth herself (who is personified to a certain extent) as likewise standing apart, distinct from the vain opinions of mankind. The one Truth concerns Being; and Being in turn is one and immutable, knowing neither beginning nor end nor any change. It is continuous and whole, encompassing all things. Nothing can exist outside it: "Being is uncreated and imperishable, complete, single, immobile and without end" (frag. 8.3–4; cf. 26–30). Clearly we are no longer dealing here with the mere physical universe, which the Ionians studied, but with all that is or can be apprehended by the mind. Nonbeing, by contrast, cannot exist because it cannot be thought. Parmenides' system operates at the level of ontology, an ontology based on pure speculative reason. The system was to prove at least as influential in its method of formulating philosophical questions as in the specific answers it gave to them. Nor did Parmenides immure himself in meditation on Being; the second part of his poem also deals with the world of opinion and appearances. It ends with a real cosmology, based on two main principles, fire and night. For the sensible world, in which men are deceived by appearances and by the limited nature of their learning, Parmenides (following the goddess) offers at least a "more likely" version of the truth (frag. 8, line 60).

The Eleatic school was to have a decisive influence on Plato and Aristotle by positing with such firmness the abstract unity of the universe; to reconcile this unity with the fragmentation of the sensible world was to be a continuing problem for philosophy. (The fact that Plato called one of his dialogues the *Parmenides* testifies to that influence.) The master had two distinguished followers. His favorite student, Zeno of Elea (not to be confused with the Stoic philosopher Zeno), baffled generations of younger thinkers with his paradoxes. The most famous is the one of Achilles and the tortoise: Achilles can never catch up with the tortoise if we consider the infinite divisibility of the distance he has to travel. The point of such paradoxes was to demonstrate the unintelligibility of movement. They were dialectical games, but "serious games," as Plato put it (*Parmenides* 137b). Another famous Eleatic was Melissus of Samos, who lived in the mid-fifth century and engaged in a critique of empirical knowledge. We have only a few fragments of his work, but he was highly esteemed in antiquity; both Plato and Isocrates quote him a number of times. A Peripatetic treatise, probably from the first century after Christ, was entitled *On Melissus, Xenophanes, and Gorgias*. In any event, the man's popularity further testifies to the wide influence enjoyed by the Eleatic thinkers.

3 · EMPEDOCLES

The last of the great Presocratic philosophers lived in the fifth century (he died about 430), and was a contemporary of the philosophers I shall discuss in chapter 5; but his cast of thought, his tone, and the problems he faces are still precisely those of the philosophers discussed above. Empedocles belonged to a noble family of Acragas (Agrigentum), in Sicily. He too was a "master of truth," a physician and healer who believed he possessed supernatural powers. This is how he presents himself in his poem the *Purifications* (*Katharmoi*); he also describes the crowds that greeted him wherever he went. "Thousands of people follow me, asking which is the path to profit; some consult me for oracles, while others wait to hear the word that will save them from various illnesses" (frag. 112.8–11). It was even said that Empedocles' death was miraculous: a voice called to him, and his body was swallowed up by Mount Aetna. He left two major poems, *On Nature* and the *Purifications*, with a combined total of some 5000 lines. Long passages have survived—about 1000 lines in all, mostly from the first poem.

The title of this first poem recalls the preoccupations of the Ionian philosophers. But whereas the Ionians tried to identify a single element from which the universe could be said to have emerged, Empedocles makes room for four "roots": earth, water, air (ether) and fire. Sometimes he gives them the names of gods. Like Parmenides' Being, these four "roots" are uncreated and eternal. But, being four, they combine with one another; and the life of the universe can be explained by their mixture and separation. Two forces preside over these transformations: love (*philotēs*) organizes and combines, while conflict (*neikos*) divides and dislocates. The universe makes and unmakes itself by alternation on a vast scale between these two forces. Under the sway of *philotēs* it tends to become the spherical and tightly unified entity described by Parmenides; under the sway of *neikos*, it breaks down into a chaos reminiscent of the change and tension dear to Heraclitus. Such are the governing principles of Empedocles' cosmogony, which he sets before his audience with the descriptive fullness of a visionary. Explaining how bodies were formed, he allows himself real flights of imagination as he evokes the genesis of limbs: "Many heads sprouted without necks; lone arms wandered without shoulders; and eyes moved through space at random, for lack of foreheads" (frag.

57). Yet this imaginary reconstruction is also an attempt at a scientific explanation; indeed, Empedocles' theory of sense perception, involving invisible "effluences" and pores, is in many respects modern.

The scientific concerns of Empedocles are combined (as in Pythagoreanism, which clearly influenced him) with a desire for purification of the soul. His second poem expresses this desire. Like the Orphics and the Pythagoreans, Empedocles believed in the transmigration of souls; like them, he recommended abstention from meat, and added other restrictions, including a prohibition of beans. He also described the realms of the world beyond, realms that he claimed he had been privileged to recall.

The power of Empedocles' cosmic vision and his initiatory fervor combine to make his poems difficult and sometimes baffling, but always striking. He is the last brilliant spark struck off by the archaic age. The archaic character of his thought may be attributable to the fact that he was Sicilian and thus had nothing to do with the new currents of thought which, since the Persian Wars, had made Athens their theater. It was in Athens that his compatriot Gorgias and the other Sicilian rhetoricians were to find fertile ground for the cultivation of their influence.

Indeed, as soon as Athens became the acknowledged center of Greek life, the spirit of her future development could be foreseen. Solon had set the example, in the midst of the archaic age, for a kind of thought based wholly on ethical and political factors—a thought for which man was truly the measure. This was the kind of thought that was to unfold in fifth-century Athens, in the field of philosophy as well as in the genres of drama and history. In fact, the humanistic tendency grew ever stronger in the course of the century, as the age of pride gave way to the age of skepticism and doubt.

3

The Early Fifth Century: The Birth of History and Tragedy

The advent of organized political life coincided with the Greek victory over the Persian invaders in 490 and 480. All Greece had been in danger; Athens had taken the leading role in the deliverance of the whole country, winning both glory and power for her pains. Her triumph marked the beginning of an era in which Greek literature was to be Athenian and essentially political, addressed to the city-state. Both traits are reflected in the two major genres to appear at the time, which were destined to survive in each of the national literatures of Europe—history and drama (the latter including both tragedy and comedy). In the first half of the fifth century each of these genres found a distinguished exponent in a resident of Athens: Herodotus, an emigrant from Ionia, and Aeschylus, a native Athenian. Both wrote about the Persian Wars, in which Aeschylus had himself fought and to which he devoted a tragedy—the earliest of the tragedies to have survived.

I · AESCHYLUS

The fact that Aeschylus is the earliest tragic poet whose work has survived should not mislead us. For the first performance of tragedy at the Athenian Dionysia was as early as 534, only nine years after his birth. Aeschylus had famous predecessors, such as Thespis, Pratinas, and Phrynichus, whose works have been lost.

The genre undoubtedly had a religious origin. The performances were part of the cult of Dionysus; and it is probable that tragedy, like comedy, was an extension of a ritual. The genre apparently did not originate at Athens (later traditions traced it to Arion, who worked at Corinth, or to choral performances at Sicyon). There was, however, a link between the beginnings of tragedy and the institution of tyranny: at Athens, tragedy took root under Pisistratus. A strong central authority, with a popular base of support, gave the ancient rites their civic dimension. Indeed, tragedy was to find its place in the life of the city; people of all classes attended, and the performances were prompted and organized by the state. The tragic poets addressed themselves to the assembled body of the people; they spoke as citizens to citizens.

47

The double origin and the double nature of tragedy help to account for its content. The plays always have a religious dimension: gods are a major object of concern and sometimes appear as characters; cult acts are portrayed, and there are meditations on the divine will. At the same time, even as they dramatize mythic material borrowed from Homer and later poets, the tragedians nearly always include representatives of the collectivity—citizens or soldiers, symbolic of the entire group for which the heroes are responsible and whose suffering is an extension of their own.

The structure of Greek tragedy made it easy to emphasize these two dimensions—the religious and the collective—thanks to the presence of the chorus. Every Greek tragedy is in fact composed of two distinct elements. The actors move about on the stage; their words are spoken (not sung), usually in iambic trimeters; and they take part in an action, or plot. But there is also a chorus of twelve or fifteen persons (perhaps originally as many as fifty), who move back and forth across the *orchestra* (a circular dancing floor in front of the stage), sing in lyric meters, and, unable themselves to participate in the action unfolding on the stage, must be content to comment on it. The chorus is thus in a position to elicit the religious meaning of the action and to punctuate it with prayers. At the same time, the chorus is easily used to represent the group—citizenry or army—whose fate is tied to that of the actors. In each play the "episodes" of dramatic action alternate with choral songs, which introduce, interrupt, and conclude that action. The introductory or entrance song is the *parodos*; the concluding song, with which the chorus exits, is the *exodos*; the other songs, numbering between two and five, are the *stasima*.

As tragedy evolved, the chorus, which must originally have been the predominant element, steadily lost its importance, while the actors become more numerous and the characters they portrayed more complex (Aeschylus was the first to use two actors; Sophocles added a third). As plots became more involved, the plays, at first grouped in trilogies, were able to stand on their own, and authors often presented three independent plays at the same festival. Yet the titles bear witness to the role of the chorus, from which plays often took their names (hence *The Suppliant Maidens*, *The Libation Bearers*, etc.). The chorus was the most original feature of Greek tragedy; and when its role became attenuated, tragedy was already in decline.

This evolution in the use of the chorus extended over the entire fifth century and involved a great number of works. Of the many hundreds of tragedies staged at Athens, a total of thirty-two have survived: seven by Aeschylus, seven by Sophocles, and eighteen by Euripides (if the *Rhesus* is to be considered his). That is shockingly few. Yet the line of development is clear; and Aeschylus, the oldest of the three tragedians, is also the one whose choral odes are the longest and whose plots are the simplest. It is in his works as well that the twofold significance of tragedy—religious and collective—is most constantly emphasized.

A · Life of Aeschylus

Aeschylus was born in 525, thirty years before Pericles and Sophocles and forty-five years before Euripides. His birthplace was Eleusis, seat of the mysteries (though that does not necessarily mean he was an initiate). He had apparently begun writing tragedies by the age of twenty-five, and won his first victory in the dramatic contest in 484. But the essential fact of his life is that he fought at Marathon in 490, and again at Salamis in 480. This fact alone is mentioned in an epitaph he is supposed to have written for himself, which simply praises him as a soldier. As it happened, the whole of his thought was to be marked by this great experience. A case in point: *The Persians*, the earliest of his tragedies to have survived, was intended to commemorate the battle of Salamis. It was performed in 472, eight years after the battle, when Aeschylus was over fifty years old. We know that he traveled to Syracuse to direct a second staging of the play, and that he wrote a tragedy in honor of the new city of Aetna (cf. Pindar's *First Pythian*). He died in Sicily in 456 and was buried at Gela; we have no reliable information about the reasons for his removal to Sicily, or about his death. We do know, however, that from 472 to 458 he worked at Athens, where his career was punctuated by frequent victories (despite the early successes of Sophocles, who defeated him in 468); his last victory was in 458, with the *Oresteia*.

B · Works of Aeschylus

According to tradition, Aeschylus wrote between seventy and ninety tragedies; seven have come down to us. For the rest, we must be content with titles, brief fragments, or reports of famous scenes recalled by others (the long, grief-stricken silence of Achilles, which opened *The Phrygians* or *The Ransoming of Hector*; the distraught period of waiting for the two divine mothers, Thetis and Eos, in the *Psychostasia* or "Weighing of Souls"). Sometimes we are lucky enough to find a new fragment, such as the speeches from the *Niobe* and the *Myrmidons* (both found in 1932), or those fragments that have given us a glimmer of Aeschylus's talent for satyr drama (a satyr play followed each set of three tragedies).

Of the seven surviving tragedies, five can be dated precisely: *The Persians* (472), the *Seven against Thebes* (467), and the three plays of the *Oresteia* (458). *The Suppliant Maidens*, long thought to be very old, is now dated with considerable probability at 463. We have no clues to the date of the *Prometheus Bound*, whose authorship has even been questioned. In addition to a complete trilogy, the seven plays include two that opened trilogies (*The Suppliant Maidens* and the *Prometheus Bound*), one that concluded a trilogy (the *Seven against Thebes*), and one that stood by itself (*The Persians*).

The Persians stands alone in several respects. It is the only surviving Greek tragedy to be based not on a myth but on a recent historical event. This was not unprecedented; Phrynichus had used the same subject in his *Phoenician Women*. But it is important to note that Aeschylus, in treating this recent event, gave it the dignity of myth. Like Phrynichus, he portrayed not the Greek victory but the Persian defeat. There is almost no action in the play: the chorus of old Persian men wait anxiously with Atossa, mother of King Xerxes, for news of the expeditionary force; a messenger discloses each phase of the Persian debacle; Darius returns from the dead, at his people's appeal, to explain the disaster; and the play ends with the return of the defeated king, amid mourning and weeping. There is nothing to puff up the pride of either side; the defeat is a collapse, which Aeschylus consistently implies is due to a decision of the gods and constitutes a punishment long held in reserve. The audience is made to tremble at the great lament for the Persians killed in battle—a sign of what the gods, in their justice, can do to men.

In the *Seven against Thebes*, war is again Aeschylus's theme. Eteocles is defending Thebes against his brother Polyneices, who has laid siege to it; it is the curse of Oedipus that his sons should clash and die by one another's hands. Again the action is sparse. There are preparations for battle, with a long description of the shields borne by the seven chief attackers and their Theban counterparts; finally Eteocles leaves the stage, going to meet Polyneices, and a little later we hear of the deaths of both. The play is filled with the anguish of the Theban women, which Eteocles respects. Aeschylus paints a strong, patriotic and pious Eteocles, who is nonetheless broken when the curse is fulfilled and the gods' will accomplished—as in *The Persians*—after a whole series of transgressions and sufferings.

The Suppliant Maidens portrays the flight of the fifty daughters of Danaus, whose Egyptian cousins want to force them into marriage. Their anguish recalls that of the Theban women in the *Seven*. The Danaids win the protection of Pelasgus, king of Argos; he is not eager to help them, but does so for fear of the gods. Despite the arrival of a threatening Egyptian herald, Pelasgus manages to protect the women. Yet their passionate attachment to chastity is itself excessive and thus anticipates their crime and its punishment, which the rest of the trilogy presumably portrayed.[1]

Prometheus Bound is set in the world of the immortals. Prometheus has incurred the wrath of Zeus by helping mortal men against his orders. In the prologue, Kratos and Bia (Force and Violence) nail Prometheus to a rock. There he is visited by the chorus of Oceanids, who are moved to pity; by their father Oceanus, who offers advice and admonitions; and by Io, herself a prey to divine wrath. In this play, then, Zeus is portrayed as cruel and tyrannical. Although the trilogy ended with a truce between Zeus and Prometheus, and the release of the latter, some scholars have found such a portrayal of Zeus shocking; when added to certain peculiarities of form (which make the *Prometheus* easier reading than the other tragedies), it has led them to

---

1. After agreeing to wed the Egyptians, all but one of the Danaids murdered their husbands on the wedding night; their punishment in the underworld, as described in later versions of the myth, was to carry water in jars perforated like sieves. There is still debate over the content of Aeschylus's second and third plays, only fragments of which survive.—Trans.

doubt that Aeschylus wrote the play. But we must not forget that all we have is the opening play of the trilogy. The atmosphere of the *Prometheus* is that of a theogony; and the *Oresteia* is proof enough that for Aeschylus order can emerge only from negotiations, gradual improvements, and a step-by-step ordering *process*. It might be added that Prometheus himself is no more blameless than were the suppliant maidens in the play of that name.

We can see from the *Oresteia* that a meaning as profound as that sought by Aeschylus needs an entire trilogy in which to unfold. In the *Agamemnon*, Clytemnestra kills the king her husband; in so doing she avenges the murder of her daughter Iphigenia. She is also, of course, acting as an adulterous woman. But she is primarily the instrument of a divine judgment, of which the chorus has presentiments throughout the play as it recalls wrongs done in the course of the Trojan War and older crimes that may have angered the gods. In *The Libation Bearers*, Orestes and Electra, at Apollo's command, kill their mother to avenge their father. On such principles, murder should always be followed by murder; but in *The Eumenides* we are shown Orestes' trial in the Athenian court of the Areopagus, founded for the occasion. (When the play was first staged, the democratic faction had recently curtailed the powers of that court.) At the trial, Athene's firmness prevails over the bloodthirsty rage of the Furies. Civic order, imposed from above by the gods, triumphs over blind vengeance. The play opens at Delphi but closes in the city of Athens, to which Athene offers her solemn advice. Thus Aeschylus's work, which begins (for us) with the Athenian victory over the "barbarian," achieved by the grace of the gods, ends with the hope that his city will also defeat, on Athene's orders and with her help, all such internal strife as may threaten it. Clearly, the civic and the religious are the two essential elements of Aeschylus's vision.

C · The Vision of Aeschylus

Having lived through the Persian Wars—the successive waves of invasion, the burning of Athens—Aeschylus describes with a rare power the brutality of war, the sacking of cities, and the deaths of soldiers. *The Persians* includes unforgettable descriptions, including that of the naval battle where the Greeks, "as if [their enemies] were fish—tuna emptied from the net—strike and hack with broken ends of oars, with bits of wreckage" (424ff.). Likewise, the women in the *Seven against Thebes* cry out in terror to see their country "prey to the clatter of hooves which draws near, flying and thundering like the invincible torrent beating the mountain's flank" (84ff.). The Trojan War haunts the *Agamemnon*; the heavy responsibility for starting it hangs on Paris and Helen, but on Agamemnon as well: "Ares, money-changer of dead bodies, has set up his balance in the field of battle; and from the pyres of Ilion he sends home to loved ones a dust heavy with cruel tears—in exchange for men, ashes, easily stowed in urns" (437–44).[2]

2. The phrase "money changer of dead bodies" is borrowed from the translation of Richmond Lattimore (see Bibliography).

Yet the war Aeschylus witnessed was a just and heroic war. Repeatedly in his plays, therefore, the tide of violence that is war is seen breaking before a determined and organized resistance, personified by a heroic leader, such as Eteocles in the *Seven* (before the curse overcomes him) or Pelasgus in *The Suppliant Maidens*—brave, pious, and thinking first of "the city." Sometimes the violence encounters a united people in control of its own affairs. Remarkably, even a king like Pelasgus is unwilling to make a decision without consulting the citizens. The chorus believes that everything depends on him ("You are the city; you are the Council"), but Pelasgus insists that this is not so: if the pollution threatens the city as a whole, "let the whole people seek the remedy" (366). Still more to the point is Aeschylus's brief reminder, in *The Persians,* that the Athenians "are no one's slaves, and subject to no one" (243).

Such passages are proof enough that Aeschylus was equally aware of what we would call domestic politics. If he condemned the tyranny of Zeus in the *Prometheus,* and proposed elsewhere the ideal of the city that is mistress of itself, he also dealt with the problems of his own day at least once in the surviving tragedies, borrowing Athene's voice to advise his countrymen. The two great hopes expressed by the goddess at the end of *The Eumenides* are that order be respected and civil wars shunned. Respect for order is embodied in the Areopagus, whose foundation Aeschylus describes with rare solemnity. The court's function will be to preserve the very principle of fear, which allows liberty to flourish without leading to disorder. Athene almost echoes the words of the Furies: "Neither anarchy nor despotism: that is the rule I advise my city to respect. Let not all fear be banished from inside her walls; for with nothing to fear, what mortal does as he ought?" (696–99). The admonition to avoid civil war is repeated several times, and in its service Athene enlists the help of the Furies, now transformed into the Eumenides or "Benevolent Ones."

Such advice is certainly related to the political developments of Aeschylus's own time; yet the many attempts to interpret his work in light of its political context, or to attribute specific stands to its author, have yielded little. Clearly he lives, thinks, and writes as a citizen; but, just as clearly, he sees political choice as preeminently moral. He is equally opposed to the hubris of conquest, the hubris of tyrants, and the hubris of unruly masses; as a citizen, he lives by the old ideal whose development we witnessed in Hesiod, Solon, and Pindar. Aeschylus cherishes this ideal all the more for the fact that the Persian Wars had just sealed its triumph, while the struggles of the young democracy threatened to jeopardize its equilibrium.

But to dwell exclusively on the human side of the ideal would be to truncate Aeschylus's vision. For what damns hubris is the verdict of the gods; what punishes Xerxes and saves the Greeks, what accounts for the deaths of Agamemnon and Clytemnestra, what guides Pelasgus, what acts, decides, and gives direction in human affairs is—always and everywhere—the will of the gods. Sometimes Aeschylus brings the gods onstage (in the *Prometheus* and *The Eumenides*); but even when they do not appear, their presence is felt: in dreams (those of Atossa and Clytemnestra); in prophetic outbursts (Cassandra's); in the return of the dead, summoned by the living (Darius in *The Persians*); in the decisive intervention of the spirits of the dead (Agamemnon in *The Libation Bearers*). The human characters, who pray and plead, are well aware of these divine powers, as are the choruses, who constantly invoke the gods or point to the workings of their will.

Aeschylus's gods, though many, are not at odds with one another; often they seem to merge into one great sovereign power, and most are mere agents of Zeus. As a result, Zeus's own power seems limitless. In invoking him, Aeschylus extends the ritual formulas with strings of laudatory epithets. The effect is very imposing: "Lord of lords, blest of the blest, supreme power of powers: from the height of your felicity, Zeus, hear us!" (*The Suppliant Maidens*, 524ff.).

A power as great as this is naturally terrifying. Zeus may be the savior; but he is above all the being whose anger can destroy anything human from one minute to the next: "Zeus hurls mortals from the height of their proud hopes into nothingness; but he does not arm himself with violence; nothing is difficult for a god. His thought is enthroned on the mountain tops, and from the height he attains his ends, without leaving his sacred seat" (ibid. 95–102). Such formidable power accounts for the continual fear and trembling in which the characters live. They never forget that within the hour Zeus can destroy them. Portents of his wrath make them tremble, as does uncertainty; even when catastrophe strikes, they cannot be sure the divine anger that provoked it is finally appeased.

Such a world would indeed be without hope if the divine wrath were not rooted in justice. But just as he shows us the violence of war breaking against the manly resolve of the defenders, so Aeschylus seems to find some reassurance in the fact that there is an order to the workings of divine omnipotence. Divine justice is anything but "simple" justice. It does not operate on the level of the individual, for the innocent are punished with the guilty, and sons may suffer for their fathers' crimes. In Aeschylus, time is seen in great blocks, and the retribution meted out in a given play may be for transgressions that go back several generations (a fact that also justifies his use of the trilogy form). From Laius to Oedipus and to the sons of Oedipus, from Tantalus and Thyestes to Agamemnon and to Orestes, long sequences are created in which new crimes delay yet aggravate the punishment. What is more, the gods lay traps for mortals they want to destroy, so that the crime, prompted by Atē (god-inflicted blindness or madness), damns the man who succumbs to temptation. All this makes divine justice something of a riddle, shrouded in mystery: "The paths of Zeus' thought reach their ends by way of thickets and dense shadows that no sight can penetrate" (*The Suppliant Maidens* 88–90). But the mystery does not stem from any gratuitous quality of divine action, and thus engenders no doubts. Sooner or later the gods will punish hubris; either the guilty man or his descendants will suffer for it. As Aeschylus sees it, this is justice; the gods' attitude is not one of mere jealousy toward those who rise too high (as the Persian Artabanus claims in Herodotus). The chorus in the *Agamemnon* specifies that it is not excessive prosperity but impious thoughts that the gods condemn. Aeschylus's work is a passionate affirmation of divine justice; there is not one play (other than the *Prometheus*, for reasons I have discussed) that does not offer ample and striking testimony to the existence of such justice. Justice is, in fact, the mainspring of the plays; because every disaster has a meaning, the characters are caught up in anguished efforts to do right, or in the horror of having done ill and recognizing their error too late. Every act has a shadow, as it were, projecting into the divine sphere; and man bears a terrible responsibility—without being, for all that, the master of his fate.

At the same time, the fact of divine justice is the very basis of morality. Fear plays the same role in man's relation to the gods as it plays in human society; and misfortune itself can be a form of instruction. Aeschylus started with a commonplace of the Greeks, to the effect that everyone learns from experience and from disappointments; but he immeasurably enhanced its meaning. At the beginning of the *Oresteia*, the old men of Argos recall the succession of gods leading up to the reign of Zeus—a succession that makes possible the notion of perfection through suffering: Zeus "put mortals on the path of understanding by laying down the law that 'wisdom comes through suffering.' When, in sleep, painful remorse drips down in the heart's sight, wisdom penetrates men in spite of themselves; and this, I think, is a beneficent violence from the gods who sit in the celestial court" (*Agamemnon* 176–84). The word "remorse" is perhaps a little too modern; but the concept goes far beyond that of simple practical experience grounded in reason. Its true scope stems from Aeschylus's faith in the gods.

D · The Art of Aeschylus

It is understandable that works inspired by such an exalted view of things should neglect all lesser considerations. The psychology of the characters carries less weight than divine intervention and is sacrificed to it; and further complication of plot would be less meaningful than the single and inexorable sequence of events by which divine wrath runs its course. Aeschylus's plays are full of long, static scenes and narrative passages, long silences on the part of certain characters, long choral odes in which the distraught chorus probes the meaning of the unfolding action.

All this implies a sense of breadth and magnitude, which blends with the majestic quality of Aeschylus's vision. The plays are arranged in trilogies, and the choral strophes in tightly structured odes, of which the outstanding example is the opening choral passage, or *parodos*, of the *Agamemnon*. In this ode the chorus alternately chants and sings no fewer than 223 consecutive lines, which fall into several different metrical sequences. Ten broad anapestic phrases correspond to the actual entrance of the chorus. These are followed by a long meditation (in the form of a triad and five pairs of strophes) on the troubling circumstances in which the Greek fleet left for Troy. The triad, in dactylic meter interspersed with iambs, solemnly evokes the omen that appeared at the gathering of the ships, and the threats that attend on it. A change of rhythm marks the invocation to Zeus, at the midpoint of the ode. Then the narrative is taken up again—with a further change of rhythm—and the sacrifice of Iphigenia is described. In this choral sequence of rare length and scope, every element is in its proper place. Another form favored by Aeschylus is the *kommos,* a lyrical dialogue in which both actors and chorus take part. The *kommos* of *The Libation Bearers,* in which Orestes, Electra, and the chorus invoke Agamemnon at his tomb, takes up 160 lines; its strophes are distributed among the speakers according to a subtly varied but highly regular order. In a sequence of fifteen metrical sections, not a syllable seems out of place.

It would be wrong to infer from what I have said about the static nature of Aeschylus's plots and the majestic quality of his verse that there is anything cold about his style; no poet is more intense or more passionate than he. Even the great lyric sequences I have evoked are charged with an almost unbearable power and violence of feeling. This power of Aeschylus's art is visible at all levels of its composition. The very simplicity of his plots allows for the sustained development of a single agony, while the single act in which it reaches a crisis stands out all the more starkly. When Eteocles leaves the stage to fight his brother, when Clytemnestra kills Agamemnon, or when Orestes kills Clytemnestra, the full gravity of the act and its implications can be felt because everything has been building up to it.

There is, moreover, little that Aeschylus is unwilling to present onstage; he deliberately seeks spectacular effects. He shows us Darius rising from his tomb, Prometheus nailed to his rock, Io tossing and turning in fear of the gadfly that pursues her. He shows us the Furies (their appearance is said to have terrified the audience). And he portrays violence at its highest pitch— the Egyptians trying to seize the Danaids by force, Cassandra in her prophetic frenzy, Orestes brandishing the sword with which he will kill his mother. Dramatic intensity is immediate, a function of what is happening onstage.

That intensity is also a function of verbal art. In Aeschylus, descriptions of battle are themselves violent; verbs crackle as they collide. Descriptions of omens, dreams, and forebodings are couched in an oracular style that heightens their agonizing solemnity. The vocabulary itself is a perfect reflection of that mixture, unique to Aeschylus, of sacred power and everyday reality. In the *Frogs,* Aristophanes made fun not only of Aeschylus's long choral sequences (914–15) but also of his rare and startling words: "Words big as oxen, bushy-browed and plumed, strange sorts of bugaboos unknown to the audience" (924–26). Aeschylus is fond of compound words, periphrases—

anything to baffle and astonish. He also plays on words, grouping several
that begin with the same syllable or juxtaposing two that contradict one another, like the "ships that are ships no more" of the Persians (680: *naes anaes*).
His sensitivity to words is remarkably keen; thus, for example—again in *The
Persians*—he piles up exotic-sounding names of the dead, evoking the grief
of the Asians in a concrete and poignant way which yet transports the Athenian audience out of its native element.

The power of Aeschylus's style lies chiefly, however, in his use of images
and the meanings he assigns to them. With Aeschylus we are at the opposite
pole from Homeric imagery. Homer used long similes, often evoking a familiar, everyday world. Aeschylus prefers brief metaphors expressing an actual
identification between two terms; by making us look at one term through the
other he reveals its nature. In human violence there may surface the kinds of
violence that animals inflict or suffer. Iphigenia struggles "like a she-goat";
the Persians are killed at sea "like tuna." Clytemnestra is the cow attacking
the bull; elsewhere she is an eel or a viper. Animals as portrayed in Aeschylus
live by struggle and pursuit. For some of the plays, master images have been
identified, most of them drawn from the animal world; J. Dumortier, for example, writes of "the animal caught in the trap," "the grip[3] of the serpent,"
"the pack thrown off the scent." Aeschylus also identifies the violence of war
or impending disaster with that of tempests, powerful sea swells, or mount-
ing waves. In this way violence and suffering are raised to a cosmic scale.

Above all, the great moral law that animates Aeschylus's work is conveyed by vivid metaphors of transgression, pollution, and crime. These run
the gamut from the most concrete images—"the clotted blood that will flow
no more," or the palace "that smells of murder and spilt blood"—to the un-
canny and terrifying hints of the transgression that "in evil men gives birth to
new license, soon or late, when comes the day marked for a new birth." The
Fury herself ushers in this new crime, this "child of ancient murders that in its
turn enters the house."

Such monstrous births are matched by an instinctive fear that gives the individual's body a life of its own. "My heart shrieks from within my limbs,"
cries Xerxes in *The Persians* (991); likewise, the chorus in the *Agamemnon*
fears without knowing what it fears: "Why this terror that rises before my
prophetic heart and stubbornly hovers around it? Why does my song, unbid-
den and unpaid, play the prophet?" (975–79). The mysterious law of divine
justice comes alive and can be physically felt; in the same way, the moral
sense awakened by this justice springs to life spontaneously and unaccount-
ably. Aeschylus's metaphors give his thought the force of revelation, im-
pressing it on us directly, without intermediary.

The art of Aeschylus is thus as concrete as it is visionary. We shall find his
successors more straightforward and easier to understand; their art will be

---

3. The French word means both "grip" and "embrace."—Trans.

very different. But they will be heirs to Aeschylus insofar as they will use myths, as he did, to investigate man's fate in relation to the gods and within the context of the city-state. The gods will seem more distant and the city more deeply divided; but the investigation will continue. It is because he began that investigation that we think of Aeschylus (in Gilbert Murray's phrase) as "the creator of tragedy."

II · HERODOTUS

As Aeschylus is the creator of tragedy, so Herodotus is "the father of history," a title conferred on him by Cicero. Like Aeschylus, he was deeply influenced by the Persian Wars. We have good reasons, then, for comparing the two. But we must not forget that chronologically Herodotus is Aeschylus's junior by quite a span. If a birth date of 485 is accepted for Herodotus, the difference in their ages is forty years; the historian was then only five years old when the battle of Salamis was fought. He knew Athens in the age of Pericles, and saw the beginning of the Peloponnesian War. He was closer in age to Sophocles, whose friend he became, than to either of the other great tragedians.

Though known as the father of history, Herodotus did not invent the genre out of whole cloth, any more than Aeschylus invented tragic drama. In the sixth century a great desire for learning had spread throughout Asia Minor, and speculations on all subjects were entertained; it was not long before purely mythological accounts of the past were called into question. At first the aim was to put such stories in order and establish sequences; the earliest "historical" works were simple chronicles, genealogies, and researches into the origins of particular cities. This genre was to survive until the end of the fifth century; its representatives include Hellanicus and those known as the Atthidographers (who wrote chronicles of Attica). Others, however, took curiosity, and the critical spirit, still farther. Herodotus had one noteworthy predecessor, Hecataeus of Miletus. Hecataeus engaged in geographic research (Herodotus mentions his sojourn in Egypt) and made a map of the world. He also wrote *Genealogies* in which he is known to have displayed a resolutely critical spirit: unwilling to limit himself, as he said, to the "tales the Greeks tell," Hecataeus set out to describe things "as they seemed true to him." Although his work itself is lost, we know from fragments that he sought rationalistic explanations for certain legends bordering on the marvelous. His concern for both firsthand information and rationalistic criticism helped make possible the transition from myth to history.

The transition finally took place under the influence of the Persian Wars. Here was a series of events affecting not a particular family or city but all Greeks and the whole of the Persian empire. It made men aware of vast sequences of political events such as the growth of the empire, and great imperatives, such as the defense of liberty or mutual aid among cities. In short, it called for a history focused on the present and on politics. These are the two characteristics of the work of Herodotus that make him the true father of history. His is certainly not a work of history as we understand it today; it does not even stand up to the intellectual demands of his successor Thucydides. Still close to the epic, it is often naive and full of the marvelous; yet it does mark a decisive break with myth and an entry into rational investigation—i.e., into history. Herodotus's work is also, incidentally, the earliest Greek prose work to have come down to us.

A · Life of Herodotus

Herodotus's life was divided between two homelands. He was born at Halicarnassus, near Miletus; the city was Dorian, and he seems to have had some Carian ancestors. The most important fact about his origins, however, is that he was educated in the crucible of intellectual curiosity that was fifth-century Asia Minor. Beyond this essential impetus, he doubtless owes to his Ionian education something of his easy grace, as well as his taste for stories and digressions.

But at an early age, after taking part with his relative Panyassis (his uncle, apparently, and an author of epic poems) in a revolt against the local tyrant, Herodotus was forced to leave his home. What we know of him thereafter is that he was a great traveler. There are references in his work to trips he made, information he collected, and objects he saw. His travels took him to Egypt, as far as Elephantine; to Babylon; to the shores of the Black Sea, into Scythian territory—and elsewhere. His work is called *Historiē*, from the Greek word for "investigation," and it is clear that his travels had a great influence on the spirit in which he approached history; not only did he "see the world," he also spoke with people and compared their traditions, identifying differences as well as traits common to all.

Among his voyages a place of honor must be reserved for the visit or visits he made to Athens. He is supposed to have read aloud from his work there and received a reward for it. He was certainly acquainted not only with Sophocles but with Pericles and the great family of the Alcmaeonidae. Finally, the visit to Athens led to his finding a new homeland, for he became a citizen of the Panhellenic colony founded, on Pericles' initiative, at Thurii in southern Italy (444 B.C.). It is not known whether he remained there. His work mentions events after 430, and his death is dated around 425. But it cannot be denied that his exposure to Athenian culture, in the era when Athens was at her apogee, fostered the political sense, the habit of discussion, and the spirit of analysis that are so prominent in the last books of his history.

B · Work of Herodotus

Herodotus took as his subject the struggle between the Greeks and the "barbarians." We might expect a simple history of the Persian Wars; but there is much more to it than this. As it has come down to us, the work is divided into nine books (each bearing the name of one of the Muses); the first Persian campaign begins only in chapter 43 of book 6.[4] Even admitting that the Ionian revolt against the Persians—described in book 5 and the beginning of book 6—is a prelude to Darius's invasion of Greece, we still have four whole books before the Ionian revolt. Are these four books then devoted to the causes of the conflict? Herodotus himself suggests as much in his opening sentence, where he says he wished to preserve the memory of the great deeds of the Greeks and Persians, and to explain "in particular what caused Greeks and barbarians to go to war with one another." This is an oversimplification, however. The first four books cover roughly the span of time stretching from the ancestors of Croesus and Cyrus, about 700 B.C., to 490. Yet the order is not purely chronological, nor is the author's aim simply to account for the outbreak of war.

Unquestionably preoccupied with the struggles between the "barbarians" and the Greeks of Asia Minor, Herodotus begins with a history of Lydia, and its king, Croesus: "This Croesus was the first of the barbarians, to our knowledge, to make subjects of some of the Greeks (whom he forced to pay tribute) and to make friends of others; he subjugated the Ionians, Aeolians, and Dorians living in Asia, and he made friends with the Lacedaemonians. Before the reign of Croesus, all Greeks were free" (1.6). Croesus, however, was defeated by Cyrus, king of the Persians, who in his turn made subjects of the Asian Greeks (1.165–70). Thus the story of Croesus leads into the relations between Persians and Greeks. In addition, the story acquires moral significance with Solon's warning to Croesus (1.29ff.), later repeated by Croesus to Cyrus (1.86). This warning sets the tone of the work and introduces its philosophy, which is imbued with the spirit of moderation. For the moral focus, in Herodotus, is at least as important as the political.

What is more, the story of Croesus interests the author for its own sake. It gives details of Croesus's family background—details comparable to those given later on the origins of Cyrus's power or on Persian customs. Herodotus is curious about the past in its own right, independent of any analysis of causes. On every subject he seeks both the earliest accounts available—those closest to the origins of a phenomenon—and the widest assortment of testimony on the customs of each nation. The Croesus story is clearly related to the conflict between Greeks and Persians, but in its details it frequently strays from that subject; it is revealing of Herodotus's tendency to mix information pure and simple with his moral, historical, or ethnographic concerns. This tendency reappears in each successive episode. Thus in tracing the growth of the Persian empire, he stops at each stage to give a miniature treatise on the history and customs of the various peoples who come under Persian rule. Egypt is the subject of book 2; then, in connection with the reign of Darius, we find an account of the Scyths and one of the Libyans, which together make up book 4. Nor is this all, for when embassies and alliances enter

4. "Books" and "chapters" in ancient works are often shorter than those names suggest to a modern audience. Chapters are often a paragraph or two in length.—Trans.

the picture, Herodotus summarizes, in long parentheses, the history of Sparta and of Athens (1.56–70 and 5.39–96). Mere chronological association inspires him to insert an account of the conflict between Sparta and Polycrates of Samos (3.39–47), as well as of the Corinthian participation in this conflict (48–53). In the latter passage he naturally speaks of Periander, tyrant of Corinth; but Periander has appeared once already, in book 1; and in book 5 (92) we find, couched in a speech, a long survey of the Corinthian tyranny.

Although Herodotus's work is centered on the Persian Wars, then, he makes many detours before settling down to describe them, and the structure of his book is more flexible than firm. It gives Herodotus the investigator room to include a mass of heterogeneous facts; but they are given in a rather archaic order in which parentheses are allowed to accumulate until at last we are brought back to the point of departure. This peculiarity of structure has led some scholars to think Herodotus may have composed the individual "treatises," or *logoi,* independently of one another, the idea of bringing them together occurring to him only later. That hypothesis, proposed long ago by F. Jacoby, would certainly account for the autonomous character of individual books; but it has fallen out of favor in recent years. Even if we abandon it, there remains a perceptible difference in tone and pace between the early, more loosely structured books and those on the Persian Wars with their tighter craftsmanship. What are we to make of the contrast? Some (like Immerwahr) would minimize it, ascribing it to the contrast in subject matter; others (like Fornara) see it as evidence of an evolution in Herodotus's style. Whatever the reason, the *History* grows more cohesive toward the end. This may be entirely due to a combination of factors: the importance of the events involved; the stir they created in Herodotus's world; the greater reliability of his sources; the probable influence of discussions he heard in Athens. The work begins in the relaxed manner characteristic of Ionia; it ends with the characteristic Athenian emphasis on politics.

Yet at no point does Herodotus put all his effort into political commentary. That was not his object; and if his opening sentence mentions the reasons for the conflict, it does so only after declaring a prior aim: to prevent time from effacing the deeds of men, so that the great actions of Greeks and barbarians "may not lose their renown." The first historian still sees it as his task to render excellence immortal—as had Pindar.

His method of proceeding is well suited to the double character (commemorative and political) of the work, and to the period he describes, which was one of discovery and of transition between two worlds.

His stance is already a decidedly critical one. In the prologue to his work, he records legendary abductions of women by both Greeks and "barbarians" (those of Io, Medea, Helen); but he does so with a skeptical irony and seeks firmer ground for his own assertions. He writes: "That is what the Persians and Phoenicians say. For my part, I do not intend to pronounce their stories true or false; but there is one person I myself know to have first unjustly attacked the Greeks, and I shall name him" (1.5). Frequently, even in passages of properly historical narrative, he has occasion to mention versions he considers doubtful. Thus at 2.123, à propos of a religious legend, he observes: "Let those who find such stories credible accept the Egyptian accounts; my sole aim in this work is to report what I was able to glean from each source." He tells the stories but withholds his own endorsement. At other times he reports several contradictory versions (e.g., Athenian and Aeginetan versions of the same incident at 5.85–88). It may be more rational to investigate the validity of sources and come down on one side or the other, as Thucydides was to do; but it is more objective to report impartially all the evidence at one's disposal. Fortunately, the evidence at Herodotus's disposal was vast, and it came not only from native informants but from his own direct observation. In book 2 (99) he cites the importance of firsthand scrutiny (*opsis*, literally "sight"), reflection, and investigation—all methods of research he had the insight to promote; rarely have they been used to such a degree by later historians. He describes geographic features, indigenous animals, and rites; he mentions the most noteworthy buildings and monuments. He even cites as evidence inscriptions he happened to see (e.g., the "Cadmean" characters mentioned at 5.59).

Herodotus's laborious documentation, however, is not always matched by an equal effort to present the material in a rational order. We may ask, in the first place, how useful it was for the author to embellish the *History* with stories he did not himself believe. Yet his own beliefs take him far afield at times, in the direction of the marvelous: he believes firmly in oracles and ••cites them freely, reports dreams (like that of Xerxes, which occupies more of book 7—chapters 12–19—than all the political causes of the second Persian campaign) and miracles (like those of Delphi, 8.35–38). Such marvels (even if Herodotus expresses reservations about some of them) remind us more of Homer than of history as we know it.

In the same way, his fondness for anecdotes about individuals readily overrides his historical sense. Few stories are as charming as the account of the way the future tyrant of Corinth was saved, as an infant, from his would-be assassins; but so much detail is hardly necessary to an understanding of the events. Even accounts of battles still emphasize individual prowess, and the analysis of tactics suffers accordingly. Finally, and most important, Herodotus still has a very imprecise notion of causation in history. The chief motive he recognizes is revenge—one of the simplest possible ways of linking an event to the one that preceded it. Undoubtedly revenge played a crucial role in a world still dominated by dynasts infatuated with honor. Yet in Herodotus's own work, alongside those simple causal sequences we find traces of more political explanations, which in our day are considered more important. His sense of historical sequence is still to a certain extent linear and superficial.

Among the signs in Herodotus of an ongoing evolution within the genre, I have yet to mention the speeches. The ancients considered the speech a legitimate technique for conveying the motives of protagonists; Thucydides' speeches are a good example. Speeches in Herodotus, however, are not always as closely interwoven with the narrative as they are in Thucydides. In this respect, Herodotus is a transitional figure between Homer and Thucydides. Many of his dialogues are in direct discourse and seem chiefly designed to suggest the immediacy of a character's presence; the technique is still anecdotal. Only the speeches in books 7 and 8, on the chances of each side's winning the second Persian campaign, are truly political speeches, giving insight into the causes of events. This difference confirms the contrast I mentioned above between the earlier and later books, and underlines the impact of the Persian Wars on Herodotus's thought—an impact that can be felt throughout his work.

C · The Thought of Herodotus

Herodotus's thought, like that of Aeschylus, must be read on two different levels; but this subtlety is more surprising in the case of a historian.

1 · POLITICAL THOUGHT

First, we find in Herodotus a number of simple, powerful political ideas. Where domestic politics is concerned, he is very much opposed to tyranny and convinced of the advantages of liberty. He describes the cruelty of the Corinthian and Milesian tyrants, and points out that the power of Athens increased as soon as she shook off tyranny (5.66 and 78). Here he sees a principle at work: "Not merely in isolated cases but as a general rule the advantages of equality are clear. As long as they were governed by tyrants, the Athenians were no better fighters than any of the peoples around them; freed from the tyrants, they moved far ahead of their neighbors. Here we have proof that as long as they were slaves, they were content to act the coward, thinking that all their work was for their master; whereas once they were free, each found it in his own interest to do his task with a will."

The Greeks' victory over the "barbarians" was likewise ensured by the spirit of discipline freely accepted—a spirit whose source was in their liberty. The famous dialogue in book 7 between Xerxes and the Greek Demaratus is a full and striking statement of this belief: Greece may be poor, but she has valor, the product of wisdom and firm laws; while the Persians are bent under the lash, the Greeks obey the law. As Demaratus puts it, "They are free, it is true, but not entirely so; for they have an absolute ruler, the law, which they fear even more than your subjects fear you" (104). Herodotus is far from systematically scorning the "barbarians." (His enlightened attitude even drew down Plutarch's accusation of "malice.")[5] But, like Aeschylus, he sees a deep and primarily political contrast between the world where power is absolute and that where liberty prevails; and the contrast explains, at least in part, the Greek victory.

5. In the essay *De Herodoti malignitate*, "On the Malice of Herodotus," in the *Moralia.*— Trans.

It remains to be said that not all Greek cities showed equal valor in the fight for liberty. If Herodotus loves the Athenians, it is for the self-sacrifice they showed during the Persian Wars: "Without straining the truth, one may say of the Athenians that they were the saviors of Greece. Whichever side they joined was sure to prevail; and because they chose liberty for Greece, they assumed the responsibility for rousing all parts of the Greek world that had refused to collaborate with the Medes" (7.139). This is the glory of Athens, whatever she may have done since. Herodotus also paints a flattering picture of the Athenian refusal of Persian offers designed to lure her away from the Greek cause (8.136–44). He puts into the Athenians' mouths the first glowing expression of Panhellenic spirit; for among the reasons for their refusal are not only the crimes of the Persians but the notion of Greek unity: "Finally, there is the Greek world, one in language and blood; there are the sanctuaries and sacrifices we share, and our common *mores*; and these the Athenians could never betray" (144). The Persian Wars gave birth to Panhellenic feeling; Herodotus gave it voice.

This explains his severity toward the indiscretions, the vacillations, and the rivalries between cities that frequently paralyzed the Greek defense. Already in book 5 he is critical of the Ionian revolt, which he sees as a product of private intrigues that were to cost all the Greeks dearly (first the Greeks in Asia Minor and later those on the mainland). At the very beginning of the first Persian campaign, the serious implications of private conflicts are evident in the feud between Athens and Aegina. During the second campaign, the Greeks split into two camps (7.132); when ambassadors are sent out by the would-be defenders, they meet with difficulties—from the Argives, for example (7.148–52), or from Gelon, tyrant of Syracuse, who is willing to help only if he is put in command (153–67); sometimes they receive false promises (as in Corcyra, 168).

In a work that is neither partisan, systematic, nor given to glossing over human failings, Herodotus manages to convey the double ideal of liberty and union. Important as these two themes are, however, they dominate his work less than do his moral and religious ideas.

2 · MORAL AND RELIGIOUS THOUGHT

The world of Herodotus, like that of Aeschylus, is ruled by the gods; but Herodotus dwells less on the justice of the gods than on the vulnerability of the mortals whose destinies they determine. In this respect he is closer to Sophocles than to Aeschylus. Also like Sophocles, he gives a prominent place to oracles, and is fond of showing how men are fooled by those they misinterpret. When Croesus asked the Delphic oracle whether he should make war on the Persians, he was told that if he did so he would destroy a great empire (1.53). He assumed that the Persian empire was meant, and went to war; but the oracle had referred to his own (1.91). A further Delphic response had told him to flee when a mule became king of the Medes, and Croesus had concluded that he would never have to flee; but the "mule" turned out to be Cyrus, whose parents were of unequal birth (his mother was a Mede and his father a Persian). Although the Pythia[6] makes it clear that Croesus's fall is in punishment for the crime of one of his ancestors (as is often the case in Aeschylus), the mistaken interpretations of the two oracles are infinitely more striking to the reader than the explanation based on divine justice.

So as not to offend the gods, Herodotus's characters—again like those of Aeschylus and the archaic poets—must avoid hubris; in Herodotus, however, hubris is not necessarily a moral failing that deserves punishment. As described in book 7 by Artabanus, an uncle of Xerxes, it is much simpler and more physical: "Observe animals of exceptional size: heaven sends down lightening to strike them and will not let them enjoy their superiority, while small animals arouse no jealousy. Consider the highest houses, the tallest trees: it is there that lightning strikes, for heaven always cuts down that which exceeds the normal limits" (7.10). In such a world, nothing is more dangerous than to trust in one's happiness. This is the gist of Solon's advice to Croesus in book 1—the advice that was to make such an impression on Cyrus: "I know the ways of divinity: it is altogether jealous of human happiness and likes to disturb it" (32). Hence the paradox that a man cannot be called happy as long as he is alive. Other examples indicate that prosperity is not only changeable but dangerous. Most striking is the case of Polycrates, tyrant of Samos, who tried in vain to rid himself of the luck that was to be his undoing. He threw a gold ring set with an emerald, which he prized greatly, into the depths of the sea, but a fish that had swallowed the ring was caught and brought to Polycrates: it is not in man's power to elude his fate (3.39–45). The best he can do is try to be just and pious, and keep his circumstances modest. He cannot be sure that will be enough, but it is a primary condition for happiness.

Herodotus's awareness of the reversals in human destiny has three important consequences for his thought and work. First, it invites a comparison with tragedy. Many episodes in Herodotus could serve as plots for tragedies; and reciprocal influences between the genres are not to be ruled out. Second, the same insight makes him see the course of history as open-ended, given to fluctuation and change. In his preface he notes: "Of the cities that were once great, most have become small; and those that were great in my time were formerly small; because I am convinced that human prosperity never stays fixed in the same place, I shall take equal notice of both" (1.5). Luck changes; the wheel turns. As Croesus puts it at 1.207, "Human affairs are on a wheel that turns and will not let the same men be always fortunate." But this wheel (kuklos) has nothing to do with the regular "cycle" in time postulated by some others; it simply means that fluctuation between good and bad fortune is the rule for all men.

6. The priestess who gave the oracular responses at Delphi.—Trans.

Finally, the sense of instability in human affairs merges, in Herodotus, with the many-sided experience of the traveler to produce a virtue no other Greek possessed to such a degree—tolerance. Herodotus knows that customs differ, that they are based on convention, and that they vary from time to time and from place to place. But he does not draw the conclusion—which others were to draw within the next generation—that every rule is relative and can thus be broken; he concludes that every rule should be respected, including those encountered abroad. Cambyses' scorn for the religious ordinances of the Egyptians was proof of his madness. While noting that everyone prefers his own native customs, Herodotus adds: "It is not to be expected that anyone but a madman would ridicule such things" (i.e., religious taboos) (3.38).

His tolerance and respect for diversity give impetus to his investigations; they are matched by an engaging sympathy for everything human. We find children in Herodotus's work—a rarity in Greek literature. He portrays great affection among family members, "barbarian" and Greek alike. Nor is his work lacking in tenderness and humor. His style may appear naive, yet it makes use of a poetic and artificial language, often reminiscent of Homer's; and it gives history a coloring of human sympathy that also brings Homer to mind.

The experience of the Persian Wars produced very different reactions in Aeschylus and in Herodotus. Where the former had seen the horror of war but also the beauty of divine justice, the latter saw an example of political complexity and of the many vicissitudes to which human life is subject. In each case, however, the experience was a decisive one and gave impetus to a new literary genre. These two genres were to develop and evolve throughout the fifth century, as Athens, open to all intellectual currents, became the adoptive home of new and revolutionary ideas.

4

Drama in the Second Half of the Fifth Century: Sophocles, Euripides, and Aristophanes

Sophocles staged his first plays in 468; his literary career began at the moment when Athens, free of the Persian threat, was becoming mistress of a vast empire and the center of Greece. When his *Antigone* appeared, the Acropolis was echoing with the sound of workmen's hammers—the Parthenon was rising. Ten years later, in 431, the Peloponnesian War began; in 404, after twenty-seven years of suffering and cruelty, Athens was to be defeated by those whom her empire had antagonized, and the days of her power would be over. During the war, new plays by Sophocles and Euripides were produced each year; but while Sophocles' work continued to reflect the harmony that had marked the peak of Athenian fortunes, Euripides, younger by fifteen years, already reflected the doubts and questionings of a period of political malaise. Comedy now developed side by side with tragedy, and it too bore witness to a growing uneasiness.

I · SOPHOCLES
A · Life of Sophocles

Sophocles' life (495?–405) was a peaceful one. Born into a comfortable family, he was a successful athlete and musician in his early youth. Cultivated and sociable, he had many friends; his witticisms were quoted and his character praised. Though he had no real vocation for politics, he repeatedly held high public office. In 443–42 he was *hellenotamias* (charged with collecting the tribute from allied cities); twice he was *stratēgos*[1] (once with Pericles, the year of the *Antigone*); and after the Sicilian debacle he was one of ten *probouloi*, special councillors charged with the preservation of the state. He also held religious office; the anonymous *Life of Sophocles* makes him a priest of Halon, a hero invoked as a healer, and he seems to have helped introduce the cult of Asclepius, for whom he wrote a paean.

Most important, his career as a playwright was marked by success from beginning to end. With his first plays he defeated Aeschylus; in all he won at least twenty victories, and always came in second when he was not first. In

1. The Greek word for a general, or military commander; in fifth-century Athens, *stratēgoi* were political leaders as well.—Trans.

409, at the age of 87, he was still taking first prize—for the *Philoctetes*. When he died in 405, the Spartan general Lysander, then in control of the Attic countryside, gave safe-conduct to his funeral procession; two dreams were said to have decreed this interruption of the war in honor of the poet. Sophocles is the tragedian par excellence, but the sufferings he portrays in his work are not his own; he seems to have been a happy man.

B · Works of Sophocles

Sophocles wrote a variety of works, including an ode to Herodotus and a treatise, *On the Chorus*. He also, of course, wrote satyr plays, one for each group of three tragedies; since 1912 we have sizable fragments of one of them, the *Ichneutae* ("Bloodhounds," describing the pursuit of Hermes after his theft of Apollo's cattle). But by far the greater part of his work consisted of tragedies. Of the 123 he wrote, seven survive, as in the case of Aeschylus. Only titles and brief fragments of the others have come down to us. Of the seven surviving plays, only three can be dated with some precision—the *Antigone* (442), the *Philoctetes* (409), and the *Oedipus at Colonus* (staged posthumously in 401). The other four are assigned, without much certainty, to earlier or later periods on the basis of literary criteria. Unlike Aeschylus's tragedies, these plays did not belong to trilogies. (Sophocles may have composed a few trilogies, however. One, called the *Telephia*, which has not survived, was ascribed to him.) Though he did not work on the grand scale of Aeschylus, Sophocles refined dramatic technique and made it less rigid; it was he who introduced the third actor and the use of painted scenery. In his plays the action is more important and includes more reversals.

The *Ajax* may be the oldest of the surviving plays. As it opens, Ajax, having planned in his bitter resentment to kill the chiefs of the Greek army that is besieging Troy, has been seized by a fit of madness and has slaughtered in their stead flocks of the army's sheep. After a prologue in which Athene shows Odysseus the demented Ajax, Ajax comes out of his stupor, in despair and covered with dishonor. His family and retainers try to persuade him to live, and are hopeful for a while, but he eludes them and kills himself. In the second half of the play there is a debate over his burial, which is finally granted thanks to the intervention of Odysseus. This juxtaposition of hope and death is the kind of reversal, frequent in Sophocles, that we do not find in Aeschylus. The fact that the play falls into two halves (it has been called a "diptych") has left it open to modern criticism, but this too is a mark of flexibility in composition.

The *Women of Trachis*, another "diptych," is close in date to the *Ajax*. The first half focuses on Deianira, who is awaiting the return of her husband Heracles; when she learns that he is bringing a new bride with him, she tries to rekindle his love by means of a magic ointment. But the drug proves to be a mortal poison, and the second half of the play focuses on Heracles—his agony, his despair, and his dying curses. As in the *Ajax*, hope and despair are juxtaposed; and the contrast between an intractable hero and a tender, fearful woman recalls that between Ajax and his captive Tecmessa. (Heracles and Deianira, however, are never on stage together.)

The *Antigone* is reminiscent in some ways of the "diptych" plays, for it continues well beyond the point at which the heroine leaves the stage: yet the unity of action is greater. Despite Creon's prohibition, Antigone has made up her mind to bury her brother Polyneices, killed in the siege of Thebes as he sought to wrest power from his brother. (The same siege was the subject of Aeschylus's *Seven against Thebes*.) Antigone debates the merits of her act, first with her sister, who is more timid than she, and again, after her arrest, with Creon. When she has been taken to her death, Creon must face the reproaches of his son Haemon, Antigone's betrothed, and the prophet Teiresias, who speaks in the name of the gods. Too late, Creon understands that he is at fault: his intention had been to preserve order in the city, but he has slighted the divine law that the dead must have burial. The end of the play leaves him overwhelmed with guilt and grief at the deaths of Antigone, Haemon, and the queen his wife.

There are distinct correspondences between this king, destroyed by the gods despite his good intentions, and the hero of *Oedipus the King*. The latter play dramatizes Oedipus's discovery that his efforts to evade an oracle have been in vain: he has indeed killed his father and married his mother, as the oracle foretold. His fall is itself the result of good intentions, for he learns the truth after ordering an investigation into the old king's death, so that a plague may be lifted from the city. It is characteristic of Sophocles that the disastrous truth should be revealed just as Oedipus has heard of his *adoptive* father's death, and thinks himself out of danger.

A similar contrast is to be found in the *Electra*. There has been much debate over which of the two *Electra*s—Sophocles' or Euripides'—is earlier; but both stand in striking contrast to Aeschylus's *Libation Bearers*. Each of the later plays is named for the heroine, and her character—her will—is behind the decision to kill Clytemnestra: the role of human will has become more prominent than that of divine intervention. Sophocles, moreover, in contrast to Euripides, has pushed to the limit Electra's grounds for despairing of Orestes' return. No longer is it simply a question of the time that has passed (while she waited feverishly but in vain): Orestes' very pretext, when at last he returns, is the claim that Orestes is dead, and Electra believes the lie. Desperate but not broken, she contemplates acting alone; at this precise moment the recognition of brother and sister takes place, and despair abruptly gives way to joy. But Electra's long solitude has awakened in her the same fierce will shown by Antigone—a will accentuated, as in the *Antigone*, by a contrast between the heroine and a more timid sister.

A similar moral decision is central to the *Philoctetes*. Neoptolemus, the young son of Achilles, is ordered by the wily Odysseus to deceive Philoctetes, whom the Greeks had abandoned many years earlier on a desert island, and to bring him back to Troy with his bow (according to an oracle, the city could not be taken without the bow). Neoptolemus is torn between his duty to the Greek army and the loyalty he feels for the unfortunate Philoctetes. Finally his sense of loyalty prevails. The young man tries to persuade Philoctetes to come of his own will, but Philoctetes is adamant in his refusal, and the intervention of the hero Heracles, half divine, half mortal, is needed to conclude the play.

In *Oedipus at Colonus,* by contrast, there are no moral debates, with the exception of Oedipus's stubborn insistence that he is innocent of his "crimes" ("I did not commit them, I suffered them," 267; cf. 273, 538–39, 964, 977, 987). But there are no conflicting duties, and the action unfolds with the solemnity of a mystery play. Blind and accursed, the old Oedipus arrives with his daughter Antigone at Colonus in Attica. He is uncertain whether he will be welcome; and he learns that each of his two sons wants to appropriate his person. As it happens, in mysterious compensation for his past sufferings, he is welcomed by Theseus; and his body, after death, is destined to preserve the country from attack. His death, at the end of the play, takes place in an atmosphere of holy exaltation.

Two themes and two sets of problems are thus dealt with by turns in Sophocles: the relation between men and gods; and the hero's moral dilemmas.

C · The Vision of Sophocles: Gods and Men

In discussing Aeschylus, I identified two sets of themes, those related to the city and those concerning the gods. The first group are of minor importance in the surviving plays of Sophocles. The second half of the *Ajax,* and more especially the *Antigone,* do include discussions of the problem of absolute authority. The *Antigone* also contains reflections on the subject of law, which have encouraged some scholars (Victor Ehrenberg, among others) to compare Sophocles' position with that of Pericles. But it must be acknowledged that what Sophocles emphasizes are religious obligations or very broad moral ones. The political life of the city-state remains in the background except as it impinges on religious duties.

The relation between men and gods is, as I have noted, a major theme in Sophocles. But it is nothing like the relation between men and gods as described by Aeschylus. In the first place, the gods are more distant. In the surviving plays, they almost never appear onstage (the sole exception is Athene, in the prologue to the *Ajax*). Likewise, their influence on human emotions is less immediate; and the principles by which they act are harder to discern.

Yet the gods make their presence known, most frequently by means of oracles. The plays of Sophocles often find their points of departure in prophecies; as the action unfolds, the characters look for the fulfilment of the various prophecies, weigh them against each other, and seek reassurance in them. Sometimes as many as three or four are cited in a single tragedy (e.g., in *The Women of Trachis,* in *Oedipus the King,* and in *Philoctetes*). Yet these oracles are not understood. Often they are enigmatic, as in Herodotus. Thus Heracles was told that he would be killed by a dead man (in fact, the drug which killed him was given to Deianira by the dying Centaur):[2] how could he be expected to interpret this? Even when the oracles themselves are clear, their application may be deceptive; thus Oedipus mistook the identity of his father and mother. To put it another way, the mystery surrounding the gods' designs does not involve a principle; it is as if a veil were lifted only halfway, and mortals were expected to guess what lay behind it. The partial disclosures of oracles add pathos to human weakness without in any way illuminating it.

Indeed, the contrast between human fate and human ignorance is a source of profound irony. It is no accident that disaster strikes at the very moment when the protagonists are taking heart. Nor is it by accident that Sophocles so often puts words of double meaning into his characters' mouths—words whose full import the speakers themselves are unaware of. Oedipus curses the murderer of Laius without knowing that he is himself the murderer, and swears to act "as if the dead man were his own father"—which is in fact the case. To the ironies of fate Sophocles adds ironies in the structuring of scenes and in the choice of words. The gods almost seem to be laughing at mankind, just as Athene in the *Ajax* makes cruel sport of the pitiful, crazed hero.

Yet in Sophocles' world view there are no signs of revolt against this divine regime. He respects the gods; and in his plays only the arrogant who are about to be struck down dare to doubt the veracity of oracles. Instead of revolt or doubt we find an overwhelming sense of the distance between gods and men. Among men, everything passes, everything changes. Sophocles says so repeatedly, in choral odes of rare nobility and power. One such marks the opening of *The Women of Trachis*: "Never has the son of Cronus, the king who ordains all things, given to mortals portions without pain. Joys and pains come to all by turns, circling, even as the stars of the Great Bear revolve. For men, nothing endures—not the starry night, not misfortunes, not riches" (126–33). The sphere of the gods, by contrast, is the sphere of the absolute, which nothing disturbs; in this respect Sophocles mirrors the beliefs of Pindar. As the chorus in the *Antigone* declares, nothing can diminish Zeus's power; "neither sleep, which charms all creatures, nor the divine and weariless months can ever conquer him." The chorus then addresses Zeus directly: "Untouched by age and time, you remain absolute master of Olympus and its dazzling light" (605–10).

The awareness of this gulf between two worlds accounts for two aspects of Sophocles' thought that at first glance might appear contradictory. First, it explains what may be called his pessimism. How can man hope, in such circumstances, to understand divine acts or escape their effects? Such acts are

2. Heracles had killed the Centaur, Nessus, with a poisoned arrow when Nessus tried to lay hands on Deianira. Before dying, Nessus had urged Deianira to preserve some of his blood, which would serve, he assured her, as a love charm.—Trans.

equally mysterious whether they are generous (*Oedipus at Colonus*) or cruel (*Oedipus the King*): a man's efforts to act rightly may be his own undoing. Or, like Oedipus, he may do wrong in spite of himself, without knowing or wishing it.

At the same time, whatever comes from the gods derives from them a sacred quality that outweighs every other consideration. A man cannot be too pious; he must put nothing before the divine ordinances. For Sophocles, the "unwritten laws" (respect for the gods, for parents, for suppliants, for the dead) are not the projections of a human consciousness or, indeed, of a Greek consciousness; they are divine laws. It is they that Antigone puts before the edict against burying her brother; and she is exhilarated at the thought that these laws partake of the permanence of the distant gods: "They are not of today or yesterday; no one knows the day they first appeared" (456–57). In the same vein, the chorus of *Oedipus the King* prays that it may never neglect the "laws begotten in the clear air of heaven, / whose only father is Olympus;" "No mortal nature brought them to birth, / no forgetfulness shall lull them to sleep; / for God is great in them and grows not old" (867–72).[3] In Sophocles, the eminence of the gods makes man's fate seem more tragic by contrast; but at the same time it increases the brilliance of the human ideal.

This brings us to another all-important aspect of Sophocles' thought that sets him apart from Aeschylus. In the absence of any clear understanding of the divine will, attention is focused on man: will he find an honorable response to the fate that threatens him? Sophocles shows us Ajax, Oedipus, Heracles, Philoctetes, even Electra at the moment when each is destroyed and brought low, though none of them can be said really to deserve such a fall; but it is at that very moment that their heroism is revealed—in the way they face the trial.

D · Characteristics and Virtues of the Sophoclean Hero

A primary feature of Sophocles' characters is the variety of positions they take, positions that are often in direct conflict with one another. This implies clear and effective characterization. After Aeschylus, literary expression had grown less rigid, and dialogue had gained in importance relative to the lyrical portion of tragedy. At the same time, the individual had gained a greater independence in society. As a result, we see more nuanced characterization, and frequent confrontations of two contrasting personalities. I have already mentioned the pairs of sisters (Antigone/Ismene, Electra/Chrysothemis) and the contrasts between husband and wife or master and captive woman (Heracles/Deianira, Ajax/Tecmessa). Elsewhere Neoptolemus's candor is contrasted with Odysseus's guile, Odysseus's prudence with Ajax's reckless passion, Odysseus's moderation with Agamemnon's harshness. All these

3. Translated by David Grene, in *The Complete Greek Tragedies*, ed. Grene and Lattimore (see Bibliography).—Trans.

characters are vividly portrayed, the individuality of each brought out by such contrasts.

Yet a qualification is in order: Sophocles' characterization does not always presuppose a psychological study that can satisfy our modern expectations. In a famous but unjust critique, Tycho von Wilamowitz (son of the well-known classical scholar) went so far as to claim that Sophocles neglected psychology to the point of implausibility when it suited his dramatic purpose. Some passages are certainly problematic. When Ajax, just before killing himself, claims to be reconciled to life, is he partly sincere and partly dishonest? Sophocles never makes it clear. Nor does he say or even imply to what extent Deianira is sincere when she claims to forgive her husband's infidelity. Equally inexplicable is Antigone's sudden shift from a bold acceptance of death to plaintive laments over her fate.

These gray areas imply no contradictions; they merely indicate that Sophocles did not care to make every link explicit in a character's motivation. For psychological investigation was not his major concern in creating characters. His characters have different mentalities because each embodies a different moral ideal, to which he or she adheres. Each knows the basis for his actions and defends his principles, making them his cause; each stands in contrast to those among whom he lives as one philosophy of life stands in contrast to others.

As a result, we come to feel that the debate on stage transcends the characters and concerns us as well. In the opposition between Ajax and Tecmessa we can see the contrast between an aristocratic ethic based on honor and a more humane ethic based on obligations to individuals. In the same play there is the debate between the Atreidae, who represent the claims of discipline, and Teucer and Odysseus, who urge respect for a dead man's former stature. The conflict between Antigone and Ismene, like that between Electra and Chrysothemis, is based on the opposite reactions of revolt and submission. The scenes in which these characters confront one another are clearly designed to weigh conflicting duties. Thus we have long speeches balancing one another, or debates in lines of crackling riposte in which antitheses—sometimes on the level of individual words or syllables—follow one another in rapid succession. Finally, each play as a whole is built from a sequence of such contrasting scenes. Antigone debates her act first with her sister and then with Creon; one is a timid ally, the other an antagonist. Later, Creon must debate *his* position with his own allies—his son and the prophet Teiresias—who find him at fault. In this series of confrontations, positions are affirmed, vindicated, and clarified; at the same time, tension builds.

Such close identification between a character and the ideal in whose name he acts implies a rare lucidity on the part of the character; yet complexity is by no means excluded. As we have seen, the sudden reversals in some characters' positions can be surprising. Neoptolemus's change of heart—his decision to embrace the right cause—is the whole subject of the play. Seldom, however, can we label a character's moral position without misrepresenting it; bad and good are usually intertwined. Creon, in the *Antigone*, defends the rights of the city-state, and his arguments are impressive; but they are also inflexible, and he tends to confuse the state with himself. Haemon and Teiresias try, each in his own way, to convince Creon of this. The truth is complex and emerges only gradually, as scene follows scene. It can honestly be said that after twenty-five centuries we are still debating the precise meaning of the conflict between Antigone and Creon. When the philosopher Hegel claims that Antigone represents the family in conflict with the state, he is oversimplifying. At different periods it has been said that Antigone stands for humane feeling as opposed to intransigence, or for the right to rebel as opposed to any abuse of power; these too are oversimplifications. In Sophocles, as in Thucydides, we find a tendency to identify the particular with the general—without, however, distorting the particular. Sophocles does not simply choose an ideal to embody in Antigone; he puts a living Antigone before us. Yet at every juncture of the plot he manages to reveal in her a set of principles and an ideal of proper conduct that together make up her unique personality. An individual and a philosophy of life can be identified with one another in Sophocles because all his characters are passionately concerned to define and to defend their reasons for living.

Among these reasons, honor takes first place. It seems to a reader of the plays that the notion of honor evolves and increasingly asserts itself. Thus we move from the altogether external honor of Ajax, made up of acknowledged exploits and finding expression in public esteem, to the internalized honor of Neoptolemus, which requires only moral courage and finds expression only in a clear conscience (to the neglect, in Neoptolemus's case, of the glory he might win, and at the risk of being misjudged by the entire Greek army). Sophocles takes us, in other words, all the way from the world of Homer to that of Socrates. The plays in all their diversity retrace this movement toward ever purer and higher values. Transcending such contrasts and such progress, however, is a fundamental trait common to all of Sophocles' protagonists; each is prepared to sacrifice everything to his honor and to his values as he understands them. These are *heroic* characters. From a fierce warrior like Ajax to young women like Antigone or Electra, all share the same resolve, the same acceptance of death, the same refusal to be swayed.

The result is that the heroes are isolated from their intimates, who misunderstand them, try to restrain them, call them reckless and unrealistic. Their acts draw down the taunts of the powerful. Ajax dies alone, killing himself on enemy soil with a sword that was the gift of an enemy. Deianira dies misunderstood and cursed by her husband. She too withdraws to die alone, as do Eurydice in *Antigone* and Jocasta in *Oedipus the King*. Antigone is condemned to die in a subterranean vault, utterly alone; she is led away amid the sarcasms of the chorus ("They are laughing at me!"). Electra can count on no one but herself to act ("I am alone"). Philoctetes has spent years alone on his island, where the Greeks want to abandon him a second time. Finally, Oedipus, at the very height of his exaltation, is left alone to face a death only he may witness.

This solitude in fact corresponds to the greatness of the hero; he is condemned to it by his insistence on an absolute. At the same time, he finds in it a sort of obligation to rise above himself with renewed strength.

Even on this point, Sophocles leaves us with an antithesis. On the one hand are the heroes, in all their greatness; on the other, their more human intimates. Naturally the spotlight is on the heroes; the brilliance, the glory are theirs. But are those who try in vain to sway them necessarily wrong? Is Ajax right to kill himself, to abandon Tecmessa, his son, and the sailors of his fleet? Is the pliancy of the more tolerant Odysseus, who can forget injuries, less praiseworthy? And is Philoctetes right to refuse so obstinately to go to Troy? The heroes, in truth, are limiting cases, proof of the nobility that can coexist with the cruelest of trials. They are not models for our emulation, any more than Sophocles' plays are disembodied sermons. They are expressions of his faith in man.

E · The Beauties of Sophocles' World

For a pessimist, Sophocles radiates a rare confidence in everything beautiful. This side of him is often revealed in his choral odes. What I have said thus far about his arrangement of scenes, his lucid dialogue, and his forceful antitheses gives an idea of his dramatic art as expressed in the spoken parts of the plays. But I have given no hint of the beauty of his great odes, which are less directly related to the action than those of Aeschylus, yet for that very reason reveal more of the poet himself. Sophocles' odes are hardly divorced from the action; but in most cases they translate the themes of the preceding episode into more universal terms, reflecting Sophocles' propensity for combining the particular and the general. In *Antigone*, for example, after the announcement that Polyneices has been buried in spite of the royal edict, the chorus sings of the greatness of human accomplishments but recalls that men are bound to obey laws; when Antigone's guilt has been discovered, it sings of the ease with which disaster strikes; after the scene with Haemon, it describes the universal power of love; and when Antigone has gone to her death, it recalls the deaths of figures from mythology. In each case there is the same broadening of focus—the same echo, in a more serene key, of the preceding action.

In this way Sophocles' odes, though far shorter than those of Aeschylus, open up broad perspectives in which we can glimpse the poet's tastes and convictions. An example is the ode in the *Antigone* that begins, "Many are the wonders in this world, but none is greater than man" (332ff.). There is no finer statement in Greek of man's preeminence, no greater praise for his discoveries and creative intelligence. In the spirit of his age, with its faith in progress, Sophocles evokes the whole series of human inventions, closing (in a vein more characteristic of his own thought) with the warning that if man uses his intelligence for ill, or against the law, it becomes ruinous.

Even expressions of grief and pain testify indirectly to Sophocles' love of life. When he wrote the poignant ode in *Oedipus at Colonus* deploring old age, the poet was in his nineties (the play was produced posthumously); it is a bitter piece, claiming that early death is best, and is often cited as evidence of Sophocles' pessimism. But behind the bitterness we can glimpse a sorrow at the loss of what made life worth living. In describing old age as "loathsome, impotent, unsociable, friendless" (1235–37), the poet may be suggesting nostalgia for the company, friendships, and happy life he had enjoyed as a younger man.

In this last tragedy, Sophocles even finds room for praise of his native Athens or, more precisely, his Attica. Oedipus comes there to die, and Sophocles takes advantage of the opportunity to describe the beauties of the Attic countryside—birds, growing things, and streams—which, together with the beneficent presence of the gods, inspire a great sense of peace. "In this land of good horses, stranger, you have found the best retreat on earth. This is white Colonus, favorite haunt of the sweet nightingale; she loves to sing in our green vales, amid the dark ivy, inviolable bower of the gods, sheltered by its thick growth of leaves from the sun and from every storm wind" (668ff.). If Sophocles is elsewhere the tragedian who most insistently recalls the fragility of human happiness and portrays heroism at its highest pitch, the Colonus ode gives us a glimpse of the happier man suggested by his biography. In the contrast he so consistently draws between man's vulnerability and his greatness, the abiding impression is that vulnerability is not paramount. The mood of Sophocles' plays is not one of despair, and he is no more "pessimistic" about man's worth than he is about the beauty of life.

II · EURIPIDES

The same cannot be said for Euripides. Born less than fifteen years after Sophocles, he nonetheless belonged to a different generation, whose minds were molded in a different moral climate. Intellectually he belongs to the age of the Sophists, and politically to the unsettled age of the Peloponnesian War.

A · Life of Euripides

Euripides was born in Salamis, almost certainly in 485. His contemporaries made fun of his humble origins, but their claims are not to be taken at face value. In any case he seems to have been dogged by misfortune. He was twice married, unhappily each time, and his circle of friends was small. He took no part in politics; and as for his plays, if they attracted much notice, they were also much criticized. The earliest were staged in 455, but not until thirteen years later did he win first prize; after this victory he won only three more in thirty-six years. His style was innovative, and he took liberties that must have shocked many spectators; Aristophanes says as much in *The Frogs*.

Eventually this uneasy truce between poet and city was broken for once and all: in 408, toward the end of the Peloponnesian War, Euripides left Athens to settle in Macedonia, at the court of King Archelaus. There he died in 406, far from his doomed city.

B · Works of Euripides

Euripides is credited with ninety-two plays; of these, eighteen tragedies (including the *Rhesus*, whose authorship has been questioned) and one satyr play have survived. The rest are known to us only through brief fragments, some quoted by ancient authors, some found on papyrus. The satyr play, *The Cyclops*, is undated. (The satyrs are the Cyclops's slaves; the dialogue is lively but joyless.) We have dates for eight of the tragedies: *Alcestis* (438—our only Euripidean play from before the Peloponnesian War), *Medea* (431), *Hippolytus* (428), *The Trojan Women* (415), *Helen* (412), *The Phoenician Women* (410), *Orestes* (408), and two that were staged posthumously: *Iphigenia in Aulis* and *The Bacchae*. The other plays fall somewhere between 431 and 412, so that all we have of Euripides' production is marked by the war; and it not infrequently bears the stamp of contemporary history, either in its details or in its impetus. A brief overview of the earlier plays will give some idea of the range of Euripides' themes.

The *Alcestis* is one of a kind. It was staged in place of the usual satyr play (hence, perhaps, the playwright's willingness to portray Heracles carousing). It is a genuine tragedy, however: Alcestis agrees to die in place of her husband Admetus; and it is only thanks to Heracles, who overcomes Death, that she returns to life and to her husband. The young wife's sacrifice is moving in its nobility, but most of the characters, including Admetus and especially his father Pheres, are quite unheroic. Despite its uniqueness, then, the *Alcestis* displays the two distinguishing features of all Euripides' plays—pathos and realism.

With the *Medea*, a new and capital theme emerges: the power of passion. Medea, abandoned by Jason, takes her revenge by killing her young rival and then cutting her own children's throats. But she does not do so without suffering and hesitation; the treatment of erotic passion brings with it the sudden psychological reversals that were to remain such an important feature of Western drama, including modern drama.

A completely different theme animates the *Heracleidae* ("Children of Heracles"), produced in 430 or sometime between 430 and 427. This is a patriotic piece, written to the greater glory of Athens. Demophon, king of Athens, welcomes the children of Heracles and shelters them from the hatred of Eurystheus. But a secondary theme recalls the *Alcestis*, for Euripides adds an account of voluntary sacrifice to the legend: in order to satisfy a divine decree, the young Macaria offers to die in place of her brothers.

The *Hippolytus* returns to the theme of erotic passion first exploited in the *Medea*. Phaedra, wife of Theseus, falls in love with Theseus's son Hippolytus; when her passion is revealed and repulsed, she accuses him falsely and kills herself. Theseus, believing her, pronounces a curse, which kills the innocent Hippolytus. In an earlier and bolder play, Euripides had made Phaedra confess her love to Hippolytus in person (as Racine was later to do). In the surviving play, the two do not even appear on stage together; but Phaedra's inner struggles, like those of Medea, are described with extraordinary power. The play opens with a speech of Aphrodite and closes with an appearance by Artemis; but the real struggle between these rival goddesses of love and purity takes place in Phaedra's heart.

The variously dated *Andromache* (between 429 and 417) again deals with passion. Andromache, who has become the slave of Neoptolemus, finds herself threatened by the jealous Hermione and her father Menelaus; they plan to kill Andromache together with her son. When they fail, Hermione fears Neoptolemus's vengeance and persuades Orestes to kill him. Threats and violence fill the play; Hermione, yielding to each of her impulses in turn, moves from arrogance to abject fear. At the same time, this is one of the plays in which Euripides uses the myth of the sack of Troy to express his deep pity for the victims of war and for the other evils that accompany war.

The same pity prompted Euripides to write the *Hecuba* (ca. 424) and, somewhat later, *The Trojan Women*. Hecuba, reduced from queen of Troy to slave of the Greeks, sees her daughter Polyxena sacrificed (though Polyxena accepts death, making her sacrifice almost a voluntary one) and avenges the murder of her son Polydorus by putting out the eyes of the traitor responsible for it. Thus the horrors of war are examined side by side with the human appetite for vengeance.

The plot of the *Heracles* (between 424 and 415) includes a shocking double reversal. It opens with one of Euripides' favorite effects—the pathos of weakness: a tyrant is on the point of murdering Heracles' family. In a coup de théâtre, Heracles arrives on the scene to save them; but a second coup de théâtre follows almost immediately: Heracles is stricken with madness and kills his own children. Euripides makes the catastrophe all the more poignant by putting the madness of Heracles at the end of all his labors. Like Sophocles' Ajax, Heracles returns to his senses and is about to kill himself; but Theseus manages to dissuade him, and he discovers a new form of courage in the will to live.

After *The Suppliant Women* (ca. 424–21—a patriotic play like the *Heracleidae* but with a strong pacifist message), come a series of plays that I do not have room to discuss in detail. In most of these the plots are increasingly complex—full of recognitions, tricks, and surprises—and take precedence over other elements. To this group belong the *Ion* (ca. 418–14?), whose young hero, pure as Hippolytus and an acolyte of Apollo, thinks he has found his long-lost father and instead finds his mother, after a sequence of unsuccessful murder attempts; *Iphigenia in Tauris* (ca. 415–12?), whose heroine recognizes her brother just as she is about to sacrifice him to Artemis and manages to escape with him, thanks to a ruse; and *Helen* (412), in which we are told that Helen was never at Troy (the war was fought for a phantom!); Menelaus finds her in Egypt and escapes with her, once again with the help of a ruse.

Roughly contemporary with these plays are *The Trojan Women*, which deals exclusively with the evils of war, and *Electra*, in which Euripides dealt, almost at the same time as Sophocles, with the subject of Aeschylus's *Libation Bearers*. With characteristic realism, Euripides gives us an Electra who has been married off to a farmer. True to his taste for emotional effects, he has her take part in the murder of Clytemnestra; then his psychology of the passions takes over and we see Electra's hate turn to remorse. Four years later, Euripides returned to this myth in the *Orestes*. Once again, realism is a dominant feature of his treatment: the Furies who pursue Orestes have become the wholly human torment of a sick man, "haunted" by the consciousness of his guilt; the verdict at his trial is no longer solemnly proclaimed by Athene but voted by a popular assembly led by demagogues. Euripides' taste for pathos reappears in Orestes' attempt to extort help by taking Hermione hostage.

The Phoenician Women (which falls between *Electra* and *Orestes*) takes up the theme of Aeschylus's *Seven against Thebes*. In Euripides, however, the two brothers appear on stage together and quarrel in their mother's presence. A corrective to their ambition appears in the self-sacrifice of the young Menoeceus. These emotional effects are enlisted in the service of Euripides' violent condemnation of the quarrels that destroy cities. The theme of self-sacrifice recurs in *Iphigenia in Aulis*, where we again find a bewildering array of doubts, debates, reversals, and expressions of pity.

Euripides' last play, *The Bacchae*, may seem at first glance to offer a startling contrast; for it depicts, in the most traditional tragic vein, the vengeance inflicted by Dionysus on the unbelieving Pentheus. The god's cult is likewise described in great poetic passages, which suggest true religious feeling; and the playwright seems to prefer this fervor to the so-called wisdom of those who argue against it. But the god thus exalted is a cruel god, and his vengeance a horrible one, for Pentheus's mother Agave returns from the Dionysian "revels" brandishing the head of her son, whom she herself has killed in her frenzy. If there is a beauty in religious fervor, it too can turn against man. The play's brutal emotional impact thus helps us see what all Euripidean tragedies have in common: the concrete presence of human suffering, whether its source be passion, war, error, or (as in *The Bacchae*) the gods. As the most conspicuous feature of Euripides' vision, this emphasis on suffering deserves to be considered first.

C · Suffering and the Portrayal of Emotion

Several different aspects of Euripides' art combine to put emotion in the foreground. First among these is the care with which he develops the psychological states of his characters. Each is individualized, and the irrational impulses of feeling are acknowledged. Whereas Aeschylus's Clytemnestra was a massive will whose chief motives remained obscure, Euripides' Medea can be known from the inside, with all her rage, her hopes, and her doubts. And in Phaedra's exchange with her nurse, full of fears, dreams, and involuntary admissions, we have the portrait of a divided soul struggling with itself—a rare spectacle in Greek literature.

Euripides paints the physical effects of strong emotion with a vividness that recalls Sappho; some of the phrases he uses of Phaedra were to be echoed, centuries later, by Racine. Phaedra's opening speech is a cry of pain: "Lift my body, raise my head. I feel as if the joints of my poor limbs were broken . . . This veil lies heavy on my head" (*Hippolytus* 198–201). Such is the force of passion, moreover, that it can banish all prudence and all respect for moral principles. Euripides does not share Socrates' view that moral failings are errors of judgment. In Phaedra's words, "We know what goodness is, and we recognize it; but we do not practice it" (*Hippolytus* 380–81); and Medea echoes her: "Yes, I feel the enormity of the act I am about to commit; but passion overcomes my better resolves." Hence the plethora of crimes and acts of excessive vengeance that fill the tragedies of Euripides.

On the other hand, the irrational nature of passions and emotions also accounts for sudden reversals of intention (another innovation in the Greek theater). Medea wants revenge and has made up her mind to kill her children, but the sight of them—their glances, their hands, their lips—make her waver more than once. Characters vacillate between acting and not acting (Medea), between anger and fear (Hermione), between hatred and despair (Electra). They may even feel surges of generosity, as in the case of Iphigenia, whose shift of mood was still shocking to Aristotle.

Euripides' psychology of the emotions and passions is one source of his emotional effects; but the reversals I have mentioned suggest that psychology is not the only factor involved. Such effects are also produced by sudden shifts in the action, and by the realism of Euripides' descriptions and tableaux.

The action is full of surprises and coups de théâtre designed to arouse in the audience the hope or despair experienced by the characters. With consummate art, Euripides stretches our fears to the breaking point and then stages last-minute recognitions. Near relatives are about to kill one another, massacres are imminent, when suddenly, just in time, help arrives. (Examples include *Andromache, Heracles, Ion, Iphigenia in Tauris,* and lost plays such as *Cresphontes, Alexander,* and *Melanippe the Wise*).

Just as he shows us these imminent murders, Euripides is continually portraying human suffering in its most concrete and intense forms. He shows us hopeless old men stretched on the ground, crushed; he shows us prostrate, utterly submissive victims. If Aeschylus's suppliant women were afraid, those of Euripides are distraught. His Electra complains of her poverty. Often the effect is heightened by the presence of children, as in *Alcestis, Medea, Andromache,* and *The Suppliant Women*—not to mention the children of Heracles, whom we see lying dead around him, or Astyanax in *The Trojan Women,* whose body is brought back to his grandmother in a scene in which cries of anguish drive home the horror: "Oh unlucky head, how cruelly the walls Apollo raised for your fathers have shorn the curls your mother loved to arrange on your brow and cover with kisses! The shining blood that seeps from this shattered skull . . . I cannot speak of the horror of it! Oh hands in which I loved to see your father's hands, you lie before me broken and lifeless! (1173–79). Memories of a happy past mingle with the brutal description of death, in a contrast that is profoundly Euripidean.

All the resources of Euripides' craft, then, contribute to the pathos of his work, which corresponds to a deep—and a deeply pessimistic—impulse in the author. Aeschylus had seen war as an ardent struggle in which the just are victorious; Euripides sees it as an evil caused by human folly, which means suffering for all. Sophocles had celebrated human heroism; Euripides often portrays men as cowardly, ambitious, or hypocritical—when they are not the playthings of passion. He sees even the gods as ruled by jealousies that make them unjust (Aphrodite in *Hippolytus,* Hera in *Heracles*) or, at the very least, cruel (Dionysus in *The Bacchae*).

The only relief in this bleak picture of the world is provided by the figures of young people who are still innocent, like Hippolytus or Ion, or who accept death with a kind of serene renunciation—Macaria, Polyxena, Menoeceus, Iphigenia. And this is the exception that proves the rule; the only ray of light in Euripides' plays shines from beyond life. More and more, in his later plays, we get a sense of the desirability of flight—from the city, from mankind, from suffering.

The qualities I have cited would be enough to suggest the originality of Euripides; but there are others, no less modern, which may seem almost contradictory to the first group. For Euripides' theater of suffering is also a theater of ideas.

D · Ideas and Doubts

In his own time, Euripides was essentially a "modern." His studies of passion, his insistence on human weakness, and his realism are all clear indications of that modernity. Because he was receptive to the intellectual currents of his time, and acquainted with some of the Sophists, he also endowed his characters with the Sophistic art of debating any issue; and he let the new ideas, problems, and doubts made fashionable by this school of thought surface in his plays.

There are thus two sides to Euripides' characterization: the most painful of emotions may alternate with the most elaborate discussion of ideas. From *Medea,* for example, we hear first exclamations—almost shrieks—and then, after her entrance, a long monologue on the condition of women. When Hecuba hears the report of her daughter's noble death, she wonders aloud about the respective importance of nature and education; and she does so immediately, at the height of her grief. Other characters produce closely argued speeches in the heat of passion. It has been said that the rhetorical brilliance of such arguments is out of place, and this is true in some cases. But feeling and rhetoric generally reinforce each other in Euripides' drama. The force of conviction, or of desire, inspires those who are pleading a cause, so that passion and intellectual analysis go hand in hand.

The presence of ideas in Euripides' work does not, however, imply unity of thought. From the very structures of the plays of Aeschylus and Sophocles one could arrive at an idea of their views of the world. Euripides, by contrast, touches on everything, debates everything, and yet manages to elude us in the end.

His ideas in the domain of politics are perhaps the least difficult to determine. At the beginning of the war he wrote some fervently patriotic plays, extolling the generosity of Athens (the *Heracleidae* and *The Suppliant Women*). Frequently an Athenian hero comes into his plays as a friend or deliverer (in *Medea* or *Heracles*, for example, or in lost plays like *Alope* or *Erechtheus*). Sparta, on the other hand, is openly attacked in *Andromache*. And yet, side by side with this patriotism, sometimes in the same play, we find a horror of war; for Euripides is an open advocate of peace. His pacifism inspires sudden tirades that cut across the plot and the myth on which the plot is based to address the audience directly. The same pacifism prompted several entire plays. *Andromache, Hecuba,* and *The Trojan Women* are devoted, wholly or in large part, to the sufferings caused by war; and the *Helen* suggests that a war has been fought for nothing. In the latter play the chorus sings: "You are mad, you who seek glory in combat, among weapons of war, thinking in your ignorance to find a cure for human misery there" (1151–54). From the patriotic fervor of the early plays to this disillusionment, the fluctuations in Euripides' thought correspond quite closely to developments in the political situation. It is hardly illogical that after so many years of war between the Greek cities, Euripides' last play should end on a Panhellenic note: Iphigenia dies for all the Greeks.

A similar evolution is visible in Euripides' treatment of domestic politics. We find panegyrics to democracy; we find, in *The Suppliant Women*, an analysis of the good and bad effects of democracy compared with those of tyranny. But then we find an ever sharper portrayal of the ill effects of individual ambition, a stumbling block to unity (as in *The Phoenician Women*), and of demagogy, which makes an unruly assembly the arbiter of every question (as in *Orestes*). These reflections of contemporary reality reveal the growing disillusionment that eventually led Euripides to leave Athens, and to write *The Bacchae*, in which the civil order is no longer paramount.

On broad political questions, then, the evolution of Euripides' views can be adequately traced. But when it comes to detail, his position varies with the vicissitudes of contemporary history, so freely reflected in his tragedies. Hence the sometimes overingenious attempts of scholars (E. Delebecque and R. Goossens, among others) to ferret out endless topical allusions in his work. The only real constant is his open-mindedness. He is severely critical of any character who treats aliens or slaves with contempt; in politics, as elsewhere, he takes the side of those who suffer.

The same open-mindedness reappears in other areas, where Euripides' criticism is even less restrained. In the literary sphere such criticism can be amusing; for example, he enjoys finding fault with a scene from Aeschylus, or replying to a scene from Sophocles. He can also be critical of the myths, which brings us to the question of his religious beliefs. His characters voice doubts, more or less irreverent in tone, running the gamut from discreet reservations to frank denials. An example is the denial that Aphrodite, "the Cyprian goddess," led Paris to Menelaus's palace: "Shameless folly is always 'the Cyprian' to mortal eyes!" (*The Trojan Women* 989). Euripides is especially critical of myths that put the gods in a bad light. His Heracles observes, "I cannot accept the idea that the gods yield to wrongful loves . . . A god who is true god has no needs; the tales that say otherwise are the wretched inventions of poets" (*Heracles* 1341ff.). Criticism of this kind is a reflection of new ideas, which are still easier to recognize when the gods invoked become those of the philosophers—as in Hecuba's prayer: "O you who uphold the earth and on earth have your throne, whoever you may be, insoluble riddle, Zeus, whether you be unbending law of nature or human intelligence, I worship you" (*The Trojan Women* 884ff.). Some Euripidean characters, like the bolder thinkers of the day, denied the very existence of the gods (as in the lost *Bellerophon*). Yet, at the same time, what tenderness we find in the Artemis of the *Hippolytus*, what elevated moral faith in the Theonoe of the *Helen*, what mystic ecstasy in *The Bacchae*! Euripides' "irreligion" is matched by a purified religious fervor, quite different from ordinary Greek religious feeling. But what does Euripides himself believe? What does he *not* believe? Does he even think the gods determine the course of events? Individual gods—Aphrodite, Hera, Dionysus—intervene in his plays, of course; but the idea of a divine will guiding the world has disappeared, and chance has taken its place. Depending on circumstances, the playwright emphasizes the power of a god or the sheer uncertainty of fortune.

The questioning of this new era in Greek thought extended to the moral sphere as well. Can virtue be taught? Does education count for more than heredity? These are among the questions Euripides formulates. In so doing, he sometimes entertains new and daring propositions; for example, the farmer who is Electra's husband is portrayed as incarnating a virtue many of the highly placed characters lack. As the fifth century approached its end, every aspect of life raised new questions, for everything was changing. Which life is preferable, the active or the contemplative? (The characters in *Antiope* debated this issue.) And what of sports? What of women? The rationalists in

Euripides' plays shower women with abuse; but some of his women characters are admirable. The truth is that Euripides touches on almost every imaginable issue, yet never pleads a cause himself: he has his characters plead them all, as the occasion dictates, which is quite a different matter.

The one feeling that does seem to reflect his own deepest inclinations—and that emerges more and more strongly in the later plays—is the pessimism his work conveys. Growing out of his pity for suffering, his disgust with politics, and his philosophic doubts, this pessimism not only prompted (in all likelihood) his own flight from Athens but also underlies his characters' fondest dreams of escape to a far country, or of retreat into art and poetry. By interweaving this pessimism, as conveyed by choral odes and the laments of victims, with the tensions generated by dramatic action, Euripides achieved a kind of counterpoint that is the most original feature of his art.

E · The Art of Euripides

The vision behind Euripides' work as a whole finds expression in certain technical innovations. Innovations of this order affect the action and its complexity. As the number of actors increased, so did the number of characters. Aside from the chorus, Aeschylus's *Seven against Thebes* required only the king and a series of messengers. *The Phoenician Women*, which deals with the same subject, brings in Oedipus's entire family: first Polyneices and Jocasta, then Antigone, Creon, Creon's son Menoeceus, the prophet Teiresias, and, finally, Oedipus himself. Simplicity is replaced by complexity, continuity by variety.

Nor did Euripides hesitate to reshape mythic materials with a free hand, adding sudden reversals at will and involving his characters in them. By such means he created new and action-filled plots. In his work we may recognize a true dramatic *technique* in the modern sense of the word, and with it a number of typical scenes, or types of scenes, that contribute to this new art. He was responsible for the introduction of long narrative prologues, designed to explain his plot innovations to the audience. As for conclusions, these strained and complicated plots would often be incapable of resolution without the ultimate appearance of a god—the deus ex machina. Between prologue and deus ex machina, both used with great freedom, he could give the action whatever course he chose. There too he relied on typical scenes; the presentation of suppliants grouped about an altar, for example, suited his taste for pathos, as did messenger speeches. Threats of murder and scenes of recognition had similar effects. By contrast, the debate scene, or *agon*, found in almost every play reflects his intellectualizing tendencies.

All this left little room for lyric poetry; indeed, Euripides' choral odes are quite short. What is more, with the exception of *The Bacchae*, his choruses have little to do with his plots. Often their songs are laments or lyrical effusions that would work just as well elsewhere. At the same time, in his concern to portray emotion, Euripides composed songs for his actors with considerable freedom. Many of his dialogues are half-sung, half-spoken; and song, as against the spoken word, always indicates a heightening of emotion. We also find solos for the actors (monodies), in which Euripides adopted the musical innovations of his contemporaries; the new music was more free-flowing than the old and better adapted to follow the development of an emotion. These various audacities that make for the "modernism" of Euripidean drama account for both its immediate popularity and the resistance it encountered.

A number of his contemporaries and imitators—little more than names to us—took the same liberties. Some, like Carcinus and his sons, were famous for their scenic effects; others, like Critias, for their bold philosophical positions. Agathon, who himself appears as a character in Plato's *Symposium* and in Aristophanes' *Thesmophoriazusae*, resembled Euripides in a number of respects and lived, like him, in Macedonia for a time. Agathon is said to have taken still farther the free invention of plots, the disjunction between chorus and plot, and the taste for metrical innovation.

Amid all these literary games, however, the real power of tragedy began to be lost. For the fourth century we have many names of plays and playwrights (Meletus, Antiphon, Chairemon, Aphares, Dicaeogenes, Astydamas), but most of these men were professional writers, trained as rhetoricians. All their works are lost, with the exception of the *Rhesus*, which was preserved because it was mistaken for Euripides' work. In reality, tragedy died with Euripides and with the greatness of Athens herself. From 386 on, revivals became a standard feature of the Dionysia; a few years later, statues of the three great tragedians were erected in the theater of Dionysus. The history of Greek tragedy extends from beginning to end of the fifth century, but not beyond.

III · ARISTOPHANES

The second half of the fifth century, which saw such a flowering—and such a clear evolution—of the tragic genre, saw a comparable flowering of comedy. Competitions in comedy grew up alongside those in tragedy. I have said nothing of Attic comedy before Aristophanes for several good reasons. The origins of the genre are ill understood; it was not officially recognized[4] at Athens until sometime in the fifth century; and not one play antedating those of Aristophanes has survived.

In Aristotle's account, comedy originated in the songs and jokes accompanying a clownish procession in honor of the god of wine. Called the *kōmos*, this procession was led by a phallic emblem and amounted to a sort of carnival. Later, actors became involved and true scenes were improvised. Comedy properly speaking appears to have developed first in areas settled by the Dorians. The earliest poet known to have written comedies was Epicharmus,

---

4. I.e., subsidized (by means of a special tax levied by the *polis*).—Trans.

who spent his life in Sicily and whose career can be traced back to the end of the sixth century. Fragments of his plays have been found on papyrus. In these we can find particular types of scenes and characters that later made their way into Attic comedy. Other traits of the genre already visible in Epicharmus are its sprightly and realistic tone and its intellectual vigor. For Attica, the first names we have are those of Chionides (mentioned by Aristotle), Magnes, Cratinus, and Crates (evoked by Aristophanes in *The Knights*). Cratinus was full of energy; Crates was more delicate. Both were writing at the same time as Aristophanes: Cratinus's *Wine Flask*, staged in 423, was a reply to *The Knights*, in which Aristophanes had accused him of drunkenness. Another comic poet, Hermippus, made a spirited attack on Pericles.

By this time, comedy was well established as a genre, with certain elements to be found in every play. Two of these elements are especially worthy of notice—the *agōn* and the *parabasis*. Both obey set forms and are composed in specific meters. At the heart of the action is the *agōn*, a debate between two opposing "camps." After a brief lyrical exhortation, the representatives of each side plead their cause—often twice each—in an *epirrhēma* made up of tetrameters. The metrical symmetry is rigorous, even if the scene includes a real battle. The parabasis, by contrast, is an interruption of the action, toward the middle of the play: the chorus, alone on stage, addresses the audience directly and acts as mouthpiece for the poet. It speaks in anapestic tetrameters; hence, this sequence is often referred to as "the anapests." It has the same sort of lyrical introduction and conclusion, and the same metrical symmetry, that we saw in the *agōn*. The *parabasis* has disappeared from the last of Aristophanes' plays; there is none in either the *Assembly of Women* or the *Plutus*.

But it would be wrong to infer from this use of set forms that there was anything stiff about Old Comedy (as the work of Aristophanes and his contemporaries came to be called). In the first place, the rest of the scenes were much freer (with rare exceptions, their meter was that of tragic dialogue, iambic trimeter). And even the fixed framework made room for the most spirited inventiveness. Old Comedy overflowed with vitality. It allowed itself every indulgence, mingling flights of lyric fancy with the most barefaced obscenities à propos of everything. Its tone was unbridled, allowing open attacks on individuals (though there were several attempts to ban the practice). It featured caricatures of assemblies as well as of politicians and other well-known figures, such as Euripides or Socrates, who were called by their own names. Such license in matters of tone was matched by a freedom of invention that made room for clownish treatment of gods, imaginary creatures (like the giant dung-beetle in the *Peace*, which takes Trygaeus to the home of the gods), or men-beasts (the wasps who, with their stings, represent Athenian jurors; the birds with whom two disgruntled Athenians go to live; even the frogs who croak in the infernal swamp). Wasps, birds, and frogs made up the choruses in these three cases and gave the plays their respective titles. The world of Greek comedy is full of variety, burlesque, and fantasy; only the farmer-hero, with his simple tastes, lends a measure of humanity and everyday reality to this motley world.

The characteristics of Old Comedy are known to us chiefly through the work of Aristophanes, the sole representative of the genre whose plays have been preserved. He was probably born in Athens about 445. Although his last dated work is the *Plutus*, staged in 388, the major part of his life and work coincides with the period of the Peloponnesian War. We know that the first of his plays to be staged was *The Banqueters* (a lost work, which, like *The Babylonians* of the following year, was not produced in his own name), in 427, shortly after the death of Pericles. We know too that many of his plays were inspired by current events: he violently attacked the demagogue Cleon, protested against the harsh treatment of Athens's allies, showed a keen pacifist spirit, and was an advocate of reconciliation among Greeks during the second half of the war. Eleven of his comedies have survived. Taken in chronological order, they cover much of the history of the war and mark its various stages.

His first surviving play, *The Acharnians*, dates from 425. Acharnae was a deme, or township, of Attica that had suffered more than most in the war, and the work is a plea for peace. Since Athens is unwilling to negotiate, Dicaeopolis concludes a personal peace treaty with Sparta; the Acharnians are furious at first, but he wins them over; and at the end of the play we see him feasting while others go hungry. Along the way, we find an account of the futile pretexts for the war and a parody of Euripides' taste for pathetic effects.

The following year saw the production of *The Knights*, the first play Aristophanes staged in his own name; it won him first prize. The play is an attack on the demagogue Cleon, who had just gained kudos (undeserved, in the eyes of Thucydides and Aristophanes) by winning the battle for Pylos. The poet shows us two servants of old Demos (the name means "the people") being tyrannized by a new overseer (Cleon). The servants learn that Cleon will be overthrown by a man still coarser than himself; they find the perfect candidate in the person of a sausage monger. Clashes between Cleon and the sausage monger ensue, followed by a flattery contest before Demos. The sausage monger wins, and Demos, rejuvenated, makes better resolutions for the future.

The Clouds (423) is an attack on Socrates, whom it quite unjustly depicts as a representative of the new fashion in ideas—i.e., as concerned with abstruse investigations of the natural world and as encouraging contempt for the laws. Strepsiades, an old and none too clever fellow who entrusts Socrates with the education of his son, lives to see the son beat him, arguing all the while that what he is doing is right. This crisis in moral thought corresponds to what Thucydides decried à propos of the same period.

The Wasps (422) condemns the structure of the Athenian law courts, which forced uneducated men into dependence on demagogues like Cleon (at the time, Cleon had just succeeded in having the daily remuneration of jurors raised to three obols). In the end, the old juror Philocleon is persuaded by his son Bdelycleon[5] to stop frequenting the lawcourts; he prepares to lead a life of pleasure instead.

With the *Peace*, in the following year, Aristophanes returned to the pacifist theme of *The Acharnians*, with a keenness enhanced by the fact that a treaty was very close to being signed. By ascending to the halls of the gods, Trygaeus manages to discover where Peace is hidden, and pulls her out of the well in which she lies buried. Everyone comes to help, including the farmers of Attica and representatives from all parts of Greece; thanks to their united efforts, Peace emerges from the well, and with her appear the goddess of the harvest and the goddess of festivals. Once again, happiness prevails.

Shortly thereafter, peace was in fact concluded.[6] We have no comedies composed between 421 and 414, however, and the one staged in 414 is a dreamlike, escapist comedy. In *The Birds*, two Athenians go to live among the birds and succeed, with their aid, in stealing sovereignty from the gods. Fantasy is everywhere—in the names of birds, in their appearance, in their legends, in their songs. The hoopoe's call to the rest of the birds (209ff.), with its imitation of birdsong ("epopopopoi, popoi . . .") and its evocation of all the various species (birds of the field, garden, mountain, swamp, etc.) offers a very rare instance of nature poetry in ancient Greek.

Three years later, shortly after the Sicilian debacle, we find Aristophanes once more in his ardent pacifist vein with *Lysistrata*, produced at the Lenaia[7] of 411. The heroine launches a mass movement of Greek women, who stage a sex strike until the men agree to make peace. We can well believe that the effects of this strike on the men were in the best tradition of the old Dionysiac processions in which the ritual phallus was carried. But the theme of peace between Greeks transcends all the buffoonery.

In the same year, at the Greater Dionysia, Aristophanes staged the *Thesmophoriazusae*, an equally colorful comedy in which women are again involved, as well as men who try to pass for women; but there is a literary side to the comedy as well, for the women are seeking revenge on Euripides, who appears as a character at the beginning.

Euripides also has a role to play in *The Frogs* (405). Dionysus, finding good poets in short supply, descends to the underworld to bring back Euripides (who had died shortly before the play's first staging, as had Sophocles and Agathon). But in the underworld he has first to judge a contest between Euripides and Aeschylus; and it is Aeschylus whom he eventually brings back with him. All these attacks testify to the novelty and (in the eyes of

---

5. Philocleon means "Cleon lover"; and Bdelycleon, "Cleon hater."—Trans.

6. This was the Peace of Nicias, which lasted for only two years.—Trans.

7. One of the festivals of Dionysus at which comedies were staged. Another such festival, the Greater Dionysia, is mentioned below.—Trans.

some) the incipient decadence of Euripides, with his Sophistic leanings; but the attacks themselves, the allusions, and the parodies are also a measure of his renown.

The Frogs is the last of Aristophanes' surviving plays from the period of the Peloponnesian War. The other two are much later in date and considerably different. The *Ecclesiazusae* ("Assembly of Women"), in 392, involves a feminist scheme to impose communism and, with it, the communal possession of women, a theme that is to recur in Plato. In Aristophanes, however, it involves forced liaisons imposed on men, with the farcical scenes to which these lead. The last play—the *Plutus*, four years later, in 388—also has a bearing on dreams of social reform, since the plot involves an attempt to cure Plutus, i.e., Wealth, of his blindness. Despite the opposition of Penia (Poverty), and despite the complaints of the wicked, who of course lose by the change, the play ends with a procession in honor of Plutus, who can see henceforth where merit lies. The plot line is less distinct than in the other plays, and the style is more austere; there is no *parabasis*. We can sense the imminent death of Old Comedy, as we can sense that of tragedy in some of Euripides' last plays.

These brief analyses can give only a very incomplete notion of Aristophanes' work, for the ancients knew of forty-four of his plays. But I have at least indicated the various points on which his interest was focused and the diversity of inspiration his work reflects. Although my summaries can give the reader an idea of the poet's personality, no summary, and indeed no translation, can convey the extraordinary richness of Aristophanes' diction. He invents words and combines them, coining for the fun of it monster words that sometimes fill a whole line of verse; he intermingles plays on words, broad jokes, lyrical interludes, parodies, and figurative language. Every passage is a stunning array of all these different techniques. Aristophanes can be frankly obscene; yet there is nothing vulgar about his style.

We do Aristophanes an injustice, then, to introduce his work in summary form. We may also misrepresent him; for perhaps we should not take at face value everything he has his characters say. Clearly he was passionately opposed to the demagogues, and to the war. Clearly he was anything but fond of the "gilded youth" with their amoralism, or the new philosophy with its subtleties, or the new art with its freedoms. But he also let himself be guided by the desire to amuse, giving a particular explanation for the war because it served his purpose, simplifying, joking, and parodying Euripides all the better for knowing his work inside out.

At least one quality, though, seems always close to his heart, independent of particular situations or pretexts for jokes. This is a love for the Attic farmer and the simple life he led, together with a deep pity for the way he seemed destined to be gulled by city slickers, especially in time of war. The peace Aristophanes loves is the peace of a return to the countryside with its palpable joys; the world he tirelessly denounces is that of war, with its ravaged fields, its poverty, and its confinement of the people—lost, duped, and wretched—inside the city walls. In this perspective, even his freshest and most cheerful tableaux can be seen as inverse images of the Peloponnesian War, whose course coincided with so much of his life and work.

There were other comic poets, contemporaries of Aristophanes, who enjoyed considerable fame and sometimes defeated him in the dramatic contests. One of these was Phrynichus, author of plays such as The Solitary, The Satyrs, and The Muses (which, like The Frogs, featured a contest between poets). The most noteworthy was Eupolis, who was a friend of Aristophanes' until a quarrel, mentioned in The Clouds, drove them apart. Like Aristophanes, Eupolis meant to use his art in the service of Athenian political life. We know that he occasionally attached Pericles; but he seems to have been less of a pacifist than was Aristophanes. Like Aristophanes, on the other hand, he attacked first Cleon and then Hyperbolus (in The Golden Age and Marikas); and he always defended the rights of allied cities harshly treated by Athens (cf. The Cities). Finally—again like Aristophanes—he portrayed (in his last play, The Demes) a descent to the underworld in search of values from the past, as embodied in great Athenian statesmen.

The same resolute political involvement can be found in Plato the comic poet,[8] some of whose plays take their titles from the names of demagogues (Hyperbolus, Cleophon). Politicized comedy, then, was a sign of the times, corresponding to the intense political life of the war years; it seems to subside as early as the first years of the next century. From then on so-called "Middle" Comedy (with authors such as Antiphanes and Alexis of Thurii) and New Comedy (with Menander) were to leave politics to the orators as they evolved toward a comic drama in which the emphasis was on complexity of plot and on character. Comedy as Aristophanes practiced it seems to have been tied, like tragedy, to the golden age of Athenian politics; neither form was to outlive that age.

---

8. Not to be confused with the philosopher.—Trans.

5

New Ideas at Athens in the Second Half of the Fifth Century

The work of Euripides and Aristophanes—discussed in the previous chapter—cannot be fully understood without taking into account the extraordinary rationalistic advances being made in the Greece of their day. These advances were most brilliant in Athens, the city that by its power and its hospitality to thinkers had become the great intellectual center of the Greek world. Many of the new developments occurred elsewhere; but in the second half of the fifth century, philosophers and Sophists were almost always guests of Athens, and it was there that their influence was decisive.

I · MEDICINE, PHILOSOPHY, AND RHETORIC
A · Medicine and Philosophy

It was at this time that medicine as a scientific discipline was born; but it did not develop at Athens. Its founder was Hippocrates, who was from Cos, an island off Asia Minor; and the two great schools of medicine were to remain those of Cos and of Cnidus (a city on the mainland just opposite Cos). Although Athens took no direct role in this effort, Athenian literature testifies to its undeniable influence on certain thinkers. Thucydides' work in particular draws inspiration from the new medicine—not only when he describes the plague, but when he analyzes political facts with the objectivity of a clinician, watching carefully for the symptoms of political disorders.

The distinctive stance of the Hippocratic school was an entirely new concern for systematic observation and for method. We can get some idea of its approach from the great mass of surviving "Hippocratic" treatises, though these are far from homogeneous as regards authorship, school, or date. A substantial effort to put the corpus in some order is underway. Yet certain trends are clear. Beginning in the second half of the fifth century, we encounter a concern to collect clinical observations (e.g., in the *Epidemics*) and a rejection of religious explanations (*On the Sacred Disease*, in which epilepsy is shown to be a disease like any other). Theories that are too general are rejected as well (*On Ancient Medicine*); and attention is paid to diet (*On Diet; On Nourishment; On Diet in Acute Diseases*) and to the effects of environment (*On Airs, Waters, and Places*).

At the same time, these treatises seek to establish a doctrine on the composition of the human body and the role of the various "humors": blood, phlegm, yellow bile, and black bile (e.g., *On the Nature of Man*). Such theories seem more antiquated to us than the method through which they were reached; they were also, of course, matter for debate. But the principle behind them is the desire to understand and to interpret. Medicine, as early as the fifth century, defines itself as a form of research.

If curiosity about the human body arose for the most part outside Athens (Cos was the seat of Asclepius, a god of healing), philosophy, by contrast, moved closer geographically to the new intellectual capital. In spirit, it moved closer to a form of reflection centered on man. Parmenides and Empedocles had proposed systematic accounts of the world; Anaxagoras, in the mid-fifth century, did the same thing, but with the difference that his doctrines were imbued with rationalism. Anaxagoras was from Clazomenae—in Asia Minor. Unlike his Ionian predecessors, he came to live at Athens, where he belonged to the entourage of Pericles. He left only after being accused (like several of Pericles' friends) of impiety. And his vision of the universe was, in fact, a rationalistic one. Plutarch, for example (*Life of Pericles* 6) tells us that when a ram with a single horn was brought to Pericles, Anaxagoras—in opposition to the diviner Lampon—proposed a purely physiological explanation. If he offers yet another general interpretation of the universe and of its origin, he explains it by the unique role of *Nous,* or Mind, and so is moving toward a focus on the role of the human mind in the organization of life.

Similar tendencies are to be found in the work of Diogenes of Apollonia, who also lived at Athens and who seems to be the object of frequent allusions in Athenian authors. His thought was not always original, however. Best known to us are his interest in medical subjects (a fragment on the veins has survived) and his taste for teleological explanations.

Democritus, on the other hand, was responsible for great advances in the direction of rationalism and curiosity about man. He was born probably about 460 in Abdera, near Thrace, and apparently lived a very long life. He traveled a great deal, and came to Athens, where, he said, no one knew him. His claim to glory is to have founded, with Leucippus, the theory known as atomism. It is hard to distinguish the contributions of each man to this theory, and even to attribute certain treatises to one or the other. But there can be no doubt about their doctrine: it was the same as that which Epicurus and Lucretius were later to expound. It was, in other words, a rationalistic system, and one in which mathematics played a large part (particularly in its account of the workings of the five senses).

In addition, Democritus—whose dates and place of origin put him in proximity to Protagoras—devoted much space in his work to man. His *Mikros Diakosmos* had to do with man, and his treatise *On Cheerfulness (Peri Euthumiēs)* is the work of a moralist, urging that the human soul be kept in order and in equilibrium. We have only a few isolated aphorisms from the latter treatise; some are remarkable for the importance they attach to what might be called the conscience: "It is in his own eyes that the man who acts shamefully should first be ashamed" (frag. 84 Diels-Kranz). Democritus even maintains, like Plato's Socrates, that he who commits injustice is more unhappy than he who suffers it (frag. 45). It is true that, because of his long life, we must assume a relatively late date for certain of his writings; in any case, his ideal of moderation is often reminiscent of Thucydides.

Those who were to have the greatest influence on Athenian thought, however, were the Sophists.

B · The Sophists

For the most part, the Sophists were not native Athenians (except Antiphon, a doubtful case, and Critias, who was not a Sophist pure and simple). Protagoras was from Abdera, Gorgias from Leontini in Sicily, Prodicus from the island of Ceos, Hippias from Elis in the Peloponnese, and Polus from Acragas in Sicily. But all of them came to Athens, and some lived there for prolonged periods. (This of course did not prevent them from traveling throughout the rest of Greece.) Protagoras was the first to arrive, towards the middle of the century; he became an intimate of Pericles and took part, at Pericles' invitation, in the foundation of Thurii (444), returning to Athens several times thereafter. Gorgias arrived as an ambassador in 427 and achieved great success with his talent for rhetoric. From that time on, he must have made frequent and lengthy stays in Athens. What has come down to us of his work is in the Attic dialect; and the Platonic dialogue that bears his name portrays him as the guest of an Athenian, treated with the utmost respect. All of Plato's dialogues, for that matter, which are our chief source for the Sophists, portray them in their Athenian employments, as well-known figures.

Their notoriety sprang from their profession, then a new and highly promising one. The Sophists were the first teachers who made it their business to instruct young men in the art of marshaling arguments, so as to prepare them for their roles as citizens. In the democratic city-state, an ever larger group of men were able to take part in civic administration, thanks to the influence they could wield through public speech. The old aristocratic education and the traditional values were no longer enough to insure success. The art of speaking in the assembly and of reasoning on political questions—"the political art" (as it is called in Plato's *Protagoras*, 319a)—was the object of the new teaching. Yet this development did not constitute what we would call a democratization of education. The Sophists charged fees for their lessons (another novelty), and considerable fees at that. Their pupils were rich, ambitious youths, who formed what amounted to a new aristocracy. Hence the somewhat disturbing aspect of the new movement; for the Sophists were masters of rhetoric, sure of themselves and of the efficacy of their teaching, drawing crowds of admiring followers. When occasion offered, they could stage brilliant public lectures, or *epideixeis*.

The Sophists' teaching was also based on a philosophical position; and the confidence in man that animated their art of debate was an important element in that position. The Sophists were rationalists, with a critical and often revolutionary cast of mind. Their interest in man led them to raise questions such as those of the relations between nature and law, justice and injustice, harmony and strife. To all these problems they brought daring views that often shook the foundations of the moral order, even when this was by no means their intention. It must be added that their doctrines varied considerably, as did their contributions to the practical art of effective speech.

1 · PROTAGORAS

Protagoras of Abdera was the first of the major Sophists to come to Athens. He was a friend of Pericles; Plutarch tells of their discussions on problems of legal responsibility (*Life of Pericles* 36), and credits Protagoras with a fine encomium on Pericles' courage in adversity. It was doubtless as Pericles' friend that he undertook to propose laws for the new Panhellenic colony at Thurii. Later he appears to have encountered difficulties in Athens; accused of impiety, he fled to Sicily and perished in a shipwreck. His influence was great, as Plato's *Protagoras* and *Meno* attest.

His works have not survived. The most famous was *Truth* (which may be identical with the *Refutations*). A relativist, not an outright atheist like Diagoras of Melos, Protagoras denied that men had any knowledge of the gods: "On the subject of the gods, I can know neither that they exist nor that they do not, nor what form they take" (frag. B 4 Diels-Kranz). As a result, the center of his universe was man. Another fragment, no less famous, affirms that "man is the measure of all things—of those that are, that they are, and of those that are not, that they are not" (frag. B1). This point of view was more than once discussed by Plato. It must be added that there are problems of interpretation: sometimes man per se (in a collective sense) seems to be meant, sometimes the individual. Where knowledge and the workings of the senses are concerned, the problem is minor (in Plato's *Theaetetus*, 171e, Socrates cites as examples "the hot, the dry, the sweet, and all other classifications of this sort"); but it becomes more serious when we turn to "the beautiful and the ugly, the just and the unjust, the pious and the impious." If everything hinges on the individual, we may ask, what norms are left? It is at any rate clear that Protagoras accepted no transcendent values and no notion of absolute justice; and in this respect his doctrine legitimated attitudes rejecting law and morality.

Yet Protagoras seems not to have adopted such attitudes himself. He evidently rescued justice—as defined by the city-state—by building on the notion of a collective self-interest. This at any rate is the substance of the myth Plato attributes to him in the *Protagoras:* the human race, poorly endowed at its beginnings, would have been doomed, even with the gifts of fire and technology, had Zeus not granted it "shame and justice, that there might be harmony and ties creating friendship within cities" (322c). The justice of cities is what permits them to survive, and in this way Protagoras defends the value of justice. He also has quite a noble idea of the role of punishment: its aim is to heal and instruct. Plato (characteristically) attributes the same idea sometimes to Protagoras, sometimes to Socrates.

So we can understand how Protagoras, relativist though he was, managed to serve as both educator and legislator. The morality he advocated no longer rested on any religious or transcendent ground; but it remained intact, thanks to the notions of self-interest rightly understood and of the body politic. These notions took the place of the former religious justification of morality, assuring it of a new defense, entirely human this time and based on reason.

Protagoras's concern for morality has been neglected or misunderstood, less because of the doctrines themselves than because his concern was called into question by his teaching of rhetoric. He was the "sophistic" debater par excellence, and was the author of a treatise called the *Antilogiae*.[1] He is known to have asserted that on every subject there are "two contrary speeches" to be made. This implies contrary theses, such as those to be found in tragedy or in Thucydides. But it also implies contrary arguments; for Protagoras taught "how to make the weaker of two arguments the stronger." Hence the brilliant and baffling art of taking up an opponent's argument and turning it upside down and inside out. From one point of view, this art can be a sound logical method, making for a more rigorous discussion. But in application it becomes dangerous; and it is understandable that Plato should have seen a rhetoric based on such devices as the great enemy—a creator of illusions and one he never tired of condemning. Protagoras himself was a moralist dedicated to the well-being of human cities; yet his philosophy and his dialectic were to pave the way for more revolutionary forms of thought.

2 · GORGIAS

Gorgias seems to have been the contemporary of Protagoras. A native of Sicily, where the art of rhetoric had just come into being with practitioners such as Corax and Tisias, he appeared in Athens as an ambassador in 427, and his eloquence dazzled the Athenians. Much of the rest of his long life (he lived to be 107 or 108) was spent at Athens, though he made many visits to other cities. His philosophic doctrines are known to us only through a fragment of his treatise *On the Nonexistent, or on Nature*, a brilliant and difficult work containing refutations of all possible opinions on being and nonbeing; it can be seen to proceed from a fundamental skepticism. Gorgias's great influence, however, stemmed not from his philosophy but from his role in the develop-

---

1. The title of his work, the *Antilogiae*, is difficult to render in English (or French, for that matter); as de Romilly points out, it can mean both "contrary theses" and "contrary (opposing) arguments." It also implies "speeches," i.e., oral (and public) debate. —Trans.

ment of rhetoric. In one of his writings, the *Helen,* we find an encomium on the powers of the spoken word, which gives a good idea of the advantages he meant to derive from them. Thus he describes the way speech acts on the emotions, comparing it to magic potions. Although he made fewer innovations than Protagoras in the area of argumentation (where he was satisfied to stress "plausibility"), he made many in the area of style, seeking out the various figures of speech that can enhance stylistic brilliance—antitheses, plays on the sounds of words, and the use of poetic vocabulary. All this lent quite a dazzle to his style; but his rhetorical effects had a profound influence on as passionate a lover of truth as Thucydides. The *Encomium of Helen* and *Defense of Palamedes* are like exercises, in which Gorgias shows off his wit; a fragment of a funeral oration gives a sample of it that is almost a parody.

Yet Gorgias was also capable of using his talent in the service of great causes. At the end of the Peloponnesian War, this Sicilian émigré living in Athens was the first to call for unity among Greeks. In this regard, Lysias and, especially, Isocrates were only following in his footsteps. Such was the burden of his *Olympicus* and of his *Pythicus* (almost certainly ca. 392). With Gorgias, the friendship within cities called for by Protagoras takes on a new dimension.

3 · PRODICUS, HIPPIAS, AND THRASYMACHUS

In the thought of these three Sophists—each of whom has a well-defined personality in Plato—the doctrines I have mentioned gradually assume more definite shapes.

Prodicus is said to have been the disciple of Protagoras. Like his mentor, he enjoyed great success and earned much money. His work is not well known to us. An important piece was the treatise called the *Horae* ("Hours"), in which he is supposed to have said that the sun, moon, and rivers, among other things, had been considered divinities because of their utility, as was the Nile among the Egyptians. These are the reflections of a Sophist drawn to ethnographic research and imbued with the relativism of Protagoras. But Xenophon, in the *Memorabilia* (2.1.21–34), gives us a different idea of the same treatise: he paraphrases the fable of Heracles' choice between Vice and Virtue, in which Prodicus apparently took it upon himself to defend virtue (as Protagoras had done), and even the value of work. Last but not least, Prodicus was a master of eloquent speech, famous for his skill in drawing distinctions between words of similar meaning.

Hippias was known for the universal scope of his attainments (derided by Plato in the *Hippias Major* and *Hippias Minor*). He worked in a variety of fields, including chronology and the training of the memory, but his originality lay chiefly in the increased weight he seems to have given to the contrast between law (*nomos*) and nature (*phusis*). He stopped short of working out the revolutionary implications of that contrast; but by referring to it at every turn, he took the relativist spirit a little farther.

Thrasymachus of Chalcedon was evidently bolder on the subject of morality. All we can attribute to him with certainty are treatises on oratorical technique; but Plato, in book 1 of the *Republic*, puts into his mouth the thesis that there are advantages to injustice, and that justice constitutes the interest of the stronger. Thus we may infer that he did not hesitate to question moral values; in this he resembles Antiphon.

4 · ANTIPHON: THE ORATOR AND THE SOPHIST

Two groups of works from the same period have come down to us under the name of Antiphon. Texts from late antiquity distinguish between the two, separating Antiphon the orator from Antiphon the Sophist. We cannot be sure this distinction is correct, though the style differs somewhat from one group to the other, and Xenophon at one point refers specifically to "Antiphon the Sophist." Given the uncertainty, it may be prudent to maintain the distinction.

Antiphon the orator does not really belong within the framework of this chapter. Yet in many respects he is quite close to the sophistic movement. An Athenian, who belonged to the oligarchic faction of the Four Hundred and earned the praises of Thucydides, he composed speeches for the lawcourts (of which three have survived)[2] as well as a collection of fictional lawcourt speeches in the purest sophistic spirit. These are the three *Tetralogies*, each consisting of four very short speeches: one for the prosecution, one for the defense, a second for the prosecution, and a second for the defense. Here we find all Protagoras's techniques for turning arguments inside out. The second tetralogy is built on the case of a young man killed in the gymnasium by a friend's javelin—the same theme which, according to Plutarch (*Pericles* chap. 36), Pericles spent an entire day discussing with Protagoras. The third tetralogy deals with a killing that took place during a drinking bout; there is a debate on the responsibility of the physician, and another on the probabilities of each man's having been the aggressor. This brings to mind the case debated by Corax and Tisias, and the arguments they put forward in favor of the strong man and the weak man (Aristotle, *Rhetoric* 2.1402a; Plato, *Phaedrus* 273b). In its general themes, then, in its choice of arguments, and in its method, this earliest example of Attic oratory seems closely linked to the teaching of the Sophists. To be sure, the speeches attributed to Antiphon that were actually delivered in court are somewhat different—more concrete, more traditional, and including, for obvious reasons, stretches of narrative; but the handling of evidence and plausibility is the same as in the *Tetralogies*, and it seems unreasonable to suggest that, here too, different authors are involved. The Sophists' teaching appears in a less disembodied form in the actual speeches; but it can be found in every line: Antiphon the orator *is* a Sophist, like the man we call "Antiphon the Sophist."

2. *Against a Stepmother, The Murder of Herodes,* and *On the Choreutēs* (= choral dancer).

Various titles and a few fragments have survived from the latter. We know that he took an interest in the interpretation of dreams and in geometric problems; but his major works were *On Truth* and *On Concord*. *On Truth* became known to us only in 1915, when large papyrus fragments were discovered. These include the boldest known extensions of the contrast between law and nature, showing how diametrically opposed the two are and demonstrating that obedience to the law, in the absence of witnesses, is contrary to the individual's self-interest: "Justice consists in not breaking any of the legal rules of the city to which one belongs. Therefore to practice justice is entirely compatible with the interest of the individual, if it is in the presence of witnesses that he obeys the laws; but if he is alone and without witnesses, his interest is to obey nature. For what pertains to law is accidental, while what pertains to nature is necessary; what pertains to law is established by agreement and does not arise of itself, while what pertains to nature is not the result of any agreement but arises of itself." In statements like these we see the relativism of Protagoras, and the contrast between nature and law of which Hippias was so fond, taken farther than ever before.

Such a position comes close to the amoral stance Plato attributes to Callicles in the *Gorgias*. For Callicles, too, there is an opposition between nature and law; for him, too, law is a convention. But Callicles goes on to take the part of nature *against* law, and to wish that a strong man might have the courage to come forward and trample on "our documents, our magic spells, our incantations, our laws all contrary to nature," and finally let blaze "in all its splendor the justice of nature" (484a).

The parallels between these two positions are proof enough that sophistic doctrines could become a powerful leaven, making conditions right for the emergence of an amoral stance and for the budding of unscrupulous ambitions. Yet the differences are no less clear than the resemblances, and have been neglected all too often. What Antiphon did was to engage in a theoretical analysis—an altogether sound one. To say that it is not in a person's interest to obey the law if no one is watching is not the same as to recommend disobedience, or even to prefer the order of nature. Antiphon recognized the conventional character of law; as far as we know, he may have found the convention a good one, and indirectly useful, more or less as it appeared to Protagoras. Callicles represents the way in which some men were able to make use of the Sophists' doctrines by distorting them; but that in no way entitles us to identify the serene philosophy of one group with the practical conclusions drawn from it by the ambition of another.

Likewise, when Antiphon says that, in a natural perspective, Greeks and "barbarians" alike are human beings, "breathing the air through their mouths and nostrils," he is hardly saying that he advocates equality among all men, whether in a particular city or in the world. A text that survives only in fragments must be handled with discretion. Antiphon is not necessarily using his ideas to advance a cause; and if he is, there is nothing in the few surviving pages to indicate what that cause might be.

The theoretical nature of his treatise *On Truth* is enough to account for his also having written the treatise *On Concord;* we need not (as some scholars have done) distinguish yet again between two authors, one of them embracing the "amoralist" position and the other rejecting it. As a matter of fact, we have a very poor idea of what the second treatise contained. The surviving passages suggest that the author was a farsighted and pessimistic student of human psychology; his bitter maxims are often reminiscent of Thucydides. He undoubtedly used "concord" in its traditional sense, for one of his dicta is that "anarchy is the worst of human afflictions." It should be clear by now that the Sophists could defend an ideal only if it was pragmatic in nature, based on the conditions of life in society. But within this framework, Antiphon speaks forcefully of "mastering and triumphing over oneself." A morality grounded in the "collective self-interest" may yet be a firm and exacting morality.

5 · OTHER SOPHISTIC WORKS

There are other works of the same period that must be seen in a similar perspective. Critias, an uncle of Plato who took part in the oligarchic regime of the Thirty, is sometimes counted as a Sophist. But he did no teaching. He was simply influenced by the spirit of the Sophists, and this can be detected in his writings (tragedies, verse descriptions of constitutions, and various shorter works). This oligarch had, in some respects, the daring of a Callicles; the way he describes the successive invention of law and of religion as bulwarks for the social order says a good deal about his freedom of thought.

There are also some short works that have come down to us without any author's name. The "Double Discourses" (*Dissoi Logoi*) consist of contrasting pairs of propositions on the good and the bad, the beautiful and the ugly, the just and the unjust. Although the author defends the existence of values, the very idea of such a debate clearly shows the influence of Protagoras. The so-called *Anonymous of Iamblichus*[3] (a text that has been attributed to various Sophists but also to Democritus and others) is an attempt to justify respect for law in the name of practical self-interest; the author does this by invoking the necessity of living in society, as well as the tranquility the law-abiding individual is sure to enjoy.

The two last-mentioned texts thus clearly belong within the current of sophistic thought. But they serve as a well-placed reminder that in the domain of morality the Sophists were still anxious to preserve values; they merely wished to change the basis for these values, with a view to humanizing them. As it happened, the shocks traditional values sustained in the fifth century were due in part to sophistic influence; but they were due above all to the po-

---

3. It bears this name because it was preserved as an insert into a work of the Neoplatonist Iamblichus (third–fourth century after Christ).—Trans.

litical crisis Athens was undergoing in the course of the Peloponnesian War. Thucydides, using the methods of analysis discovered by the Sophists, was to reveal the full gravity of this crisis.

II · THUCYDIDES

At a time when the art of speaking and debating was in full flower, thanks to the Sophists, and when medicine was becoming a rational and scientific discipline, Thucydides, working in Athens, had the insight to apply the same intellectual standards to history, thereby transforming the genre so recently created by Herodotus. But the difference between the two historians must also be accounted for by the fact that Thucydides was Athenian and had been brought up in a city where politics took precedence of everything else and where power was at its high-water mark. Herodotus's history concerned itself with ethnography, religion, and edifying anecdotes; that of Thucydides is entirely political. Herodotus's work took both Greeks and "barbarians" into account, showing an interest in all and in each; that of Thucydides is focused solely on the Peloponnesian War, the war between Sparta and Athens, through whose vicissitudes he lived as they took place: the Athenian experience fills his horizon.

The two outstanding traits of his work come together, I might add, in his choice of subject: it was the Peloponnesian War that had claimed his passionate attention; but this was also the sole area in which his standards as a scientific historian could be met, for direct inquiry and systematic criticism were made possible by the fact that such recent events were involved.

A · Life of Thucydides

Thucydides' life is known to us chiefly from the glimpses of it in his work, although the history is unusually sparing of personal information. We learn at least that he was Athenian, and an adult when the war began (5.26.5); he served, moreover, as *stratēgos* in 424 [see chap. 4, n.1]. His birth must fall somewhere in the neighborhood of 465 or 460. The name of his father, Olorus, was that of a Thracian king whose daughter Miltiades had married; so Thucydides may have been related to the illustrious family of Miltiades and Cimon.[4] He may also have owed his Thracian connections to family ties; he himself acknowledges that he owned operating rights to gold mines in Thrace and "for this reason had a certain influence with the most prominent men on the mainland" (4.105.1).

His connections were to prove useful to him at the time of his exile, which cut his life into two parts. In the first of these, he lived a full Athenian life. He received a first-rate education (we find the names of Anaxagoras and of Sophists such as Gorgias and Prodicus among the teachers assigned to him by tradition), and is said to have attended a reading of Herodotus, which

---

4. Prominent Athenian *stratēgoi*. Miltiades was a commander at Marathon; Cimon was a great naval commander and political opponent of Pericles.—Trans.

made a lively impression on him. At all events, from the moment the war broke out he had decided to be its historian (1.1.1). Obviously politics held a passionate interest for him. We can get some idea of his opinions from the fact that he warmly praises the democratic regime of Pericles (2.65), but also the "mixed" regime of 411 (8.97). We know that when the plague broke out in Athens, he was striken with the disease (2.48.3). When the cities of Chalcidice were in danger, he was sent there as *stratēgos* (4.104); but he failed to prevent the town of Amphipolis from being taken. As a result, he was indicted, convicted, and banished.

From that time on, in exile, he was a historian only. He devoted all his time to gathering information from both camps: "It happened, moreover, that I found myself exiled for a period of twenty years, after my command at Amphipolis, and was able to observe what was happening on both sides, especially on the Peloponnesian side, thanks to my exile; so I had the leisure to arrive at a somewhat more accurate view of things" (5.26). His practical experience was a direct help to the historian, while his failure in the practical sphere proved an indirect advantage to his work.

We do not know whether he returned to Athens after 404, when at the end of the war general amnesties were issued. Though fanciful and contradictory versions exist, we do not know when or how he died; he seems to have lived some years beyond 404. We are equally ignorant of the conditions under which his work assumed its present shape. It is unfinished; it should have covered the period through 404 but stops short in 411. From the earliest books on, we find references to the latter part of the war, and even to the final defeat of Athens. We can thus assume that he took notes from the very beginning, but only began the actual composition after 404. Yet he portrays as his own original judgment the recognition that a single war was involved, though there were ten years of war and then a long period of shaky peace before the Sicilian expedition and the resumption of hostilities. So it is natural to assume that at the time of the first peace treaty, he began a draft, which he reworked later—a hypothesis that is confirmed by points of detail. We cannot be more specific than this. It is impossible to identify any clean break between the earlier drafts and the reworkings; and the unity of the work—even if it was built up in successive layers—obliges the reader to adopt a global view that is admirable in its coherence.

B · Work of Thucydides

Thucydides' work is a history of the Peloponnesian War, the war that between 431 and 404 pitted the two great Greek states, Athens and Sparta, against one another and mobilized on one side or the other almost all the Greek cities. As I have noted, the work is incomplete and does not cover the end of the war. What has survived consists of eight books (this division was not made by Thucydides). The first is devoted to the causes of the war. The actual conflict begins at the opening of book 2, and the narrative follows its course from year to year throughout the first ten years of war, that is, up to the Peace of Nicias, concluded in 421 (5.24). After a few years of peace, however, the war was to resume; thus immediately after his account of the treaty, Thucydides inserts a second preface, in which he defends the assertion that a single war is involved, despite the years of interruption (which are described briefly in the remainder of book 5). Books 6 and 7 together form a unit, with its own introduction and conclusion, devoted to the Sicilian expedition (415–13). The eighth book, which presents compositional difficulties, describes the developing struggles in the Aegean, the revolts of Athenian allies, and the civil war at Athens; the book comes to an abrupt end in 411.

Two things about this structure are particularly striking. In the first place there is the prominence given to the Sicilian expedition. Strictly speaking, this event might have seemed independent of the war between Athens and Sparta; and yet it brought about not only the resumption of the war but a debacle from which Athens was never to recover. The rash imperialist venture ended in disaster, and it is this fact that Thucydides wants to bring to his readers' attention. The two books on the expedition are highly polished, filled with speeches, and frequently moving. They stand out so clearly from the rest of the history that scholars have occasionally tried to see them as a true monograph. But their finished quality is, rather, an expression of Thucydides' interest in Athenian imperialism, and in the tragedy of his city's fall from power.

The other feature of the history that immediately strikes the reader is the importance of the first book. Thucydides' primary aim is to explain, to make others understand; and the whole of book 1 is devoted to the causes of the war. After a preface demonstrating the importance of the war he has chosen to chronicle (and looking back, the better to prove it, as far as the period before the Trojan War), he explains his methods; then, as early as chapter 23, he turns to the question of causes. He distinguishes between the motives and origins of particular disputes on the one hand (illustrated by the episodes of Corcyra and Potidaea) and what he calls "the truest cause" on the other. "In fact," he writes, "the truest cause is also the least acknowledged; in my opinion, it was that the Athenians, by their growing power, aroused the fears of the Lacedaemonians and thus forced them into war" (1.23.6). This level of explanation leads Thucydides next to sketch out the making of the Athenian empire, from the end of the Persian Wars to the Peloponnesian War. Finally, the chances of each side's winning are weighed and measured at length, in analyses that balance one another: the two speeches of the Corinthians and Corcyraeans at Athens; the four speeches (of the Corinthians, the Athenians, a king of Sparta, and an ephor) at Sparta; and then the speeches of the Corinthians at Sparta and of Pericles at Athens. The intellectual rigor Thucydides brings to his political analyses is in evidence throughout this section.

The rest of the narrative is laid out year by year, even season by season, with meticulous care. But there is nothing annalistic about it, for Thucydides takes care to cut out unnecessary detail, to organize his material, and to focus the reader's attention on the most important episodes. These episodes are of two main types. First, there are the accounts of battles, which appeal to the former general and strategist in Thucydides; he anatomizes them with a rare decisiveness. For this purpose he has the commanding officers on both sides explain their battle plans beforehand, and arranges it so that their arguments match and complement one another; then he sees to it that his own account of the facts bears some relation to these plans, so as to reveal their strength or weakness as it emerges. The most remarkable of the battle narratives are those of naval battles—Patras and Naupactus in book 2, and the struggle for Syracuse in books 6 and 7.

Alongside the battles, Thucydides gives pride of place to the negotiations from which alliances or defections emerge; and if the accounts of sea battles prove the naval superiority of the Athenians, who controlled the sea, the political negotiations, by contrast, often reveal the weakness inherent in their empire, because of the unpopularity Athenians earned by their imperial power. In most of the political analyses, in fact, we find the same emphasis that was suggested by the prominence given to the Sicilian expedition: Thucydides' reflections are almost always focused on the Athenian empire and on the problems of power. He even portrays Pericles as analyzing her resources—and that as early as book 1, where we find a whole theory of the limitless possibilities associated with supreme sea power. In book 2, again in Pericles' words, Thucydides gives us a great speech in praise of Athens and her empire (the Funeral Oration); but the speech is also a warning against the risks presented by the hostility of her subjects. Nearly all the episodes on which Thucydides focuses his reader's attention are, in varying degrees, related to this problem.

Book 2 is largely concerned with Pericles' difficulty in getting the Athenian people to accept his tactic of remaining on the defensive (a tactic corresponding to the nature of Athenian power); the Athenians are enthusiastic and downcast by turns. Yet their naval power is vindicated at Patras. The greater part of book 3 is divided between the episodes of Plataea and Mytilene. Plataea is the faithful ally destined for a tragic end; Mytilene is the rebellious city, forcing Athens to face the problem of repression (in the speeches of Cleon and Diodotus). Adjoining these two episodes is a terrifying account of civil war (prompted by the events in Corcyra).

In book 4 Thucydides singles out the episode of Pylos, which might have led to a peaceful settlement; but the Athenians resisted, out of "a desire for more." The same book treats of Sicily, where a movement was already afoot to resist Athenian hegemony. And at the end of book 4 the Spartan general Brasidas begins to implement his policy of encouraging the subject cities to break away from the Athenian empire. The fears aroused by such defections finally forced Athens to negotiate. But she had not learned her lesson: Athenian ambitions in Sicily were to revive the problem of imperialism with new sharpness, and give it a still more serious turn. Finally, just before the two books on Sicily, Thucydides inserts an extraordinary dialogue between the Athenians and the inhabitants of Melos, a small neutral island they intend to subjugate with no justification whatever, merely because they want to make a show of force. This dialogue, which concludes book 5 (and is the only dialogue in the history), deals with every aspect of the politics of force, including the moral or religious ideas that sustain or condemn it, and the circumstances that make it both necessary in the short term and dangerous for the future.

Seen in this light, history becomes a profound reflection on politics. In the work of Thucydides we find not only the actual adventure of two enemy cities but an intellectual adventure, in which a true philosophy of power gradually unfolds. This form of history obviously implies a rather uncommon notion of historical truth.

C · Historical Truth

Where accuracy is concerned, Thucydides is aware that he is setting new standards. About the facts of the war, he says, "I did not think, in recording them, that I should trust the chance informant any more than my personal opinion: either I was present myself or I made inquiries of others about each point, with all possible precision. And it was difficult to determine just what the facts were, for the witnesses to each event gave versions of it that varied according to their preference for one side or the other, and according to their memories" (1.22.2–3).

It goes without saying that such research can be carried out only with difficulty and with constant vigilance. The difficulty increases when the object of investigation is in the past; and in his backward look in book 1 (the "Archaeology," 1.2–21) Thucydides undertakes the search with a rationalistic zeal shot through with pride. He refuses to use Homer directly, but uses as supporting evidence what can be gleaned from the poems about the practices of Homer's day; he adds observations of an archaeological nature and comparisons to the development of other peoples; in short, he launches into a critical demonstration, worthy of the skillful argumentation of the Sophists. With recent events his difficulties were lesser, and careful investigation was enough to ensure more trustworthy results. In spite of repeated efforts, it is still hard to catch Thucydides in error.

His respect for facts is visible even in the manner of his narration. Except in two or three passages, he never speaks in his own name: he means to let the facts speak for themselves, to respect strict chronological sequence, and to disappear behind a perfectly objective flow of narrative.

His use of speeches, which in this respect shocks our modern sensibilities, is undoubtedly connected—at least on one level—with the same wish for objectivity. At first glance the device seems hardly objective, for Thucydides does not claim to cite the exact content of the speeches; in his words, he only wants "to express what, in my opinion, the speakers might have said to best suit the occasion—keeping as close as possible, where the general import of a piece was concerned, to the words that were actually spoken" (1.22.1). Given the necessity of reconstructing in certain cases, it may have appeared more economical and more accurate to put the analyses into the mouths of the protagonists, whose words and acts may thus be followed without mediation, as if they were characters in a tragedy.

Yet it is clear that the use of speeches, for Thucydides, fulfills a requirement beyond that of simple objectivity. Just as in discussing the causes of the war he distinguishes between the "incidents or specific disagreements" and the "truest cause," so he means to go beyond mere accuracy in order to arrive at a deeper truth. What he seeks is the meaning of events and the secret of their interconnection. For this purpose he selects and eliminates detail, outlines a structure, and so arrives at a more general level of meaning.

It is impossible to overemphasize how much Thucydides *leaves out* of his account. He eliminates not only what he believes to be false but what he finds uninteresting. In his history there are no oracles or legends; but neither are there any anecdotes. There are no descriptions that do not serve an explanatory purpose; no portraits of individuals; nothing, in fact, that deviates from the strict circumstantial account of the war. There is nothing on the domestic politics of Athens, nothing on social conditions, nothing on the rifts between groups or individuals.

Even in the narrative itself, Thucydides abridges. To make the points he considers essential more striking to the reader, he passes over the rest in silence. For him, the cause of the war is the growth of Athenian power; the series of incidents that led to actual combat remains secondary. So he omits even a bare account of the Megarian Decree, to which some traced the origin of the war; he is satisfied to mention it in passing. He even omits whatever gossip may have been in circulation about the misconduct of Pericles or Aspasia,[5] or about scores to be settled. Within each episode he proceeds in the same way. Sometimes we are sorry, for we would like more documentation; but Thucydides' history is anything but a sheaf of documents.

His intention is to pick out the essential elements of the unfolding action and to organize them so that they express the meaning not only of that particular action but of others that may resemble it. "If those who desire a clear view of past events—and of those future events that, in virtue of their human character, will prove similar or analogous—should find my researches useful, it will be enough: they are intended as a treasure for all time rather than a showpiece for the audience of the moment" (1.22.4). The same Thucydides who, having suffered from the plague, describes it with care so that those

---

5. Aspasia, the mistress of Pericles, was a gifted and unusually well-educated woman, often attacked by comic poets and political opponents of Pericles.—Trans.

who might see it recur should "profit by previous experience and not have to face the unknown" (2.48.3) speaks of the war that engulfed his homeland with the same clinical rigor—but also with the same ambition to achieve a knowledge that should be lasting and universal in its implication.

Thus, although he was prudent enough never to draw conclusions, and although he had the greatest respect for the complexity of facts, a genuine reflection on politics lies at the heart of Thucydides' history. And the attention that men of different centuries, grappling with war and imperialism, have consistently paid to his work is an indication that, in some measure at least, he has won his bet. It is a bold enough bet to warrant our investigating the philosophy behind it and the means it employs.

D · Thucydides' Philosophy of History

Thucydides' very undertaking assumes that there is a permanent and unchanging element in human nature. At times he refers to this element directly (as at 3.82.2). "Human nature," where it appears in the history, seems to be made up of unreflecting passions; it draws man into error by making him always want more, and by encouraging him to hope, only to leave him suddenly discouraged. It is reflected equally in the rash decisions of the Athenians and in the blindness of their rebellious subjects. These somewhat passive tendencies, often attacked in speeches, are constants of a sort. "As the crowd is wont to do," "as often happens after a stroke of good luck," "as often befalls thoughtless people": formulas like these punctuate the work, underpinning both its moral pessimism and its analytic soundness. Thucydides has no illusions whatever about mankind; disinterested motives find little room in his work, serving rather as specious pretexts. In the same way, his speakers are always denouncing the emptiness of their opponents' moral pretensions. This should hardly surprise us since the historian himself is capable of pitilessly exposing the atrocities of civil war (3.82ff.) or the moral insensibility of victors (5.85ff.).

What is more, the gods are missing from Thucydides' world. He may have believed in them; we do not know. But it is certain that, unlike Aeschylus or even Herodotus, he did not believe that the gods took a role in history, either to punish the guilty or to rescue the innocent. Their absence lends a still darker shade to the picture Thucydides draws.

Yet this is not the whole picture. For if we are made aware of the tendencies and temptations to which human nature is prone, it is because the speakers in Thucydides cite them. And the speakers do more than this: they denounce them, anticipate their effects on the enemy, and urge compatriots to be on guard against them. In other words, they use them as a basis for lucid forethought, a guide to rational and effectual conduct. Irrational temptation is man's weakness; the knowledge of its effects is the backbone of his intelligence. The same can be said of Thucydides' own attacks on these unreasonable habits: he does so to help others "see clearly," so that, in future, men's action may profit by experience, as one profits by the knowledge of a disease.

Thus we find in history side by side with blind impulses, a reasoning faculty capable of calculation and foresight. The historian allows us to glimpse, behind each event, this clash between affective tendencies and the reason that resists them, between the blindness of the passions and the lucidity that can take their measure in advance. Leaders, if they are good ones, know how to look ahead. Thucydides praises this quality in Themistocles (1.138.3) and Pericles (2.65.5 and 13). Most important, he constantly shows us the art of prevision at work. Speeches precede action and always analyze its probable outcome; the narrative tells whether the analyses are correct. The strategy recommended by Pericles, for example, is based on a calculation, and his various speeches are so many arguments to prove that if Athens adopts his strategy, she must triumph. Similarly, before each battle the generals analyze the situation and outline the reasoning behind their plans (based on anticipation of the enemy's attitude), or explain why they expect to win. Bad generals (like Cleon, whom Thucydides dislikes and judges harshly) do not calculate enough, and their opponents reap the benefit. The Spartan Brasidas is a good example of such an opponent. At Amphipolis he explains to his soldiers the mistake Cleon seems to have made and the way he, Brasidas, intends to profit by it. He uses expressions such as "I shall explain to you," "I surmise," "we can anticipate that . . ." (5.9). The narrative, of course, proves him right.

It is possible, then, for man to gain some control over events. Even a setback, in this perspective, becomes a lesson and permits progress. But the struggle between lucidity and the easier alternative is a never-ending one. In reading Thucydides, some critics are most impressed by the failures of reason (as is Stahl), others by its successes (cf. my own book, *History and Reason in Thucydides*). The historian himself reduces the ongoing war to this moral and intellectual struggle but, according to his wont, draws no conclusions; he leaves the judgment to us. In any case, his pessimism seems to find an important counterweight in the prominence he gives to reasoned knowledge. His work radiates the pride of an age that in every field was discovering the potential of reason.

Finally, even where action is concerned, Thucydides gives us not only dark moments and disheartening scenes but also some images of dazzling success. Athens may have been a brutal conqueror (a fault for which many, including Aristophanes and Stesimbrotus of Thasos, chided her); but Pericles' Funeral Oration in book 2 protrays her in all her distinction and in the splendor of a civilization proud of its own achievements. Thucydides was certainly not forced to include such a speech in his work. By doing so, he corrected his reader's final image—the image Pericles himself repeatedly evokes, claiming that "the memory [of Athenian power] will be preserved eternally" or that "her brilliance in the present, together with her glory for the future, will remain forever in the memories of men" (2.64.3 and 5). Ruthless as Thucydides' analysis can be, it nonetheless reflects the glow of those Athenian achievements of which the city had been justly proud in his youth. At the same time, his work makes use of all the intellectual and literary resources that were another source of its pride.

E · The Art of Thucydides

Thucydides' history is constructed like a working drawing. The speeches stand in a precise relation to the narrative and to each other; most commonly, two contrasting speeches are placed one after the other, matching one another point for point and allowing the reader to see both sides of a question. This art of ranging arguments against one another, of bringing them into collision and overturning them, undeniably corresponds to the teaching of the Sophists; it was Protagoras, after all, who taught the art of making the weaker argument appear stronger—in other words, of using against one's opponent the very facts on which his position is based. The speakers in Thucydides are constantly doing this—Corcyraeans against Corinthians, Plataeans against Thebans, Cleon against Diodotus, Alcibiades against Nicias, and many others—but with a difference: what was merely a rhetorical trick to the Sophists' pupils becomes in Thucydides a means of analysis and discovery. As each question is put on trial, so to speak, the debate between opposing speakers allows the reader to gauge the advantages and disadvantages of each position and eventually to identify the correct assessments, the mistakes, and the part played by chance. From these double analyses a system emerges that is both complex and complete.

At the same time, in order to lend force to his analyses, Thucydides neglected none of the techniques popularized by the Sophists that might strengthen an argument or increase its impact on an audience. This is true of the speeches, at least, in which we find rare and poetic words to catch our attention, antitheses (like those of Gorgias) to focus it, and distinctions between synonyms (like those of Prodicus) to refine it. Sometimes in the more elaborately worked passages the figures of speech come thick and fast, in a somewhat artificial style recalling that of Gorgias. More often the figures and contrasts are meant to strengthen the argument. The balance sheet between Athenians and Spartans drawn by the Corinthian ambassadors may serve as an example, even in translation. As the Corinthians put it to the Spartans, "They are innovators, quick to imagine and to carry out their ideas. You concentrate on preserving what you already have; you invent nothing, and your action falls short even of what is necessary. They move boldly without reckoning their strength, run risks without stopping to think and are optimistic in bad situations; but your way is always to do less than your strength warrants, to mistrust even the soundest deliberations, and in bad situations to tell yourselves there is no way out" (1.70.2).

In addition to these stylistic traits borrowed from the Sophists, Thucydides' own love of general observation causes him to pile up abstract words and infinitives and participles used as substantives, which allow for more condensed and more universal reasoning. Such abstractions are to be found even in passages of pure narrative, where the style is for the most part quite different, lacking the brilliance displayed in the speeches. But there is something moving about the way each sentence traces the mind's effort to organize the various aspects of reality. Thus we find whole series of causal expressions, juxtaposed or combined, and layers of explanation one on top of the other. The sentences are often long, yet they have none of the regularity of a periodic style. Most frequently we find two or three causal clauses of different kinds preceding the verb. Here is an example, following Thucydides' word order: "The Plataeans, since they realized that the Thebans were within the walls and that the town had suddenly fallen into their [= Theban] hands, taking fright and reckoning the invading troops much more numerous (for they could not see, as it was night), made up their minds to make terms" (2.3).

While every facet of the work, from the structure of episodes to details of style, reflects the working of a subtle and abstract intellect, it would be a mistake to conclude that the history is a purely intellectual and "cerebral" work. For the protagonists themselves describe their reasoning and their calculations; it is they who explain their fears and hopes, their plans and expectations. Knowing them, we follow every turn of the action with full awareness of its implications. As with tragedy, it is because we are involved in the action and privy to its workings that the outcome can have its full emotional resonance. Thucydides is, moreover, fully capable of heightening dramatic effects when the occasion calls for it. His description of the plague is clinical, but also tragic. His description of civil war is lucid and profound, yet powerfully emphasizes the horror of domestic violence. The debacle of the Sicilian expedition is set out with technical rigor; yet emotion is to be found in it as well—for example, in the varied feelings of the onlookers during the last battle (7.71.2-3); or in the contrast between the abject despair of the retreat and the exhilaration that had marked the expedition's departure (75.6-7); or, finally, in the historian's own conclusions, emphatic and somber (87.5-6). Intelligence, in Thucydides, is responsible for maintaining and heightening the interest of the work. The sobriety he imposes on himself hardly implies coldness—far from it. He was a contemporary of the Sophists and physicians, but of the tragedians as well; and there can be no doubt that in his eyes the catastrophe of Athenian power was the deepest of tragedies. Indeed, his work, which conveys so well the confidence in man that marked the "Periclean Age," is also in a way its death certificate. Athens had owed her flowering to the Persian campaigns; she was never to recover from the Peloponnesian War.

6

Attic Oratory of the Fourth Century

The early fourth century gave Athens a breathing space in which to collect herself and ponder the lessons of her defeat before having to defend her liberty against the Macedonian threat—a defense that was to prove vain. For the Athenians, most of the fourth century (up to the death of Alexander in 323) was a time of reflection, which saw the proliferation, in prose, of political and philosophic doctrines.

This reflection took place on several different levels. The first was that of practical life: the fourth century was the century of Attic oratory, and Demosthenes' career corresponds exactly to the crisis of Greek liberty. Other authors kept a greater distance, advising their contemporaries largely in treatises in which they set forth their doctrines: this was the case with Isocrates and (at least partly) with Xenophon. Still others devoted themselves exclusively to philosophical reflection, to which they brought a new dimension: it was the fourth century that gave the world Plato and Aristotle. I mention the distinction between levels of thought and between genres because it has dictated my assignment of authors to particular chapters. But it should be clear that this distinction is one of convenience and does not correspond to any chronological development. Oratory, political thought, and philosophy begin at almost the same time, that is, at the beginning of the century; from then on, however, each genre follows its own course. So Demosthenes will be discussed before Xenophon and Plato, although his political career began the very year Xenophon died and only eight years before Plato's death. It is merely the grouping by genres that puts Demosthenes before the other two, in the chapter on oratory.

Oratory, which occupied such an important place in classical culture, in fact falls entirely within the limits of the fourth century if we consider only Athens and the works that have survived. In one continuous blaze, Attic oratory—both forensic and political—played itself out between the end of the Peloponnesian War and the death of Alexander.

There were great orators before the fourth century, of course; but their works have not survived, and the speeches recast by Thucydides, after his own fashion, can scarcely give us an idea of the originals. Indeed, it seems that no one thought of preserving and publishing speeches until after the Peloponnesian War, when the effort to perfect rhetorical techniques (carried out during the war years) had ensured the independence of oratory as a literary genre. Even then, only a small portion of the output was preserved. Where political speeches are concerned, we have nothing before Demosthenes, whose career began in the mid-fourth century. With lawcourt speeches we are a little more fortunate: Andocides and Lysias were active at the turn of the century (between fifth and fourth); Isaeus was somewhat later, but still belongs to the first half of the fourth century. For this reason I begin with forensic oratory, which, indeed, accords with the essential aims of rhetoric. As for epideictic oratory (showpieces) and theoretical studies, these appear chiefly in connection with Isocrates and his rivals. Since Isocrates was a teacher of "philosophy" as well, this last form of oratory will be considered, with Isocrates himself, in the following chapter.

I · FORENSIC ORATORY

The first Athenian whose lawcourt speeches have been preserved was not a professional but a man whose life was spent in long legal debates over one famous incident. His name was Andocides.

1 · ANDOCIDES

Andocides was implicated in the mutilation of the herms[1] in 415. The son of Leogoras, he belonged to the noble family of the Kērukes, whose oligarchic leanings he shared; he belonged to a club or faction (*hetairia*) hostile to the democracy. It was probably to cement their association by some joint sacrilege that this group went ahead with the mutilation, which threw Athens into an uproar just before the departure of the Sicilian expedition (415). Thucydides describes the tension of the moment and tells how a suspect finally agreed, in return for personal immunity, to confess and to name those responsible (6.60). The suspect was Andocides, and the affair was to cast a shadow over the rest of his life. When an edict was passed against those guilty of impiety, his immunity did not prevent him from being denied access to the agora,[2] financially ruined, and forced to quit Athens. Between 414 and 403 he sued for the right to return, and then to remain. Two of his three surviving speeches look back to the incident of 415. (A fourth ascribed to him, entitled *Against Alcibiades*, is an imaginary speech about a vote of ostracism between Nicias and Alcibiades; it is certainly not the work of Andocides.)

---

1. The herms were sacred columns (originally, all were dedicated to the god Hermes), bearing human heads and male genitalia.—Trans.

2. Because the agora, or central square, of a Greek city was the site of temples and images of the gods, those convicted of impiety—who were considered ritually impure—might be excluded from it. Because the agora was also the civic center and marketplace, a man who could not enter it was prevented from doing business and from taking part in the political life of the city.—Trans.

In the earliest of the surviving speeches, *On His Return* (ca. 410), Andocides asks to be allowed to return to Athens on the strength of services rendered—and of those he may yet render. His attempt failed. He was able to return when the general amnesty was issued at the end of the war; but new difficulties, and new legal proceedings, were in store for him. The speech *On the Mysteries* (number 1 in the traditional sequence) dates from 399. Andocides had been accused of taking part in the mysteries and of entering the agora, despite the edict against those guilty of impiety. This time, after a major trial, he was finally acquitted. In his speech he makes a point of the fact that although his *hetairia* was guilty, he himself had neither agreed to the plan nor helped to carry it out. The third speech, *On the Peace*, is from the period after he had regained his rights. It refers to a negotiation with Sparta in which Andocides had taken an official role (in 392–91). It also marks the end of this brief period: the Athenians were unhappy with the terms of the treaty, and sent Andocides into exile once again.

The three speeches are thus closely connected with Andocides' own life and the scandal that had marred it. Indeed, the best thing about them is the personal, direct tone of the narrative passages. When he tells of his night in prison, of the pressures on him, and of his doubts, Andocides touches us. We see him overwhelmed: "I thought to myself, 'Unhappy man! Fallen as I am into the worst of straits, shall I let my relatives perish unjustly—let them be put to death . . . ? Or shall I tell the Athenians what I heard from the mouth of Euphiletus himself, who devised the crime?'" (1.51).

In his argumentation, however, Andocides is generally dry and unoriginal. In some cases the apparent banality of his arguments may be due to the fact that others imitated him (certain passages of *On the Peace* seem to be recapitulated in Aeschines' speech *On the False Embassy*). Even so, nothing rises above the level of textbook arguments and petty, abstract lines of reasoning, of which we find purely theoretical examples in Antiphon and for which the many treatises of the day must have furnished models. It is as if an orator could not be natural or spontaneous until his technique had been mastered by thorough training.

The Alexandrians included Andocides in the canon of the ten best orators. His talents would scarcely warrant this honor, were it not that he must be credited for being one of the pioneers. We have a sense of immeasurable progress when we turn from him to his contemporary, Lysias, who was the Athenian equivalent of a professional lawyer.

2 · LYSIAS

The important fact about Lysias's life is that he was not an Athenian citizen although he lived in Athens. He was thus excluded from political life and became a "logographer," one who wrote legal speeches for others.

We are well acquainted with his family background. His father Cephalus had come from Syracuse, and owned a large shield-manufacturing business in Athens. Lysias tells us as much in his speech *Against Eratosthenes*; and Plato sets the opening of his *Republic* in the house of this very Cephalus, whom he portrays as surrounded by a brilliant circle, including Socrates and some of the Sophists. This atmosphere of wealth and urbanity accounts for both Lysias's education (in Athens and then in Italy, where he studied with Tisias, the great teacher of rhetoric) and his graceful tone. But the political crisis at the end of the war, and the measures taken against metics[3] by the regime of the Thirty, ravaged his family. Lysias himself, who must have been about thirty-five at the time, barely escaped arrest; but his brother was arrested and put to death, and their fortune was lost. From that time on, Lysias had to make a living by his gift for rhetoric. He did so until his death, sometime between 380 and 360.

The body of his work was enormous: some of the ancients listed more than four hundred speeches, of which thirty-five have come down to us (some of these are fragmentary or spurious). Almost all are speeches to lawcourts, composed for clients. But there are exceptions, even if we exclude his career as a teacher of rhetoric, about which we have only indirect and uncertain testimony; for we have epideictic works attributed to Lysias, as well as a very personal speech composed in his own behalf—the speech *Against Eratosthenes*.

The epideictic speeches, or "showpieces," are of doubtful authenticity and mediocre quality. They are the *Funeral Oration* and the *Olympiacus*, to which may be added, with many reservations, the *Eroticus*, or speech on love, quoted (and attributed to Lysias) by Plato in the *Phaedrus*. The last-mentioned speech defends the notion that it is better to grant one's favors to a lover who is not in love. The proposition is in the sophistic taste, while the style resembles that of Lysias; but the whole is more likely to be a pastiche than a quotation. All we can conclude from it is that Lysias also on occasion wrote in this genre of the imaginary speech on paradoxical premises. The two other showpieces are a different case. Their style, heavily influenced by the Sophists, is not that of Lysias's forensic speeches, though the contrast may be attributable to the difference of genres. The *Funeral Oration*—in praise of the Athenian dead and of Athens (a genre of which we have several examples)[4]—could not have been *delivered* by Lysias since he was not a citizen; but he may perhaps have composed it. As far as ideas are concerned, it is plausible to attribute the three epideictic pieces to Lysias. The *Funeral Oration* is quite comparable to Isocrates (there are close parallels to his *Panegyricus*), but the democratic note would be appropriate to Lysias. Likewise, the *Olympiacus* urges harmony among Greeks, as Gorgias had recently done; but the attacks on Dionysius of Syracuse are more likely to be Lysias's.

---

3. Resident aliens of privileged status who had some of the legal rights and responsibilities of Athenian citizens.—Trans.

4. Some of the better-known, mentioned above, are that of Gorgias and that attributed to Pericles by Thucydides.—Trans.

Whatever the case, these two speeches are more important as documents in the history of ideas than as literary works. The first dates from shortly after 393, the second from 388 or 384.

On the other hand, nothing could be more personal than the speech *Against Eratosthenes*; as it happens, this unusual piece also provides a kind of digest of the most characteristic traits of Lysias's thought and talent. It has to do with the episode that disrupted his life: Eratosthenes was one of the thirty tyrants responsible for the arrest and death of his brother in 404 and for the confiscation of the family fortune. The Thirty had been overthrown shortly thereafter by the exiled democrats. After their fall, an agreement had been reached prohibiting legal actions against them; nevertheless, Lysias found an opportunity to attack Eratosthenes in 403 and, with him, his political associates, including Theramenes, who was more moderate than the rest but whom Lysias hated for having negotiated the disastrous peace of 404. The most moving part of the speech is that which traces the circumstances of the death of Polemarchus (Lysias's brother). In its stark simplicity, the tale seems to prefigure all the cases of collective and arbitrary legal action history has known.

This exemplary quality stems in part from the warmth of the convictions that underlie all of Lysias's work. Lysias was a democrat, and his experience in 404 only reinforced his opinions. He forgives nothing and condones no compromises. His attacks on Theramenes are sufficient testimony of this; he seems to hate hypocritical moderates even more than extremists. Nor is it hard to find similar opinions in the speeches he wrote for others. Undeniably, he wrote on occasion for aristocrats, as in the speeches *For Mantitheus* (16) and *For a Citizen Accused of Subverting the Democracy* (25); but he defends their innocence and so cannot be said to contradict himself by pleading their cause. Elsewhere in his work (if we exclude oration 20, *For Polystratus*, which is certainly spurious) we can find nothing that deviates from his democratic ideal. Oration 34, for example, which is not forensic, opposes restricting political rights to landholders. Oration 13 (*Against Agoratus*), like the speech against Eratosthenes, is an attack on a man who took part in the events of 404; it is also an attack on Theramenes, whom it brands a traitor. Nor are such comments lacking in other speeches. Though designed to please the jurors, these comments also seem to correspond to the author's own views.

Yet the force of his opinions, in *Against Eratosthenes*, is all the greater for his deliberate restraint in expressing them: what he gives us are the facts, very simply told. The cruel and arbitrary action of the Thirty is reported without bombast; details of the victims' flight are presented in brief dialogues, without comment ("I said to Peison, 'Will you spare me for money?' 'Yes,' he replied, 'if you pay enough' "); the meanness of the prosecutors is conveyed in concrete details, likewise without comment—as when the tally of confiscated wealth concludes with this minor but revealing act: "Polemarchus's wife had gold earrings, which were hers when she first entered the house [as a bride]; Melobius pulled them from her ears" (19).

Lysias's reserve, often laced with irony, and his feeling for concrete detail, may be found in all the speeches, along with his art of adapting to the client's character (*ēthopoiia*). This is why the speeches offer such a vivid picture of Athenian life at the time. There are street scenes involving drunken youths, and shops where patrons stop to chat, as the poor invalid of oration 24 reminds his audience: "You're all in the habit of dropping in at different shops—one at the perfumer's, one at the barber's, one at the shoemaker's." There are scenes within doors as well—for example, in the house of the unfaithful wife whose husband is the speaker in *On the Murder of Eratosthenes* (oration 1; not the same Eratosthenes); he tells how his wife used the baby's crying as an excuse to go downstairs, locking him in upstairs, where he began to think: "I recalled that the doors opening on the street and on the courtyard had creaked that night—something that had never happened before—and that my wife seemed to be wearing powder" (17). This familiar world, naive at times, likes to think of itself as well disposed to order; and Lysias's art tends to make it both vivid and likable.

His art is in fact more subtle than it appears at first glance. It consists in presenting the facts as simply as possible, but in such a way that the jurors will be strongly inclined to take a particular view. The sole aim left to argumentation is that of countering such claims as the opponent may make; and Lysias does so without elaborate attention to form or dialectic, in the interests of an artless plausibility. Thus, when the deceived husband defends himself against the charge of premeditated murder, he piles up evidence for the plausibility of his story, and his very hypotheses assume concrete shape: "And then, do you think I would have let my guest go home? . . . Isn't it likely that I would have sent word to my friends during the day, and asked them to gather at a house nearby? . . . If I had planned the whole thing, tell me, wouldn't I have posted servants?" (40–41). The arguments in favor of plausibility have lost the baldness we saw in Antiphon and Andocides, and taken on a tinge of spontaneity and simplicity. These last two traits are also reflected in Lysias's effortless and limpid style. With him, forensic oratory becomes more than a technique; henceforth it is a literary art.

3 · ISAEUS

We cannot say the same of Isaeus. Little is known of his life: he is said to have been born in Chalcis, and was called the pupil of Isocrates and the teacher of Demosthenes. But none of this is certain. Further, our opinion of Isaeus may be biased by an accident of fate: his only surviving works are speeches on inheritance cases. There are eleven of these and nothing more, except a long fragment of a speech protesting the deletion of a man's name from the citizenship rolls (the *Defense of Euphiletus* 12); the theme is virtually the same. It must be admitted that such discussions of complex situations involving legal and family status are not in themselves very attractive material.

However that may be, Isaeus certainly lacks the grace of Lysias. Yet the tradition that he was Demosthenes' teacher corresponds to a virtue his predecessors lacked: cogency of argumentation. Isaeus can reduce a case to one or two clear arguments, which he then repeats, varies and reuses in different forms. He can also quote the laws and comment on them decisively. Finally, he can throw an obvious fact into high relief by accumulating pieces of evidence only to emerge at last with a brief and abrupt conclusion that compels acceptance. Isaeus scarcely has the literary grace of Lysias, but he has something of the power (though applied to a sterile subject matter) that will unfold in Demosthenes.

II · DEMOSTHENES

Demosthenes' life was closely intertwined with that of Athens, and his work punctuates the phases of their common history. Among the stages of his life, only his youth was private; and among his works, only the speeches on civil cases are unconnected with the adventure of his city's struggle for her independence.

A · Life and Work of Demosthenes
1 · YOUTH

Demosthenes, of the deme Paeania, was born in 384, more than half a century later than Lysias and Isocrates. His career as an orator, like the careers of Lysias and Andocides, took its impetus from a misfortune: because of his father's death when he was only seven, he was entrusted to the care of guardians, whose dishonesty eventually forced him to take action against them. So he studied oratory to be able to do so. He pleaded his own cause (five speeches have come down to us), and his ultimate success encouraged him to make this his career. The story goes that he was overwhelmed, as a boy, on hearing the trial of a great orator, Callistratus of Aphidna.

So he went to work. He worked on his diction (with pebbles in his mouth), his voice (by declaiming as he ran), his gestures (by speaking in front of a mirror). But he also worked to develop his mind. He is said to have been Isaeus's pupil, to have copied Thucydides' history by hand eight times, to have been a disciple of Plato and of Isocrates. One thing is certain: he was imbued with the history of Athens and often reflected the moral ideas that were emerging in his day. He made use of his talent in a career as "logographer," or speech writer for others (like Lysias or Isaeus); but he used it still more as a political orator, taking part in public litigation or delivering speeches in the assembly. His first political speech dates from 355, when he was barely thirty years old.

2 · BEFORE PHILIP

The *First Philippic* dates from 351. The four years preceding it were filled with a series of speeches that still lack the passionate consistency of the following period but show us his positions in the making. He arrived on the political scene in the heyday of Eubulus,[5] who put moderation and thrift before everything else; from the beginning, Demosthenes seemed to put the concern for a moral ideal before that for economy.

Against Androtion, in 355, is a violent attack on a man who had violated the civil rights of individuals in order to collect overdue taxes. *Against Leptines*, in 354, is a similar attack on a man who had tried to repeal certain tax exemptions, thereby undermining respect for pledges and tarnishing the city's honor. *Against Timocrates*, in 353, is virtually a continuation of *Against Androtion*, for Timocrates was trying to protect Androtion by urging measures of doubtful legality. In Demosthenes' view, the measures thus taken were inimical to respect for law and to the democratic spirit of the state. These three speeches also offer early glimpses of general principles on foreign policy, such as the importance of the navy, of alliances, and of the national honor. Indeed, Demosthenes had begun to speak on such questions even before *Against Timocrates*. His speech *On the Symmories*[6] was delivered in the fall of 354; it was to have dealt with the Persians, but the young Demosthenes boldly shifted his ground, urging that the Athenians take advantage of current rumors to build up their striking force by reforming the organization of the trierarchies (which financed the outfitting of ships). Thus he appealed to the Athenians' mettle without specifying in what cause they were to use it. The following year, in the speech *For the Megalopolitans*, he declares himself ready to oppose Sparta and prevent her from destroying people who are not allies of Athens—this in the name of the unconditional ideal of the independence of cities. Some months later, the forensic speech *Against Aristocrates* opposes a decree that would have shown undue favoritism to a Thracian prince, thereby threatening traditional Athenian control of the Chersonese. A further speech of the same kind, delivered somewhat later, is *On the Liberty of the Rhodians*; it urges Athens to support Rhodes in the name of the natural alliance among democracies.

All these speeches seem designed to build up a national resistance to vague and shifting threats; the threat that was Philip of Macedon would give this attitude a focus and a raison d'être, mobilizing all the orator's energies from then on. At once the utilitarian realism Demosthenes had adopted in his early speeches (borrowed, perhaps, from Thucydides) was to subside before the passion inspired by the sense of his country's danger.

3 · THE STRUGGLE AGAINST PHILIP:
FROM 351 TO THE PEACE OF PHILOCRATES

Philip had ruled Macedonia since 359; he had begun making inroads into Greek territory at Amphipolis, Pydna, and Potidaea. In 353, taking advan-

---

5. Eubulus, as theoric commissioner, controlled Athenian finances between 355 and 346.—Trans.

6. The symmories were groups of wealthy citizens responsible for the outfitting and upkeep of specific numbers of ships.—Trans.

tage of the Third Sacred War,[7] he had moved into Thessaly. Checked on that front, he turned to the northern Aegean. It was at this juncture that Demosthenes delivered, at short intervals, the *First Philippic* (351) and the three *Olynthiacs* (349). The *First Philippic* is a rousing call for resistance. The young Demosthenes had not hesitated to take the floor first; and he took the opportunity to pile up appeals, reproaches, and urgent warnings. He called for a great outpouring of effort—an army with a large citizen contingent, which should be prepared to move in immediately at the first opportunity. The opportunity was to loom up before him with the threat to Olynthus, the major city of Chalcidice, which Philip had at first tried to beguile by flattery. Passionately and stubbornly Demosthenes insists that this is the best of all opportunities. He calls for reinforcements to be sent to Olynthus, and even proposes a reform of the "theoric" fund, a mainstay of Eubulus's policy.[8] Finally he insists that Philip's power, built on injustice, cannot endure: to oppose him, Athens must rise at last from her humbled state and be once more what she was in the past; she must be reborn.

Here we have all of Demosthenes' great themes. He had burned all the bridges that still linked him to the pacifists. But his efforts were not crowned with success. Olynthus fell, through treachery, in 348, and soon thereafter (346) Athens concluded the Peace of Philocrates with Philip. Demosthenes accepted it; he had no choice. We know this from his short speech *On the Peace*. It should also be noted that *Against Midias*, his violent attack on a personal enemy (the wealthy Midias, who had slapped his face at the Greater Dionysia of 348), was never delivered. Demosthenes could tell when the propitious moment had passed. Yet three years later he was to return to the subject of the peace treaty, in his speech *On the False Embassy*. As early as 346 he had brought an action against his fellow ambassadors, in particular (with the help of a certain Timarchus) against Aeschines. Aeschines had responded with an action against Timarchus, and other trials had intervened; hence the three years' delay. But the delay softened neither Demosthenes' bitterness nor his passionate anger. He denounces Aeschines as one of those traitors who throughout Greece are working for Philip; this he calls a true disease of the Greeks, a disease Philip deliberately fosters. Clearly, the defeat that had forced acceptance of the peace of 346 had simply put a temporary halt to the struggle; Demosthenes was ready to take it up again.

7. The last of a series of wars among members of the Delphic Amphictyony, a league of Greek tribes pledged to maintain the cult of Apollo at Delphi. The motives for these wars were basically political rather than religious.—Trans.

8. Eubulus sought to divert funds for military operations into public works and other civilian projects; Demosthenes wanted the money spent on rearmament. *Theorika* were allowances paid to poor Athenians to enable them to attend dramatic festivals, but these allowances were only one item paid for out of the "theoric" fund.—Trans.

4 · THE STRUGGLE AGAINST PHILIP:
FROM 346 TO 338

Three strong speeches mark this renewal of the struggle and Demosthenes' fresh attempt to alert his fellow citizens. The *Second Philippic*, in 344, denounces Philip as the enemy of Athens, the only city capable of defending the Greek cause. The speech *On the Chersonese*, in 341, refuses to take seriously the blame that might attach to the Athenian *stratēgos* Diopeithes, and counts as serious and decisive only Philip's wrongs, past and future, toward Athens. In the same year, the *Third Philippic* (on the subject of Euboea) goes so far as to conclude that a state of war already exists between Philip and Athens. In the name of this struggle, all three speeches call for severity to traitors; even more important, they call for a burst of energy from the Athenian people, who must regain a sense of their responsibilities.

The burst of energy was forthcoming, in some measure at least: Diopeithes stayed in the Chersonese, an expeditionary force was sent to Euboea, and Demosthenes became the arbiter of Athenian policy. But the speeches he delivered at this decisive juncture are lost to us. The last of his political speeches to survive, the *Fourth Philippic*, could not have been delivered in its present form—it is a curious mixture of borrowings from other speeches, with three fresh passages in which some details betray the will to find support at all costs. This trait at least tallies with what we know of Demosthenes' bold policy: to oppose Philip, he did not hesitate to form an alliance with the Thebans, who were so disliked at Athens. We know, of course, that nothing came of his efforts: the battle of Chaeronea, in August of 338, marked Philip's definitive victory. From then on, Athens was subject to the kings of Macedonia.

Although we lack the speeches delivered at the time, we do have—as in the case of the earlier campaign—a major retrospective speech, composed several years later on the occasion of a political trial. This is the most famous, and the most personal, of Demosthenes' speeches, the *De Corona* ("On the Crown"), which dates from 330 but deals with earlier events and with his policies in general. The trial stemmed from Ctesiphon's proposal to grant Demosthenes a gold crown for the generosity of his contributions to the rebuilding of the city walls. Aeschines attacked the proposal, and the matter was brought to trial; in fact, Demosthenes' entire political career was at issue. Never did he show more authority or soundness of judgment than in this trial. By a deft stroke of composition, he saved for the end (following a false epilogue and a scathing attack on Aeschines) a whole block of events in which he had distinguished himself—the period of the Theban alliance and the final effort to resist Philip. To this he devotes nearly a hundred paragraphs (160–251). He repudiates nothing of what he has done. He recalls the situation after the surprise attack on Elatea, when he alone had the courage to address the Council. Again and again he asks, "What else was there to do?" He points out, at the very least, what harm was avoided thanks to his policy. Finally, in a sudden burst of feeling, he declares that he was in the right, despite the ultimate defeat: "Even if the future had been visible to all, if all had known it in advance, if you, Aeschines, had foretold it, and had vouched for it with shouting and clamor (when in fact you didn't breathe a word)—even then our country should not have abandoned this course of action if she set any store by her glory, our ancestors, or posterity" (199).

In this speech the great tradition of Athenian prestige—which Pericles, in Thucydides' history, had claimed would survive her power—is taken up again to striking effect after her defeat, in an idealism that leaves no room for doubt or regret. The Athenians must have been moved by it: they voted for Demosthenes, approving after the fact a policy that had led them to disaster.

5 · THE END OF DEMOSTHENES' LIFE

Unhappily, the *De Corona* is not the end of the story. Demosthenes lived eight more years, in an Athens subject to Alexander. From these years we have only a forensic speech of limited significance, *Against Aristogeiton*, whose authenticity has been challenged (I refer to the first speech by that name; there is a second, still more suspect). We know at any rate that Demosthenes took part in an attempted uprising; that he was involved in some doubtful dealings (he is said to have taken money from Harpalus, an agent of Alexander); and that he took hope once more in 323, at the death of Alexander, but was forced shortly thereafter (322) to flee and to commit suicide by taking poison. His life was of little account before the struggle with Philip; it was of no more account afterward; and his work as an orator was closely bound up with that struggle.

6 · THE SPEECHES IN CIVIL CASES

Only the civil law speeches remain marginal. Except for the speeches against his guardians, they are all "logographer's" work, composed for clients. Of these we have thirty-three in all under Demosthenes' name, but only ten or so are likely to be his; it is particularly difficult to sort them out because the author's personality recedes before that of the person for whom each was written. In general, these speeches are lucid and clear-cut, but with none of the traits that make for Demosthenes' power in the political speeches—a confirmation that this power is linked to the intensity of his convictions. The intensity, in turn, is reflected in the supreme brilliance of his style.

B · The Thought and Style of Demosthenes

Demosthenes' fate was that of all who have passionately identified themselves with causes: during his lifetime, he was both praised and dragged through the mud, and twenty-five centuries later he is still not judged with equanimity. Some try to prove that he was nothing but a traitor, a "bought man." Some attack the blindness of his policy, based on a patriotism whose focus was the city-state and thus unfit to gauge the new unifying forces that were emerging (and that Isocrates anticipated). To others, by contrast, he appears as the symbol of every resistance movement, of independence in all its forms. It may be said to his glory that he is still invoked in discussions of current events.

Leaving factual circumstances and personal preferences aside, the eloquence of Demosthenes is clearly based on several firm ideas in the moral and political sphere. Demosthenes was a democrat; but for that very reason he believed the real remedy for all ills was a strengthening of the democratic character. To that end he insisted on two things: respect for the law, and the people's willingness to shoulder their responsibilities.

The passages on law, common in the political speeches, have an uncommon brilliance. For a Greek, the identification of law with democracy was virtually self-evident; but at a time when respect for the law was waning, Demosthenes found striking terms in which to recall this identification. One of the most clear-cut passages is *Against Midias* 221ff., which shows that law not only ensures the individual's safety in the street but protects the very authority of judges. The strength of the law proceeds from the citizens' determination to respect it: "This is how you make for the strength of the laws, just as they make for yours" (par. 224).

But the law outlines a way of life, not a policy: policy is the work of the people, when gathered in assembly. Demosthenes never tires of repeating that what ruins policy is the people's subservience to demagogues who flatter them. Here again the idea is not a new one, but Demosthenes gives it new life. He knows how to evoke the plight of free speech, which is banished from the speaker's platform while the people amuse themselves, encouraging "men who are traitors to offer their slanders and insults." Meanwhile, little by little, the people lose their sovereignty: "Formerly, you paid taxes by symmories; now you make policy by symmories: the orator is the leader, under him is the *stratēgos*, and there are the Three Hundred[9] to shout approval on one side or the other; the rest of you divide yourselves between the two camps" (*On Organization* 20 = Olynthiac 2.29). The people are "reduced to the rank of servant, of subordinate"; they are "tamed, domesticated." Last but not least, they are hindered by their own lack of will, and follow the path of least resistance. Lucidity and the will to act elude them simultaneously. All this Demosthenes tells the people, with bitter reproach. In his view, the orator, that is, the statesman, must shoulder many duties. One is to tell the people the truth; a second is devotion to the city. Others are the ability to anticipate—to foresee the course events will take from their beginnings—and the refusal ever to shirk one's obligations, which for the orator are like those of a soldier at his post.

9. The three hundred richest citizens, who took a leading role in the affairs of the symmories.—Trans.

A revival of values is thus in order, both for the people and for politicians; and in this respect Demosthenes is truly an "educator of the people" (in the words of Werner Jaeger). Once restored, these values would restore in turn the reputation Athens had formerly enjoyed, which Demosthenes never ceased to believe she might enjoy again. It was the Athens of the Persian Wars he would have liked to see reborn, with Philip taking the role of the Persian king. He longed for her glory, her preeminence, her brilliance. The continual contrast between this lost but recoverable greatness and the wretchedness of the present accounts for the urgency and tension so intrinsic to his oratory. All the means at his disposal are used in the service of this unvarying idea.

His composition is free enough to throw the main points into relief; we saw evidence of this in the *De Corona*. This freedom extends to the very details of his speeches: often the opening remarks boldly shift the question at issue. Even when he follows an organized outline that has been subtly pondered, he always gives the impression of yielding to spontaneous inspiration. Sometimes it is difficult to make out the different parts of a speech, so strong is the impression of a single unifying movement. Yet we know there was nothing improvisational about Demosthenes' art.

Still more than his freedom of composition, the sheer force of his style radiates power. Nothing in the earlier orators—at least in those we know, with their more polished, concise, and intellectual manner—prepares us for this style. Most remarkable is his way of combining abruptness with the extended period, brevity with breadth. The impression of abruptness and brevity comes first from the force of the words themselves, a product of their colloquial, concrete nature. We have already seen it in expressions such as "You make policy by symmories." Often such concrete terms emerge as sudden images. Thus we find (*Philippic* 1.26): "Like the makers of clay figurines, you choose your generals for show, not for war." Or he compares the allocations of the theoric fund to the diets permitted by physicians, "which give no strength but merely keep the patient alive" (Olynthiac 3.33). In places, such images crowd one another, varying from one line to the next, as if the vividness of the impression or the urgent need to communicate it demanded this constant change. Occasionally Demosthenes shifts suddenly into direct discourse or dialogue. Sometimes this is merely artful presentation, designed to highlight a particular point ("Where are provisions going to come from? . . . From the sky? . . . That is an impossibility," On the Chersonese 26). Sometimes it is a way of pointing out that there is no solution, as with the series of six questions followed by inadequate answers in On the Chersonese 17. Sometimes too it can be a sarcastic way of unmasking the intentions of an opponent, Demosthenes putting hypothetical words into his mouth.

This impetuous boldness, this intensity and brilliance, were stigmatized by Aeschines, who attributed strings of absurd and incoherent images to his rival: "They are pruning the city; someone has surreptitiously hamstrung the democracy; we are sewn together into mats, threaded like needles into tight places" (*Against Ctesiphon* 166). Aeschines adds that Demosthenes "spun in circles" at the rostrum. But such facile criticisms neglect the fact that these sudden bursts are sustained by a style that also includes the opposite qualities. For Demosthenes also composes long periods, which are solemn and powerful. As examples I could cite the famous opening of the *De Corona*, with its prayer to the gods, or the passage in the *Second Olynthiac* (23–26) in which he demonstrates that Philip's success is not surprising; the only surprising factor is the Athenians' attitude. In the latter passsage the development extends over twenty-two lines, marked by verbal motifs that recur at intervals ("It is not surprising . . . and for my part I am not surprised: on the contrary, it would be surprising if . . . But what surpises *me* . . . *That* is what surprises me"). Such sentences obey a continuous rising rhythm, which seems to carry conviction by its very self-assurance.

Naturally, these two types of sentences alternate in Demosthenes: the brief remarks, unanswered questions, and mordant images are suited to criticism of an attitude or attacks on an opponent, while the longer sentences, sweeping or emphatic, come into their own when the orator wants to evoke an ideal or rise to a view of the whole. Above all, just as the heart of his inspiration is in the contrast between past and present or between ideal and reality, so the deepest originality of his style is in his way of combining both tones in a single sentence. For example, he often builds a period slowly and with dignity, accumulating clauses of increasing importance, only to surprise his audience with a sudden brief conclusion whose obvious truth is overwhelming (as in *For the Megalopolitans* 8, *Chersonese* 6 and 49–50, *Midias* 48–50). These sudden conclusions correspond to the emergence of a proof, or of a threat; they reinforce by contrast the importance of their message, and confront the audience with a fact that sweeps away all reservations.

Clearly, Demosthenes' eloquence presupposes a consummate grasp of the techniques of oratory. But these techniques are fused, in his work, into an inner current or thrust that derives all its value from the importance of the campaign in progress. His style matches the absolute and passionate quality of his commitment. As it happened, the apex of Athenian political oratory— which was reached in Demosthenes—coincided with the crisis that was to swallow up the city's independence. It is only an apparent paradox that the ideal of Athenian patriotism should have found its most fervent expression at the moment when it was waging its last vain battle.

III · ORATORS CONTEMPORARY TO DEMOSTHENES

Almost all the great political orators of the fourth century belonged to the same generation. Demosthenes was born in 384, and Demades at about the same date; Hyperides, Lycurgus, and Aeschines were born five or six years earlier, and Phocion thirteen years earlier. What is more, Hyperides, Phocion, and Lycurgus all died within five years of Demosthenes. The flowering of Attic oratory is thus clearly linked to the city's great crisis.

1 · AESCHINES

Because he was an adversary of Demosthenes, Aeschines will always be compared to him. It is from Demosthenes' speeches that we learn of Aeschines' humble origins, his brief career as third actor, his fine voice. All three of his surviving speeches deal with the two major political episodes I have mentioned in connection with Demosthenes: *Against Timarchus* is an attempt to block Demosthenes' charges about the handling of the embassy of 346, and *On the Embassy* is Aeschines' response in the same case; *Against Ctesiphon* is the speech of accusation that opened the case of the gold crown, tried in 330. In their strictly antithetical speeches the two orators trade insults, give different versions of the facts, and defend opposite policies.

Where Demosthenes wanted a struggle, Aeschines, an adherent of Eubulus, dreamed of peace, entente, and fiscal restraint; he tended to promote accommodation with Philip. In Demosthenes' eyes this was sheer treason, and he made the charge openly in *On the False Embassy.* He was no less harsh in his condemnation of Aeschines' role at Delphi, where his speech against the Locrians of Amphissa brought on the Sacred War and Philip's advance to Elatea. Aeschines tried to defend himself on both these counts, acknowledging that events had not taken the turn he expected. But his policies were undeniably ambiguous. It is not surprising that the Athenians barely acquitted him in the case of the embassy, and refused to take his lead in the case of the crown; nor is it hard to understand Demosthenes' hatred of him.

The two men were, moreover, of very different temperaments, a fact reflected in their speeches. With Aeschines there are never any surprises in composition or chronological sequence. At the same time, he enjoys leisurely discussion of points of law; he takes a calm, steady tone, uninterrupted by the dazzle of images or the urgent flow of reproofs. His only exclamations are those of an intellectual in a moralizing vein—for example, at the end of *Against Ctesiphon*, his invocation of "the Earth, the Sun, Virtue, Reason, and that Education by which we know good from evil." A moderate, Aeschines is cold, circumscribed, without flights of eloquence and without great ideas. In every respect he is the opposite of Demosthenes. This of course scarcely proves that it would have been a bad idea to reach an accommodation with Philip.

What to do about Philip became, in fact, the object of the great debate that split the fourth-century orators into two camps.

2 · THE FACTION OF RESISTANCE

We know of this faction through some speeches of second rank, falsely attributed to Demosthenes (*On Halonnesus*, from 342, and *On the Treaty with Alexander*, from 335), but primarily through those of two major orators, Hyperides and Lycurgus.

Hyperides was at least as strongly in favor of resistance as was Demosthenes, and it may have been his refusal to relent that made him attack Demosthenes under Alexander, during the Harpalus trial (this was the context for his speech *Against Demosthenes*). Otherwise the two men were allies; Hyperides obtained the conviction of Philocrates after the truce that bore his name, and proposed public rewards for Demosthenes. They died in similar circumstances.

Hyperides was a brilliant and dynamic man, who readily became an object of gossip. His taste for women was well known, and his defense of the courtesan Phryne caused quite a stir.[10] He did not limit himself to political oratory: of his work, partially recovered in the second half of the nineteenth century thanks to papyrus finds, six speeches survive, of which four are forensic, written for clients (only *For Euxenippus* is complete), and one is a showpiece (another *Funeral Oration*, delivered in 323).

In his forensic speeches, this comrade-in-arms of Demosthenes recaptures the brisk and lively tone of Lysias (e.g., in *Against Athenogenes*, which describes the misfortunes of a credulous farmer fallen victim to a swindle). But Hyperides can also argue as well as Isaeus (as in *For Euxenippus*); and in his *Funeral Oration* he finds ringing tones, worthy of Demosthenes, in which to extol the resistance and stigmatize the shame of Macedonian domination. In him we have Lysias, Isaeus, and Demosthenes combined—or in succession. The treatise *On the Sublime* was later to compare him with the victors in the pentathlon, who excel in the combination of events without coming first in any one; their strength is in the variety of their talents.

Lycurgus was of the same faction, but of a completely different temperament. Born into a prominent aristocratic family, the Eteobutadidae, he chose to serve his country as an administrator. His name is especially associated with the attempts at recovery following the defeat at Chaeronea, when he managed the finances of Athens for twelve years. He implemented an austerity program, but one that also called for reorganization and large public-works projects. He was honest and fiercely devoted to virtue, and would tolerate no weakness in himself or in others; in the unruly fourth century, his personality recalls the more or less mythic figures of the past, such as Solon or Aristides.

This intransigent virtue finds forceful expression in his only surviving speech, *Against Leocrates*. Leocrates had left Athens just after the battle of Chaeronea to settle first in Rhodes and then at Megara. Such conduct was obviously in bad taste, to say the least, and the mass mobilization ordered by the Athenians at that time made it look like desertion. But to accuse the man of treason, as Lycurgus did, seems excessively harsh. Yet in Lycurgus's view, forsaking Athens at that juncture was tantamount to bringing about the city's fall: "What worse treachery could he have practiced against his city, since as far as he was concerned he left her in bondage to the enemy?" (78). The excessive quality of this charge is in itself a measure of the value Lycur-

---

10. He is supposed to have bared her bosom in court.—Trans.

gus put on good citizenship. Like Demosthenes, he wanted to see a revival of the traditional values of an earlier Athens, including the self-sacrifice (described in history and in myth) of each citizen for the good of his homeland. More particular to Lycurgus was the desire to see this ideal citizenship from the past combined with reverence for the gods. At a time when the old ideal of the city-state was about to go down for the last time, it can be said for Lycurgus that he tried to revive the spirit behind that ideal. In the light of subsequent events, his stubbornness becomes almost touching.

Nor was the "patriotic" faction the only one in which the political crisis brought out virtues worthy of the past. The period of the battle of Chaeronea and its aftermath was a time of civic revival, even in the other camp; Phocion is perhaps the finest example.

3 · ORATORS OF THE MACEDONIAN FACTION

In the pro-Macedonian camp, two men in particular made their mark; and they stand in complete contrast to one another.

Demades was of relatively humble origins; he was the son of a boatman, and boasted of having had no teacher but the rostrum. A brilliant extemporizer, he never published his orations; but the vigor of his style—largely due to his use of images—was well known. His quips and bons mots were quoted, and a few have come down to us. As a rule, they are brutally concrete and powerfully evocative. Demades was an orator outside the mainstream, whose eloquence was achieved in spite of—and in defiance of—the norm.

Phocion, by contrast, was a man of good family, as reserved as Demades was impudent. The latter, as a prisoner, had won Philip's favor by a stroke of luck; Phocion was elected *stratēgos* forty-five times, and tried to revive the tradition whereby the roles of orator and general were fused in a single charge. A serious and upright man, he was executed by being forced to drink hemlock, as was Socrates. Plutarch found Phocion worthy of inclusion in the *Lives*, where he is paired with Cato of Utica. He must have been a brilliant speaker; his quoted sayings are stern and biting, and Demosthenes called him "the cleaver of my speeches." But his convictions were those of a realist, and denied him the flights of oratory in which some others indulged. The heroes of the anti-Macedonian resistance he compared to cypresses, which are big and lofty but bear no fruit. For his part, he thought of the fruit; and if anything can be held against him, it is that he stood for reality rather than for an ideal no longer attainable.

The end of Greek independence marks the end of great Greek oratory. At most we may add Dinarchus to those named above; and the differences between him and them are revealing. Dinarchus was a Corinthian by birth and hence not a political orator but a "logographer" who did legal business only in other men's names. Apparently he published about a hundred speeches, of which three remain (two of them incomplete). All of the surviving speeches were composed for the Harpalus case, and one is specifically against Demosthenes. They are sober and quite impersonal works, in which imitations of other orators can be detected. The decadence of Attic oratory begins with this man, who, unlike his predecessors, was not personally involved in the cases he pleaded. We can understand why Dionysius of Halicarnassus said of political oratory: "After the death of Alexander of Macedon, it began to lose its strength and to wither away little by little; in my day it had almost completely disappeared."

7

Reflections on Politics and History: Isocrates and Xenophon

While the orators tried to instruct the people directly, and the philosophers shunned the assembly to rebuild the world in thought, two men of the fourth century took an intermediate position. They wrote treatises in which they sought to advance a practical wisdom accessible to every man capable of reflection. A comparison of their ideas reveals many similarities; not so a comparison of their lives, though both were Athenians born between 440 and 430.

I · ISOCRATES

An overview of Isocrates' life clearly indicates the two areas in which he was active. The first was rhetoric. His father owned a flute-making business, and Isocrates grew up in a comfortable milieu; he was apparently a follower of Socrates and a pupil of such Sophists as Prodicus and Gorgias. But at the end of the war, his father found himself bankrupt. So, like Lysias, Isocrates became a logographer (he lacked the necessary talents for a career as an orator). We have six of the speeches he wrote in this capacity. Then in 393 he opened a school of rhetoric, and quickly published several manifestos stating his position vis-à-vis other teachers of his time. These include the theoretical treatise *Against the Sophists*, and two short treatises demonstrating his approach to conventional ("school") subjects—the *Helen* and the *Busiris*. But we can better evaluate the principles behind his teaching if we consult a later work, the *Antidosis* (354), a speech for the defense in a hypothetical trial. Here, Isocrates reviews what he means by rhetoric and by philosophy—two terms that in his view cover a single phenomenon. This teaching was to prove highly popular, and many prominent men, Athenians and foreigners, are said to have been pupils of Isocrates.

But Isocrates was not satisfied with this success and soon entered another sphere, that of politics—not everyday, practical politics, but the politics of Greece as a whole and the principles that should guide it. He brought out a steady stream of writings on the subject: the *Panegyricus* (380), in favor of Athenian hegemony; *On the Peace* (356), attacking the city's imperialistic tendencies; the *Areopagiticus* (355), advocating a return to a moderate form of democracy; the *Philippus* (346), urging Philip to make peace among the Greek states and lead them against Persia; and finally, just before his death, the *Panathenaicus* (339), expressing the hope that Athens will come to exercise an important role once again in alliance with Philip. Nor is this all, for during the same period Isocrates was composing short pieces in which he gave his opinions on specific political issues (e.g., the *Plataicus*, published between 373 and 371, and the *Archidamus*, somewhat later). In some of the short works he also offers advice to princes, particularly to Nicocles of Cyprus, as in *To Nicocles* and *Evagoras* (Evagoras was Nicocles' father). A different piece called the *Nicocles* is in the same vein but may not be the work of Isocrates; *To Demonicus*, undoubtedly spurious, is addressed to a private citizen. Isocrates also corresponded with princes; we have letters he wrote to Dionysius of Syracuse, to the children of Jason of Pherae, to Archidamus, and to Philip (letter 2, dating from 344), among others. Without leaving home, he made himself the champion of a great political cause—the unification of Greece, to be sealed by joint action under the leadership of a capable ruler. The defeat at Chaeronea must have saddened his last days; he died shortly thereafter, at the age of 98. But it is clear that he had played as great a part in the political sphere as in the field of rhetoric.

A · Rhetoric

When Isocrates opened his school, the only teachers of rhetoric were Sophists, who taught the art of "speaking well" with a view to sheer effectiveness, whatever the cause to be pleaded. Many had written treatises, now lost. After the great Sophists discussed above came men like Evenus of Paros, Theodorus of Byzantium (cited by Plato), Alcidamas, and Polycrates. Alcidamas was a pupil of Gorgias, whose surviving works include *On the Sophists* and a hypothetical indictment of Palamedes; he was particularly concerned with achieving brilliance in improvisation, and on every subject took a position antithetical to that of Isocrates. An extreme case is Polycrates, author of an *Indictment of Socrates*, who also wrote an encomium on Busiris, the Egyptian tyrant who murdered or ate his guests. And why not? After all, Polycrates also wrote in praise of cooking pots and pebbles. This kind of rhetoric was to turn Plato against rhetoric in general, which he considered a fomenter of lies. Isocrates, for his part, resolutely opposed such speeches and those who taught others to write them. Unlike Plato, however, he did not condemn rhetoric per se; in this regard he occupied an intermediate position between the Sophists and the philosopher.

Indeed, Isocrates believed that the art of speaking well was also the art of thinking well. This was why he could claim that rhetoric and philosophy were one. He did so advisedly, on the basis of a coherent system of thought. In his view, speech and the conviction it carries are our sole criteria of truth, even as they are the sole means of progress, understanding, and civilization. In a passage that appears twice in his work (*Nicocles* 5–9 = *Antidosis* 253–

57), he describes the power of speech as the source of man's superiority: it allows men to live together, to create cities, laws, and inventions of all kinds. It also makes precision possible, and control over thought: "It is thanks to speech that we can teach the ignorant and test the learned; for we consider precise language the surest evidence of sound thinking." In Greek, after all, *logos* is both word and thought.

It goes without saying that to "speak well," in this view, is not what the Sophists and teachers of rhetoric meant by that phrase, that is, to deploy a set of hackneyed formulas with a view to success of a practical order. It is, rather, to express in clear form ideas that deserve approval. And this can be achieved only if the speaker cultivates his powers of reflection.

Isocrates can profess such notions solely because he takes a particular view of human knowledge. His view is lucid, yet very different from that demanded by a thinker of Plato's stamp. For Isocrates does not believe in the possibility of philosophic certainties. To his mind, the investigations of philosophers are fruitless; he prefers to offer "reasonable opinions on useful subjects." He is satisfied, in other words, with that "opinion," or *doxa*, which Plato was to judge so harshly from a philosophic perspective. Isocrates is not in search of absolute truth, much less a new kind of truth; what he calls wisdom is the art of arriving at ideas that can be adopted to good purpose. He refuses likewise to believe in a "science of the good," but thinks it worthwhile to improve human life in the practical order by affirming received values: the philosophers "urge men to practice a virtue and a wisdom not only unknown to others but which they themselves cannot agree upon; I urge men to practice a virtue that all men recognize" (*Antidosis* 84).

For Isocrates, then, learning to speak well is learning to arrive at ideas and advocate values that will be endorsed and prove effective. This ability, moreover, will win for those who acquire it the esteem of their fellows; for the opinion of the community, which is the sole criterion of truth and goodness, is also the finest recognition for one who has proved worthy of it. Here we have the consummation, as it were, of Isocrates' philosophy: censure will be focused on those who are unjust, and esteem on those who are good, so that virtue will be its own reward—an idea that recurs in his political philosophy.

We have to do, then, with a system of thought that limits itself resolutely to practical wisdom—a fact that explains Isocrates' latent polemics with Plato, as well as a reciprocal irritation conveyed by slight but discernible allusions in each man's work. In practice, however, Isocrates' teaching was opposed primarily to that of the Sophists, who were teachers of rhetoric like himself. What set him apart from them was his more moderate and accommodating nature.

Of the three elements necessary to the mastery of any discipline (natural gifts, theoretical training, and practice), Isocrates considered the second distinctly inadequate. Success, in his eyes, depended in large part on natural talents, which needed chiefly to be developed; to this end, practical training was the essential means. Isocrates had no faith in "instant" formulas: after a discussion of the "general themes used in speeches," he moved on to exercises. The pupil had to learn to choose arguments befitting the occasion and arrange them in a complete speech; to help him, the teacher provided models and critiques. It was a training akin to the French tradition of *dissertations* and *explications de texte*.[1] Students who followed it would, he believed, learn to think and speak better, and hence to live better. In this respect, Isocrates was the founder of humanistic education as we know it.

His own speeches are examples of what he recommended to his pupils. It is hard to get a sense of this from the speeches he wrote for the courts (though these too contain general themes characteristic of him, such as the praise of convention and of concord in *Against Callimachus*); but his short pieces in the sophistic manner are very revealing. Thus, for example, Gorgias had written a defense of Helen and Alcidamas a defense of the Egyptian tyrant Busiris; in each case the author had pleaded for acquittal even while acknowledging the defendant's crimes. Isocrates took up the same subjects and composed his own *Helen* and *Busiris*. Far from approaching them as matter for court trials, however, he cited all the noble and elevated themes that could be associated with these two characters, and passed over their faults. His praise of beauty, in the *Helen*, is still famous; but with it he included an encomium on Theseus and another on the unity among Greeks in the Trojan campaign—a unity for which Helen was indirectly responsible.

It was this tendency that moved Isocrates to aim yet higher. Following the example set by the epideictic and "Olympic" speeches of Gorgias and Lysias, he cultivated the genre of the "Panhellenic" oration, full of advice for the cities and lessons drawn from history. In these speeches he set out to deploy in a just cause all the resources of his art, including those devices whose aim is not to deceive but "to help and to charm one's auditors while educating them" (*Panathenaicus* 246). Other resources include masterful composition, a pure, polished, and harmonious diction—a style, in short, that seems more appropriate to "metrical pieces with musical settings than to speeches in lawcourts" (*Antidosis* 46).

By conferring such dignity on the prose treatise, Isocrates created a particular literary tone, which has come down to us by way of Cicero. His periodic style, with its balance, breadth, and appeal to the ear (always avoiding hiatus, for example), became a model for all subsequent Attic orators and their emulators. But Isocrates saw these formal qualities as meaningful only in the service of the political and moral cause he sought to champion for the good of the Greeks.

---

1. The French use the word *dissertation* to mean a school essay of fairly rigid form. The *explication de texte* is an interpretative essay—also highly structured—on a short literary passage.—Trans.

B · Politics

One of the great innovations of Isocrates' political thought (and of fourth-century political thought in general) is its focus on Greece as a whole rather than on Athens.

1 · ATHENIAN POLITICAL LIFE

In the whole corpus of Isocrates' work there is a single discourse on the domestic political life of Athens: the *Areopagiticus* (written ca. 356–54). He is careful to explain that he is broaching the subject only because the city's internal policies threaten to destroy her position in Greece. Thus the domestic reform he seeks is a necessarily roundabout way of furthering a Panhellenic policy. The speech takes its name from the court of the Areopagus, which Isocrates would like to see reinvested with its role as guardian of morality. This fact alone is a clear indication that, fearing the excesses of the democracy, he desired a return to the "ancestral constitution" called for by the moderates and previously championed by Theramenes.

Although he suggests several reforms in that direction (such as substituting indirect election—election from a picked slate of candidates—for the choice of officials by lot), Isocrates' chief emphasis is on moral reform: "Cities are well ordered not by decrees but by mores." He hopes for a truce between rich and poor, and for a rebirth of civic spirit. In former days the Areopagus had imposed the old virtues of respect for others and moderation (*aidōs* and *sōphrosunē*); without these, Athens cannot hope to secure her rightful place among the Greek states. Even when he approaches domestic policy, then, Isocrates' impulses are primarily those of a moralist; even in a domestic context, he thinks of Greece as a whole.

2 · THE PANHELLENIC PROGRAM

His greatest concern, in fact, was to promote a Panhellenic policy—a policy based on the idea that all Greeks are brothers and should be united in common enterprises. The idea was not a new one. It had taken shape during the struggle against the Persians and been voiced, if only in passing, by Herodotus, Aristophanes, and Gorgias. The enhanced authority of Persia (thanks to the "King's Peace" of 386) was destined to revive it; and the Peloponnesian War had demonstrated the dire effects of disunity. As early as 380, then, the idea was to appear full-blown in the *Panegyricus*, and Isocrates was never again to lose sight of it.

For him, unity among the Greeks and war with Persia went hand in hand: "It is impossible to have a secure peace unless we wage a common war on the barbarians—impossible for the Greeks to live in harmony until we have won our advantages from the same source and run risks facing the same foes" (*Panegyricus* 173). In this way the unity and greatness of the Persian War period would be revived; at the same time, those Greeks still under the Persian yoke could be freed, and others enriched through the occupation of new lands. Success would be easy, because of the "barbarians' " cultural inferiority. All that was needed was to find the proper leadership, or hegemony, in order to coordinate the efforts of the Greeks. With a backward glance to the Persian Wars, the obvious suggestion was to entrust the leadership to Athens.

3 · THE CLAIMS OF ATHENS—AND HER MISTAKES

The *Panegyricus* sets forth Athenian claims to hegemony (claims reiterated, in part, in the *Panathenaicus*): her cultural superiority, her services rendered during the Persian Wars, and the fact that her rule over the Greeks had, on the whole, been relatively mild. The sole caveat was that her new hegemony should be still more so, taking care never to infringe on the rights of allied cities. As it happened, soon after the *Panegyricus* (and probably under its influence) the Second Athenian Confederacy was created, under Athenian leadership and in the spirit of Isocrates' proposal—without tribute, garrisons, or dispatches of Athenian settlers to the cities. It did not win the acceptance of the allies, some of whom made war on Athens, and in his disappointment Isocrates chided the Athenians for their mistakes in a speech *On the Peace*. The mistakes all came down to an abuse of authority; they were the same mistakes as in the past—the very same that had been the undoing of Athens, and of Sparta after her. By comparing the points of view expressed in the two speeches (the *Panegyricus* and *On the Peace*), we discover a whole theory of power and a philosophy of history—both of which recur in all of Isocrates' subsequent works.

4 · POWER AND HISTORY

Isocrates' theory of power, like his theory of rhetoric, is grounded in the importance of opinion. The only guarantee of lasting power is the affection and loyalty (*eunoia*) a powerful entity can inspire among its neighbors. A state that treats other peoples badly, by contrast, earns their hostility, and this hostility ultimately overwhelms the state. The way Athens received the hegemony of the Greeks, of the latter's own will, at the end of the Persian Wars is an example of the more fortunate outcome; the way in which she lost her empire illustrates the less fortunate sequence of events.

In *On the Peace*, Isocrates is able to add a further proof of his theory: Sparta, having succeeded Athens as the dominant power in Greece, also made herself hated and soon lost her power. And why should this surprise us? Supreme power went to the Spartans' heads and led them into the same mistakes: "As befits those corrupted by the same desires and the same disease, they undertook the same ventures, made comparable mistakes, and fell at last into similar misfortunes" (104). Their situation was that of any tyrant, whose very power destroys him, and who, having earned his subjects' hatred, falls into the worst misfortunes.

This doctrine implies that to survive, any power must be attended by justice and mildness. Isocrates never tired of saying so to the princes he addressed. He also said so forcefully to Philip, in whom he hoped to find a leader for Greece who would also be a benefactor. The dream of a mild and generous authority, grounded in the esteem of the people, may also be found in Xenophon. But with his clear-cut and somewhat simplistic feeling for antitheses, Isocrates took this dream for a bona fide lesson of history. He was not himself a historian, but he obviously reflected on history and argued from it (though he interpreted it on the basis of present need and sometimes drew different conclusions from one speech to the next). In so doing he instituted a new form of speculative thought. It should not surprise us, then, that there were historians among his pupils. Chief among these were Ephorus (of Cumae) and Theopompus (of Chios). Unlike Thucydides and Xenophon, they were not men of action but intellectuals like Isocrates; also like him, they were conscientious moralists. Their taste for meditating on history with an eye on the interplay of virtue and vice is surely the legacy of Isocrates.

5 · DOCTRINE AND APPLICATIONS

This "program" in all its specificity, combining such clear-cut theories and historical experiences, occupied Isocrates fully from 380 to 338 and accounts for the apparent contradictions in his thought. It was because the program never varied that his opinion of Athens did. Optimistic in 380 when she held power over no one, severe in 355 when she had clashed with some of the cities in her new confederation, laudatory again when (ca. 340) Philip's hegemony seemed to eliminate all danger of Athenian imperialism—his judgment of facts varied with the situation; but his theory was invariable.

Similarly, after arguing for the hegemony of Athens, Isocrates turned to various princes as potential leaders. Then, seeing Philip establish a foothold in Greece, he had hopes for him. At first he hoped Philip would be moved by Athenian moderation (On the Peace 22). Disillusioned on that score, he next tried to enlist Philip's power in the service of his Panhellenic program. It is interesting to note that the Philippus, in which he charged the Macedonian king with this mission and expressed confidence in him, dates from 346, the year of the Peace of Philocrates. Isocrates moved beyond Athenian patriotism because everything, in his eyes, had to be sacrificed to his program, itself unalterable. This program also explains why Isocrates, while consistently extolling Athens at the expense of Sparta, sometimes expressed a concern not to alienate the latter. At the end of the Panathenaicus, a young pupil with Spartan sympathies offers his opinion; his words may leave the reader somewhat confused, but they convey a tentative tolerance worthy of one who advocated Greek unity.

Isocrates' stubborn patience may appear naive to us; his moralizing arguments, his way of repeating and parading them, his confidence in virtue and in mankind can seem highly unrealistic. Yet his thought, or the thought he echoed, was not a tissue of empty dreams. The Second Athenian League seems to have been inspired by it, as was the political attitude of Timotheus, a pupil of Isocrates who for a time was influential in Athens. And if Philip had seemed at first an intransigent conqueror, the Confederacy of Corinth, formed shortly after Chaeronea—and shortly before Philip's own death— was intended to bring the Greeks together and lead them to war in Asia while granting them certain rights, as Isocrates had recommended. Isocrates' dream of Greek unity likewise corresponded to the newly emerging tendency to form leagues and confederations. The city-state had in fact been superseded; only, as ill luck would have it, the power passed to a conqueror who had little respect for the Greeks. Isocrates would appear more realistic if there had been no Alexander.

II · XENOPHON

Xenophon, like Isocrates, moved beyond the bounds of the city-state—and that quite literally, in the course of his own life, which was infinitely more adventurous than that of Isocrates. In his thought, Xenophon also shared some common points with Isocrates, though he worked in different fields.

I · LIFE OF XENOPHON

Xenophon was born into a wealthy family. Though educated for an active life, he became acquainted with Socrates and listened to his discussions; a part of his work would later be devoted to Socrates. But in the defeated Athens of the early fourth century, he was tempted by other horizons. In 401 he enlisted with a group of Greeks (one of whom was his friend Proxenus, a Boeotian) to travel to Asia and defend the cause of Cyrus the Younger against his brother Artaxerxes. Cyrus was killed in the battle of Cunaxa, near the Euphrates, and the Greeks had to retreat across Asia Minor, through hostile territory. This retreat of the "Ten Thousand" was an adventure in which Xenophon was able to demonstrate his talents as a leader; he describes the whole episode in the *Anabasis*. In the course of it, he grew attached to the Spartans, and upon his return he joined the entourage of the Spartan king Agesilaus. The attachment was such that when Athens fought against Sparta, Xenophon was on the Spartan side. This was in 394, at the battle of Coronea.

As might be expected, he was exiled from Athens; and he lived for more than twenty years in a Lacedaemonian milieu. The Spartans granted him a small estate at Scillus, near Olympia, and he became a gentleman farmer, working at the same time on a variety of prose works. The *Oeconomicus* helps us to form an idea of the life he led there and of the way he managed his house and lands.

In time, Sparta, defeated by the Thebans at Leuctra, arrived at a rapprochement with Athens (371). Xenophon, whose small estate had recently fallen into enemy hands, benefited by the rapprochement: his exile was repealed. His sons served in the Athenian army, and one of them, Gryllus, died in its ranks in 362. Xenophon himself probably returned to Athens and took an interest in his city's finances, as the treatise *On the Revenues* (after 355) would indicate. He died shortly thereafter, but not before putting the finishing touches to his major works. It is not easy to say when each of these was begun or which was written during any given period of his life. Attempts at a precise chronology have been made (e.g., by E. Delebecque); but whatever the circumstances under which they were begun, reworked, and completed, these works provide a kind of direct testimony bearing on Xenophon's personal history and that of his time, including the ideas and men contemporary to him.

2 · XENOPHON'S ACCOUNTS OF HIS LIFE AND OCCUPATIONS

Xenophon was one of the first authors to publish a work in the vein of the war memoir—namely, the *Anabasis*. The book (almost certainly published under the pseudonym "Themistogenes of Syracuse") sets out to tell of Cyrus the Younger's campaign against his brother. By the end of the first book, however, the battle of Cunaxa and the death of Cyrus have already taken place; the remaining six books describe the adventures of the Ten Thousand in Asia and their return. The narrative is lively and direct, full of the most concrete geographic and ethnographic information (which Herodotus would not have been ashamed to acknowledge), all gleaned from personal observation. The work also contains character portraits, such as those (in book 2) of the three contrasting *stratēgoi*—Clearchus, Proxenus, and Menon. Finally, Xenophon's personal recollections give the story an individual flavor: the scene in which the Greeks at last catch sight of the sea (4.7) is justly famous.

But if the author's presence in his work adds a certain charm, it also clearly introduces concerns that are not those of the historian. The *Anabasis* is a defense of Xenophon himself and of his ideas. He does not hesitate to put himself emphatically in the foreground, demonstrating his abilities as a leader. With naive self-satisfaction—quite the opposite of Thucydides' restraint—he offers himself as an example of the good leader (a leitmotif of all his works) who knows how to make himself both feared and loved. (By contrast, Clearchus was too harsh and Proxenus too indulgent, so that the soldiers were lacking in loyalty to both.) The good leader also knows how to pay attention to the slightest details of provisioning, weapons, and military drill; and he gives the example in everything. He knows, finally, how to take religion into account, and signs and omens as well. Many episodes in Xenophon's narrative, and many of his own speeches, which he quotes, are designed to bring out one or the other of these qualities. As a result, his personal reminiscences, often concrete and colorful, also smack of the edifying example—a feature all his writings share.

It is noteworthy, in this respect, that the very same doctrine can be found in a treatise dealing exclusively with family life in peacetime—the *Oecono-*

micus. The *Oeconomicus* takes the form of a dialogue, and Socrates appears in it, but only to help describe the way Ischomachus manages his estate and trains his young wife in her duties as mistress of the house. Here too we find a very concrete and lifelike picture, which includes the hierarchy of servants, the care of crops, and even the proper organization of cupboards. The characters and manners of individuals are also depicted: Ischomachus's young wife, obedient and eager, is described in a way that seems charming if one is not too confirmed a feminist. But at the same time, the description of the estate brings Xenophon himself on stage in an obvious way, with the pride he took in filling these household functions, so different from those that figured in the *Anabasis*. Ultimately, transcending both Ischomachus and Xenophon himself, the same doctrine appears: the good administrator and the good mistress of the house must know how to inspire fear and love; this is how they will win the greatest zeal, and the best return, from each of their subordinates. Xenophon, for that matter, is perfectly aware of the correspondences between domestic arts or agriculture and the arts of war or politics. Just as order is equally necessary in a household and in an army (8.4), so good management of a house and of a country are comparable: "One who can teach the art of being a good master can also teach the art of being a good king" (13.5).

The *Oeconomicus* has no overt bearing on Xenophon's life but evokes it indirectly. It can be grouped in this regard with the short treatises in which he recorded his experience and advice on subjects that were dear to him. Thus he wrote on equitation (*On Horsemanship*), on hunting (*The Art of Hunting*, a work whose authenticity has sometimes been contested), and on the art of command in the cavalry. This soldier and country gentleman was also—like many aristocrats—a horseman, who did not neglect to praise the various equestrian pursuits as the best of educations. Xenophon the squire had no desire to be anything but what he was. And yet this squire was also a true historian.

3 · HISTORY OF GREECE AND POLITICAL WRITINGS

Xenophon even aspired to be Thucydides' continuator. His history, which covers the years from 411 to 362, begins where Thucydides' ends and indicates as much by its opening words, which are "After that . . ." Xenophon's history is called the *Hellenica*, and the title alone shows that it lacks the unity of action we found in Thucydides' history with its focus on one war. Xenophon's title also indicates that political life was tending more and more to be that of Greece as a whole rather than of a particular city-state.

The work is made up of two distinct parts; the first describes the end of the Peloponnesian War, somewhat—but only somewhat—in the manner of Thucydides. This is augmented by an account (2.3.9 through the end of book 2) of the regime of the Thirty and the crisis that put an end to it in 403. Already in the latter account we can see points of contrast with Thucydides: individuals play a greater role, and the sober character of the analysis is blurred. Indeed, as the rest of the work shows, Xenophon had none of Thucydides' outstanding qualities. His historical explanations are poor, his speeches have no causal function, his chronology wavers, and he even omits important facts—it was pointed out long ago that he mentions neither the battle of Cnidus, nor the creation of the Second Athenian League, nor the founding of Megalopolis to prevent Spartan expansion. These omissions may not be innocent. Xenophon is the friend of Agesilaus and of Sparta—in the greater part of his work, at least—and his history is not altogether impartial. He does, however, condemn the Spartan destruction of the Cadmea (the citadel of Thebes); but with a philosophy of history more worthy of Herodotus than of Thucydides, the pious Xenophon acknowledges that the gods have punished that crime.

If he lacks Thucydides' virtues, Xenophon has others—those that are visible in the *Anabasis* as well: his feeling for the concrete and for striking episodes. The account of Theramenes' death, full of visual and conversational detail, is one of the finest examples of his skill in creating moving scenes. The speeches in Xenophon may add little to our understanding of the facts; but when they deal with an idea he cares about, they are forceful enough to make it compelling. The most striking case is that of the rapprochement between Athens and Sparta in 371 (6.3–7.1). For Xenophon the Athenian and friend of Sparta the subject was tailor-made to please him; he introduced a whole series of speeches leading up to the reconciliation (there are three at 6.3) and making arrangements for the collaboration of the two peoples (e.g., the speeches of Procles at 6.5.38 and 7.1.1). In these, each speaker has his own tone and style (which was not the case in Thucydides), and all offer arguments in favor of the policy of rapprochement, which Xenophon must have endorsed. Recognizing the superiority of Athens in naval force and of Sparta in land force, the speakers point out that an alliance between the two should constitute an almost irresistible power.

The *Hellenica* is Xenophon's only work in the genre of history; it is also the only historical work from this era to have survived. We can only note that at least some tendencies of the lost works chimed with the spirit of the *Hellenica*. (An apparent exception is Ctesias, whose lost works on Persia and India seem to have belonged rather to the Herodotean tradition.) In 1906, however, classicists were delighted by the discovery on papyrus of several pages from an anonymous work, the *Hellenica Oxyrhynchia* (after the name of the town where it was found). The events discussed are those of the year 395, and thus appear to belong to another continuation of Thucydides. The quality of these few pages (which date from the second quarter of the fourth century) makes us greatly regret the loss of the rest. We have still fewer fragments from the works of Isocrates' pupils. But it is characteristic of the period that Theopompus—like Xenophon—should have produced a continuation of Thucydides called the *Hellenica*, and an account of the years 359–36 in a long work entitled the *Philippica*; in the latter title, the name of a man re-places that of Greece. As for Ephorus, he was the first author of a *History* with claims to universality: he began with the arrival of the Dorians in the Peloponnese and ended with the advent of Philip. History in the fourth century took its point of departure in Thucydides, but sought greater breadth and universality.

Xenophon's historical work is thus an important one. With it may be grouped three short treatises deriving from the same interests.

The *Hellenica* gives a very favorable account of the Spartan king Agesilaus; but that was not enough for his friend Xenophon, who reworked the material relating to the king and made it into an encomium, the *Agesilaus*. From a literary point of view, this little work devoted to an individual antici-pates somewhat the genre of biography. From the point of view of ideas, be-yond Xenophon's admiration for Sparta and Spartan virtues, it offers yet an-other application of his ideas on the art of government; more than anyone, Agesilaus possessed the mildness blended with severity that wins a leader the devotion of all his subjects.

Xenophon's Spartan sympathies are also conveyed in his short treatise the *Constitution of the Lacedaemonians*. The genre consisting of descriptions of constitutions existed before Xenophon. We have a somewhat singular exam-ple in the *Constitution of the Athenians* that was preserved among Xeno-phon's works but dates from the beginning of the Peloponnesian War or per-haps a little earlier. This piece by an opponent of the democracy is in fact a polemical work, claiming that the domestic and foreign policy of the Athen-ians has a certain logic to it and always tends to guarantee the authority of the "bad" over the "good."[2] The text is unpolished, terse, and rather archaic in expression; it is an argument rather than a description. The various *Consti-tutions* that followed—and those of Critias in particular—must have been quite different. But Xenophon's, at any rate, is descriptive, and one of our best documents on life in Sparta. What he describes is not so much a consti-tution (in the modern sense of the word) as a way of life; he focuses on the so-cial and moral practices so peculiar to, and characteristic of, the Spartans, as well as on their military organization. His admiration for the virtues of Sparta is obvious. Yet a final chapter speaks of the changes that have under-mined the system. This is a kind of postscript, of later date and inspired by new experiences; but there is room for doubt as to its interpretation.

The two foregoing pieces are related to forms of history; the treatise *Ways and Means* is not. It is a program of economic development for Athens, writ-ten at the end of Xenophon's life when his prudence and conservatism coin-cided with those of Eubulus. But the concrete description of the resources he proposes to develop makes the piece a document on Athenian life. It serves

---

2. The terms here translated "bad" and "good" also carry the social connotations of "low-born" and "high-born."—Trans.

too as a reminder that Sparta did not have a monopoly on Xenophon's interests.

If the two last-mentioned works betray a seriousness and even an austerity corresponding to Xenophon's practical sense, the surge of admiration that made him write the *Agesilaus* surfaces once again in a work whose only historical element is its setting, and which is actually a novel—the *Cyropaedia*.

4 · HISTORICAL FICTION

Historical fiction, soon to come into its own with the romance of Alexander and the Greek romances in general (long before the extraordinary success it enjoys today), begins, for all practical purposes, with Xenophon. In the history of literature, this conservative with a penchant for moralizing proved an innovator. The work is called the *Cyropaedia*, or "Education of Cyrus,"[3] a title that clearly conveys the author's intent to edify; but it is actually an account of Cyrus's whole life and of the virtues he continued to practice until his death in 529. The setting, then, is roughly historical. But Xenophon took remarkable liberties with the historical facts: his Cyrus merges the kingdoms of Persia and Media by wholly peaceful means, without a hint of the conflicts that set him against members of his own family; and he dies in his bed, bidding noble farewells, instead of being killed in battle. Clearly, Xenophon is improving on the facts in order to present his hero in a more edifying light.

In this way he can make him a still more shining example of the art of governing—Xenophon's obsession in all his works. For that matter, he did not pick Cyrus haphazardly; Herodotus had already spoken of Cyrus's mildness, and said he was like a father to his subjects. This mildness and generosity are amply illustrated in the work; and one might think that Xenophon's ideal was based on the same ideas we found in Isocrates. But the difference is that Cyrus was first and foremost a conqueror, and it was his technique of conquest that interested the soldier in Xenophon. Xenophon's Cyrus has the virtues to be found in Agesilaus or in the *Anabasis*: he knows how to punish and reward, to keep an eye on everything—even the health of his troops—and to demonstrate his own superiority on occasion. He also knows how to use his very mildness to win new allies, inspire devotion in his men, and get them to rally. Thus the successive episodes of his conquest illustrate the just victories that are the reward of a good leader.

But—and here we find another contrast to Isocrates—the "doctrinal" aspect of the work is closely intertwined with the concrete and lively account of an adventure. In it we find the kinds of precise details that give the *Anabasis* its value; we also find local color. Above all, we find Xenophon's special art of presenting well-defined personalities in all their particularity. He even allowed himself the pleasure of including episodes that are at least as touching as they are edifying. An example is the story of the beautiful Panthea,

---

3. I.e., Cyrus the Great (600?–529 B.C.), not the man Xenophon fought for in 401.—Trans.

which is interwoven with the narrative in several books of the *Cyropaedia*. A captive princess in the custody of Araspas, Panthea excites a violent passion in her keeper, which Cyrus handles wisely: he pardons Araspas, for he knows the power of love, but he protects Panthea, who has thoughts only for her husband. His goodness wins Cyrus the help of the husband, who dies in the king's service. The despair of the princess, who kills herself so as not to outlive the man she loves, inspires the king's pity and respect. Love has made its appearance in history; and surely this entitles us to call the *Cyropaedia* a historical novel. The work, which could move the reader with its romantic touches while at the same time offering an idealized image of the good king (and, incidentally, a model for anyone with ideas of conquering Asia), enjoyed an incredible success that lasted for centuries. Alexander knew it backwards and forwards; the Romans in Cicero's day read it avidly; and, thanks to Xenophon, Cyrus was destined to remain one of the most popular models of royalty in later literature.

Similar to the *Cyropaedia* in this respect is a little dialogue with no claims to historicity, the *Hieron*, which portrays a conversation between the Sicilian tyrant Hieron and the poet Simonides. It is in fact a study of the cares that beset tyrants, and thus corresponds to preoccupations also voiced by Isocrates (in *On the Peace*) and Plato (at the end of the *Republic*). The difference is that in Xenophon's piece the tyrant's troubles are purely practical (his unpopularity, for example, makes it impossible for him to travel or to have friends). The idea that a change in attitude would transform this tyranny into a happy kingship links the dialogue with the *Cyropaedia*.

Indeed, in the diversity of their subject matter all the treatises, narratives, and dialogues of Xenophon express related ideas. What is more, they all reflect the new horizons of the fourth century—political views no longer confined to the city-state, the concept of monarchy, the psychology of the individual. I might add that his language, which is clear and controlled, already exhibits certain characteristics of the "common" dialect (*koinē*) that was soon to prevail. But if these traits are the signs of new times, Xenophon also wrote a series of works in which he tried to be faithful to the years of his youth in Athens. These are the works that he devoted, many years after the fact, to Socrates.

5 · THE STORY OF SOCRATES

Besides the *Oeconomicus*, in which Socrates takes a very subdued role, Xenophon's works devoted to Socrates include, first and foremost, the *Memorabilia* (in four books), and, of secondary importance, the *Apology* or *Defense of Socrates* (whose authenticity has been contested) and the *Symposium* (which seems a fairly free composition). Though some of these works, including the beginning of the *Memorabilia*, may date back to the years at Scillus, they were not finished until later, at the time of the rapprochement with Athens. In any case they were written at some distance from the events, and many details may have been suggested by earlier works: Plato was far from being the only disciple of Socrates to write about his teacher. (Some of the others were Euclides of Megara, Antisthenes, and Aristippus of Cyrene; see the beginning of chapter 8 below). Their works have been lost, but some of the titles recall those of Plato.

Since the only remnants of this Socratic literature are the testimonies of Plato and Xenophon, it is natural to compare them. The difference is obvious: Plato's Socrates is a bold thinker who invents a new way to formulate questions and always traces things back to their essences; Xenophon's is a virtuous and reasonable citizen, who preaches a morality in everyday life that is primarily practical. The value of this double testimony has long been debated. It is probable that Plato, whose own philosophy continued to deepen throughout his life, occasionally projected some of his own ideas onto the portrait he drew of his teacher, or that he tended to cull from past conversations the points that echoed his own thought. By the same token, it is no less probable that Xenophon, who was primarily interested in practical life and never a philosopher, simplified the meaning of Socrates' teaching and retained chiefly what he was able to understand or appreciate.

Whatever the case, the Socrates he portrays is a simple man of simple virtues: a pious man, of course (a point Xenophon stresses from the beginning), who believes the gods are concerned with man's welfare and who advocates, among other things, self-control, respect for law, gratitude to parents, mutual aid between brothers, and friendship. In keeping with Xenophon's taste, this Socrates also recommends learning to be an army officer and a cavalry commander (3.1–4); he even preaches on behalf of the conservative virtues, calling for a return of civil harmony and praising the influence of the Areopagus in former days—as Xenophon might have done. Nor does he ever neglect the sense of practical utility dear to Xenophon. The only surprise is that such a moderate Socrates could have caused so much commotion and stirred so many passions in all who approached him.

These various themes—which, when all is said, are surely authentic in part—are almost always presented in the form of short dialogues; the interlocutors include Sophists such as Antiphon, Prodicus, and Hippias, or members of Socrates' entourage, such as Glaucon and Charmides. The dialogues are lively, clear, and always brief (only two or three pages each); here too, the more closely the external features correspond to those of Plato's dialogues, the more striking is the contrast in inspiration and depth of thought. Xenophon, despite his Socratic writings, is no more a philosopher than Isocrates. Both were preoccupied with practical wisdom; but philosophy as Plato defined it is something else altogether.

8

Philosophers of the Fourth Century: Plato and Aristotle

INTRODUCTION: SOCRATES

Socrates does not really belong in a history of literature, for he wrote nothing. Nor does he belong in a chapter on the fourth century, for he lived in the fifth. He was born in 470, between Euripides and Thucydides, and died in 399, at the dawn of the new century. I have chosen to describe his role here because, although a contemporary of the Sophists (with whom we see him conversing in Plato), he opened a new era in Greek thought. All the philosophers of the fourth century invoke him either directly or indirectly. Among those whose accounts of him survive, only Aristophanes (who presents a caricature of him in *The Clouds*) wrote in the fifth century. The two witnesses to his teaching, Plato and Xenophon, wrote after his death, in the fourth century. It was in the fourth century too that the teachings of the so-called "Socratic" philosophers (whose doctrines, I might add, differed considerably) began to circulate. The "Socratics" included Euclides of Megara (whose ideas were related to Parmenides' doctrines on Being), Antisthenes (a moralist who stressed the role of effort), Aristippus of Cyrene (who defended the value of pleasure in due proportion), and Aeschines of Sphettus (the author of very lively dialogues). Socrates, in the fifth century, broke ground for all the philosophical reflection of the fourth.

Thanks to those who spoke about him—and portrayed him as speaking—in their works, we think of him as an eminently familiar being, one with whom we might have lived. We know of his role in certain battles of the Peloponnesian War, and of his exemplary behavior as a citizen: he refused to associate himself either with unjust votes (after the battle of Arginusae) or with illegal policies (under the thirty tyrants). We are familiar with his habit of talking philosophy in the streets of Athens, with his physical ugliness, his irony, his stubbornness, his patience as a "midwife" to minds. And we know of his trial and of his death, which was to haunt all his followers, before coming back to haunt so many others threatened or caught up in an unjust death.

The man's extraordinary importance in the history of ideas stems from two features of his thought. The first is his exclusive interest in ethics. Where Ionian philosophy had tended to deal with the world as a whole, Socrates the

Athenian was concerned with man only; he took to its logical conclusion the tendency already perceptible in Anaxagoras and his follower Archelaus. Second, within the field of ethics, he displayed a new and imperious insistence on truth. While the Sophists were teaching the art of illusion mongering, he, the Athenian, was forever asking questions, seeking definitions, and—the better to elucidate moral problems—furnishing multiple examples from everyday life, which offered useful analogies.

It may be that in Socrates' thought the questions outweighed the doctrines. At most we can glimpse, through all the conflicting testimony, the fundamental intellectualism that made him assume (in contrast to Euripides) that one cannot recognize the good without embracing it, and that to be better is also to be happier. Yet his taste for asking question after question undoubtedly explains both his influence and the judgment against him. It was because he seemed to question everything that he was suspected of disrespect for virtue and for the city's gods—when in fact this questioner cited Apollo's oracle as his authority[1] and considered the quest for virtue his only aim. But it was also because he forced everyone to ask himself questions, to examine them closely and come to grips with them, that this unparalleled teacher had so many followers, all so different from one another. He was content to set them on the right path; and in Plato's case the path was to lead very far indeed.

I · PLATO

Plato's thought was nourished at its beginnings by the teaching of Socrates; it was also stimulated by the death of Socrates, which Plato himself (in the Seventh Letter, whose authenticity is now virtually unchallenged) describes as a turning-point in his life.

A · Life of Plato

Plato was born at the beginning of the Peloponnesian War (428–27). Through his mother he belonged to the Athenian aristocracy; he was related to Critias and Charmides, both of whom were associated with the thirty tyrants in 404 (they sometimes appear in the dialogues, as do Plato's two brothers, Adeimantus and Glaucon, major characters in the *Republic*). Plato undoubtedly received the full education of a young aristocrat and, like many of these, apparently planned a career in politics. Then he met Socrates. The eager devotion with which he drew and redrew his teacher's portrait is proof enough of the hold this encounter had on him. We can well imagine what his teacher's death must have meant to him. He left Athens for several years, going first to Megara to be with fellow followers of Socrates, then to Egypt and Cyrene to meet other scholars. When he returned to Athens (in 395 or thereabouts), it was unthinkable that he should take part in the government of a

---

1. The oracle had said that Socrates was the wisest man in Greece.—Trans.

city that had reached such a depth of corruption. Where politics was concerned, his only thought from then on was to reconstruct in the mind an ideal city, founded on knowledge of the Good. He opened a school in the gardens of Academus in 387, when he had already published several dialogues. His teaching there was the chief occupation of his life, until his death in 347.

Plato left Athens again several times, however. Convinced that man's troubles would end only when pure and authentic philosophers should come to power, or when sovereigns should have access to true philosophy, he put his hope in the tyrants of Sicily. He first went there (in 388, just before he opened the Academy) intending to meet the Pythagorean scholars of Tarentum, especially Archytas; but he was invited to visit Dionysius of Syracuse, and made a disciple of the young Dion, Dionysius's brother-in-law and son-in-law.[2] The trip ended badly, and Plato was even sold as a slave.[3] But a hope had been born—a hope that accounts for a second trip, twenty years later, after Dionysius's death. It began well: the younger Dionysius, his father's successor, at first semed full of enthusiasm. But before long he banished Dion; and Plato himself had some difficulty leaving the country. A final attept, in 361, began with the same euphoria but was equally unsuccessful. The just city Plato had imagined would never see the light in his lifetime. Yet it remained for him one of the goals of the philosopher's work, as well as the means by which philosophers might escape the risk of corruption by their environment to attain, by long and expert effort, the contemplation of the Good itself.

B · Works of Plato

Plato's work consists of thirty-five dialogues, together with a few admittedly apocryphal dialogues and a collection of letters. Some of the thirty-five (especially the *Alcibiades Major, Second Alcibiades,* and *Hippias Major*) have also seemed suspect, and their authenticity has been contested. The dates of composition have not been precisely fixed; scholars try to estimate them on the basis of various criteria (references to events, progress in the elaboration of the doctrine, changes in stylistic habits). Despite the differences of opinion resulting from this imprecision, we can make out in the series of dialogues an evolution and a deepening of Plato's thought. The early dialogues are intended primarily to formulate problems; they sometimes end with a question, in the Socratic manner. These are followed by a series of great works—the *Phaedo,* the *Symposium,* the *Phaedrus,* and the *Republic*—in which the essential themes of Platonic thought appear and in which literary grace is fused with a remarkable thrust of intellectual discovery. Platonic dialectic next tackles problems of a more technical nature, and the dialogues that follow are harder to read (this is true of the *Parmenides,* the *Theaetetus,* the *Sophist,*

2. Dion married his own niece, the daughter of his sister Aristomache and Dionysius.— Trans.
   3. He was ransomed immediately by a friend.—Trans.

the *Statesman* (*Politicus*), the *Philebus*, the *Timaeus*, and the *Critias*, which will not be discussed here). Plato's last work is the long dialogue of the *Laws*, in which he takes up once again, on a more concrete level, the political program that had appeared in its ideal form in the *Republic*.

1 · THE EARLY DIALOGUES

We cannot be sure that the *Apology* is the first Platonic dialogue; some think that Plato may have begun to write before Socrates' death, while others (including A. Lesky) put this short work among the last of the early group. It would deserve to stand first, however, as the most direct homage Plato paid his teacher after returning to Athens. The work closes with the condemned man's charge to the jury; Socrates speaks serenely of death, which he does not fear. Here, despite the great simplicity of tone, there is a foretaste of the nobility we shall meet again in the *Phaedo*. The *Crito* too is lit from within by the picture of Socrates awaiting death; this is the dialogue in which he refuses to leave Athens, out of fidelity to the city's laws.

Many of the other dialogues of this period are attempts at definition. In each case we watch Socrates discomfit interlocutors who mistakenly thought they knew what they were talking about—for example, in the *Laches* (where the subject is courage), the *Euthyphro* (piety), the *Lysis* (friendship; this may be a somewhat later work), and the *Charmides* (prudence or temperance [sōphrosunē]).

Three dialogues written in this period, or at the end of it, stand out from the rest. The first is the *Protagoras*. Here Plato portrays with charming verve and irony the success enjoyed by the great Sophists, in particular by the very greatest, Protagoras. Socrates, having accompanied a young enthusiast who wants to become a student of Protagoras, innocently asks the great man what he teaches. As Protagoras claims to be able to make men good citizens, Socrates raises the question (often asked at the end of the fifth century, and having serious implications for the Sophists) whether virtue can be taught. Protagoras replies with a myth demonstrating the importance of political virtue, and with a more subtle commentary; but in the following discussion difficulties arise, and the speakers' positions are reversed. No resolution is reached, and we are left with the irony of Socrates and his belief in the oneness of virtue, which he sees as always tied to the intellect.

The *Gorgias* goes farther and seems very close to the great dialogues of Plato's maturity. The subject is rhetoric (hence the title, Gorgias being second among the Sophists and the greatest rhetoric teacher of his day). But the issue, of course, is the ethical role of rhetoric. Gorgias admits that rhetoric does not aim at the true, but he considers it a tool that may be used well or badly. This would seem to have serious consequences. Polus, one of Gorgias's pupils, shows more mettle than his teacher, and it becomes clear that the very ends of human life are at issue: Polus admires the power the orator can wield, but Socrates thinks it worse to commit injustice than to suffer it. A third character then enters the dialogue (an unknown—almost the only such in Plato); his name is Callicles. Pushing the proposition to its limits, he contrasts a justice based on formal agreement with the "just according to nature"—in other words, the victory of the strongest. The debate grows strained. Callicles is insolent; several times he gives us to understand that someday Socrates, with his refusal of all common sense, might well find himself insulted, accused, and condemned to death. Such allusions obviously lend a tragic resonance to the debate, which closes with a calm statement by Socrates (who is ready to meet death serenely) and a myth about the judgment of the dead in the underworld. This highly important dialogue thus reflects in all its acuteness the crisis of values at the end of the fifth century and the irreducible opposition between two goals—success in political life (as promosed by the Sophists), and exclusive reflection on the good (as practiced by Socrates).

The *Meno* again takes up the question whether virtue can be taught, and brings into the discussion the theory of *anamnēsis* or "recollection,"[4] which assumes the immortality of the soul. The physical presence of Socrates is still essential here; it is in the *Meno* that we find the simile of the stingray, which Socrates resembles in his mysterious ability to "numb" his interlocutors. Yet the dialogue lacks the richness and distinctiveness of the *Gorgias*. The same can be said of certain other dialogues from this general period—the *Menexenus*, a parody of a funeral oration; the *Ion*, which makes fun of the poets and their commentators; the *Euthydemus*, an attack on two Sophists; and the *Cratylus*, an extended play on etymologies. Of the dialogues mentioned thus far, only the *Gorgias* is on a par with the great philosophical dialogues of Plato's "maturity" (as we call it), which were probably composed at intervals during the fifteen-year period from 385 to 370.

2 · THE GREAT PHILOSOPHICAL DIALOGUES

The three great philosophical dialogues share, above all, a perfection of literary form and a determination to emphasize Socrates' influence.

This is true of the *Phaedo*, which takes place on the very day of Socrates' death; he is in prison, surrounded by his friends, and their last conversation turns on the immortality of the soul. The imminence of death and the grief of his followers make Socrates' own serenity stand out poignantly; he looks upon death as a liberation from the body and its tyrannies. Near the end we encounter a new myth about the destiny of souls after death. The dialogue closes with a very brief and restrained account of Socrates' last moments.

The atmosphere of the *Symposium* is wholly different—full of life with its dinner parties, drinking, jokes, and social graces. The *Symposium* also has

---

4. I.e., the theory that the soul beholds the Ideas before it is joined to the body, and after its descent to earth "recollects" or recognizes the Ideas as they can be discerned in material things.— Trans.

an original format: it consists of a series of speeches on love by different characters, whom Plato portrays and parodies with ready wit. In a second section it is Socrates' turn to speak, and the tone changes; soon (201d) he is speaking alone, quoting the account he says he has heard from a wise woman named Diotima, which presents love as an aspiration toward, and an initiation into, the Beautiful and the Good. A third and final section suddenly introduces the enfant terrible among Socrates' followers, the young Alcibiades, who arrives drunk, crowned with ivy and violets. He describes—in a sort of concrete application of the preceding speech—what Socrates has meant and still means to him, enlarging on the love that this man, ugly as Silenus, is capable of inspiring, and on his apparent invulnerability to every temptation. In the small hours of the morning only Socrates is still awake, still pursuing his inquiries among the empty tables, without a trace of fatigue.

In the *Phaedrus*, which again has to do with rhetoric, Socrates is faced not with a great teacher but with a timid and enthusiastic young man, with whom he has left Athens for a walk along the banks of the Ilissus. They stop to rest by a plane tree and a chaste tree (*agnus castus*), near a spring sacred to the nymphs. The poetry of the place and its power of inspiration are mentioned several times. Although the dialogue is ostensibly about rhetoric, the example chosen is love. The point of departure is a speech attributed to Lysias on the expediency of granting one's favors to a lover who is not in love. In two attempts to correct this view, Socrates offers a first speech on love (237a–241d), which grows ever more inspired, and then a second speech (243e–257b), presented as a retraction. The second is an encomium on love, tied to the glowing description of our immortal souls and of their struggle to rise and free themselves (the soul resembling a driver with a team of two horses, one good and one bad). This great passage brings to the dialogue of which it is the core an exceptional radiance and a new form of poetry.

I have emphasized the literary quality of these three dialogues; yet the reader will understand even from the briefest summaries that the Platonic system is already present in them in its entirety, with its dualism, belief in the immortality of the soul, and perpetual striving—within a lifetime and from one life to the next—to contemplate the Good without the trammels of the body. Plato traces this upward movement using both the rigor of his arguments and the lure of poetry; in similar fashion, the soul simultaneously obeys dialectic and love. The dialogues to follow will be largely devoted to analyzing the nature of this "participation" of the sensible world in the world of ideas, or to solving the problem of the number of the ideas and their unity. A further task will be to establish the procedures of that dialectic the *Phaedrus* describes as essential, whose role is to rise from the particular to the idea so as to return to the particular by a clear and rational sequence of steps. But even before clarifying these points, Plato will produce another great dialogue of similar brilliance, devoted this time to politics—the *Republic*.

3 · THE REPUBLIC

The *Republic* consists of no fewer than ten books. Its subtitle is *On Justice*; indeed, the first book, which serves as an introduction (and may have been composed before the rest, for separate publication), is an attempt to define "the just." The discussion continues in a less dialectical and more serious vein in book 2; it is here that Socrates proposes to seek what constitutes "the just" by considering first the "large letters"—the city as a whole—and only afterward the "small letters," i.e., the individual. The whole account is in fact political, but the dialogue establishes a rigorous equation between the city and the soul of each man. The limited size of the city-state and the natural solidarity among its members made such an identification easier.

Books 2–4 describe the formation of cities and the education of the guardians (in music and gymnastics); this discussion leads to the notion, expressed in the second part of book 4 (427e ff.), that the city contains three elements, to which the various virtues correspond—wisdom for the rulers, courage for the warriors, and temperance for all—while justice consists in each person's doing his job without encroaching on the spheres of others. In the individual, reason, "anger," and desire are the three corresponding elements; and justice requires that each part of the soul, like each class within the city, fulfill its function without disturbance or encroachment.

Books 5–7 put forward the premises—so difficult of acceptance—that a healthy city presupposes. The common possession of women and children is shocking enough, and the rule of philosophers still more so. But it is to the latter premise that we owe the far-reaching analysis, at the heart of the *Republic*, of the philosopher's role and education. This analysis ends, in book 7, with the myth of the cave: the philosopher will have torn himself away from the shadows of the cave in which we live so that he can turn toward the daylight, climb the path toward the outside world, and finally raise his eyes to the Sun itself—in other words, to the Good. Having done so, he will go down again to help others, renouncing the joys of contemplation out of love for justice.

Books 8 and 9 return to the subject of injustice, that is, to the flawed forms of government, which Plato represents as succeeding one another in a steady, declining trend—timocracy, oligarchy, democracy, tyranny. Each is destroyed by the corruption of that which constitutes its principle. There is a kind of man corresponding to each kind of government, and the two are described side by side. Just as the worst government is tyranny, so the unhappiest man is the tyrannical man, whose passions rule him: here we come back to the familiar ethical analyses of Socrates. But Plato also manages, in these two books, to sketch bitter caricatures of the various regimes whose flaws he observed in his own lifetime.

Book 10 returns to two rather disparate points. The first is a condemnation of the poets. Plato wants none of them in his ideal city because of their bad moral influence, and because their art of simple imitation works in a manner contrary to philosophy. We can sense that his rejection of the poets is all the more severe because he had a greater love for them, and felt their seductive power more keenly, than most men do. The dialogue ends (like the *Gorgias* and *Phaedo*) with the idea that virtue is rewarded after death, and a new myth is introduced to describe the rewards. This time the myth (as ostensibly told by Er the Pamphylian, who came back to life twelve days after his death) opens broad perspectives on the very structure of the universe and the way souls choose their reincarnations.

Thus in the *Republic* everything is brought together—politics (a critique of the present and a dream of a better world); ethics and psychology (the parts of the soul and the evolution from one form of corrupt state to another); metaphysics (the allegory of the cave and the final vision). This coherence and interpenetration are characteristic of Platonism, which always presents itself as a system. As for the political program, Plato emphasizes the fact that it is barely feasible—barely feasible but, in the last analysis, not impossible. It is also characteristic of Platonism to propose a model in this way—something perfect but remote; a source of inspiration, at the very least, and an object of contemplation, like the Good or the Ideas. But this also explains why Plato was to return to more practical views at the end of his life, in the *Laws*.

4 · THE LAWS

In a summary as brief as this we may pass over the technical dialogues named above, although their importance for philosophy properly speaking is crucial, and although the *Timaeus*, with its cosmology, was perhaps the dialogue that had the single greatest influence on ancient philosophy. But it is harder still, in moving from the *Republic* to the *Laws*—even in a rapid overview—to avoid at least mentioning the *Statesman* (*Politicus*). Ostensibly it is only a search for a definition, in the dialectical mode; but it resembles the *Laws* and the *Republic* in offering a myth about the Golden Age and the birth of states. It also introduces two new ideas: a man possessing the "science of kingship" would be superior to written laws; and the chief concern of such a man would be to interweave the various temperaments of men, which are like the warp and weft of a fabric. Instead of the concern for absolute order expressed in the *Republic*—an order in which all differences are suppressed— we find here a concern for living unity and for harmonization, which respects differences.

The dialogue of the *Laws*, for its part, comes down to the level of everyday reality. The passion of the greatest dialogues is missing here, and Plato must have died before he was able to put the finishing touches to the work. It is made up of twelve books and an appendix, the *Epinomis*, which deals with wisdom and with the science of numbers, but whose authenticity is hotly disputed. In the rest of the work, Plato—or, rather, the interlocutors he sets before us (of whom Socrates is no longer one)—propose to found the best possible city-state. The object is no longer (as in the *Republic*) the ideal city, to be ruled by philosophers, nor (as in the *Statesman*) a man who should possess the "science of kingship"; in the absence of these unlikely conditions, all the authority in the city is here conferred upon the laws. Nothing is neglected in this dialogue: we find a critique of flawed governments (which, in the shape of a simplified historical analysis, fills book 3); observations on the site to be chosen, the number of citizens, and the education and games of young children; a concern to introduce the laws with preambles; and the essential outlines of the legislation itself. The program is as full as that of the *Republic* was sketchy. Yet the dialogue stays on the level of political and social facts. Even moral observations are relatively rare and limited in scope, while the aims of the system promoted in the dialogue are much less ambitious. The *Laws* no longer requires, for example, that goods be held in common; but it establishes a class system based on wealth, with all sorts of rules and limits designed to avoid excesses. Nor does it aspire to a city that would live in unity according to the directives of the Good; instead, it sets up precise rules for education to make the citizens as good as possible, and creates a whole series of tribunals (the highest being the "nocturnal council") to head off any threat of corruption before it is too late. Such strictures have made some readers think of this as a totalitarian and oppressive regime; but it is important to recognize that Plato espoused such a system only because he could find no path leading to his ideal world; the surveillance he proposes is merely the other face of a limitless dedication to justice and the common good. For that matter, if the city in the *Laws* leaves little room for liberty or tolerance—because Plato had been permanently marked by the excesses of the Athenian democracy, which invoked those values—his philosophy in general displays a perpetual openness to a form of progress and an ideal that the individual may pursue in hope and wonder. Plato is only "oppressive" in cases where it seems indispensable to him; and, even there, he would prefer to convince and instruct, as his teacher Socrates had done.

C · Plato's Means of Expression

It is impossible to sum up in a few sentences the general content of Plato's thought. His way of expressing that thought, however, can give some notion of his most original and characteristic tendencies.

1 · THE DIALOGUE FORM

After Plato, and into modern times, the dialogue form has occasionally been used for philosophical works; in most cases the form is an embellishment, a way to make thinking agreeable. Plato must bear some of the responsibility, for his dialogues are first of all charming scenes—lively, ironic, and tender. Each interlocutor has his own personality. Those who oppose Socrates are often insolent, self-confident, and condescending. His followers are timid, sincere, surprised; and Socrates' way of gently making fun of them is inimita-

ble. This irony of tone, incidentally, is not what we refer to as "Socratic irony": the latter phrase is used to describe his way of forever asking questions,
as if he were really in ignorance and really expected to be enlightened. But
the irony of tone reinforces this other irony, evoking amused sympathy, affection, and a critical spirit all at the same time. Further, everything in a dialogue is made to count: pauses and interludes mark the chief divisions; backtracking in the argument conveys the difficulty of grasping the truth; gestures
and settings harmonize in subtle ways with the themes of the inquiry.

To be sure, these altogether external resources bring the thought to life
and make it more accessible; yet clearly there are other reasons for Plato's
choice of the dialogue form. The first is a concern for intellectual rigor. In
Plato, Socrates often calls himself "forgetful": he cannot remember long
speeches in order to criticize them afterward. This feigned incapacity hides
the idea that dialogue alone permits us to follow an inquiry step by step,
without letting anything pass that has not been accepted and verified. Socrates also says at times that the sheer number of witnesses to a fact is worthless;
he values only his own judgment and that of his interlocutor: "If I do not win
your testimony, and yours alone, in favor of my arguments, I shall consider
that I have done nothing toward the resolution of our debate—nor will you
have done anything, for that matter, if you do not win the support of my testimony, mine alone, and send the other witnesses packing" (*Gorgias* 472b–c).
For these two reasons, a dialogue, which lets nothing pass and requires the
assent of the interested parties, is the surest form of inquiry into truth. The
Sophists, apparently, had sometimes practiced a kind of teaching by question and answer ("eristic"); but we may assume it amounted to training in the
art of debate. In this respect, eristic resembled the uninterrupted speech of
which the Sophists were past masters and which played a part in the political
life of Athens. But such speeches amount to an art of deception; the dialogue
has the very opposite function, and there is nothing accidental about the fact
that it can even be identified with dialectic. Nor is it by accident that those
who debate with Socrates have so much trouble conforming to his rules. Plato applies these rules with such strictness that a lay reader sometimes has difficulty finding his way through the minutiae of the argument's progress; or he
may look with a certain sense of superiority on the endless string of "yesses"
demanded at every step—here a "certainly," there an "it's obvious," "very
true," or "undoubtedly." These roundabout ways and these "yesses" show
clearly that the Platonic dialogue is not an artful way of decking out ideas
but a demanding and rigorous method for arriving at a few truths that may
be fixed and accepted with certainty. The very choice of form is an expression
of philosophic objectives.

What is more, by garnering assent at each step like this, the dialogue combines intellectual rigor with another characteristic aspect of Platonism. Plato
shows us all these different characters—rivals or friends, followers, great
men or mere youngsters—being led to a kind of involuntary conversion,

forced to reexamine not only their definitions but their practical intentions and their ideas about the ends of human life; he portrays them as reticent, astonished, compelled to accept Socrates' conclusions; and in so doing he gives us a whole series of precedents and models that force us to reflect and show us something of the way. In the early dialogues the chief aim is to produce the astonishment that is the beginning of philosophy; in later ones, the interlocutor is taken farther, and a whole world is offered for his discovery. But in every case this series of impulses, whether carried through or merely set in motion, is a kind of protreptic, inviting the reader to follow the same impetus. The importance, in the myth of the cave, of turning and climbing toward the light; the concern with "planting" dialectic in souls at the end of the *Phaedrus*; the role of love in the *Phaedrus* and *Symposium*—all this confirms how important, in Plato's eyes, was the act of turning minds in the direction of philosophy. The dialogues are so many illustrations of that act.

This points to another virtue of the Platonic method of exposition (added to intellectual rigor and compounded with it): the virtue of suggesting even as it proves. It is on such grounds that one can justify the presence of myths at the ends of these thorny, almost scholastic debates.

2 · THE MYTHS

Plato's myths, of which I have already cited the most important in my summaries of the *Gorgias*, the *Phaedo*, and the *Republic*, have been the object of many studies with respect to their content as well as their sources or function. The surprise is that Plato, who was so concerned with intellectual precision, should have juxtaposed to his proofs these more or less fictional accounts of a world we can know nothing about. The *Gorgias* myth—the simplest of all—is thus introduced as a "fine tale": "You will perhaps take it for a story (*muthos*)," says Socrates to Callicles, "but I take it for a true account (*logos*); and it is as truths that I give you the things I am going to speak of" (523a). This undoubtedly reflects Socrates' respect for religious tradition; but it also reflects a desire on Plato's part to hold out a possibility and a hope at the limits of reasoned effort. The details may be naive, but the point is to illustrate the immortality of the soul, for which Plato elsewhere gave rationalistic arguments.

His recourse to such beliefs—which is not a part of yet stands side by side with his reasoned arguments—corresponds to two essential characteristics of Plato's thought. The first is the presence of the divine. Obviously for him there can be no question of the anthropomorphic and motley gods of Olympus. But he always indentifies the Good with divinity, and progress toward the Good with what he calls "assimilation to God" ("Flight [from the mortal sphere] is to make oneself as much like God as possible," he writes in the *Theaetetus* (176b), "and one does so by becoming just and holy through lucidity of mind"). Thus Plato's rationalism is grounded in a kind of faith. A second and equally important characteristic of Platonism is always to suggest something beyond what has been shown and taught. In a passage in the Seventh Letter, which has raised many doubts and misgivings, Plato says he has never himself written about his most serious interests: "There is no way, in fact, to express them in formulas, as is done in other fields of study; rather, it is when one has kept company with these problems for a long time, when one has lived with them, that the truth suddenly flares up in the soul, as light flares up from a spark, and grows from then on by itself" (341c). It is obviously inappropriate to build too much on a single sentence, or to construe Platonic thought as an esoteric mysticism. Yet we have references to an oral teaching of Plato, which is said to have dealt with the One (the lecture *On the Good*); and we know that in the *Phaedrus* he prefers the spoken word to the written. So there is always something that lies beyond the text. The sentence from the Seventh Letter is understandable in the context of a philosophy whose very medium of expression indicates that proof always leads us to a contemplation that transcends it.

Nor are these two aspects of Plato's work—the rigor of the dialogue form and the illumination suggested by the myths—kept separate from one another; for it is a distinctive feature of his work to establish correspondences, proportions, and gradations at every level.

3 · CORRESPONDENCES AND PROPORTIONS

Certain Oriental influences may be detectable in the myths; but whatever we decide on that score there is no doubt that the whole of Plato's thought was profoundly influenced by mathematics. He was himself passionately interested in mathematical research, and appears to have had connections with the famous mathematician Theodorus of Cyrene as well as with the astronomer and mathematician Eudoxus of Cnidus. Theaetetus, who gave his name to one of the dialogues, was a young mathematician, a student of Theodorus. Plato was also interested in Pythagorean philosophy, in which the study of number played a great part. This diverse group of thinkers concerned themselves with problems such as that of irrational numbers and the roots of integers. Mathematics is the form of intellectual training that Plato, in the *Republic*, puts just before dialectic. And, when there is occasion, he includes in the dialogues analyses borrowed from mathematics: hence geometry serves as a test to prove the theory of recollection in the *Meno*; and the transition from the perfect to the imperfect forms of government in the *Republic* (8.546b) is attributed to ignorance of a perfect number, defined in formidably mathematical terms.

The privileged status he accords mathematics is also reflected, in a general way, in Plato's mode of expression. It is reflected first, of course, in the rigor of his arguments, and in his way of sometimes handling concepts as mathematicians handle numbers. But it is reflected too in his taste for expressing relationships among ideas as equations of a mathematical nature. The strict correspondences he draws, in the *Republic*, between parts of the soul, elements of the city's population, and virtues rest somehow on the same method of analysis. The clearest example is undoubtedly the system presented in the *Gorgias*, where a whole series of concepts are arranged in coordinated pairs. Distinctions are made between the arts pertaining to body and to soul, between those designed to build up in advance and to repair, and especially between those tending to produce real improvement and those that are mere flattery. The correspondences may be reduced to the following diagram (the arts of flattery are below the line):

$$\frac{\text{gymnastics}}{\text{adornment}} = \frac{\text{medicine}}{\text{cookery}} = \frac{\text{legislation}}{\text{sophistry}} = \frac{\text{justice (at law)}}{\text{rhetoric}}$$

Plato comments on these relationships as if he were a mathematician. Similarly, in the myth of the cave, the knowable world is divided into steps or stages. There is a progression within the visible world, or world of opinion, from images and shadows to real beings. A similar progression within the intelligible world leads from the knowledge that rests on hypotheses to the direct knowledge of principles and ideas. Finally, the same relation is also to be found between the visible world and the intelligible world. What emerges is a complete system, which commentators often elucidate with the help of mathematical proportions or geometric diagrams. What is more, this system includes the whole of the universe. Such a vision confirms the influence of mathematics on Plato's thought; but at the same time it reveals how the notion of proportion could provide a link and a series of stages between vague forms of knowledge, rigorous intellection, and, at the very top, contemplation. For Plato it was not enough to reconcile these different attitudes with one another; he links them one to another and invites us to move through each in turn.

4 · STYLE

These complementary attitudes are reflected in the complementary qualities of Plato's style. I shall not describe that style here. Suffice it to say that it combines the most perfect transparency and intellectual rigor with the warmth of poetry. Translations always make Plato sound heavier than he really is. Since he pays close attention to his choice of words, their very juxtaposition often has an immediate significance in the Greek that no translation can preserve. On top of this he has a taste for irony, pastiche, and subtle plays on ideas. At times his sentences expand until they burst free of the intended structures. This happens every time he evokes the happy state of souls after death, or the philosopher's joy, or the radiant influence of the Beautiful and the Good. It can also happen when he is struck with indignation in the course of blasting the tyrant, attacking the ambitious, or describing the way the crowd corrupts young men. I am going to quote one of his sentences, chosen virtually at random, on the rapt contemplation of beauty; it will serve to illustrate not only the warmth of his style but also the major themes of this philosophy that is at once dualistic, idealistic, and fueled by an endless aspiration toward the transcendent. In Plato's words, contemplation is a kind of initiation, "a mystery [= rite] we celebrated in the wholeness of our true nature, untouched by all those ills that awaited us in later days; and whole, simple, motionless, and happy were those apparitions the initiation at last revealed to our gaze in a pure and gleaming light, because we were pure and did not yet bear the mark of this tomb we now carry about with us under the name of 'body,' attached to it as an oyster is attached to its shell" (*Phaedrus* 250c). The mainspring of Platonism is reflected in such a sentence.

II · ARISTOTLE

With Aristotle, we find ourselves in Plato's footsteps (he was Plato's student) and at the same time in a new world, which is no longer as strongly centered on the city-state. At all events, it is no longer centered on Athens; Aristotle himself was a native of Stagira, in Chalcidice, and spent only a part of his life in Athens.

1 · LIFE OF ARISTOTLE

Aristotle was born in 384, when Plato had already opened his school, and died in 322, shortly after the death of Alexander. His father was a physician to the king of Macedonia, which may have awakened his interest in the natural sciences. After his father's death he was raised by a man from Atarneus, in the Troad; undoubtedly this accounts in part for the long visit he later made to that region. But it was to Athens, and to Plato, that he came to complete his education. From that time on (probably 367), he was a philosopher, and his life falls into three distinct periods—the first stay in Athens, the Assus period, and the second stay in Athens.

Arriving in Athens at the age of seventeen, Aristotle followed Plato's course of study until the latter's death in 347–in other words, for a period of twenty years. He was thus deeply imbued with Platonic thought in its later phases, and doubtless took part in the work of the school. This is not to say that he had no criticisms to make or new interests to develop—his work proves that he did. But we must always remember that his philosophy took Plato's philosophy as its point of departure and was molded by it in many ways.

After Plato's death, his nephew Speusippus succeeded him as director of the school; Aristotle had no further reason to stay. Two of Plato's students had established themselves some time earlier in the Troad, at the court of Hermias, the dynast of Atarneus. Hermias was a former slave who had become a ruling prince, and took an interest in philosophy—a hopeful case for a student of Plato. Aristotle went to live in his province, at Assus, where he stayed three years; he became Hermias's admirer, adviser, friend, and relative by marriage. Then, in company with his student Theophrastus, he went to Mytilene, the young man's home. In 343–42 he was summoned to Macedonia to serve as tutor to the young Alexander. We should like to think that the philosopher had some influence on the young prince, but there is no evidence that he did; and the policy of cultural fusion between Greeks and "barbarians," so dear to Alexander, was radically at odds with Aristotle's teaching. Yet relations between the two men were good, and Aristotle even obtained Alexander's promise that the city of his birth would be restored. We do not know how Aristotle took the execution of his nephew Callisthenes, who was put to death by Alexander for refusing to worship him; but that occurred considerably later, in 327.

Meanwhile, in 335–34, his mission as tutor fulfilled, Aristotle returned to Athens, which was thenceforth under Macedonian rule. He had probably made return visits earlier, but this time he went back to stay. He opened his own school, the Lyceum; and since he taught while walking with his followers in the paths on its grounds, his students were called Peripatetics (from *peripatos*, meaning "a walk"). In the morning he instructed pupils in specialized subjects, and in the afternoon addressed a wider public. In this way he taught for thirteen years, until the death of Alexander, which set off a wave of strong anti-Macedonian feeling. Aristotle was threatened with prosecution, left Athens, and died almost immediately thereafter. He left a will, which we can read in Diogenes Laertius (5.11); in it he made gifts to all and named as successors his favorite pupils, beginning with Theophrastus.

2 · ARISTOTLE'S WORK AS A WHOLE

Aristotle's chief legacy was a body of work that is both sizable and, in some respects, difficult to reconstruct. We know it consisted of two sorts of treatises—one group designed for publication, the other for use within the school (whence the name "esoteric," which means nothing more than this) and thus written without the slightest concern for literary polish. As fate would have it, all the works intended for publication have been lost. We have at most their titles (three ancient catalogues of Aristotle's work are extant; one is in Diogenes Laertius). Most of these were probably early works, still close to Platonism; we may even mention, in passing, titles that are identical with those of certain Platonic dialogues, including the *Menexenus*, the *Symposium*, and the *Sophist*. Others, to judge by a few surviving fragments, already marked a distance from Plato; an example is *On Philosophy*, apparently composed in Assus. We have indirect knowledge of some others, such as the *Eudemus* (which deals with the immortality of the soul) and the *Protrepticus* (portions of which may be found in Iamblichus). At all events, this great loss accounts for the mediocre literary quality of the Aristotle that has come down to us; once he was considered a good writer.

As it happens, all that remains of his work has been preserved in strange and roundabout ways. His didactic writings were bequeathed to Theophrastus and, after Theophrastus, to the son of another pupil who had been with Aristotle in Assus. This person is said to have hidden them in a basement room at Scepsis, near Assus, from which they were recovered (in a rather poor state of preservation) only in the first century. At that point they began to be recopied, and in time they were also translated into various languages, including Arabic. The editor of Aristotle must often resort to these translations to reconstruct the state of the older manuscripts—whose original was itself flawed. This hardly simplifies the restoration of the text, and adds yet another obstacle to our enjoyment in reading Aristotle.

To make matters worse, these esoteric or "acroamatic" writings, as they are sometimes called (from *akroasthai*, to hear), were lecture notes, which could be reused, modified and amplified. As a result, the problem of dating, not only for individual works but for the different parts of each work, is particularly acute where Aristotle is concerned. In response to this problem, the German scholar Werner Jaeger put forward a series of suggestions in 1923. For each of the major works he sought to reconstruct an original version and a series of revisions which, taken together, indicate a real evolution in Aristotle's ideas, tending to free him progressively from Plato's influence. To give just one example, in Jaeger's view the *Politics* originally consisted of books 7 and 8, written at Assus; books 2 and 3 were added by way of introduction; books 4–6, much more historical and concrete, are clearly later, as is book 1. Such reconstructions are naturally subject to revision, and various reactions to Jaeger's somewhat simplistic scheme appeared after the publication of his book (those, for example, of F. Dirlmeier, I. Düring, and, in France, R. Weil, who agreed with Jaeger's overall scheme but arrived at a more subtle reconstruction of the *Politics*). Whatever conclusions the individual scholar may reach, however, no one can write about Aristotle without keeping the character of his works in mind, or without taking some account of the questions Jaeger raised. And if the way in which Aristotle gradually set himself apart from Plato cannot always be traced in the details of editing and interpolation, it is nonetheless clear that the idea of such a development should shape our overall understanding of Aristotle and any presentation, however brief, of the content of his work.

The difference between the two philosophers is indeed that which Jaeger saw between the different parts of the *Politics*: where Plato always subordinates everything in the physical order to the Idea, the Good, or the One, Aristotle attaches a much greater importance to the physical world in all its actuality and diversity. This contrast is visible in every work and in every doctrine, as well as in the very diversity of Aristotle's interests. Plato was concerned only with ethics and with politics. If he spoke of rhetoric, it was to contrast it with ethics or to enlist it in his search for truth; if he spoke of the soul, the gods, love, or death, it was always to raise the question of how a man ought to live. Aristotle, on the other hand, was a scientist as well as a philosopher in the strict sense of the word; and, in addition to works on ethics and politics, he left writings on logic, physics, and various sciences. To bring out more clearly this broadening of research and the encyclopedic aspect it suddenly assumed, I have treated separately the writings which, by their subject matter, fit most readily into the Platonic perspective, saving for the end everything which, by the very choice of subject, conveys Aristotle's originality. This grouping is in no way chronological.

3 · ETHICS AND POLITICS

The Aristotelian corpus contains three treatises on ethics: the *Nicomachean Ethics* (in ten books), the *Eudemian Ethics* (seven books) and the so-called *Great Ethics* or *Magna Moralia* (two books). The last of these is certainly the work of a pupil and later in date. The authenticity of the *Eudemian Ethics* has been contested, but it is plausibly Aristotle's. The first two treatises are apparently named after their editors (Nicomachus was Aristotle's son, and Eudemus of Rhodes was his pupil); three books are repeated in both of these works (*Eth. Nic.* 5–7 = *Eth. Eud.* 4–6). The *Nicomachean Ethics* is both the fuller and the more original of the two. The ideas it upholds are reminiscent of Plato's: it offers a comparable hierarchy of "goods" and a comparable end or aim for human existence, putting the theoretical or contemplative life at the summit of human aspiration. Yet in his way of approaching the subject, in the content he assigns it, and in his idea of virtue, Aristotle has moved away from Plato.

Aristotle approaches moral values as so many givens; he offers us a reflection on mores (Greek *ēthē*). And where each of these values is concerned, his aim is not exhortation but definition, and above all classification. For example, when dealing with justice (in book 5), he establishes a whole series of distinctions corresponding to the different applications of justice in human affairs; there is universal and particular justice, distributive and corrective justice, justice through reciprocity, household justice, natural and legal justice, and so on. We found nothing of the kind in Plato; and if Aristotle's account lacks warmth, it also implies an exceptional lucidity. Many of his analyses have subsequently served as points of departure for the speculations of other philosophers, up to and including those of modern times.

The same concern for exhaustive classification reappears in Aristotle's very notion of what the virtues are and in the scheme he follows in describing them. Whereas the first two books are devoted in a very general way to the definition of happiness and virtue, the following books examine all the different virtues in succession. He begins, to be sure, with the major traditional virtues: courage, temperance (*sōphrosunē*), justice, and the intellectual virtues. But he closes with two full books (8 and 9) on friendship; and he inserts between temperance and justice a whole series of virtues related to life in society, of which Plato had nothing to say (e.g., amiability, wit, liberality). Here too we find the Platonic framework widening, under the pressure of more realistic considerations; the presence of these virtues corresponds to a greater acceptance of cities as they are and of men as they are. I might mention that they belong, like friendship, to the realm of feeling, whose autonomy Aristotle was more willing to acknowledge than Plato had been.

I should add that in his teaching on the virtues Aristotle introduces several ideas that reveal the same realism and acceptance. The first is the idea of the mean: every virtue is in fact a kind of equilibrium between excess and defect. Thus courage, for example, will be found halfway between an excess of fear, which is cowardice, and an excess of confidence, which is recklessness (2.2.1104a). This idea could only have taken root and become systematic in a man with a passion for classification—and in a man who, less demanding than Plato, no longer saw the virtues as eternal Ideas reigning in the absolute.

The same shift is perceptible in what Aristotle says about the role of habit. He states this principle as early as the opening of book 2: "It is neither by nature nor contrary to nature that the virtues arise in us; rather, nature has given us the capacity to receive them, and this capacity is brought to maturity by habit" (2.1.1103a). Thus we must acquire good habits from our earliest youth. To put it another way, virtue for Aristotle is no longer simply a matter of *nous* (intellect) and its mastery over the human soul, as it was for Plato; the help of time and circumstances is required. In this way Aristotle combines intellectualism with empirical realism. Some of the virtues themselves take on a more modest appearance in this new light. Thus, side by side with wisdom or speculative knowledge (*sophia*), Aristotle gives an important place to prudence (*phronēsis*)—henceforth a thoroughly practical wisdom.

These modulations, deviations, and shifts make for the originality of Aristotle's thought. They are all the more apparent when we turn to the sphere in which Plato had most unmistakably turned his back on reality—that of politics. Of his works for the general public, Aristotle had devoted several to this sphere. These included a treatise in two books called the *Statesman* (*Politicus*), one "On Justice" and one "On Kingship." Today we have only the *Politics* (in eight books). But the contrast between Aristotle's and Plato's ways of approaching political philosophy will be obvious if we recall that Aristotle had collected, or had had his students collect, an enormous amount of preliminary documentation, including various "Constitutions," "Barbarian Customs," "Tables of the Laws of Solon," and more. In order to speak about politics he brought together a mass of information that was both precise and diversified. Here again, the way of proceeding is characteristic.

These various collections have been lost. In 1891, however, the Aristotelian *Constitution of Athens* was found on papyrus. The work is far from flawless; but with its two parts, historical and descriptive, it forms a striking contrast to the other *Constitutions* we have (those of Xenophon, for example, or of the pseudo-Xenophon). It is more technical, pays more attention to institutions, and does a better job of combining history and theory. This little work is a source we must use with care, but on some points it is irreplaceable. When we think of the number of such documents Aristotle collected, we can see here too how his very method should have led him to undertake, in the *Politics*, a thorough revision of Plato.

Book 1 of the *Politics* shows the least divergence from Plato, for it deals in the abstract with the definition of the state and with its formation. Aristotle does not break with his own time here, insofar as he sanctions slavery; indeed, this is one of the few ancient texts that take the trouble to justify a usage that was generally taken for granted. What is most Aristotelian about book 1 is the way the existence of states is given as natural: the city-state is an extension of simpler groupings (couple, family, village); it corresponds to a properly human tendency, for man is a "political animal" (1.2.1253a), i.e., a being naturally inclined to live in the communal setting of a city or *polis*. In book 1, then, we may recognize not only Aristotle's penchant for classification but his respect for the affective element in man and his sense of the bonds society creates.

Book 2 is a critique of philosophical systems that propose an ideal form of government—beginning with that of Plato. Aristotle vehemently opposes the idea of the common possession of goods or of women and children. Indeed, he rejects the notion that a city might be founded on the similarity of all men; in his eyes, a city is made up of diverse elements and must be dealt with as such. If private ties were abolished, moreover, the result would be not a true solidarity but a general indifference. For Aristotle, ownership and affection are lively and powerful feelings, which the city needs and should make use of. We recognize the familiar contrast between the two philosophers; but here it has taken the form of a frank and acknowledged opposition. Aristotle's realism cannot brook the extreme and theoretical nature of Plato's constructs.

In book 3 we come to a classification of the different forms of government. It differs little from the traditional classification, and the principle of distinguishing between healthy and corrupt regimes had already made its appearance in Plato. But Plato, though he had sketched out various modes of classification, was interested primarily in the progressive corruption of the sequence of regimes. Aristotle, on the other hand, was the first to propose a complete and clear classification, made up of six regimes: three healthy ones, distinguished by the number of rulers (monarchy, aristocracy, and *politeia* or "republic"), and an equal number of corrupt regimes corresponding to the first set, in which the rulers no longer have the common interest at heart (tyranny, oligarchy, democracy). Aristotle enlarges on and refines this scheme, for he admits the existence of mixtures and intermediate states, of which he saw many examples. In his discussions of the various regimes, Aristotle was likewise less concerned to propose an unattainable ideal than to define the dangers each regime must avoid and the best means of avoiding them. The means are examined separately in each case; Aristotle intends his assessment to be concrete and objective. Book V[5] even includes an examination of the

5. Cited by De Romilly as book 8. The books of the *Politics* have been numbered in several different ways; the passage concerned is in book 5 of most standard editions and English translations.

causes of revolutions in the different types of government; the result is a kind of sociology of power. Here Aristotle takes full account of institutions in their technical aspects. Thus he distinguishes three powers within the state (deliberative, executive, and judicial); thus again he contrasts laws with decrees, and gives careful accounts of the organization of power and the role of magistrates. This concern for technicality is the basis for political science in the modern sense of the term; and such are the criteria on which Aristotle bases his preferences and his advice.

In his very definition of the best form of government, we again encounter his own characteristic tendencies, quite different from Plato's. Politically, his praise of the *politeia* connects him with the tradition of moderate democracy (which he praises, incidentally, in the *Constitution of Athens*); Plato had none of this indulgence for democracy and recognized only its flaws. Philosophically, the *politeia* dovetails with Aristotle's taste for the mean, to which I have referred in my discussion of his ethics. To be sure, a good regime is defined in the first place by the rule of law and by concern for the common good. But the best way to institute and maintain such a regime is to devise a mixture. Aristotle's *politeia* is a mixture of aristocracy and democracy, a "mixed" constitution; the idea was to play an important role in later political thought. What is more, in Aristotle's view the best prop of a regime is the middle class, which has neither too much nor too little and is thus more reasonable and moderate: "Where the middle class is numerous, the fewest factions and disagreements arise among the citizens" (4.9.1296a).

Finally, though Aristotle, like Plato and all Greek thinkers, attaches great importance to education and to the laws, he links the importance of these elements to the role of habit. It is habit that makes for the force of law (2.9.1267a), and habit that presides over the education of the young (books 7–8); thus Aristotle's model city will take responsibility for the education of all, and will do so in the spirit of its own constitution. Where Plato built an ideal model, Aristotle tries to spell out the practical means of improving politics, by taking account of what is both reasonable and possible. To put it another way, he discusses ethics and politics in the capacity of an observer who seeks to account for everything. So it is not surprising that he should see ethics and politics as only two facets of an infinitely broader inquiry—one animated throughout by the same concern for objective analysis.

4 · OTHER FIELDS OF THOUGHT

Aristotle took an interest in everything, from the most abstract to the most concrete of disciplines.

Logic and dialectic.   Logic was for him the instrument (*organon*) of all intellectual work; he left a series of works that are the first attempts we have at systematic thought in this genre. They consist of the *Categories* (whose authenticity has been questioned, at least for some passages), the *Peri Hermēn-*

eias or *De Interpretatione* (also open to question), the *Prior Analytics*, the *Posterior Analytics*, and the eight books of the *Topics*; to these must be added the *Sophistical Refutations*, which point out the deceptive character of some arguments used by the Sophists. The most remarkable features of this group of works are Aristotle's analysis of the syllogism (in the *Prior Analytics*) and his theory of demonstration, or proof. All other branches of knowledge presuppose the application of these principles and procedures.

Physics.   Physics, as Aristotle understood the term, covered a much wider field than the physics we know. Its aim was to determine how and why things originate and change, take shape and alter their shape. Aristotle dealt with it in the eight books of the *Physics* (which first discuss basic principles and then movement), as well as in the short treatise *On Generation and Corruption*. To these we may add the *De Caelo* ("On the Heavens"), in four books; it opens with a discussion of the stars, but soon turns to a more general treatment of physical principles. The motion and orbits of the planets are obviously among the subjects with which physics deals, and Aristotle offers a theory about them: he posits a round and motionless earth in the center of the cosmos.

Metaphysics.   The very name of metaphysics comes from the collective title given to the treatises on being that came "after physics" in the corpus of Aristotle's work. These are the thirteen books of the *Metaphysics* (the appendix to book 1 is a later composition, and book 4 was placed where it is by the editors). In the work as a whole, the idea of movement predominates (in the beginning, the divinity was the sole "mover"). Of prime importance is the fact that Aristotle abandons the Platonic theory of Ideas and Plato's strict dualism; for him, the relationship between body and soul is the same as that between matter and form, or *eidos*. Matter takes on form by degrees, and there is a whole range of intermediate stages between raw matter and pure form. In the same way, form (*eidos*) is combined with matter, whereas the Platonic "Idea" was separate from it. It goes without saying that these doctrines are complicated wholes, incorporating technical discussions, and that their subtleties cannot be summarized in two or three sentences.

Things are simpler when we turn to the last two areas of Aristotle's interest: the sciences and literature.

The sciences.   Plato was an avid mathematician; Aristotle, whose taste was more concrete with respect to the sciences as well, specialized mainly in natural history and biology. But he also took an interest in all the curiosities of the physical world and the world of the senses. In natural history, as elsewhere, he looked for classifications. We have some examples of these in his treatises *On the Parts of Animals* (a textbook of comparative anatomy), *On the Generation of Animals*, and the long treatise called the *Zoology* (or *History of*

Animals, "history" here meaning no more than our "inquiry"), in ten books. With these I should mention the less important works *On the Gait of Animals* and *On the Movement of Animals*. In all, the amount of information contained in these books is considerable. Aristotle's students took part in the research; Theophrastus was one such participant. The *Parva Naturalia*, or "short treatises on natural history," tackle some of the curiosities of human biology (e.g., sense perception, sleep, dreams, longevity or brevity of life). In these works, metaphysical concerns are combined with the most meticulous observation. Other treatises examine curiosities of the physical world—the *Meteorology*, for example, which deals with the realm between moon and earth, or the piece *On the Nile Floods* (whose authenticity has been questioned). And this is without counting the works no longer considered Aristotle's but which at least testify to the interests of his school—e.g., the *Problemata*, the treatises *On Colors*, *On Plants*, and many others.

These works have obviously been superseded, and are more important as testimony to the development of scientific notions than as authoritative works; such is the law of scientific inquiry. This is not the case with Aristotle's works on literature.

Literature.   Plato banished the poets from his city, and either condemned rhetoric or equated it with dialectic and the search for truth. Aristotle, by contrast, wrote works on both *Poetics* and *Rhetoric*.

The *Poetics* has been one of the most influential of his works. It originally consisted of two books; only the first (on epic and tragedy) survives. A further token of Aristotle's interest in literature was his published treatise *On the Poets*, which, like all the published works, has been lost. The same interest produced the *Homeric Problems*. And among the works of documentation he supervised was the *Didascaliae*, an account of the dramatic contests including the names of prize-winning works and the circumstances in which the plays were produced. Here again, his research was carried out on a wide scale.

The *Poetics* includes many valuable definitions, which are the starting-point for the vocabulary of literary criticism; it also includes classifications indicating the relations between the different genres (epic, tragedy, and comedy). One of the most famous of these analyses is that assigning to tragedy the aim of producing pity and fear. Beginning with this observation, Aristotle was led to defend the tragic emotion in terms that have elicited much comment. Plato had considered that emotion pernicious; it fostered feelings one should sooner learn to check. Aristotle's reply is that tragedy, by eliciting pity and fear, effects a "purging" (*katharsis*) of these emotions (1449b). The word is apparently to be taken in a sense more medical than moral. Indeed, it is based on a more complex psychology than that which Plato took as his starting point: it implies that, by permitting oneself these feelings in imaginary cases, far from fostering them in real life one is freed of them. The quarrel with Plato could not be clearer.

It must be admitted that the author of the *Poetics* sometimes surprises us with his judgments. His analyses are of a technical nature and essentially deal with the handling of the plot (reversals, recognitions, etc.), which seems to leave Aeschylus out of account. In the sphere of psychology, Aristotle emphasizes coherence and plausibility—and is thus led to censure the sudden reversals sometimes staged by Euripides (in *Iphigenia in Aulis*, for example).

Such choices stem from Aristotle's effort to deduce *rules*. Many of those that guided dramaturgy for centuries come from him (e.g., the rules of plausibility and unity of action). Aristotle's rules do not form as imperious a code as that which ruled French drama of the seventeenth century; but the latter owes a great deal to them, as do all subsequent works on poetics.

The *Rhetoric* enjoyed a parallel and comparable influence: it did for oratory what the *Poetics* had done for tragedy. The question of the value of rhetoric was an important one. The censure of Plato (who contrasted it with philosophy) and the spread of Isocrates' teaching (which identified it with philosophy) required Aristotle to take a stand. Characteristically, he acknowledged that rhetoric had its place and proceeded to define its rules, some of them entirely practical; but he also analyzed the difference between it and dialectic so far as reasoned argument was concerned. He took a lifelong interest in the subject. He published a treatise called the *Gryllus, or On Rhetoric*; he also gathered vast documentation, for his lost works included a *Collection of Rhetorical Handbooks*. This is undoubtedly how a treatise called the *Rhetorica ad Alexandrum* came to be grouped with his works; it was apparently written by Anaximenes of Lampsacus, one of Isocrates' pupils, and consists of practical advice.

Aristotle's method is different and more far-reaching. In book 1 of the *Rhetoric*, after defining rhetoric in relation to dialectic, he goes on to classify (as we might expect!) the various genres of oratory—deliberative, forensic, and epideictic—and to identify the subject matter and aims of each. Book 2 is devoted to the passions and emotions on which speeches play, which the orator must know (anger, friendship, fear, shame, the willingness to oblige, pity, indignation, etc.). Then Aristotle considers once again the form of reasoning proper to rhetoric—not the strict syllogism of science or dialectic but a reasoning that merely aims at acceptable probabilities. Aristotle calls it the enthymeme. He classifies its different forms before moving on to the *topoi*, or general lines of argument, and finally, in book 3, to composition and style.

It should be clear that in its precision the *Rhetoric*, like so many of Aristotle's works, provides a vocabulary for inquiry of a technical order. In particular, it bridges the gap between ordinary practical advice and research into logical problems. As always, Aristotle sought to uncover the mainsprings of an intellectual activity rather than to defend or attack the activity itself; and he broached this passionately debated question with the lucid calm of a scientist.

In sum, then, there is something encyclopedic about his work, which helps to explain the considerable influence he has enjoyed. After him we will not find this conjunction of all the disciplines; instead there will be specialists—scientists, philosophers, literary critics. The diversity of his interests highlights still further the fact that a single cast of mind can so easily be recognized in each of his undertakings. The desire to classify, to monitor, to "place," and to formulate in terms of philosophical or epistemological issues everything that has a bearing on man and the world—this is the point of departure for Aristotle's eminently personal enterprise.

In Plato and Aristotle we thus have the maturation and supreme achievement of two different forms of philosophy, one oriented toward inner meditation and exalting the care of the soul, the other oriented toward a reasoned and descriptive ordering of things in the world. The complementarity is all the more striking when we recall that one of these men was the other's student.

9

The Hellenistic Age

We call "Hellenistic" the age that began with the death of Alexander in 323 and lasted until the beginnings of the Roman Empire. The name was designed to evoke the diffusion of Hellenism into non-Greek countries and the exchanges that resulted. From the perspective of literary history, we see in this period a movement counter to the one that in the fifth and fourth centuries had drawn everything toward Athens. Menander was an Athenian, but his plays, unlike those of the dramatists discussed above, were not intended for Athenian festivals only. Soon the prestige of Alexandria eclipsed that of Athens: Theocritus was a Sicilian who lived in Alexandria; Callimachus was from Cyrene and also lived in Alexandria, where, under Ptolemy II Philadelphus, he did important work at the great library. Polybius, still later, was from the Peloponnese but was brought forcibly to Rome, where he stayed for many years.

In the Hellenistic world—a world no longer bounded by the city and one in which city-states in general played an ever-diminishing role—literature became more independent of politics. New Comedy took no political stance, and rarely contained topical allusions; neither Theocritus nor Callimachus wrote political poetry; the philosophers were in search of an ethic for the individual, and said of the wise man that he "had no homeland." It would take the interest of the historian and, above all, the growth of a powerful new political entity—soon making itself felt even in Greece—to bring back, with Polybius, the old concern for the problems of states in general.

I · MENANDER

The beginning of Menander's career coincides exactly with the beginning of the Hellenistic age. Born in 342–41, he staged his first play (the *Orgē*) in 321, two years after Alexander's death; he seems to have lived until 293. In his youth he knew the young Epicurus, and attended Aristotle's school, where he made the acquaintance of Theophrastus. So he is a good representative of the spirit of the new schools. He was apparently invited to Egypt and to Macedonia, but remained in Athens. The invitations are a sign of the times, while his refusal keeps him within the Athenian tradition.

Until the beginning of the twentieth century we had only uncertain and in-direct knowledge of Menander. There were fragments of his work quoted by other authors, as well as Latin imitations (those of Terence—*The Andrian Woman, Heautontimorumenos, The Eunuch,* and *The Brothers*—are quite faithful, and those of Plautus more freely adapted); there were also com-ments and words of praise from ancient authors. Then the papyrologists be-gan to restore Menander to us. A first series of important finds occurred in 1905. But the major discovery was that of an entire play, the *Dyskolos* (= "The Misanthrope"), published in 1959 by Victor Martin. From then on, editions and commentaries multiplied; *The Samian Woman* and *The Shield* were recovered. Other finds followed: four years after the *Dyskolos*, long passages of *The Sicyonian* were published in Paris by A. Blanchard and A. Bataille; then fragments of the *Misoumenos* were published in England by E. G. Turner. We can probably expect more good surprises from this quar-ter: Menander's very popularity accounts for his presence amid the "scrap paper" that found its way into the Egyptian tombs. And we are told that Menander wrote 108 comedies.

Some of these comedies today are scarcely more than titles. Excluding the *Dyskolos*, those of which we have the best idea are the *Epitrepontes* ("The Arbitrators"), *Perikeiromenē* ("The Shorn Girl"), and *Samia* (*The Samian Woman*); we have between 300 and 600 lines from each of these plays. Taken together with other fragments and summaries, this material allows us to vi-sualize Menander's dramatic art and reassures us that the qualities observ-able in the *Dyskolos* were not unique to that play.

1 · ACTION IN MENANDER

A comedy by Menander is quite unlike the plays of the Old Comedy. The imaginative freedom is gone, as are the fixed structures within each play (*parabasis, agōn,* etc.). The chorus has lost its role altogether and is reduced to providing musical interludes dividing the play into acts, or into parts that henceforth deserve that name. Each comedy includes a prologue, in the form of a long monologue (in the *Dyskolos*, it is spoken by the god Pan); this monologue, like those of Euripides, explains the sometimes complex circum-stances of the action, which then unfolds from act to act. Clearly plot has be-come an essential element, as in the last tragedies of Euripides.

To some extent, the plots reflect the troubled times in which Menander lived: they constantly involve unidentified children, some born in the ab-sence of a father who is on a distant voyage, some kidnaped, some aban-doned and raised by the chance comer. But to Menander these upheavals merely furnish pretexts for misunderstandings he can ravel and unravel. On this basis he puts together the most complicated plots one could wish; and, like Euripides, he loves the theatrical effects of last-minute recognitions. His frequent use of courtesans complicates matters further by adding jealousy to the pot, so that his imbroglios have still greater repercussions.

In *The Arbitrators* a young couple is separated because the wife has borne a child shortly after the wedding; the young husband is indignant, but he had raped his wife during a festival before the wedding, without knowing who she was. A harp girl he takes up with out of spite then complicates things by posing as the mother of the child. To make a long story short, there is a fine string of misunderstandings before the happy reconciliation.

In *The Shorn Girl*, a pair of abandoned twins have been entrusted to two different families. One day the brother (who has been brought up a free and rich man, and knows nothing of his past) kisses his sister (who knows everything); her hair is cut by the man she lives with, who is furiously jealous. In the end this man marries her, in an atmosphere of euphoria regained.

In *The Samian Woman*, a child is again at issue, this one born while the master of the house is away and replaced by another. All kinds of suspicions result: the master suspects his own son of having cuckolded him with the Samian woman. In fact, one child has died, and the survivor, whom the Samian has passed off as her own, is the child of the son and—the very woman who is chosen to be his wife!

Chance, or *Tuchē*, plays a major part in all of this, and Menander does not fail to point to its omnipotence, blindness, and malice (his friend Demetrius of Phalerum also had thoughts on the subject). Yet the author's artistry plays an even greater role, and the constant play of misunderstandings offers him a comic device that quickly becomes conventional. It would be so, at any rate, were it not for the diversity and subtlety of his characterization; in some cases, characterization even supplies the subject of the play, as in the *Dyskolos*.

2 · CHARACTERS IN MENANDER'S COMEDIES

The *Dyskolos* (a fairly early comedy for Menander, dating from 316) is from beginning to end a burlesque of a cantankerous and misanthropic personality. Cnemon, a grumpy old man, has taken an aversion to his fellow men and decided to flee their company; he bullies all who approach him. This is particularly trying to Sostratus, who is in love with Cnemon's daughter. The turning point comes when Cnemon, while trying to recover a bucket and spade from the bottom of a well, falls in himself—and cannot do without the help of others for a change! As it happens, he is fished out by his stepson and Sostratus, after which he is all agreement on the subject of marriages. His personality does not change, but he at least admits his error: "I wouldn't have believed that in all the world there was a single creature capable of acting disinterestedly, out of sympathy for his neighbor."

The portrait of the "atrabilious" man is thus the very subject of the comedy. Nor can we doubt that this attempt to describe and delimit human types was characteristic of Menander. He was a friend of Theophrastus, author of the *Characters*; and we may note that some of the titles of Menander's lost plays correspond to characters in Theophrastus (*The Rustic, The Supersti-*

tious Man, The Flatterer). Menander also bequeathed to world drama a certain number of "types," or typical characters, who were part of the society of his day and who, thanks to him, have become classic: the lover, the soldier, the sponger, the cook—and above all the slave (often named Daos), that bold and ingenious slave who lectures his young masters, comes up with expedients, and pulls the strings of the plot, all without losing a very realistic sense of where his own advantage lies. Molière's valets, twenty centuries later, are modeled on Menander's slaves.

Yet the existence of these typical, recognizable characters in no way excludes variety or subtle psychological nuances; far from it. No old man, young lover, or slave is ever exactly like another. At the same time, the vicissitudes of the plot produce bursts of feeling, which are portrayed even as they arise. Politics has disappeared in the comedies of Menander; but it has been replaced by psychology. Like the tragedies of Euripides, Menander's plays are rich in monologues. Some are funny, like that of the lover in the *Dyskolos* who, having disguised himself as a farm worker, returns from the fields dog-tired, regretting his premature zeal, and yet comes back for more: "Why? I can't say, no, by the gods!" (line 544). Others are touching, like the remorseful speech of the young husband in *The Arbitrators*, who learns that his wife, whom he has accused unjustly, is faithful to him after all.

One trait characterizes Menander's world as a whole: it is a civilized and affectionate world. The misanthrope of the *Dyskolos* is something of an exception to the rule, but this is precisely because the play is intended to criticize his failing; and though his language is bitter, it is far from offensive. Likewise, Menander's slaves can be insolent and waggish, but they are no longer a pretext for the obscene jokes of which Aristophanes was so fond. Graciousness and basic courtesy almost always prevail among Menander's characters, just as a supple discretion prevails in his style. These traits faithfully reflect his ideal of human behavior.

3 · HUMANITY IN MENANDER

The *Dyskolos* is a case in point: those who lack a sense of human solidarity owe it to themselves to acquire one. Men need one another, and the most admirable human quality is precisely that proper to man, "humanity." Cnemon lacks it, and is described as "a man with too little humanity" (*anthrōpos apanthrōpos*, line 6). By contrast, the man who lives up to the human ideal touches us; as a famous fragment puts it, "What a charming creature is man, when he is a man!" (frag. 484 Koerte). A number of other aphoristic lines illustrate the reciprocal ties this virtue weaves among men: "No one is a stranger to me if he is virtuous" (frag. 475 Koerte); "That's what it is to live: not to live for oneself alone" (frag. 646 Koerte). Finally, there can be no doubt that Terence is translating or adapting Menander when he says, in the *Heautontimorumenos*, "I am a man, and nothing human is alien to me."

This sense of fraternity among men suits the new age, in which man's horizon is no longer bounded by the city-state; it reflects the cosmopolitanism of the philosophers who were Menander's contemporaries. But such a feeling had been expressed earlier by Aristotle; and his school may well have been the source of Menander's ideal, insofar as he recommends making a practice of mildness and tolerance. For these are the new virtues of this new world: *The Arbitrators* is an attack on impetuous anger and an example of forgiveness, understanding, and reconciliation. So is *The Shorn Girl*. The plays of Menander are constantly presenting us with family attachments, marks of affection, friendships. There is even a kind of affectionate familiarity toward slaves; and even harp girls and courtesans show signs of delicacy. The tact and grace of Menander's art are tailored to this new ideal of human relationships. The civic spirit of earlier centuries has yielded its sway to a more flexible private life, in which affection comes into its own.

These traits surely account for the considerable popularity Menander's work enjoyed; the copies found in Egypt, the statue carved by Praxiteles' sons, the Latin imitations by Plautus and Terence, and Plutarch's commentaries all testify to his popularity, which was long-lived. Archaeologists have recently uncovered a whole series of mosaics in Mytilene that are illustrations of Menander's comedies; they date from around 300 and help us to picture the way the plays would have been staged at that time.

4 · OTHER WRITERS OF NEW COMEDY

For us, Menander has eclipsed all the other writers of New Comedy—some of whom, it must be said, often bested him in the dramatic competitions during his lifetime. Philemon is the best known of these. Syracusan by birth and Athenian by adoption, he spent some time at the Egyptian court. He lived from 361 to 262. Diphilus also enjoyed great fame. Apollodorus of Carystus modeled his work closely on Menander's. All three wrote comedies that were imitated by Plautus or Terence. Their works, of which we have only slim fragments, subscribed to the same esthetic as that reflected in Menander's— the only difference being that the first two also wrote comedies on mythological subjects, as had the poets of the preceding generation; it is characteristic of Menander that he should have avoided these.

II · THE PHILOSOPHIC SCHOOLS

Philosophy, which had reached the height of its glory at Athens, in the work of Plato and Aristotle, continued to be centered in Athens, and the various schools took their names from the places they occupied in that city. The Platonic school continued to be known as the Academy, after the gardens of the hero Academus; Aristotle's followers were the Peripatetics, or "Walkers," of the Lyceum (a covered walk in Athens); the Cynics, followers of the Socratic philosopher Antisthenes, apparently got their name from the gymnasium of Cynosarges, where Antisthenes taught. Soon there appeared the two great schools that were to follow; and if the Epicureans were named after their teacher (though the "Garden" was known as their meeting place), the Stoics were named for the "Porch" or portico (*stoa* in Greek).

Yet in the Hellenistic period most of these philosphers were no longer native Athenians; Aristotle himself was not. They came from the most diverse places, and many were former slaves. It should not surprise us that the systems of thought they developed were centered less and less on the city and the collectivity while becoming increasingly concerned with individual autonomy. At the same time a cosmopolitanism was arising that suited the new political conditions. It is characteristic of these troubled times that the various philosophic systems sought less to pursue the notion of an ideal world than to define a way for the individual to escape external upheavals through inner tranquillity. This was true of the older schools—the Academy, the Peripatetics, and the Cynics—and still more so of the newer ones—the Skeptics, the Stoics, and the Epicureans—which tended to eclipse the former group.

Yet at the beginning of the Hellenistic period Aristotle's school had several brilliant representatives. Theophrastus, who came from Lesbos, was Aristotle's first successor; and while he is best known for the *Characters*, this short, moralizing work was only a very small part of his output. Like his teacher, he studied metaphysics, physics, natural history, rhetoric, and poetry. We still possess two of his treatises on botany. His broad interests were characteristic of the school (Clearchus excepted), and Theophrastus cultivated them so well that he died a famous man.[1] He was succeeded as director of the school by Straton of Lampsacus, and then by others who are less well known. But already in Theophrastus's time we can observe the Peripatetics' taste (which they never lost) for the various aspects of concrete reality. Aristoxenus of Tarentum, another pupil of Aristotle's who likewise produced a vast body of work, distinguished himself in the field of music theory; his study of both harmony and rhythm led him to take an interest in the Pythagorean tradition. He also wrote biography, a genre that was then relatively new. As for Dicaearchus, another pupil of Aristotle's, his chief interests were history and geography (one of his works was a book on *Life in Greece*). It is not surprising, then, to see the Peripatetic school maintain ties with political life. Demetrius of Phalerum, who governed Athens for a time,[2] had been a student of Theophrastus (and had himself written on politics); and Straton of Lampsacus, Theophrastus's successor as head of the Lyceum, was brought to Alexandria by Ptolemy to serve as a tutor.

Meanwhile, the Academy was carrying on the Platonic, and even the Socratic, tradition. It did so rather timidly until the advent of Arcesilaus of Pi-

1. According to Diogenes Laertius (5.41), the whole city of Athens turned out for his funeral. —Trans.

2. In the capacity of *epimeletēs*, or governor, under the Macedonian king Cassander.— Trans.

tane, who became the school's director in 268 and who emphasized the imperfections of sense perception as a source of knowledge. But it was only much later that the school regained some of its authority, thanks to men who taught in Rome in Cicero's day—men like Philo of Larissa and Antiochus of Ascalon, who brought a considerable eclecticism to the Platonic tradition.

The school of the Cynics had an influence of a different order, a matter more of tone and mode of expression than of content. To this school we owe the diatribe, a work of propaganda combining satire and polemic. The first Cynics were Diogenes (a man from Sinope who was to win lasting fame for his rejection of all conventions and comforts alike) and his pupil Crates. Their successors, Bion (a freedman from the Pontus), Teles, Menippus (a former slave from Syria), and others, wrote violent satires in the tradition of Hipponax, and thus had a definite influence on Roman satire: *Menippean Satires*, the title of a work by Varro, recalls the name of Menippus.[3] From a philosophical perspective, their demanding moral stance and rejection of convention found at least some echo in the greatest school of the Hellenistic period, that of the Stoics.

The work of the Old Stoa begins with Zeno and continues with Cleanthes and Chrysippus. Zeno was from Citium (a Phoenician settlement in Cyprus); he should not be confused with Zeno of Elea, who lived at the beginning of the fifth century. Zeno the Stoic seems to have lived from 333 to 262 (give or take a few years; the evidence is elusive, especially for his date of birth). He came to Athens as a young man and was at first a student of the Cynic Crates. In 301 he began his own teaching, for which he accepted no payment. He apparently wrote a great deal, but his work is lost. Cleanthes of Assus (in Asia Minor) arrived in Athens around 282, a robust and poor man. He was a faithful successor to Zeno. We have his *Hymn to Zeus*, a work of rare nobility. After a series of internal clashes, the leadership of the school passed to Chrysippus, a native of Cilicia, who lived until the end of the third century (he died between 208 and 204). He had been trained in the Platonic school, and came away with useful experience in dialectic, which he turned against his former teachers. He wrote much, like Zeno—in fact, even more than Zeno; almost nothing has survived. We know he took an interest in logic, sense perception, the emotions, providence, and fate. He gave Stoicism its clarity as a system—whence the saying, "Without Chrysippus, there would have been no Stoa."

The history of Stoicism does not end with Chrysippus; but in virtue of his formative role I may here characterize its spirit, which was well established from his day on. To characterize its spirit is not of course to analyze its system, which is based on a logic and a description of the universe not easily penetrated by the layman. The essential facts are that the Stoic universe is one, and that there reigns in it a Logos emanating from God and ruling over

3. Works of prose satire in English (those of Jonathan Swift, for example) and in other modern languages are sometimes assigned to the genre of "Menippean satire."—Trans.

all of nature. The necessity that dominates the world and expresses its structure is both fate and providence at once. Wisdom, then, is to use one's mind to perceive this order of nature, and to live in accordance with it. Indeed, in Stoicism there is no longer a contrast between nature and reason; the two coincide.

The Stoics distinguish among things that are good, bad, and "indifferent," relegating to the last category health and sickness, beauty, wealth, shame, and poverty; their value depends on the use one makes of them, which should be guided by reason. Passion is an unreasonable impulse, a sickness of the soul, caused by error. One must act so as never to let oneself be troubled by passion. The wise man attains this goal. He alone has all the virtues; he alone is truly free. He knows how to distinguish between what depends on him and what does not. He waits for death with an untroubled heart. He escapes the tyranny of the passions and the vicissitudes of fate alike. It goes without saying that such a man's horizon is not bounded by his native land. He acts in conformity with the order of the world, but he is also a "citizen of the world." Naturally, the general run of mankind can only begin to approach this somewhat inhuman ideal, by showing prudence and by choosing "appropriate" conduct.

By the sheer force of its ethical demands, this philosophy soon spread to the four corners of the world—to Babylon, to Alexandria, and then to Rome. It was in Rome that it enjoyed a second flowering (the Middle Stoa) with Panaetius (185–112) and Posidonius (135–51), before culminating in the Stoicism of the imperial age, exemplified by Seneca, Epictetus, and Marcus Aurelius.

Panaetius was born in Rhodes and studied philosophy in Athens, but went at an early age to Rome, where he made friends with Scipio Aemilianus and many other Romans. He was primarily a moralist, and had emulators who wrote in Latin; in the De Officiis, Cicero acknowledges himself one of these. Posidonius came from Apamea, in Syria, and was the student of Panaetius; he founded a school in Rhodes. But he stayed in contact with Rome. Pompey was among his friends, as was Cicero, who sought him out in Rhodes. We find his influence in many fields, for in addition to his ethical works and studies of the gods (used by Cicero) he produced geographical and historical works (cf. chap. 10, sec. II, below). It was through the intermediary of these two men, natives of Rhodes and Syria, that the legacy of Greek philosophy penetrated Roman thought and provided it with its fundamental ethical principles. And through their agency, by imperceptible stages, that legacy survived into the Renaissance and even into our own times. Many of the names I mention here are little known to the general public; but it is thanks to such men that the word "stoic" has entered our modern language.

The same is true of the word "epicurean," which has acquired a meaning almost opposite to "stoic" and rather different from what the doctrine itself implied. Epicurus was from Samos but was an Athenian citizen. Born in 341, like Menander, he came at an early age to Athens, traveled a good deal, and then returned to settle in Athens, where he opened his school in 306. From there his philosophy spread throughout the Mediterranean; he died at the height of fame in 270. His teaching, in other words, was contemporary to that of Zeno (give or take a few years). His work is scarcely better preserved than his rival's. We know that he had irresistible charm as a teacher, and that he wrote treatises of all kinds—on nature, on the highest good, and on justice, among other subjects. All these are lost; and the three letters preserved by Diogenes Laertius are to be used with caution. Epicurus also published selected quotations and maxims, some of which have come down to us. These scraps would be little indeed if we did not have the testimony of several followers and continuators. Some charred papyri from Herculaneum, for example, have yielded texts by Philodemus of Gadara (second half of the first century B.C.) including summaries and quotations from Epicurus. An inscription from the vicinity of Lycia has likewise revealed the great principles that the Epicurean Diogenes of Oenoanda wanted to bequeath to his fellow citizens (A.D. 200). Of course, all such evidence taken together is not worth the testimony of the Latin poet Lucretius (first half of the first century B.C.).

The foundation for Epicurean doctrine was the atomism of Democritus— revised, either by Epicurus or by one of his disciples, to include the notion of the *clinamen*, which causes atoms to "swerve," bringing them into contact with one another. This world is the opposite of the Stoics' world: in it, chance alone rules over matter; it obeys neither providence nor reason. Epicureanism is also contrary to Platonism, for it is a form of materialism and precludes the notion of an immortal soul. But these very qualities were meant to allow men to dismiss their fear of the "beyond" and to ensure their serenity (*ataraxia*). Epicurus's chief aim, in fact, was to tear man away from his irrational fears and teach him to win peace. Such a process requires effort. In this perspective we can understand how, on the basis of diametrically opposed visions of the world, Epicureanism and Stoicism could arrive at ethical beliefs that are similar in some ways. For the serenity that is Epicurus's goal implies—as in Stoicism, though for different reasons—a mastery over the desires and passions. Pleasure is indeed the criterion of happiness; but this pleasure has little to do with the disorderly pleasures of the senses. The Epicurean rids himself of love, which ought not trouble man; he avoids political life; he prefers to concentrate on the gentle joys of friendship (we know that Epicurus himself maintained a model friendship—almost a legendary one— with his disciple Metrodorus). In sum, then, "God is not to be feared, death is nothing to us,[4] the good is easy to obtain and suffering easy to endure" (Usener ed., p. 69). For Epicurus, as for the Stoics, the wise man is free and sufficient unto himself.

---

4. Literally, "nothing we can *feel*." Some of these maxims are also to be found in book 10 of Diogenes Laertius (see, e.g., chaps. 124–25, 133, and 139).—Trans.

To be sure, a relative indifference to society's rules regarding pleasure and decency could leave an impression of the Epicurean that was sometimes prejudicial; and the acceptance of pleasure as an axiom (which recalls Aristippus) could also lend itself to misapprehension or broad interpretation. But in its fundamental principles, Epicureanism demanded self-mastery and firmness to a greater degree than most outsiders were willing to believe.

Nor should misapprehensions like this surprise us. The schools I have described were forever at odds with one another. Epicureanism clashed with Platonism (as we can see in the case of the Epicurean Colotes, whom Plutarch attacked); it also clashed with Stoicism. The schools were close competitors; we even hear of an Athenian embassy to Rome in 156 that included the head of the Academy (Carneades), a Peripatetic, and a Stoic. For that matter, Carneades had moved so far from Plato's own position that he created a scandal by denying the importance of justice.

The Skeptics did not wait until things had gone this far to poke fun at the spate of quarrels and doctrines: Pyrrho was already making a name for himself when Aristotle died; not long afterward, his follower Timon of Phlius made an easy target of the philosophers' "battle royal" in his *Silloi*. In the Skeptics' view, it made more sense to suspend judgment, limit oneself to the evidence of the senses, and observe moderation in one's views. This empiricism was to lead to the true skepticism of the imperial age—that of Sextus Empiricus.

In the meantime, the rival schools may also have profited by the bracing influence of competition. However that may be, the Greece of the Hellenistic age bequeathed to Rome a living heritage of doctrines and aspirations; no other aspect of Greek culture was to be as successful in adapting to, and developing within, the Roman milieu.

There were only a few new contributions to Hellenistic philosophy from outside these major systems, i.e., from outside the Athenian tradition. Of these I must first mention, for the record, some pseudo-Pythagorean writings whose date and authorship have been much debated, but which may go back to the third or second century. This literature—most of it now lost—was of a scientific cast and invoked the Pythagorean tradition.

The most interesting contributions, however, were to come from the Jews. Alexandria was the obvious point of contact between the two cultures, for many Jews lived there. For their use, the Hebrew scriptures were translated into Greek by the "Seventy" (whence the name, Septuagint, by which the translation is known).[5] A short treatise has survived which celebrates the appearance of this translation: the *Letter of Aristeas to Philocrates*, almost certainly written toward the end of the second century. It describes how Ptol-

---

5. According to legend, Ptolemy Philadelphus commissioned seventy-two Jewish scholars from Palestine to produce a translation of their Law for the library at Alexandria. A more fabulous version has it that they produced individual translations which miraculously proved identical.—Trans.

emy welcomed the translators and offers, à propos of this event, a real dialogue on the subject of the good king. From then on, texts written in Greek were added to the Bible: cultural exchange had become a reality.

At the very end of the Hellenistic period, or rather under the empire, the philosopher Philo, known as Philo Judaeus or Philo of Alexandria, became a living example of this dual cultural allegiance. We know when he lived thanks to an embassy he undertook to Rome in A.D. 39. His Greek learning was genuine and unaffected; he wrote very good Greek; and he was imbued with Greek philosophy—his religious beliefs were influenced by Platonism. Yet all his works are devoted to the presentation, defense, and interpretation of the Jewish faith. Thus it happens that we have many treatises of his (over thirty) whose tenor is very Greek but whose religious content is genuinely biblical. Among them are *On the Creation of the World*, *On Abraham*, and *On the Sacrifices of Cain and Abel*. Sometimes Philo uses the allegorical method—a Greek method—in his interpretation of the Bible. With exegesis properly speaking (of a narrowly technical kind at that) he combines the apologist's concern to reach a wide public (as in the *Life of Moses*).

Such an orientation is characteristic of Alexandria, which was long to foster religious aspirations of all sorts while the great rationalistic systems of traditional paganism were being developed at Rome.

III · ALEXANDRIAN POETRY

Athens remained the city where comedy flourished and philosophers gathered; but poetry followed the trend that was bringing about the creation of new cultural centers. Thus the new center for poetry was Alexandria and the court of the Ptolemies. This court encouraged intellectual activity. Soon Alexandria had a Museum (for the research and scholarly exchanges fostered by the Muses), an observatory, a botanical garden, and, most important, a library—even two. The Attalids likewise founded a library in Pergamum, and the two dynasties competed with one another in the acquisiton of texts. The story goes that every ship to arrive in Egypt had to hand over its books. We hear of purchases, and of "loans" that were never returned. The goal, according to one text, was to gather "all the books ever published in the world." Once collected, these had to be restored, copied, and catalogued. Famous scholars—true philologists[6]—presided over this work. Zenodotus was the first; then came the poet Apollonius of Rhodes and the historian and geographer Eratosthenes (who measured the circumference of the earth);[7] their successors included Aristophanes of Byzantium and finally Aristarchus, whose name become synonymous with scholarly criticism. It was these scholars who, using critical methods, edited and established the texts of the Greek poets: Zenodotus and Aristarchus were the great editors of Homer, and Aris-

6. The root meaning of "philologist" is "lover of words" or "lover of learning."—Trans.

7. See below, sec. VII(1). We cannot say how accurate his result was because we are unsure about his unit of measure.—Trans.

tophanes of Byzantium edited the lyric and tragic poets, among others. The Alexandrians were also interested in grammar; the city saw the birth of countless treatises and commentaries, culminating in the vast work of Didymus on the subject. In sum, until the middle of the second century—when the Ptolemies became at once less hospitable and less powerful—Alexandria was a cultural center of incredible vigor.

In such an atmosphere it was natural that poetry should hold a place of honor; but poetry also took on a new quality: it became the work of scholars, sophisticates, men of letters. Callimachus and Apollonius of Rhodes both lived at Alexandria in the first half of the third century, and both worked at the library. Theocritus came to the city during the same period, as did the scholarly poet Lycophron. This properly Alexandrian vein found its chief exponent in Callimachus.

1 · CALLIMACHUS AND APOLLONIUS OF RHODES: THE SCHOLARLY SCHOOL

Callimachus was born shortly before the turn of the third century into a noble family of Cyrene, a Greek colony on the Libyan coast. In Alexandria, he was at first a simple schoolmaster; but before long he was entrusted with an important cataloguing job at the library. He drew up the lists (*Pinakes*, or "Tables") of authors and works, in 120 volumes. The criticisms on points of detail that Aristarchus and others made of these lists are trivial, and demonstrate the rigorous standards of these scholarly circles.

But Callimachus was not only a scholar; he was a poet, and his poetic oeuvre (composed between 280 and 240, approximately) was sizable. We are told that he produced 800 volumes—and what is left of all these works will fill only one. But thanks to various finds on papyrus and wooden tablets, and to summaries likewise found on papyrus in 1934, we can form a fairly clear idea of his work and talents. He was a scholarly poet, varying meter and dialect to suit the genre in which he was writing, scrupulous in his prosody, and interested in the whole ancient heritage of myth and ritual, which he loved to explicate and mine for congenial images. He was also a court poet, readily mingling praises of the royal family with his evocations of ancient legend. The best preserved of his works are the *Hymns* and the *Aitia* ("Origins").

In their external form, the *Hymns* remind us of the Homeric Hymns. Through the manuscript tradition, six hymns have come down to us (one each to Zeus, Apollo, Artemis, and Demeter; one on Delos; and one on the bath of Pallas). Only that on the bath of Pallas is in elegiac meter. The dates and tones are quite diverse. But whatever the differences among them, all are far removed in inspiration from the older hymns, whose simple faith they no longer share. Instead, they offer a series of anecdotes or genre scenes, sometimes spiced with humor and always graceful. The author's taste for curious details of cult is evident at every turn.

In this last respect the *Hymns* resemble the *Aitia,* a long poem in four books, written in elegiac meter. Here the poet, dreaming, questions the Muses about heroes and gods. The opening—the meeting with the Muses on Mount Helicon—is obviously based on Hesiod; but in Callimachus the Muses' revelations take on a familiar and entertaining cast. The great subjects of the classical age are avoided, while the poet concentrates instead on a series of anecdotal details that seem almost to belong to the province of folklore. Some examples from book 1: Why, in Paros, do men offer sacrifice to the Graces without flute music and without garlands? In memory of an episode from the life of Minos. How are we to interpret sacrifices that include curses? These recall an episode from the story of the Argonauts. In every case, what we have here are local curiosities and little-known legends; one of the rare fragments to have survived is a pretty tale of love (Acontius and Cydippe), which Ovid later retold. It hardly seems necessary to seek a single theme running like a guiding thread through the whole work; instead, variety is the rule. For that matter, Callimachus always refused to work on the grand scale. He preferred brevity—the discrete and perfect detail. Thus he declared in the *Reply to the Telchines*[8] that he preferred the narrow path to the highway, and the cicada's song to the braying of asses.

The *Reply to the Telchines,* a piece of literary polemic, may have served as a prologue to the *Aitia,* but only if the prologue was a later addition, for in it the poet speaks of his age and his white hair. The elegiac poem called the "Lock of Berenice" may have been added to the same collection in similar circumstances; it extols the offering made by Queen Berenice upon the triumphal return of her young husband, Ptolemy III Euergetes, in 246–45. This poem was translated into Latin by Catullus.

There is of course no way of knowing the original relationships among these poems, nor does it much matter to which collections they belonged. Whatever the subject, Callimachus always composed in small, discrete scenes. His surviving works include fragments of elegies (on themes other than love), some iambic poetry, and some epigrams (preserved in the Palatine Anthology, discussed below). It seems that even the closest thing to an "epic" poem he composed, the *Hecale,* presented the ancient myth (that of Theseus and the bull of Marathon) in a succession of brief sketches done in a graceful, intimate manner. Although Theseus is the hero, the poem is called the *Hecale* after the poor old woman at whose house he stops; and a passage found on a tablet seems to have introduced birds that could speak. The poet's very erudition gave him a sense of familiarity with the legends and made the legendary world seem close and accessible.

Nor do the qualities I have cited in any way prevent the inclusion of a personal note in his work. Callimachus speaks of heroes and gods, but he also finds room, in the digressions characteristic of his work, to speak of his home

---

8. The Telchines were a legendary race of sorcerers, said to have been the first metalworkers. Callimachus refers to his critics as "Telchines" because of their malice.—Trans.

town, Cyrene; of his gratitude to his noble patrons; and of his literary enemies. His life and his reading blend into one another: Callimachus is a true "man of letters" in the modern sense of the phrase.

He had a student who was also a scholarly poet, Apollonius of Rhodes, who despite his name is thought to have been born in Alexandria. He was apparently Zenodotus's successor as director of the library, as well as tutor to Ptolemy III Euergetes. But things took a turn for the worse when he gave a first public reading of his great poem, the *Argonautica*. It was disastrously received; he quarreled with Callimachus and went to Rhodes in self-imposed exile. The welcome he received there would account for his being remembered as Apollonius "of Rhodes." But except for these broad outlines we know little about his life; the ancient testimony is contradictory. The date of his birth is uncertain. Nor do we know whether, after winning acclaim in Rhodes, he returned to Alexandria; some say he did, but they may well be in error. We are equally ignorant of when he died.

What we do know is that he was the author of the *Argonautica*, a long poem which he undoubtedly revised in Rhodes (the ancient sources speak of two successive editions). And this poem, for once, has been preserved in its entirety. It is a continuous narrative in four books, devoted to the long voyage Jason and his companions made to Colchis to bring back the Golden Fleece. The theme was ancient: it had been part of the Homeric "Cycle," and had inspired many tragedies and other poems (notably Pindar's *Fourth Pythian*, but also whole epics that are lost to us). Yet even as he retold the old story, Apollonius took advantage of the opportunities it offered for incorporating various other legends. The subject of the first two books, for example, is an extended voyage in which every stage is an occasion for summoning up some mythological episode. Thus the stopover in Lemnos offers a pretext for evoking Hypsipyle and the crime of the Lemnian women;[9] a little farther on we encounter Phineus, the ill-fated prophet whose food is snatched from his lips by the Harpies. Many lesser-known legends are also included. This is the work of a man bred on mythology, who enjoys retelling picturesque tales. I might add that he is also wont to linger over geographical details; the description of the return voyage, in book 4, combines that interest with mythology in an imaginary geography.

In this learned curiosity we may recognize the tastes of Callimachus. And, although Callimachus was opposed in principle to a poem of such length, the mode of composition provides a variety that should have satisfied him. The two men traded allusions, imitations, and protestations; but from our perspective, the resemblances between them are more striking than the differences.

---

9. According to the myth, the women of Lemnos were slighted by their husbands and avenged themselves by killing all the men on the island; Hypsipyle alone spared her father, the king.—Trans.

Just as he shared his teacher's scholarly curiosity, Apollonius also shared with him the tendency of the age to prefer a world that was human rather than grand. Apollonius's heroes, like Callimachus's Theseus, are far removed from the greatness of their literary forebears. Jason is like a traveler alarmed by the scale of his enterprise: "Now I am bent under the burden of extreme fear and intolerable anguish—afraid to navigate these seaways that chill the blood, and afraid when we come to land, for there are only enemies everywhere" (2.627–30). Phineus, whom I mentioned above, is a poor old man in a shabby house. Heroes and gods have come closer to the level of the average man. There is even a touch of irony in some of Apollonius's descriptions of them.

It is from this angle that we can see an ultimately realistic work emerging from a poem replete with literary allusions—a poem that imitates Homer and borrows his stock scenes among gods, in battle, and at sea. The heroes of the *Argonautica* inhabit a natural world that is often accessible, closely observed, and brilliantly described. Their feelings too are described from the most human of angles; but this does not rule out either complexity or strength. The example of Medea, with her stirrings of love and her violent emotions, is most often cited, as it deserves to be. Drawing inspiration now from Euripides and now from Sappho, Apollonius composed a picture of love that was to enjoy considerable influence.

Apollonius wrote other works—collections of learned poems on the founding of cities, epigrams, a scholarly work on Homer, a poem about a city near Alexandria (Canopus). The fact that the *Argonautica* alone survived is an index of the poem's importance, and may testify as well to the presence of those accessible and human feelings that allow it to speak more directly to readers.

The same cannot be said for the work of Lycophron, a Euboean who came to Alexandria at about the same time and was known as a scholar and tragedian. We have an epic poem of his composing, the *Alexandra*, which consists of a long prophetic monologue; it is written in oracular style, and is deliberately obscure.

Yet the realistic vein and the "tableau" drawn from concrete daily life undoubtedly suited the taste of the age: the work of Theocritus is proof that they did.

2 · THEOCRITUS AND HERODAS:
THE SCHOOL OF THE FAMILIAR AND REALISTIC

Theocritus wrote in various genres; he composed hymns and epigrams, for example. But his renown stems from the fact that he created a poetic form destined for fame: the idyll (from Greek *eidullion*, "short piece," "short poem") and pastoral or bucolic poetry (from Greek *boukolos*, "herdsman"). He had predecessors in this area who expressed themselves in satyr drama or dithyramb; but it was he who gave the genre a form that could compel lasting interest.

We know little of his life. Parts of it were spent in three places: Syracuse, the island of Cos, and of course Alexandria. All three places are meticulously described in his work when the occasion arises. He was born in Syracuse, and among his surviving poems we find an idyll called *The Syracusan Women*, or *Women at the Festival of Adonis* (Idyll 15); another, called *The Graces* or *Hieron*, praises that prince [likewise a Syracusan] and seeks his patronage (Idyll 16, probably dating from 275). It is clear too that Theocritus owes much to the genre of the mime, one of whose practitioners had been a fifth-century Syracusan, Sophron. But Theocritus did not remain in Syracuse. We know that he lived for a long time in the island of Cos (near Asia Minor), as Apollonius did in Rhodes. He often mentions natives or traditions of Cos, and idyll 7 (the *Thalysia*) takes place on that island. Finally, like all the poets of his day, Theocritus came to Alexandria to seek the patronage of the Ptolemies. The Syracusan women of idyll 15 are attending a great festival in Alexandria; idyll 17 is an *Encomium of Ptolemy* and seems not much later than the appeal to Hieron (a date of 270 has been suggested). We also have a fragment of a poem entitled *Berenice*, after one of the queens of Egypt who bore that name (we cannot be sure which). The dates are all very much in doubt. Theocritus may have stopped at Cos before going to Alexandria; it is probable that he returned there afterward; but in any case his stay at Alexandria was during the heyday of Callimachus, the great age of Alexandrian poetry.

Certain characteristics of his art clearly indicate a connection between the two men. His preference for short poems (of between 50 and 150 lines) is in the spirit of Callimachus, as is his habit of portraying the heroes of mythology in an intimate and human manner (e.g., *The Child Heracles*). His depiction of love invites comparison with Apollonius, and some passages (outside of the bucolic poems) are reminiscent of the *Argonautica*. But the originality, and the clearest success, of Theocritus consist in his choice of a pastoral setting and his adoption of a rustic realism. We can trace back to him that line of shepherds destined to survive even in modern literature: the Daphnises, the Corydons, the Tityruses and their ladies, shepherds concerned with poetry and musical contests, love-struck and tender shepherds—but shepherds nonetheless, milking their ewes, making their cheeses, laboring in the sun, and sometimes even believing that work is the most important thing in life. What is more, Theocritus took pleasure in rendering with amused fidelity the naive speech of his shepherds and of his characters generally. The result was a mixture of realism and artistic convention, comic drama and lyricism, unique to Theocritus. It is present in all the idylls; two examples will show as much.

The Syracusan Women begins like a comedy. Many of the idylls are dialogues, for that matter; 4, 5, and 10, for example, portray conversations between goatherds and shepherds or between reapers. In *The Syracusan Women*, the speakers are the two women of the title, who are minutely observed. From the very first lines a realistic tone is struck: the wife complains about her husband; there is the baby to look after and the little servant girl's faults to deplore. Then the two women leave for the festival, are caught up in the crowd, talk to an old woman, and are put in their place for talking too much. Yet the poem ends with the beautiful hymn to Adonis heard by the two women: comedy turns into lyric.

Idyll 2 (*The Sorceresses*), very different in structure, likewise reconciles realism with poetic transposition. It describes in concrete terms the passion of a poor girl, abandoned by her lover, who resorts to magic ritual in an attempt to lure him back to her. Theocritus hides no detail of her humble and credulous life. But he describes the intensity of her feelings in a way that again recalls Sappho and Medea; at the same time the rite itself (described in the poem), with its magic refrain, makes an incantation of the story as a whole.

All the forms of love may be found in Theocritus: love for boys and for women, hopeless passions—like that of the Cyclops for lovely Galatea—and happy courtships accompanied by carefree drinking. This variety may also be found in the poets after Theocritus, like Moschus of Syracuse (second century) and Bion of Smyrna, who wrote both pastoral poetry and genial mythological tales. But the originality of Theocritus resides in the fact that all his love stories end in song—a song quoted in the poem and admired by the characters, which resolves the action into harmonies and whose beauty is a joy to all. In this way Theocritus combines a taste for the familiar with a form of aestheticism; and the result is that his characters, so real on one level, also belong to the fictional world of literature.

In this respect the poems of Theocritus differ greatly from the mimes that were his point of departure. The fact is obvious if we compare him to Herodas. Herodas was neither the first nor the only writer to compose mimes. I have already mentioned the Syracusan Sophron in my discussion of Theocritus. Hipponax of Ephesus, a still earlier writer of iambic poetry, was famous for his freedom of expression. He introduced a meter known as the choliamb (or "limping iamb"), which Theocritus, Callimachus, and a certain Phoenix of Colophon used on occasion. Herodas had the idea of adapting this meter, suggestive of mockery, to the mime; the result was the *Mimiambi*.

Herodas lived in Cos, where, as we have seen, Theocritus spent some time. The dates seem to coincide, for we find references in Herodas to events that took place between 270 and 221. Since 1890, thanks to a papyrological find, we have fairly large fragments of his mimes. They are dialogues, like some of Theocritus's idylls, but much more realistic and harshly satirical. There are scenes from everyday life—women visiting a shoemaker, for example. But for the most part, Herodas's cast of characters is rather unsavory: procuresses and pimps, cruel and jealous women (one woman is seen hounding a slave who was more than just a slave to her), married women obsessed with sexual gratification. The theme of visits between gossips, which we saw in Theocritus, recurs, but the talk turns to much less decent pursuits than celebrating a festival. Herodas is a pitiless moralist; if he distorts reality, it is not to elicit greater harmony from it but to produce a caricature of it.

3 · DIDACTIC POETRY: ARATUS AND NICANDER OF COLOPHON

Callimachus and Theocritus resemble one another in their taste for brief, intimate scenes; but in his taste for erudition and for scholarly explanations, Callimachus is closer to Aratus. All these men belonged to a single milieu; one of Callimachus's epigrams, in fact, defends the work of Aratus. Born in Cilicia, Aratus spent time at the Macedonian court (under Antigonus Gonatas, who became king in 276); it is not known whether he came to Alexandria. A philosopher and mathematician, he incorporated the astronomy of his day into a poem called the *Phenomena*. His other poetry was occasional verse, now lost. But the *Phenomena* was widely known and highly regarded; scholars quoted it and wrote commentaries on it; and it survived. Written in hexameters, it is a little over 1000 lines long. Though Hesiod's influence is perceptible, Aratus's chief sources of inspiration were the doctrines esteemed by his contemporaries: the opening is a kind of hymn to Zeus, which recalls that of the Stoic Cleanthes, and the last part deals with meteorology in a way reminiscent of Theophrastus.

The popularity of the "scientific" poem is also reflected in Nicander of Colophon, who produced examples of it and helped to promote the genre. The ancient references to this author are ambiguous and contradictory, but we know he lived in the second century. Two hexameter poems of his have survived—the *Theriaca*, on remedies for animal bites, and the *Alexipharmaca*, on antidotes. One of his sources was Apollodorus, who wrote on these topics in Alexandria. The form of the poems is rather abrupt. Another poem, now lost, dealt with metamorphoses, a theme well suited to Alexandrian tastes and one that Ovid was to take up in his turn. Nicander wrote many other poems and works of prose as well.

This kind of popularization for an educated public appears to have been well received; as evidence we can cite many names—Philostephanus of Cyrene, Eratosthenes, Apollodorus of Athens, Phanocles, Parthenius, and Euphorion of Chalcis, among others. Eratosthenes and Apollodorus were genuine scholars, and also wrote in prose. Eratosthenes' *Hermes*, written in hexameters, evoked both the god's legend and the harmony of the spheres; Apollodorus's *Commentary on the Catalogue of Ships* and his *Chronica* (a work of chronology), in iambic trimeters, are more erudite still. The scholarly poetry of the Hellenistic age merely embellished learning by presenting it in a more studied and elaborate form. In this perspective, it is closely related to the scientific and historical literature that flourished at the same period—a fact that allows us to turn directly from one genre to the other.

Yet it would distort the picture to disregard the fact that all the poetic genres were in use at the time. Plays continued to be written; Lycophron of Chalcis, for example, produced historical dramas and satyr plays in addition to the *Alexandra*, the poem I mentioned above. In another sphere, the epigram came into great favor, as we can judge by surviving inscriptions; but epigrams did not necessarily lead to inscriptions, and in the Alexandrian period the genre developed a life of its own. Its practitioners included Callimachus and Theocritus, as well as men like Asclepiades of Samos (mentioned by Theocritus) and Heraclitus of Halicarnassus (to whom Callimachus devoted an elegy); still later there were others, including Meleager of Gadara. These little poems were often gathered into collections, and some at last found their way into the two great collections assembled in the Byzantine era, the "Planudean Anthology" and the "Palatine Anthology" (the latter, put together around 1060, was only rediscovered at the end of the seventeenth century). Thus the Alexandrians tried their hands at all the poetic genres, though they proved more successful in some than in others.

IV · NATURAL AND HUMAN SCIENCES

Greek prose of the Hellenistic period no longer fits the categories of the preceding age. Political oratory, which had been so important, disappeared, as did essays on current political questions; oratory became the business of rhetoricians. Conversely, as learning became more specialized, all sorts of scholarly writings, scientific publications, and technical discussions appeared. Though lost to us today, these played a major role in the history of ideas. The sole surviving work was of a kind to win the attention of a wider public because it dealt with history; even then, it might have been lost had its subject not been the political entity destined to supplant the squabbling Hellenistic monarchies and establish a new order: that of Rome.

1 · THE MASS OF LOST WORKS

The lost works are many; I can only mention a few names to suggest the fecundity of the new genre.

Where oratory is concerned, suffice it to say that a reaction set in against the long-standing ascendancy of Atticism. A group of rhetoricians from Asia Minor, the first of whom was apparently Hegesias of Magnesia, founded a movement that has been called Asianism; they turned their backs on elegance and on the periodic style to court surprise effects, figures of speech, and the magic of the verb. By contrast, the Rhodian school opposed Asianism and embraced logical inquiry. Along with the debates about form and style, others appeared, which soon took pride of place: these had to do with various exact sciences.

Geography, which we have already seen featured in the poetry of Apollonius of Rhodes, may have owed some of its popularity to the far-flung expeditions of Alexander. During the same period, Pytheas of Marseilles set off to explore the northern parts of Europe; his accounts were met with astonishment. In the Alexandrian period, the most distinguished geographer was Eratosthenes. He was a native of Cyrene, like Callimachus, and a director of the Alexandrian Library—a charge he assumed in 246, having studied at Athens in the interim. I have already mentioned him as a poet; he also wrote on comedy, and did important research on chronology. But he applied his solid scientific training primarily to geography. By measuring shadows with the aid of a sort of sundial called a *gnomon*, he calculated the circumference of the earth. The tradition of scientific geography was firmly established from that time on; we find it again in Posidonius.

This kind of geography obviously had close ties with astronomy. I have mentioned the role of astronomy in Aratus's poem the *Phenomena*. The great name in this field, however, was that of Hipparchus, a man from Nicaea in Bithynia who, as it happened, found himself in a position to criticize Aratus. He worked in Rhodes and in Alexandria and seems to have been acquainted with Babylonian astronomy. Concerned about exactness of observation (a sign of the times), he perfected measuring instruments (including the diopter), and his calculations of the movements of stars are a high-water mark in Greek astronomy. He even discovered the precession of the equinoxes—and this in the second century B.C.

Such astronomy presupposes mathematics. Indeed, early in the third century a man working at Alexandria had laid the foundations of geometry. This was Euclid, author of the famous *Elements*, which was the authoritative work in the field for centuries. Euclid established the principles of plane geometry, algebraic geometry, irrational numbers, and solid geometry. His work was continued by Archimedes. This Syracusan, who died in 212 when his city was taken by the Romans, has won lasting fame for his mechanical inventions and for his role in the defense of Syracuse; but Archimedes was primarily a pure scientist, whose studies included *The Quadrature of the Parabola*, *The Measurement of the Circle*, and *On Spirals*. After him, Apollonius of Perge pursued similar lines of research (on *Conics*, for example). Acoustics, optics, and algebra were other topics of interest; this branch of the history of literature is "literary" no longer.

As if in compensation, history was becoming *more* literary as it took a somewhat different form. The historian Duris of Samos (who lived from 340 to 270, approximately, and whose works include a history that begins with Philip of Macedon and ends with Pyrrhus) was already complaining of the lackluster style of the Isocratic school; he called for a more dramatic and colorful form of history—even if that meant a less accurate form. When it came to drama, Alexander's conquests and the various upheavals that ensued—which brought new cities into the sphere of political life—were a powerful stimulus to historians. The end of the fourth century and the beginning of the third saw a succession of *Histories of Alexander*, written by men who had accompanied him and occupied positions in his retinue. This was the case with Ptolemy I, who drew on his own experience, supplemented by the *Ephemerides* or diary of the royal command; his *History of Alexander*, now lost, was later used by Arrian. There were similar works by less important men such as Onesicritus, Chares, Marsyas of Pella, Aristobulus, Nearchus, and many others. Hieronymus of Cardia recorded the period immediately following, in which he, likewise, had played an active part. But if these researchers were serious and objective, the very appeal of the figure of Alexander was also destined to influence the writing of history, and in a very different way—one that coincided with the taste of Duris. For the conqueror's adventures and matchless talents were an open invitation to the development of fictionalized and rhetorical history. The rhetorician Hegesias, whom I have already mentioned for his contributions to rhetorical technique, wrote accounts of Alexander inspired by the new taste; so did Clitarchus. From that point it was a short step to leave history altogether, as we can see if we turn to what is called the *Romance of Alexander*—a piece formerly attributed to Callisthenes, which survives in a late version. This work, which was translated into Latin and Armenian, included largely imaginary descriptions and made use of letters written with all the freedom proper to fiction. Nor was this the end of the story, for the French Middle Ages would be so taken with various "romances of Alexander" that some scholars have seen in them the origin of the French verse form called the "alexandrine." After providing a focus of interest for the historians of his own age, Alexander thus became, in time, a hero of fiction.

Meanwhile, history moved on. After Alexander we come to an age of many historians, whose works are almost all lost. These works included *Hellenica* (histories of Greece as a whole) in the manner of Xenophon; local histories (e.g., of Lycia, Egypt, and India); monographs on individuals or memoirs (like those of Pyrrhus or Aratus)—not to mention the renewed interest in Attic history (e.g., Philochorus) and the theoretical works (that of Euhemerus, for example, who sought to "rationalize" the myths).

Timaeus is a special case. Born at Tauromenium, in Sicily, in the mid-fourth century, he was forced into exile as a result of political activities. He then lived in Athens for many years. His *Histories* (in thirty-eight books, only fragments of which have survived) dealt with the Western Greeks up to the death of Agathocles of Syracuse (in 289); an addendum seems to have covered later events, up to the outbreak of the First Punic War. With Timaeus, then, we can see the focus of interest beginning to move west, before coming to rest on Rome. Where method was concerned, however, he seems to have approached his subject quite differently from Polybius, who was harshly critical of him. Timaeus was trained in Athens by a student of Isocrates, and Polybius considered him too "bookish" a historian. Apparently he also adopted the tone of moral censure favored by the Isocratic school; Polybius has vigorous complaints to make on this score as well. In fact, Timaeus is chiefly known to us through these criticisms, which, though they may be somewhat unfair, help us to gauge the originality of Polybius.

2 · POLYBIUS

Like Timaeus, Polybius had no connection with Alexandria. He was born at Megalopolis, in the Peloponnese, around the year 200 B.C. (or a little after), when the importance of Rome already outweighed that of any other power in the Mediterranean world. Victorious in the Second Punic War, the Romans were engaged in a struggle with Philip V of Macedonia. Greece was thus directly in their path and had a direct interest in the outcome. Flamininus's proclamation of Greek liberty took place in 196 B.C., and Perseus's defeat at Pydna in 168.[10] As it happened, Polybius, who had taken an active part in the politics of his city and of the Achaean League (of which Megalopolis was an influential member), was brought to Rome in 167 with other prominent Achaeans suspected of hostility to Rome. But he was well received in his place of exile and soon felt at home there. Admitted to the circle of the Scipios, he acquired great influence over the young Scipio Aemilianus. He also knew Laelius, Cato, and many others. He even had permission to travel, and he took advantage of it. He returned to Greece only in 150, and shortly thereafter was with Scipio at the siege of Carthage; his definitive return was not until 146, after the conclusive victory of Rome and the sack of Corinth. From that time on he worked as a peacemaker[11]—and historian—until his death at the age of eighty-two.

We can understand how his experiences should have focused Polybius's full attention and powers of reflection on one unprecedented event: the irresistible advance of Roman power. He declares repeatedly that all his historical writings are intended to explain this phenomenon; and we may take him at his word. "Can anyone, indeed, be so blind and so indifferent as to take no interest in the question of how, and by virtue of what form of government, the Roman state has succeeded—without any precedent—in extending its dominion over nearly the whole of the inhabited world, and that in less than fifty- three years?" (Histories 1.1). I might add that Polybius, by adopting this focus, was linking up with a solid tradition of Greek historiography: Herodotus and, to an even greater degree, Thucydides had already taken an interest in the genesis of the power of states; each had already had the sense of living through events of unusual significance; and each had found that sense a compelling reason to describe his experience in a history.

Yet in the establishment of Roman power there were new and unique features, of which Polybius was fully aware. In the first place, the Romans encountered not one people that did not eventually yield to them; and Polybius, Mediterranean that he was, could speak easily of their sway over "nearly all the peoples of the earth." Second, as their dominion spread successively to the various peoples the Greeks had known, it caught them up in a common destiny—which suggested to Polybius that they should be included in a common history: "For the originality of my subject and the remarkable thing about the times we have just lived through is this: Fortune has directed almost all events in a single direction, and has forced all human affairs to ori-

10. Flamininus was the Roman general who defeated Philip V; Perseus was Philip's successor.—Trans.

11. The sack of Corinth ended a short and catastrophic Greek bid for independence from Rome. Polybius used his position of influence with Rome to mitigate the punishment of Greece.—Trans.

ent themselves toward one and the same goal. Thus the historian, for his part, ought to make it possible for his readers to take in at once glance the mechanisms Fortune has put into play so as to produce all these effects simultaneously. Indeed, it was this above all that gave me the idea for this study and persuaded me to undertake it" (1.4). Polybius points out that partial histories can give us no better understanding of universal history than detached limbs can give of a living thing: "History is truly interesting and instructive only if it allows us to observe the entire network of events in their interdependence, together with their similarities and differences." (1.4) This clear objective accounts for both Polybius's choice of subject and his method of exposition. Nor is it unrelated to his very conception of historical method.

When I speak of Polybius's choice of subject, I refer of course to his major work and not to his secondary works, now lost—though most of these had some relation to the former (such as the biography of Philopoemon, the great Megalopolitan statesman, or the monograph on the Numantine War, waged by Scipio Aemilianus in 133). There were other short pieces as well. But Polybius's *Histories* are a sizable work, including forty books and originally meant to cover the growth of Rome in the fifty-three years referred to above, i.e., from the beginning of the Second Punic War (221) to the victory over Perseus (168). In fact, the period covered is longer than this: in the first place, the first two books, by way of introduction (and by way of taking up where Timaeus left off), discuss the years between the beginning of the First Punic War and the Second (264–21); then, too, having declared that he would end his account with the year 168—and having begun his work with this intention—Polybius felt it was necessary to continue up to the complete surrender of Greece in 146. Thus the work actually covers some 120 years—those that saw the establishment of Roman power. But the *Histories* have not survived intact; we have the first five books in their entirety, books 6–16 in abridged form, and only fragments (though some are sizable) of the remaining books.

The new idea of political unification, to which the advance of Rome gave rise, dictated the manner of the work's composition. Thus Polybius sets out to integrate the events taking place in different parts of the Mediterranean, using the technique of "interweaving," or *sumploke*; Rome is of course the hub from which everything radiates and toward which everything converges. For the most part, from book 7 on, Polybius keeps to an annalistic framework, discussing the events of each year region by region—those in Sicily, for example, followed by those in Asia, Greece, or Spain. By and large, with some exceptions, each book covers two years. But there are several, outside of the introductory books, that constitute self-contained analyses, such as book 6 (on the Roman constitution) and book 12 (on geography and on criticism of previous historians). I shall discuss these below.

It is probable, and even certain, that Polybius went through several drafts in composing such a work and that it contains revisions; but the history of its composition has not lent itself to any serious hypotheses. On the other hand, the principles that guided its composition are clear enough, for Polybius knew exactly what he thought should be expected of a historical work, and the originality of his own is largely due to this idea. Yet there are points of comparison between his idea and that of Thucydides, who invoked similar principles. Like Thucydides, but in contrast to the tragic or rhetorical historians of his own day, Polybius aspired to utility rather than entertainment. He often speaks of the benefits to be derived from his work. But for history to be beneficial, it must be (as he says) "pragmatic"; that is, it must be objective and must confine itself to facts. This much is pure Thucydides; where Polybius departs from his predecessor is in making these facts and this objectivity more limiting and more concrete. He uses speeches only rarely, and then briefly, when he has sure documentation; he is severely critical of the technique as used by Timaeus, who rewrote speeches "as if he were doing a school exercise on an assigned topic" (12.25a). Polybius also demands precise technical information. In the same book (12.25e), when stipulating which studies are necessary to the historian, he puts immediately after book-based research the practice of "visiting towns and sites, rivers and ports—in short, noting all particular features as well as distances by land and sea." He prefers on-site research to book work, and often informs the reader that he took care to verify his information "on location," the better to understand what took place. He did so for Hannibal's famous crossing of the Alps, for example. He is similarly careful about military facts, be they questions of armament or of tactics; nor does he confine himself to general principles, as Thucydides did, but describes everything at close range. His analysis of the Romans' military organization (6.19–42) is exceptional in this respect.

In his concern for technical objectivity, then, Polybius is already a modern historian. He is modern too in the way he handles political history. Thucydides saw the conduct of states as illustrations of great psychological laws; but Polybius says that one of the essential factors behind the sudden growth of Rome's power was the peculiar nature of her constitution. This idea is one of the crucial theses of his work. It explains why book 6 occupies such a prominent place—just after the victory of Hannibal at Cannae, when Rome is in great danger, and just before she begins to rally. Polybius believes that great danger furnishes the best opportunity for judging either a character or a constitution. So he interrupts his narrative and devotes a whole book to the description of the Roman constitution. The account is far from being perfectly controlled. We can see in it traces of various doctrines defended by the fourth- and third-century philosophers, especially those of Aristotle's school. First there is the notion of a cycle of constitutions; then, more important, the notion that the best constitution is a "mixed" one—the kind Rome has, which provides for a balance of powers (among consuls, Senate, and people). The powers may reinforce one another or check one another, and this, in Polybius's view, is the secret of Rome's power (1.64.1; 3.2.6; 6.2.9; 6.18.4). Polybius did not invent the idea of the "mixed" constitution. But here too, in his choice of detail and in the role he ascribes to political mechanisms, he established a new and modern kind of history.

Such are the original aspects of Polybius's work. He had other ideas too, of course, on the subject of history. Thus he drew a clear distinction between the beginning of an event and its cause, or between the cause and the motive adduced (3.6: *aitia* and *prophasis*). Here we are strongly reminded of Thucydides—but this in itself detracts from Polybius's originality; and he does not always apply the distinction with equal insight.

There is no denying the significance of Polybius's innovations in the genre of history. Neither his thought nor his talent, however, are above criticism. His thought is often ill defined, as it is on the subject of constitutions and their cycle, or on the role of Fortune; he often invokes the latter in his reflections but then tries to set it aside at other junctures to make room for individual worth (as in the case of Scipio Africanus, 10.2). The lessons he so readily draws from history are often quite ordinary pieces of advice—elementary counsels of prudence. Nor is the picture he gives us of Rome always as penetrating as we could wish (he was, after all, a Greek), or as solid as we could wish. He paints admirable portraits of Scipio, with his lucid clemency and native ability, and he admires Roman politics; but he condemns minor faults without giving any clear indication what he thought of his friends' cruelty in Carthage, Corinth, or Numantia. True, his history has not come down to us intact. But it is possible too that his role as friend of the Romans interfered somewhat with his judgment. Finally, he writes rather heavily, using an abstract vocabulary in which we can sometimes detect the wording of the original documents; his tone is slightly sententious and lackluster. This Greek who appointed himself historian of Rome has none of his homeland's traditional elegance.

Such reservations, however, in no way diminish his worth—or his influence, which was considerable. The Roman Livy was to use Polybius and imitate him. Other historians took his work as a point of departure, writing *Post-Polybian Histories*. This was the case with Posidonius and later with Strabo. For us, Polybius also illustrates the evolution of Greek literature. As was intimated in connection with the philosophers, Rome was taking the place of Alexandria; henceforth it was to be the true capital of Greco-Roman culture.

10

Perspectives on the Roman Age

It is not easy to find a unifying element in the Greek literature of the Roman age, which is spread over several centuries and over a variety of countries—all those the Romanized world came to include. Some of the writers of this period were from the coast of Asia Minor (Dionysius of Halicarnassus, Quintus of Smyrna); others were from still farther away—from Phrygia (Epictetus), Bithynia (Arrian, Dio Chrysostom), and Commagene (Lucian), not to mention Egypt (Plotinus) and Sicily (Diodorus). Greece proper produced few authors, but managed to produce the only one whose personality positively commands our attention—Plutarch.

Yet the unity that neither time nor place provides can be found to some extent in the genres. To all appearances, the time of creative spurts is past, as is the time of action and political independence. The Roman age is an age of prose writers who devote themselves to reflection—historians, philosophers, rhetoricians. Yet it is an age still capable of producing new genres, which reflect a lively interest in individuals, both in their adventures and in their psychological makeup. The two major such genres are biography, which takes its place beside history, and fictional narrative—the romance properly speaking, or the short fictional tale in the manner of the second great writer of the period, Lucian.

These characteristics will account for the divisions I have adopted in the present chapter, in which I no longer observe a chronological order. The reader will note the absence of poetry from among my headings. Poems continued to be written; but many have been lost, and what we know of them suggests that they were not particularly inspired. Only two names deserve mention, and they come very late in the period: Quintus of Smyrna and Nonnus of Panopolis (in Egypt). The former wrote a *Sequel to Homer* in fourteen books, which survives intact; in the epic mode, it relates the events that fall between the *Iliad* and the *Odyssey*. Quintus apparently lived in the fourth century after Christ. Once again we are dealing with an imitation, rather didactic in nature; its innovations are modest. As for Nonnus, he was the author of the *Dionysiaca*, a more original epic describing Dionysus's expedition to India. Its forty-eight books have been preserved intact. Nonnus

191

lived in the fifth century after Christ. Religious inspiration lends force to his poem; since the beginning of the Alexandrian period, Dionysus had assumed an important role in Greek religion. Yet Nonnus is still imitating Homer, "the haven of all great poetry." Nonnus had emulators, one of whom was Musaeus (not to be confused with the legendary poet of ancient times, often associated with Orpheus). This Musaeus was the author of a poem that has come down to us; in hexameters, it tells the sad tale of the lovers Hero and Leander. But on the whole the age of great poetry is clearly past. In the Roman period, Greek poetry is no longer alive—it merely survives. I shall have nothing further to say of it in this book.

I · PLUTARCH

I begin this chapter with Plutarch because of the special place he occupies in literary history thanks to his personality and the volume of his work; chronologically speaking, Diodorus Siculus, Dionysius of Halicarnassus, and Strabo all preceded him.

1 · LIFE AND WORK

Plutarch was born shortly before A.D. 50 and died in 120 or shortly thereafter. His birthplace was Chaeronea in Boeotia, the little town near Mount Parnassus where Philip had once defeated the Greeks. Plutarch was to spend nearly all his life there. As a young man, however, he went to complete his studies in Athens, which was still the city of philosophers. There he was a pupil of the Platonist Ammonius, and, as his work shows, he always remained faithful to his teacher. He went on long voyages as well, and made the compulsory stay in Rome. But he came back to settle in Chaeronea, was married there, and lived there until his death.

Plutarch's life in Chaeronea is well known to us from his works. It included three main elements, which blended with one another. First, there was his life as a citizen; Plutarch was from a noble family, and himself followed the tradition prescribing that a well-born man serve his city. He held various positions in Chaeronea. At the same time he maintained friendships with many Romans, and acquired Roman citizenship. The second major element of his life was religion, centering on Delphi, which is not far from Chaeronea. Plutarch held priestly offices there, and his work is full of reflections on the god of Delphi, Apollonian prophecy, and related topics. Thus he divided his time between Chaeronea and Delphi, becoming a citizen of the latter as well (the Delphians honored him with an inscription after his death).

But the essential element of Plutarch's life was his private life, which he lets us glimpse in his work; the importance of this sphere is a mark of the new age. We see him with his wife Timoxena and with his children. Theirs was a life of familial tenderness. Plutarch had an exalted sense of conjugal love and respect for women, as his dialogue *On Love*, the *Erotikos*, amply proves. And the *Consolation to his Wife* radiates tenderness. In addition, Plutarch led a sociable and hospitable life in Chaeronea, surrounded by friends who, like himself, loved to discuss philosophy. His dialogues reflect the atmosphere of these talks, and his moral counsels often refer to specific conversations. His work also gives us the names of his friends, Greek and Roman. All of them aspired to wisdom, but to a serene and genial wisdom, which Plutarch's work as a whole tends to put forward as an ideal.

His work is copious. Though more than half has been lost, it amounts to twenty-five volumes in Amyot's translation. It consists essentially of two parts: the *Parallel Lives* and the group of treatises known under the collective title of the *Moralia*.

The *Parallel Lives*—which in each case pair the life of a Greek hero with that of a Roman—include twenty-two pairs of lives. Those of Epaminondas and Scipio are lost. We also have four individual lives, and the "Catalogue of Lamprias" cites quite a number of others that have not survived (including lives of poets and philosophers). It was to the *Parallel Lives* that Plutarch owed his great fame and influence. Yet they represent only half of his extant works and only a fraction of his intellectual interests.

The *Moralia*, in their diversity, give a fuller picture. Yet it must be acknowledged that the two series of works are closely related: we find in the *Moralia* a wealth of historical examples, and in the *Lives* a wealth of comments, digressions, and philosophical observations echoing the problems dealt with in the *Moralia* and reflecting the same body of ideas. These problems are of various kinds, and not all have to do with ethics. Among the works that justify the collective title are treatises devoted to virtues and vices. Examples include *On Moral Virtue*, *On the Control of Anger*, *On Tranquility of Mind*, *On Brotherly Love*, *On Talkativeness*, and *On Being a Busybody*. To these may be added the dialogue on love, the *Advice on Marriage*, and the *Consolations*. Some of these titles bring Seneca to mind: the similarity of genre should allow us to grasp the affinities between the thought of the two men.

Elsewhere in the *Moralia*, ethics take second place to metaphysics. This is true of the treatises that inquire into the nature of fate, for example, or into the delays of divine justice; in the same category are those discussing the premises of Plato's *Timaeus*, or of the Stoics, or of Epicurus. Here again we may gauge the relation between Plutarch's positions and those of the philosophers he examines. The so-called Delphic treatises fall halfway between philosophy and history, since they deal with problems of a fairly concrete nature; there is one *On the "E" at Delphi*, others *On the Pythia's Responses* and *On the Cessation of Oracles*. But many others are akin to history: collections of famous sayings; reflections on Alexander's success or on the glory of the Athenians, even on the suitability of engaging in politics when one is old. Some deal with literature—for example, *How to Read the Poets* and *On the Malice of Herodotus*. Some even deal with altogether concrete problems relating to the moon, to animals, to the principle of cold.

The *Moralia*, then, reveal a universally curious mind, steeped in books and doctrines, raising all the questions that interested the cultivated men of the age. Plutarch's treatment of these questions, by contrast, is hardly ever bookish. He often uses the dialogue form; anecdotal examples abound; but we also find examples drawn from his personal life or from his reading, and digressions meant to put forward a given taste or idea that was dear to him. If the *Lives* claim our attention because of the novelty of their literary form and because their contents are so rich in history and psychological insights into the heroes they evoke, the *Moralia* offer a fuller understanding of the thought and ideals of their author.

2 · THE LIVES

The idea of writing biographies existed before Plutarch. Some scholars would put the origins of the genre much farther back; in any case, we find works devoted to a single man—such as Xenophon's *Agesilaus*—as early as the fourth century B.C. Aristotelian philosophy, in turn, delighted in seeking out anecdotes illustrative of virtues or vices. Before long, history itself was focusing on the role of great men, such as Alexander or the Roman emperors. But Plutarch was the most illustrious representative of the genre.

He did not consider himself a historian. He says so explicitly in his *Life of Alexander*: "I am not writing histories but biographies, and it is not mainly in the most striking actions that virtue or vice is revealed. On the contrary, a small detail, a word, or a joke is often a better index of character than combats resulting in thousands of deaths, or the most important pitched battles and sieges" (1.2). Plutarch's concern is the analysis of character, and his instrument is the revealing anecdote or phrase. But his concern for psychology goes hand in hand with—or, more accurately, proceeds from—a concern for ethics. Plutarch does not write, as biographers do today, for the sheer pleasure of better comprehending human reactions; the thought of good and evil never leaves him. And while he is not blind to the ultimate failings of his great men—failings he always indicates in passing—he clearly hopes primarily to highlight virtues and to give his readers a taste for them. He explains as much in speaking of Pericles: "We must then seek out what is best; nor should we limit ourselves to contemplating it, but make this contemplation food for our minds. In fact, just as that color is suited to the eye whose freshness and delight stimulate and nourish the vision, so our power of thought should be directed to sights that draw it, through pleasure, to its own proper good. Such sights are actions inspired by virtue, which beget in men who examine them an emulation and a zeal urging them to imitation" (1.3–4). Plutarch's biographies have the appeal of lively and anecdotal stories; they are a form of history that brings us into intimate contact with great men; but at the same time they seek to implant, and succeed in implanting, a kind of confidence in man.

Such a design would have been remarkable in itself. But Plutarch added a further dimension to it by presenting these biographies in Greek/Roman pairs. The genre of the comparison was much used at that time in the schools of rhetoric. But the idea of drawing parallels between the great men of Greece and Rome also takes on meaning in the context of the contemporary situation generally. Rome had supplanted Greece in the political sphere and with that had assumed primacy even in the spheres of art and thought. This did not imply bad relations between Greeks and Romans. Plutarch was as friendly to the latter as Polybius had been, and must have been delighted in every respect to see Hadrian prove well disposed toward Greece. But his friendship was devoid of servility and left Plutarch faithful to the Greek past. This is why he brought together, and drew parallels between, the two worlds destined to be linked from then on, and treated as equal the great accomplishments of Greece and Rome. His deliberate choice thus confirms the existence of a civilization that is not Roman but Greco-Roman.

I should add that he never forces the parallels. The two heroes paired in each case are comparable because of a political situation, a character trait, or a certain reputation; but Plutarch makes no effort to draw comparisons between the details of the two lives. After describing each man separately, he is satisfied with a few brief paragraphs of comparison (*sunkrisis*). Sometimes even these are missing, either because he never wrote them or because they have been lost. The paired lives are naturally of uneven quality, and this may hinge in part on the characters of the subjects; some are better known or more engaging than others. But all the *Lives* exhibit common characteristics that proceed from their author's fundamental intent.

Plutarch did not mean to be a historian; and there are times when he loses his grip on historical interpretation. For example, it is enough to compare his Pericles with that of Thucydides to see that he has let himself be misled by inferior sources; he attributes to Pericles all the petty and selfish motives that Thucydides overrules with such authority—motives that do not even square with what Plutarch says elsewhere. On the other hand, we learn a wealth of details from Plutarch that are not to be found in Thucydides. All the little concrete particulars, the gossip, and the famous lines that bring Pericles to life come from Plutarch. He may not be a historian, but history cannot do without him. Then too, he generally drew on a variety of sources. He did not look for political interpretations; but he obviously did earnest and honest research on the kinds of facts that interested him.

I should add that what may seem somewhat trivial where history is concerned—Plutarch's taste for the anecdote and the "little story"—becomes a source of pleasure in a literary perspective. Nothing could be livelier than his narrative: he makes us see and hear the characters. Never is the flow of narrative impeded by factual detail or historical criticism; the reader is caught up in it as he might be in a novel. And this is the more remarkable in that Plutarch's style has nothing brilliant about it. It is pure, and avoids hiatus, as becomes a good classical author; but the sentences are long, often too long; and neologisms of a philosophic cast, which make the analysis subtler, also make it less graceful. Nonetheless, the narrative leaves an impression of briskness, life, and spontaneity—the very impression rendered by Amyot's French translation, which is still fresh after 400 years.

The impression is probably also due, at least in part, to Plutarch's way of letting us see his own reactions, and to the conviction with which he admires, praises, or deplores. He makes no attempt to hide this conviction, which is communicated directly to the reader. And with it are communicated Plutarch's tastes and ideas.

3 · PLUTARCH'S IDEAS

The whole of Plutarch's thought is animated by his fidelity to Platonism, whose idealism—in every sense of the word—he retained. In reading Plutarch, we are constantly reminded of details of Plato's works. Yet Plutarch also felt the influence of later doctrines and took positions on them. He knew and discussed Epicureanism. Above all, he knew and discussed Stoicism. He was well informed about it and, while sometimes critical of the philosophy, felt its attraction deeply. The Stoics were opponents he respected, and their thought was a precious reference point to him in formulating his own. Like the Stoics he believed in "daemons"; but he imagined them differently, and connected them with a dualistic conception of the world that had nothing Stoic about it. Similarly, if his ethics approach the Stoic ideal, he also acknowledges—in contrast to the Stoics—the existence of feelings and of the affective element in man. This leads him to espouse a gentler and more humane ethics. Plutarch in fact expressed different opinions on philosophical issues from time to time, as he investigated, read, and pondered; and it can be difficult to formulate his beliefs in precise terms. As a result, his leanings and his ideal conception of life have remained the more important elements of his thought.

In this ideal conception a special place is reserved for the family. I have already pointed out the importance to Plutarch of conjugal love, and various other treatises evoke the affection between brothers or between parents and children. In a more general way as well, Plutarch likes to see gentleness prevail in relations among people. He holds it to be a natural feeling—for, as he says, "Unless we fly in the face of nature, we cannot live without friends, without human contacts, as solitary beings" (*On Brotherly Love* 479c). He says too that "there is in the soul a propensity for affection: it is made to love" (*Life of Solon* 7.3). But this natural feeling is also a duty. We must train ourselves to be gentle, tolerant, and patient. We must treat everyone with respect, women as well as men, even slaves, even animals. All this is part of the wise man's serenity—a more human and approachable serenity than that of Stoicism, or even of Plato, as the reader can see. Yet the ethical system involved is by no means an undemanding one. The *Lives* and the *Moralia* constantly convey a sense of the effort we must exert on ourselves in every sphere so as to make steady progress toward wisdom.

This ideal conception of how to live, which Plutarch himself likes to identify as Greek, does indeed have its roots in a long-drawn maturation process of Greek culture; but, over time, that culture became more humane. Plutarch's unique merit is undoubtedly his ability to combine, in a way that at first seems paradoxical, a taste for greatness and a cult of "famous men" with a taste for human tenderness in its day-to-day reality. One serves as a corrective to the other but at the same time reinforces it. This balance is yet another of the qualities that helped to ensure Plutarch's exceptional popularity in antiquity, during the Renaissance, and in the neoclassical period.

II · THE HISTORIANS

The Greek historians of the Roman age, though inferior to the great Greek historians like Herodotus, Thucydides, and Polybius, also enjoyed considerable influence. This influence had more to do with the information they conveyed than with their literary merits.

1 · FROM 100 B.C. TO A.D. 100

The beginnings of the Roman period—in other words, the first century before Christ and the first century after—were the richest part of the period for historical writing. Like Plutarch, and indeed like Polybius, the authors are historians of the Greco-Roman world and sometimes reflect a similar concern to draw parallels between the two cultures. A brief overview of their activity reveals many blanks corresponding to works now lost.

Such is the case with the two authors who were Polybius's direct continuators, beginning their works at the point where he left off. The first of these is the philosopher Posidonius; his historical work in fifty-two books, which covered the period from 144 B.C. to 85 B.C. or a little after, is now lost. The second is Strabo, who was primarily an eminent geographer. His geographical work, of a scientific precision remarkable for its day, has survived; but his *Historical Studies*, which were voluminous, are lost.

The same is true of two slightly later historians, whose work would have been interesting as the testimony of "outsiders": Nicholas of Damascus and Juba of Mauretania. Nicholas of Damascus held posts in the retinues of Mark Antony and then of Herod, king of Judea, and concluded his career at the court of Augustus. He was something of a philosopher, wrote biographies (one of Augustus in particular), and composed a great universal history in 144 books which dealt with the kingdoms of the Orient, Greece, and Judea but also included portions of Roman history. Juba was the king of Mauretania, the second of that name. He spent his youth as a hostage in Rome before coming into his kingdom. He undertook to satisfy his curiosity on all kinds of subjects, and ancient authors cite a variety of works by him; but he also wrote a history of Rome, which is often mentioned approvingly by the ancients. I could draw out the list of lost works in the fields of history, geography, and ethnography (that, for example, of Alexander Polyhistor); but it will be better to confine myself to the two men of this period whose works have been preserved.

The first of these is only incidentally a historian. Dionysius of Halicarnassus was mainly a theorist on style and a literary critic; in this respect he belongs with the rhetoricians. But he also left a work on Roman antiquities, which spanned the history of Rome from its beginnings to the Punic Wars; the first part of this (a little more than ten books) has survived. Dionysius had no critical sense and used the ancient annalists indiscriminately, embellishing their testimony with speeches and with all the devices of rhetoric. Yet on many points his testimony is still precious to us.

Diodorus Siculus was a much better historian, though he too was heavily dependent on his sources. Born at Agyrion, Sicily, about 90 B.C., Diodorus is known only through the vast work to which, he tells us, he devoted thirty years of his life. He prepared himself to write it by traveling (we know he went to Egypt shortly after 60 B.C.), and most of all by reading, largely at Rome: "Having been born at Agyrion, in Sicily, and having gained a considerable knowledge of the Latin language because of the Romans' close and frequent relations with that island, I carefully consulted the documents preserved over so many years by the Romans, in order to elucidate the history of this great empire" (*Bibliotheca* 1.4). The sentence clearly says that the work was based on library documentation, and that in large part it was focused on Rome. Yet it is not a history of Rome but a universal history; Diodorus aimed at nothing less than an encyclopedic account, stretching from the fabulous origins of the world to his own day and embracing Greeks, Romans, and "barbarians" alike. The outline of his work (which included forty books) is revealing in this respect. He begins with Egypt, Assyria, Chaldea, Media, India, etc.; the first six books bring us to the threshold of Greek history properly speaking (just after the Trojan War). The following books—through book 17, on Alexander—seek to establish correspondences, in broad swaths, between events in Greece, Rome, and other countries (as these interact with Greece or Rome). The final books are more detailed but parts of them are lost; the surviving portion ends with the year 302.

We can gauge from this outline the labor it must have taken to gather such heterogeneous facts and to relate them to one another chronologically. It was an extraordinary attempt at integration, which by comparison with Polybius marks a new broadening of perspective: the unification of the world implies a greater extension of history. It is not surprising that history on such a scale must become scholarly history, based on the work of predecessors.

The resulting method has a number of serious drawbacks: Diodorus is tied to his sources and generally follows them very closely (to the extent that we can often recognize them, and identify facts borrowed from, say, Ephorus, Duris, Phylarchus, or Polybius). He is frequently lacking in critical rigor and historical insight. Thus the entire opening section of his work has to do with mythological material, which he accepts without argument—in contrast to the classical historians, who had eliminated all such baggage as more than a little dubious. Indeed, the very nature of Diodorus's work, of his method and of his mind, is a function of new circumstances. In contrast to his predecessors the citizen-historians, caught up in the specific but limited vicissitudes of their city-states, Diodorus is a scholar with no political commitment who finds himself suddenly faced with a vast world and humbly seeks to bring some order to its motley past.

In this respect he stands in contrast to the Jewish historian Flavius Josephus, born in A.D. 37. Though he wrote about his country's past (in the *Jewish Antiquities*), Josephus also chronicled the war which the Romans waged on that country in his own day, and composed an *Autobiography*.

2 · THE SECOND CENTURY AFTER CHRIST

Like Josephus, Arrian and Appian chose clearly delimited subjects, and Arrian was a man of action. He was born at Nicomedia, in Bithynia, about A.D. 95 (and was to live until ca. 175); he took part in politics and in several wars, and devoted some of his works, now lost, to his country and to these wars. He became famous for two works, only one of which—on Alexander's Asian campaign—is historical. Out of loyalty to Xenophon he called it the *Anabasis* and divided it, like his original, into seven books. It has the merit of being based on early and sober accounts by men who took part in the campaign, especially Ptolemy (cf. chap. 9, sec. IV, 1, above). The account in the *Anabasis* can be supplemented by the short piece called the *Indica*, in which Arrian tells of the voyage of the fleet Alexander sent under the command of Nearchus from the mouths of the Indus to the Persian Gulf. Here too Arrian went straight to the best sources: he used Nearchus's own account. What is more, he checked it against those of other witnesses and chose among them on the basis of plausibility. Nor was he loath to digress: drawing on his broad experience, he could interweave the information he gathered with comments and comparisons from his own store. The work is picturesque. Arrian wrote it in the Ionic dialect, perhaps out of another literary loyalty which led him to share the habits and interests of Herodotus.

Xenophon remained Arrian's true exemplar, however. Like Xenophon, he sought to supplement his historical work with a sustained interest in philosophy. Having heard the teaching of Epictetus, he wanted to preserve a record of it; and it is, in fact, through Arrian that Epictetus's philosophy has come down to us. Arrian wrote eight books of *Discourses* (inspired, perhaps, by the *Memorabilia*?), four of which have survived, and a *Handbook* (the *Encheiridion*) summarizing his teacher's thought. His fidelity to his sources in the field of philosophy is as invaluable as in the field of history; and his discretion is greater still. The *Discourses* are usually published under Epictetus's own name, so faithful are they to his tone and style.

Appian is less Greek and more Roman than Arrian. Born in Alexandria, he lived in Rome and wrote a *History of Rome*. It was a voluminous work (twenty-four books). Parts have been preserved, and we know the plan on which it was organized: it dealt with the histories of different peoples in the order in which they happened to become involved with Rome. It reserved a prominent place for the history of the Civil Wars, which fills books 13–17 and has survived intact, complete with a special preface. If, on the whole, Appian proves a sensible but rather limited historian, he is a good source of information for the period of the Civil Wars. He also marks the term of the development that had tended to give ever greater prominence to the power of Rome, even in Greek works. Appian is really a Roman historian writing in Greek.

The same is true, three-quarters of a century later, of Dio Cassius, who like Arrian was a Bithynian by birth; he was also related to another famous Bithynian, Dio Chrysostom or Dio of Prusa. Dio Cassius (Cassius Dio Cocceianus) lived from 155 to 235 and held high office under Commodus and the emperors that followed. He was even consul at the same time as the emperor Alexander Severus in 229. Turning to the study of history, partly at the encouragement of Septimus Severus, he threw himself without delay into a vast enterprise, which was to take many years (he speaks of ten years just to assemble the materials). He completed it at the end of his life, in his native country. It was a *Roman History* stretching from the origins to A.D. 229. The work consisted of eighty books and followed an annalistic (year-by-year) order. Books 36–60 (from B.C. 68 to A.D. 47) and parts of the final books have survived. For the latter we have summaries or selections from the Byzantine era (the final books were recast by Xiphilinus and abridged by Zonaras; and a collection of excerpts was made at the behest of Constantine Porphyrogenitus in the tenth century). Dio's history is decidedly favorable to the monarchy and readily extols the clemency of the emperors. It is curiously attentive to dreams and omens. At the same time, it devotes considerable space to speeches; these are long and somewhat bombastic, with occasional flashes of brilliance. Dio meant to imitate Thucydides and also, to some extent, Demosthenes. His influence in France, in the seventeenth and eighteenth centuries, should not be underestimated.

Dio Cassius was not the last Greek historian. I should mention, for the third century, Herodian and his *History of the Successors to Marcus Aurelius*; loyal in its admiration of the empire, Herodian's work at least has the virtue of dealing with events he witnessed. I should mention Dexippus and his great *Chronicle* extending from prehistory to A.D. 270; he also wrote a *History of the Goths* (*Scythica*) dealing with the recent invasions (238–70). Dexippus was an Athenian of noble birth who held public office in Athens. His work is largely lost; only some speeches from it survive. I should also mention Eunapius (ca. 345–420) and his chronicle of the years 270–404; Olympiodorus, who took up where Eunapius left off; and, finally, Zosimus, who brings us to the end of the fifth century. Rather than pursue in detail this history of history, which is becoming a kind of litany of names, I find it more useful to indicate two tangential developments, both of great importance.

The first concerns technical writings on strategy and on historical geography. In strategy, which had found a distinguished exponent in Aeneas as early as the fourth century B.C., the best example is Polyaenus and his collection of *Stratagems* in eight books. Published in 162, it consists of a series of short narratives, and has been preserved. In historical geography one great name stands out, that of Pausanias, who in the second century wrote a famous *Description of Greece* in ten books. Organized by location, the work is a kind of tour guide; it gives descriptions of the sites and works of art still to be seen in Pausanias's day, and adds all kinds of brief asides on geography, history, and mythology, thus mingling book learning with direct experience. The work is, in a way, a very appropriate one with which to close this overview of the Greek historians of the Roman age: it displays the meticulous erudition, the taste for compilation, yet also the real curiosity of the period; and it considers the Greek sites in the form they assumed from then on: that of a culture belonging entirely to the past.[1] One has the impression that Greek culture, in this period, was suffering from inner exhaustion; if there were clear achievements, we have only indirect knowledge of them.

On the other hand, a great renewal could be expected as a result of the rise of Christianity; indeed, the new religion did give birth to a new kind of history, whose very content was different. I should mention at least two new forms of historical activity that grew out of it. One of these was modest in nature but destined to endure for a long time: the writing of lives of the saints. Saint Athanasius, bishop of Alexandria, who lived from 295 to 373 and wrote many theological treatises, set the example with his *Life of Saint Anthony*. The other form was broader in scope, as it involved the history of the Church itself. This was a history in the margins of history, so to speak: it no longer centered on politics, a fact that made all the difference. Eusebius of Caesarea, another fourth-century Christian, was its most celebrated representative. Eusebius lived from 265 to 340; he was a bishop and enjoyed the favor of the emperor. His writings included religious treatises, orations, panegyrics, and a *Life of Constantine*. His most important works were the *Chronicle*, which sought to situate Christianity in the history of the rest of the world, and the *Ecclesiastical History*, in ten books, which traced the history of Christianity from its beginnings to 323 and included the succession of bishops as well as accounts of the martyrs, persecutions, and synods.

The new subject matter Eusebius brought to history entailed changes of method. In the first place, this new material had to be related to history in general. And its origins extended back in time, so that it posed problems of chronology. To reconcile biblical traditions with secular history would always be one of the most difficult tasks of Christian chronology. Second, in its

1. In this respect Pausanias's work may be grouped wth the great scholarly collections that are such precious sources for us, such as the *Deipnosophists* of Athenaeus (third century), Stobaeus's *Anthology* (fifth century), and the *Suda*, formerly cited under the name of Suidas.

presentation the new material called for an intermingling of doctrine and narrative—whether the topic at hand be theological debates or the interpretation of events in light of divine providence. Such history was necessarily tinged with apologetics. Finally, to fulfill his apologetic aim the author was led to amass proofs, suggestive facts, and references, so that his history accumulated the documentation traditional history had omitted.

This new orientation was to develop side by side with the old for several centuries without any reciprocal influence. Ecclesiastical history continued to be written in the fourth and fifth centuries, by Theodoret among others. But it was destined always to remain a separate genre. At the end of this survey of Greek historians, the new genre helps us to gauge, by contrast, the degree to which traditional history was bound up with politics and power. It was in that older form, established by Herodotus and Thucydides, that history was to survive into our own day.

III · RHETORIC

As often happens in periods when political responsibility is in eclipse, questions of literary expression predominated under the empire. Rhetoric became an essential part of education, and the debates between schools gave rise to a sizable body of works. The polemic between Asianism and Atticism, which had begun in the Hellenistic period, continued to occupy men's minds. For a time, there was a strong reaction to Asianism; Cicero's influence obviously contributed to it. For this early period I may mention two names and an anonymous work.

The first name has already come up in my survey of historical writing—Dionysius of Halicarnassus. This scholarly man was, like Cicero, an Atticist, but one who admired Demosthenes more than Lysias. He left behind him some short treatises, and in particular some critical studies of Demosthenes, Thucydides, and the principal Attic orators. The *Letters to Ammaeus* are studies of the same type; one deals with Demosthenes and Aristotle, the other with Thucydides. In them, Dionysius dispenses praise and blame, sometimes following the text sentence by sentence, commenting on each phrase with a rather dogmatic stiffness and expressing shock at the most original qualities of each man.

Dionysius's contemporary and friend Caecilius of Calacte (in Sicily) was also an Atticist, and a still more sober one, for his admiration was chiefly reserved for Lysias. One of his contemporaries said of him that he loved Lysias better than himself, and hated Plato even more than he loved Lysias! This judgment gives a revealing glimpse of the dogmatic element in Caecilius's taste. He wrote a treatise *On the Characteristics of Ten Attic Orators*, as well as studies of specific authors or branches of rhetoric (*On Figures of Speech, On the Sublime*); these have been lost.

As if in compensation, we have part of an anonymous treatise bearing the same title as one of Caecilius's lost works, *On the Sublime*. It was long attributed, incorrectly, to Longinus. We may date it to the middle of the first century after Christ; it seems to be a reply to Caecilius's treatise. While for Caecilius style was everything, the author of *On the Sublime* emphasizes sublimity of feeling and thought.[2] He defends Plato against his detractors, and praises the beauty of lyrical flights, metaphors, and naturalness of expression, while excusing "flaws": "It may be necessarily the case that low and mediocre minds, because they never take risks or attempt the highest peaks, most often escape flaws and blunders, while great minds are prone to fall from the very fact of their greatness" (33.2). Thus the treatise *On the Sublime* heralds a movement toward more emotional, irrational, and romantic tastes, which were to be those of the so-called Second Sophistic in the course of the second century.

The "Sophists" in fact played a considerable role under the empire. They taught rhetoric, but they also taught men to think, and in this capacity went about lecturing, exhorting, advising princes, and taking positions on points of literature, religion, ethics, and politics. Often they traveled from city to city, like men of consequence. In their case, the term "Sophist" has none of the connotations of our modern term "sophistry"; they were simply "teachers."

Yet some of them reverted to the ways of the original Sophists in choosing to demonstrate their skill on paradoxical or bizarre topics. The great Dio of Prusa, who would later be called "Chrysostom" ("the golden-mouthed"), wrote encomiums on the parrot, on the gnat, and on hair (a fragment of the latter survives); but that was not all he wrote. Born in A.D. 40 (in Bithynia), he belonged to a prominent family and became a famous teacher. Then he was exiled for fourteen years because of his friendship with a relative of Domitian's, and found in this trial a stimulus that led him to deepen his thought and adopt some of the doctrines of the Stoics and Cynics. He died about A.D. 120. Eighty speeches attributed to him have survived (not all are authentic). Some are addressed to cities (e.g., Rhodes, Alexandria, and Tarsus); others discuss the virtues a king should have; still others extol an ethical ideal of moderation. Dio possessed a sort of Socratic irony as well as strength and true sublimity of expression. For several centuries he was immensely popular. Many of those who came after were directly or indirectly his students, including Favorinus, Herodes Atticus, and Aelius Aristides.

Aelius Aristides lived in the second century and was without a doubt the most famous "Sophist" in this age that produced so many of them. Born in Mysia in 129, he spent most of his life in Smyrna, which he praises in several works, and died about 189. He most admired Isocrates, the defender of rhetoric, and like Caecilius attacked Plato, who had taken his stand against rhetoric. The treatises *On Rhetoric* and *On the Four* (i.e., the great men of Athens—Miltiades, Cimon, Themistocles, and Pericles) are replies to Plato, six

---

2. The Greek for "sublimity" is *hupsos*, literally "height," "elevation."—Trans.

centuries later. Like Isocrates, Aristides wrote a *Panathenaicus*; like Isocrates, he pleaded the cause of concord. He also wrote occasional pieces and
speeches on fictitious events. In all, fifty-five of his speeches have survived.
The most curious and personal are the six books of *Sacred Discourses*, in
which he speaks of himself, his illnesses, and the miraculous cures he received from Asclepius at Pergamum. Aelius Aristides believed in dreams,
prophecies, and premonitory signs: this follower of Isocrates had a taste for
the irrational.

This taste would prove characteristic of the Second Sophistic. The men
who belonged to the movement were Asians for the most part, fond of bombast and of playing the magician. Among them Nicetes was from Smyrna,
Lollianus from Ephesus, Scopelianus from Clazomenae, Hadrianus and
Maximus from Tyre, and Polemon from Laodicea. Almost all looked to Gorgias and his stylistic figures rather than to the restraint of Attic style. They
cultivated the seductive charms of poetic speech, enhanced by metaphors
and declaimed in an "inspired" manner. Many of them readily affected
trances or states of holy rapture. Sophists though they were, they did not
limit themselves, in their art, to the reasoned techniques of speech.

We are familiar with these characteristics thanks to the work of Philostratus. There were in fact several men by that name, all related to one another in
various degrees, who wrote during succeeding periods of the empire; as may
be imagined, this creates some confusion about the authorship of particular
works. But the two important pieces known as the *Lives of the Sophists* and
the *Life of Apollonius of Tyana* were the work of the second Philostratus, a
man who lived from about 160 or 170 to 245 or thereabouts; in Rome, he was
a protégé of the empress Julia Domna, wife of Septimus Severus (herself a
Syrian and daughter of a priest of the Sun).

The *Lives of the Sophists*, which begins with Gorgias and continues
through the Second Sophistic, is the source that best conveys the histrionic
and inspired tendencies characteristic of the new oratory. The *Life of Apollonius of Tyana* moves immediately into the world of magic or miracle. It is a
work in eight books, devoted to a thaumaturgist of the first century who
claimed connections with the Pythagoreans. Philostratus's work portrays
this miracle worker as a divine being; it describes his voyage to India (where
he witnessed all sorts of wonders), his passage to Alexandria and then to
Ethiopia (where he met the Gymnosophists)—not to mention his miraculous
escape from prison in Rome. The book was later compared with the Gospels.
It is certainly not worthy of the comparison. But it is a good index of the ill-
defined aspirations toward mysticism and the supernatural that the Asian
provinces brought, in the early third century, to the steadily weakening empire. These aspirations account for the growing popularity of Oriental cults
(the cult of Mithra and the cult of Isis and Osiris), and were indeed to find
some sort of fulfillment with the appearance of the Christian religion.

The sophistic tradition did not die out upon the appearance of Christianity; on the contrary, it enjoyed a revival in the fourth century under the aegis of the emperor Julian. By that time, Sophists and Christians had established relations with one another and were engaged in a dialogue. I therefore discuss these developments at the end of the chapter, after introducing the early Christian authors.

IV · THE ROMANCE

The romance, precursor of the novel,[3] was born in the first century after Christ; it grew up on the periphery of history and rhetoric. To the former it owes its narrative framework, to the latter its sense of fictional situations and its art of illusion. It also owes a great deal to the plots of New Comedy. Yet its characteristics make it a distinct genre, with its own precise requirements. The first is that every romance be the story of a couple in love but separated by a thousand circumstances, which entail long voyages for both before the final reunion. Indeed, the titles of most Greek romances consist of the two lovers' names (*Chaereas and Callirhoe, Daphnis and Chloe*, etc.; similarly, the *Ephesiaca* is another name for *Habrocomes and Anthia*, as the *Aethiopica* is for *Theagenes and Chariclea*). The more fearsome and protracted the adventures, the more laudable the fidelity and the more touching the joy when love at last finds its reward. (It is possible that the notion of the lover's quest is traceable in part to Oriental influences.) The genre is thus much more precise and distinctive than what the word "romance" implies to a modern ear; yet modern romances and novels have their antecedents in these early works, written in Greek during the Roman period.

The beginnings of the Greek romance are partially lost to us; we have only traces (some of which go back to the Hellenistic period) of narratives that were presented as historical but were fictional in content. Such are the "romances" about Troy (which laid claims to historicity, at least if we may judge by the somewhat later Latin narratives attributed to Dictys and Dares), or the adventures of Ninus and Semiramis (of which we have short papyrus fragments, and in which love already occupies a prominent place). The framework could also be geographical, as in the *Voyages of Iambulus* (quoted in part by Diodorus Siculus) or the *Marvels beyond Thule* (imitated by Lucian; a summary of it has survived).

Then, in the second century after Christ, we encounter true romances, which have survived. *Chaereas and Callirhoe* is a romance in eight books, written by Chariton, who was born at Aphrodisias in Caria. He portrays characters from the family of Hermocrates (the Syracusan of the fifth century B.C.) struggling with the king of Persia and his satraps; there are in-

---

3. In French, *roman* means both "romance" and "novel." These are usually considered two distinct genres, though the novel developed out of the romance.—Trans.

trigues, jealousies, a feigned death, robbers—all the devices of the adventure novel are already enlisted in the service of this romance.

The *Ephesiaca* is the work of Xenophon of Ephesus. This romance, in five books (perhaps ten originally), relates the adventures of Habrocomes and Anthia, who set off on a voyage to avoid the effects of a threatening oracle. Naturally a storm comes up, followed by shipwreck and pirates; the young couple is separated, and both fall into situations that try their virtue sorely; yet they manage to escape. The premises of the story, however, are drawn from actual conditions in the Mediterranean world at the time, and the fantastic is beginning to yield to a more novelistic vein.

The *Aethiopica* (or *Theagenes and Charicleia*) is the work of Heliodorus, a Phoenician from Emesa; it probably dates from the third century. Charicleia is a young Ethiopian princess who has been abandoned by her mother and raised at Delphi; Theagenes is in love with her. In obedience to an oracle, both leave Delphi; they are shipwrecked, fall into the hands of robbers, and become the objects of fearful passions (the wife of the satrap of Egypt falls in love with Theagenes). They are on the point of being sacrificed to the Sun in Charicleia's native Ethiopia when they are recognized, freed, and joined in marriage. The opening of the tale is lively, the characters diverse, the genre scenes brilliant. It might be said that the author succeeds in giving life to the most artificial and conventional material.

With these three romances, very similar in kind, I should list others; some have been lost (like the *Babyloniaca* of the Syrian Iamblichus, not to be confused with the philosopher of that name) and others preserved (like the *Adventures of Leucippe and Cleitophon*, by Achilles Tatius, narrated in the first person by the hero, whose adventures take him from Syria to Egypt and from Egypt to Asia Minor). By and large, all these romances betray the same taste for travel and imagined adventures that found expression in works such as the *Life of Apollonius of Tyana*. The capital difference is the role of love. And there is one romance, somewhat different from the rest, in which love has a still greater role and from which travel adventures have been eliminated: Longus's *Daphnis and Chloe*. As the characters' names indicate, this is a pastoral or bucolic romance; in French it is often referred to as *Pastorales*. Lost at birth, Daphnis and Chloe are raised by shepherds, in Lesbos. They meet of course with the customary adventures: Daphnis is carried off by marauders, Chloe is the object of a cowherd's advances, Daphnis inspires an untimely passion in a certain Gnathon, and so on. But the countryside—the same countryside we found in Theocritus—enfolds eveything in its atmosphere, and the descriptions of rustic life give the story a more concrete presence, not lacking in charm. There is also, in the description of awakening love, an unconscious but compelling sensuality. Chloe's love for Daphnis comes upon her when she helps him to bathe, and finds him beautiful; from then on, without knowing what has happened to her, "she [has] no taste for anything; her eyes no longer [obey] her; Daphnis's name [is] always on her lips." Daphnis, for his part, is moved by a kiss: "It was as though instead of a kiss he had received a burning sting; he suddenly grew sad, shivered, and tried to check the beating of his heart; he wanted to look at Chloe, and when he did, a flush spread over his face." We can see that the Lesbian shepherd is faithful to his island's poetess; here Longus speaks with the voice of Sappho. These original qualities of the romance, together with its relative brevity (it is only four books long), account for its exceptional popularity. Amyot and P.-L. Courier translated it into French; Goethe thought Longus greater than Virgil; and the work was a source of inspiration both to the painter Corot and to the composer Maurice Ravel.

At about the same time that the romance began to flourish, a taste for love letters was spreading. Indeed, the writing of fictional letters in general became quite the fashion. Alciphron was remarkably successful at it, and a collection of 118 of his letters has survived—a series of genre paintings in prose, as it were. It was natural that love should make a place for itself in this genre as well, until in the fifth century it became predominant in Aristaenetus's collection of fifty letters, steeped in literary allusion and pastiche.

This double taste for love and imaginary narrative is yet another mark of an era in retreat from reality. It conveys the same escapism to be found in our detective novels; but in a different civilization it took a different form: the Greek literature of the empire seeks escape in the refinements of a culture that imitates itself.

V · LUCIAN

Lucian is the incarnation of all the diverse tendencies I have noted in the Greek literature of the Roman era. Like Plutarch, he wrote many short treatises on a variety of questions, often moral questions. Second, he was a professional Sophist, and left works characteristic of the interests of the Sophistic. But he also wrote imaginary narratives for pleasure and amused himself by imitating the romances that were all the rage. By a rather remarkable paradox, however, his chief concern was to lampoon the age in which he lived, with its philosophy, its history, its rhetoric, its romances, its taste for the irrational. He was both a faithful representative of his age and a harsh judge of it. In this respect he is doubly qualified to close this all-too-brief review of the era.

I should add that—as another paradox would have it—this impeccably Attic writer, whose works are used to teach modern children to read Greek, was a "barbarian" by birth: this Syrian from Samosata himself learned Greek at school. He was born around 120 or 125; and he himself tells us (in *The Dream*) how he was first apprenticed to an uncle who made statuettes. After being beaten for breaking a stone slab, he gained permission to study with some Greek teachers of rhetoric (thus "Culture," *Paideia*, wins out over "Sculpture" in the debate which, as he tells it, was to decide his future). Indeed, he was soon a Sophist himself, teaching throughout Greece, Italy, and

Gaul to great acclaim and writing for show, as the Sophists did. Then, about 160 or 165, he grew tired of this life and broke with rhetoric. Again we have his own description, in *The Double Indictment, or Trials by Jury*, of the "trial" in which Rhetoric charges him with ingratitude for leaving her and taking up with the Dialogue. At this time Lucian came to settle in Athens, where he frequented philosophic and intellectual circles. It was not his first contact with philosophy; at Rome he had known the Platonist Nigrinus (he devoted a dialogue to him—*Nigrinus, or The Portrait of a Philosopher*). He may have found the spirit of the Cynics and the memory of Menippus's satires (mentioned in the last chapter) more to his taste: Menippus is a character in various dialogues by Lucian (he appears in ten of the thirty "Dialogues of the Dead"). But Lucian's chief reaction to these philosophers and their debates was to elicit laughter at their expense. In his writings of the Athenian period, which make up the bulk of his work, he pokes fun at them and their doctrines—and at human foibles generally. He had found his own voice, his genre, his tone. Yet after twenty years of this brilliant and waggish existence he gave it all up again—he left Athens. We know less about his last years—only that he became a traveler again, and then held a post in Egypt before his death at the end of the century.

His literary production is sizable and extraordinarily varied. Eighty-two works bearing his name have survived. Without the shadow of a doubt, this collection includes works that are not his (such as the treatise *On the Syrian Goddess*, which describes, in the Ionian dialect, religious observances scarcely to Lucian's taste); on the other hand, we certainly do not have his work in its entirety. He wrote something in almost every genre, even poetry (short dramatic pieces and a collection of some fifty epigrams). We may pass over the latter, as we may pass over his strictly sophistic writings, works of sheer virtuosity (*Encomium on the Fly, The Consonants at Law*, hypothetical trial speeches such as *The Tyrannicide*). There remains a whole series of pieces in which this imaginative moralist criticized the foibles of those around him.

Sometimes his criticism is purely literary, as in the little treatise *How to Write History*, where he makes fun of the contemporary craze for writing history. He also mocks authors who "spend their time showering praises on princes and generals, raising those of their own nation to the skies and tearing their enemies down," or who produce fabulous tales and grandiloquent prologues that are mere copies, some more skillful than others, of earlier authors' works. Lucian's criticism is reasonable; he does a good job of pinpointing the faults of his age.

He also makes fun of contemporary romances in the *True Story*: he takes it upon himself to write one in his turn—as he says, "not wanting to be the only man who failed to take advantage of the freedom to make believe." In his story, he specifies, *nothing* will be true; and there follows an account of fantastic voyages—first to the moon, then into the stomach of a gigantic whale, then to the Isles of the Blessed and the land of dreams. The mainspring of the work is parody, but Lucian's talent makes it engaging in its own right.

The irrational character of many of his contemporaries' works drew down harsher mockery from Lucian. Two of his pieces should be contrasted with the *Life of Apollonius of Tyana*, discussed above. The letter *On the Death of Peregrinus* mocks the latter's sensational suicide and the fund of hypocrisy that never seemed to fail him; the credulity of the age stands fully revealed at the end, when the death of the unprepossessing Peregrinus becomes a kind of apotheosis, complete with miracles. The piece entitled *Alexander or The False Prophet* is likewise the story of an imposter who feigned mystical raptures, practiced prestidigitation, gave out oracles, and made Rome buzz with his feats. Lucian's criticism of him is particularly harsh, and undoubtedly justified. This criticism, I should add, was extended to less unusual forms of credulity as well: Lucian has often been compared to Voltaire, and, like Voltaire, he detested superstition. His little piece *On Funerals* disparages funeral rites and the beliefs they imply; and his irreverent portrayal of the gods is done in just the spirit we would call Voltairean.

But with these attacks on credulity I have already moved from Lucian's critique of literary fashions to his critique of beliefs and doctrines. In this sphere, it should be noted, he reserves his most virulent attacks for the philosophers, with their abstruse doctrines and their quarrels. A characteristic title is *Philosophies for Sale*: in a short comic scene, Zeus puts the representatives of the major philosophical schools up for sale; the doctrines of each, summarized by an outsider, seem outlandish and ridiculous. The same philosophers reappear, with others, in *The Fisherman, or The Dead Come to Life*; this time Philosophy is their judge, and the bait used to catch them is gold. Comparable attacks may be found in the *Timon*, in which a philosopher with a long beard is caught red-handed trying to satisfy his greed, and especially in the *Icaromenippus*. This dialogue, like the *True Story*, uses the premise of a voyage "beyond the clouds," to where Zeus lives; but the point here is that from so high up and so far away, men's follies are more visible. First Menippus stops along the way to look back at them; then, on reaching Zeus's abode, he watches the god carry on his work of world administration, wrestling with the contradictory or absurd wishes of men. But of all these evils, one of the worst is again the attitude of the philosophers, "that lazy race, quarrelsome, vain, short-tempered, gluttonous, fantastic, bloated with pride and insolence." There can be only one solution: Zeus decides to use his thunderbolt.

It should be obvious from these summaries that Lucian's real charge against the philosophers is that they are vainer and more absurd than other men while sharing all the rest of their faults. These short pieces and dialogues are more original in form than in content.

In fact, the ideas involved are simple and reasonable. Lucian parades before us the ludicrous "types" of a society—the parasite, the misanthrope, and all the rest. Two themes recur frequently, for Lucian freely rails against the vanity of wealth and the vanity of wishes. The theme of wealth appears, for example, in *The Dream or The Cock*, a dialogue between a cobbler who dreams of striking it rich and his cock, who turns out to be Pythagoras reincarnate and opens the cobbler's eyes to the cares of rich men. (We recognize here the theme of La Fontaine's fable, *The Cobbler and the Rich Man*.) The same notion resurfaces in *Timon or the Misanthrope*, in which Poverty and Wealth appear (as in Aristophanes' *Plutus*). We find it yet again in *Charon, or The Onlookers*, in which Charon[4] takes a day off and observes the misfortunes of the rich and powerful. As for the futility of wishes, an idea that surfaces in several of the texts I have already discussed (the *Icaromenippus*, and even the dialogue of *The Cock*), it is the central theme of the dialogue entitled *The Ship, or The Wishes*, in which each character foolishly indulges in impossible wishes.

Lucian's "wisdom" would be a little thin if it were not set off by a lively and charming form. The dialogue was a well-established genre in Greek literature before his day—we need only recall the dialogues of Plato—and this tradition doubtless explains the suitability of the form for a writer who wanted to discuss ideas. But Lucian's dialogues are very different from Plato's. They have the sarcastic irony of the Cynics' satires and the gay spontaneity of New Comedy. In this respect they usher in a new literary form; and Lucian was conscious of this, for he declared repeatedly that there had previously been no similarity of tone between the dialogue and comedy, and that he had been the first to bring them together. In the *Double Indictment*, for example, he says that the dialogue, before he took it in hand, looked venerable but not very ingratiating to the reader: "I began to teach him to walk on the ground like a man; I washed off all the grime that covered him, and by forcing him to smile, I made him more agreeable to the spectators. But above all, I paired him with comedy, and by this connection assured him of the goodwill of the audience, who until then had feared his bristles and no more dared to touch him than they would a hedgehog" (34).

Even in Plato's hands the dialogue had portrayed characters who were no longer living, but these were described as they had been in life. Lucian's fame largely rests on his dialogues among gods and among the dead. Like his imaginary travelers who go off "beyond the clouds," Lucian's dialogues go off into unreal worlds, and thereby open up increased possibilities for themselves. Many writers, in France and elsewhere, were to emulate him; Fontenelle and Fénelon, to name only two, wrote *Dialogues of the Dead*.

Nor should we be surprised to find such men among his posterity. Toward the end of classical Greek literature, Lucian, who was not Greek and lived in an age that had nothing "classical" about it, displayed even in his innovations a kind of polished, classical grace. And yet the world in which he lived,

---

4. The ferryman who, in Greek mythology, carried the souls of the dead across the Styx to Hades.—Trans.

which is reflected rather faithfully in his work, was a world in transformation and in disarray, ready to collapse in every sector.

VI · PHILOSOPHY

Before I describe the appearance in Greek literature of the absolutely new element that was Christian literature, it is only proper to recall that over against these works of history, romance, and rhetoric, philosophy continued to develop and was evolving in a profoundly original direction, of which Lucian gives us little idea.

This is not altogether true of scientific investigation: the age of great discoveries was past. Yet research continued in a variety of fields. At about the time of Marcus Aurelius, astronomy was enriched by the famous system of Ptolemy, which took its place in the series of discoveries stretching back to the Alexandrian age; and in the same period medicine produced a famous name, Galen, who compiled a true critical summa of the knowledge that had been assembled in his field. He was from Pergamum, and the breadth of his learning was exceptional. His bibliography included no fewer than 153 works; many have survived, either in Greek or in Latin or Arabic translations, and not all are on the subject of medicine. I should add that by the second half of the first century after Christ the roster of pharmacology included a name destined for lasting fame, and a work that has come down to us—that of Dioscorides. Although these names were important during the Middle Ages, they were few in number and clearly did not represent a major revival of scientific learning.

Certain philosophic doctrines, on the other hand, enjoyed a remarkable expansion and took on new coloring. Skepticism remained marginal; yet it did produce one of its greatest exponents during this period, Sextus Empiricus ("the Empiricist"),[5] who lived toward the end of the second century and was a resolute foe of all dogmatists, scholars, and rhetoricians. The violence of his attacks on the power of reason may in itself be a sign of the times in which he lived. A more clear-cut revival is apparent among the Stoics and, more particularly, the Platonists.

The leading representatives of Stoicism at this period were a Phrygian slave and a Roman emperor. The slave, Epictetus, lived during the reigns of Nero and his successors. His master had him educated, and later, after his manumission, Epictetus began to teach Stoic philosophy, first in Rome and then in Epirus. He had many followers; Arrian took it upon himself to disseminate his thought by publishing the *Discourses* and the *Handbook*. From Stoicism, Epictetus retained chiefly the ethical teachings and, within ethics, gave pride of place to the notion of the sage's liberation. His love of humanity seems to reflect the new era. The emperor Marcus Aurelius (121–80), though

5. The epithet identifies him as a member of the "empirical" school of physicians, the *empeirikoi.*—Trans.

a Roman, often wrote in Greek; his major work is his *Meditations*, a kind of journal of his inner life around the years 170–74. Here he expresses an ideal of serenity, acceptance, and aspiration to imitate God; most striking is the personal accent he gives to this ideal, as if he is not only preaching but living it. Stoic philosophy was becoming less and less doctrinaire, and ever more interested in the inner life of the individual. At a time when Christianity was beginning to spread, non-Christian philosophy was already assuming some of the characteristics of the faith and of its dialogue with God.

As for Platonism, it was so powerfully renewed from within that for this era we must speak of "Neoplatonism." The man responsible for the internal renewal was Plotinus. He was born in Egypt in 204; after devoting his youth to studies in Alexandria, he came to teach in Rome, where despite his success he led an austere and unpretentious life. He died in Italy at the age of sixty-six. All his life he continued to teach and to keep a disorganized record of his reflections. His follower Porphyry later published these reflections, editing them as six series of nine treatises each, called the *Enneads* ("Nines").

Plotinus was a follower of Plato; he cites him as an authority, and uses Plato's works as the point of departure for his own reflections. It should be noted, however, that he did not retain all of Platonism. What mattered to him above all was its first step, which dissociates the sensible world from the world of ideas, finds the former inferior, and seeks to free itself from it as much as possible. Liberation from the body and assimilation to God, as described in the *Phaedo*, are the very heart of Plotinus's thought; and the notion of the revelation of the Good in its ineffable nature, as we find it in Plato's Seventh Letter, delimits the ultimate aim of that thought.

By putting this aspect of Platonism first, however, Plotinus added a new dimension to it and gave it a much more mystical cast. Like Epictetus, he sought complete detachment from the sensible world, to be achieved through a form of asceticism; this was to lead not only to a contemplation of the Good, as in Plato, but to a true union with it. The imitation of God was an end acknowledged by Plato and Marcus Aurelius; Plotinus added the idea of true communion with God, achieved through ecstasy. Nor was this aspect of his thought a mere question of emotional coloring. It entailed belief in everything that could serve as intermediary between man and God—rites, astrology, belief in "daemons." So it came about that Neoplatonism was far less rationalistic, and more religious, than the Platonism from which it claimed descent. It was no longer concerned with dialectic or political thought; it had broken with the actual to seek "the beyond" at once, in the present moment.

This revised form of Platonism played a major role in the culture of the empire, and in many ways seems characteristic of that culture. Some scholars have tried to depict it as an effect of Oriental influences, and it is indeed possible that such were involved. Plotinus had lived in Alexandria and made no secret of his desire to know the wisdom of Persia and India. Yet his elaboration of Platonism seems largely a function of the new era in which he lived.

After all, Oriental influences were in themselves an effect of the growth of the empire. Similarities among the doctrines of different schools point to a ferment in the sphere of ideas and to shared aspirations. The insistence on the individual's spiritual quest and the disappearance of political philosophy correspond to the new political situation. Above all, the mysticism that surfaces in Neoplatonism corresponds to both the longing for escape and the taste for the irrational that were then becoming widespread. These new tendencies, visible in both Plotinus and Marcus Aurelius, clearly prefigure the imminent triumph of Christianity.

The name of Plotinus cannot be dissociated from that of his follower Porphyry, who not only published his teacher's writings but wrote his biography as well. Porphyry, the great prophet of Neoplatonism, completed the work of transforming philosophy into a "science of God," or *theosophia*. He was also interested in the history of philosophy and the lives of philosophers (a discipline in which Diogenes Laertius—from Laerte in Asia Minor—had recently won recognition); we have a *Life of Pythagoras* from Porphyry's hand as well. Most important—and a new departure in the pagan works of the time—he felt it necessary to defend his teachers' thought against the new religion: he wrote a piece called *Against the Christians*. With this third-century man (who lived from 223 to 303, and was a native of Tyre), a dialogue is finally joined between pagan and Christian thought. And it was high time: Porphyry had been a student of Longinus but had also known a great doctor of the Church, Origen.

The Neoplatonist trend outlived Plotinus and Porphyry. At the beginning of the fourth century it was represented by the Syrian Iamblichus (who also wrote a *Life of Pythagoras*); his treatise *On the Mysteries* purports to be the work of an Egyptian priest and reveals the ever more religious and "orientalizing" cast of philosophy. Neoplatonism was also destined to influence the emperor Julian. In the fifth century it was represented in Athens by Proclus (410–85), who was born in Byzantium. Among Proclus's works we find *Elements of Theology*, a *Commentary on the Timaeus*, and a study *On Platonic Theology*; these titles eloquently convey the double inspiration behind his thought. But he was more dogmatic and less fervid than his predecessors. With Proclus, Neoplatonism was becoming systematized—and frozen.

The mysticism that had surfaced in it made a further appearance in a series of writings related to Neoplatonism, which may be traced to the third century. The writings are called "hermetic" because they were handed down under the name of Hermes Trismegistus, a sage or god said to have made revelations to the Egyptians (later, the invention of alchemy was attributed to him). The literature that developed around this legendary character was to paganism what Gnosticism was to Christianity. It included an acceptance of dualism and discussions of various doctrinal points in a search for the means to a closer union with God. Oriental influences can be detected in it; they are still more obvious in the *Chaldaean Oracles*, a work of the same genre dating from the reign of Marcus Aurelius. The age as a whole was inclined to religion, mysticism, and mystery. It rediscovered Plato because of the divorce he postulated between body and soul; but its Plato was a Plato without reason and without the struggle for clarity—a Plato who was Apollonius of Tyana's contemporary and who, in a world on the verge of ruin, was possessed by a desire to escape at any cost, though his "flight" was toward God. In some respects, Neoplatonism was not so far removed from Christianity as to prevent its being put to use by the Christians.

VII · THE CHRISTIANS

It would be impossible to present the history of Greek Christian literature here, even in abbreviated form. This literature was in full flower from the first to the fifth centuries and comprises a large body of notable works. Furthermore, despite the possible points of contact I have just indicated, its problems, its points of reference, its intellectual framework, and even its traditions are different from those of classical Greek literature. As Christian historians were only interested in the history of the Church, so Christian thinkers were only interested in their religion, in revelation, and in Holy Scripture. At most we may venture to cite Synesius of Cyrene (370–413) as the author of sophistic works in the traditional mold—but these works preceded his conversion, and were followed by others of an entirely religious nature. If one was a Christian, in that period, one was nothing else. Early Christian literature, which is sui generis, must therefore be studied in works devoted to it alone. I have included this overview only because it seemed impossible, in discussing the pagan thinkers, to omit all mention of the Christian efflorescence, which dates from the same centuries and to which the pagans were often responding; but I offer only a very schematic frame of reference.

For this reason I will pass over the earliest Christian writings in Greek that have survived, which consist of letters and apologetic works, scarcely venturing outside the genre of occasional writing. At the end of the second century, however, major authors appear, whose intellectual ambitions are far-reaching and who set out to use the heritage of Greek culture in defense of Christianity. Thus we may observe a sort of exchange taking place. While religious aspirations were developing in pagan thought, the literary traditions of paganism were being incorporated into Christian writings.

The most representative figure of the late second century is Clement, called Clement of Alexandria because he came there to study under a former Stoic who had converted to Christianity, and because he taught there himself from 190 to 203. The persecutions of Septimus Severus put an end to his teaching. He probably died around 215. This enormously learned man put all his erudition at the service of his faith. He left a variety of works, three of which (despite differences in length) make up a kind of sequence—the *Protrepticus*, the *Paedagogus* ("Tutor"), and the *Stromateis*. The titles of the first two speak for themselves. "Protrepticus" means "exhortation." This relatively short work is addressed to minds that are still undecided or less than adequately imbued with the faith; it invites them to reject paganism with its materialism, contradictions, and immorality. The *Paedagogus* is addressed to converts and consists of a series of counsels designed to teach them to live according to the new ideal. Finally, the *Stromateis*, a work in seven books, is addressed to Christians, for whom it tries to elucidate all the doctrinal problems Christianity can raise. It treats of a variety of themes (*stromateis* means tapestries) and is more straightforwardly theological.

This progression is characteristic of Clement's own mind. He means to fight paganism, but without breaking his ties to Greek philosophy. On the contrary, he arranges a sort of transition from Greek philosophy to Christianity. He sees the former as a kind of preparation, a propaedeutic, and thus takes pains to rehabilitate it for the benefit of religion. In his writings we find a great many references to pagan philosophy and a deliberate effort to bring reason into conjunction with faith. This effort alone gives his teaching the status of a true Christian humanism. Conversely, his work establishes Christianity within the province of Greek letters. The fact that he was Origen's teacher only increases his importance.

Origen was an Alexandrian Christian who at an early age displayed a double passion for study and for the Christian faith (and this during the very height of the persecutions). Born in 185, he was already teaching as a young man (under twenty years of age); but in 232 he had to leave Alexandria after being convicted of heresy. He then taught in Caesarea, and later in Tyre, where he died at the age of seventy, having managed to survive a variety of persecutions. Like his teacher Clement, Origen made room for pagan learning: his teaching began with dialectic and the sciences, and rose in stages to encompass philosophy and theology. He also took up the principle (once adopted by Philo) of distinguishing between the material and the spiritual meanings of a text, thereby admitting allegorical interpretations. This was undoubtedly the source of the propositions that were condemned as unorthodox (e.g., the inequality of the three divine Persons, which was also to generate the controversy over Arianism).

But the condemnation itself proves that Origen was much more of a theologian than Clement had been. And he was a scholar as well. He produced an edition of the Scriptures in Hebrew with several parallel translations, as well as scholia, homilies, and running commentaries on various points. He did not hesitate to raise the most difficult questions about revelation or about the incarnation, and in so doing he provided a model for the exegesis of sacred texts. His treatise *On the Fundamental Doctrines* (which survives in Latin translation, as *De Principiis*) is in the same spirit. At the same time, Origen was a polemicist like Clement—though much more systematic and dialectical. Under the Antonines a Platonist named Celsus had written a treatise, the *True Account*, attacking the Christians. Origen took it upon himself to draft a reply, *Against Celsus*, which has been preserved. Its eight books, written shortly before 250, contain a severe and resolute critique of Greek philosophy, which Origen found ill adapted to the mass of humanity.

Origen was discussed, condemned, listened to. Works were written both for and against him. Yet these debates remained academic, and it was not until the following century that the most talented of the Christian writers began to make themselves heard.

The fourth century opens with Eusebius, whom I have already mentioned as a historian (at the end of sec. III above) but who also produced exegetic and apologetic works. In two great works, the *Praeparatio Evangelica* in fifteen books and the *Demonstratio Evangelica* in twenty books, he criticized the non-Christian theologies and demonstrated the correspondences between the facts of the Gospel and Old Testament prophecies. Like his historical works, these represent a scholarly gathering of facts and quotations rather than a body of critical or philosophic thought.

In the course of the fourth century, however—a century whose beginnings witnessed both the triumph of Christianity (with Constantine's victory at the Milvian Bridge, in 312) and some of its bitterest internal struggles (over the Arian heresy, condemned in 325)—there appeared the great works of Christian evangelization, exhortation, and exegesis, to which Greek learning added a true literary luster. Some of these doctors of the Church were not only spiritual leaders but true men of action: the Church had become a "great power."

The first in date was Athanasius, patriarch of Alexandria and the most stubborn antagonist of the Arian heresy; in opposition to Arius's followers, he championed the consubstantiality of Father and Son. Nor was the struggle confined to the plane of ideas; during this troubled period, Athanasius was by turns honored and exiled, recalled and dismissed by the emperors. Only the years immediately preceding his death in 373 were relatively peaceful. His work, not unexpectedly, reflects some of these quarrels. It includes several attacks on Arius's followers as well as justifications and defenses of his own position. Athanasius also wrote a *Discourse against the Hellenes*, a *Biography of Saint Anthony*, and *Pastoral Letters*. All in all, he was a fierce partisan of strict orthodoxy, forever returning to the notions of the unity of God and the divinity of the Word. More direct and single-minded than the other authors I have discussed, he moved farther away from Greek philosophy. At the same time, he had something his predecessors lacked: a bold and impassioned eloquence that brings to mind the tradition of Greek oratory—albeit in the service of a very un-Greek cause.

The task of defending orthodoxy next passed to the town of Caesarea—where Eusebius had been bishop—and to the province of Cappadocia, which in the fourth century took on a great importance for religion: Saint Basil, his friend Saint Gregory of Nazianzus, and his brother Saint Gregory of Nyssa were all Cappadocians. Basil himself was born in Caesarea; it was there that he first met Gregory of Nazianzus; and he too served as the city's bishop.

Basil the Great was born in about 330 and died in 379. The son of a rhetorician, he had a solid classical education and studied in Athens under Libanius (discussed below). Then he entered religious life, becoming a bishop in 370. After Athanasius's death he was the staunchest champion of orthodoxy, unchallenged in his authority as a leader of the Church. But he was more tractable by temperament than Athanasius, and more interested in ethics than in theology. One of his most original initiatives was the development of monastic life in Asia Minor, where he organized communities for which he established rules. His large literary output, like that of his predecessors, included dogmatic works. But he expressed himself in a more original vein in three sets of writings deriving from his work as a preacher: the *Homilies*, often on ethical questions; the ascetic writings, which correspond to his interest in monastic life, for which they establish rules; and finally the letters. In the homilies we see him in his role as teacher, making very simple commentaries on the Scriptures (for which he claims direct belief, without allegory or transposition) and marveling at the beauty of the world. His letters form a collection numbering 366 (not all are genuine); they were written between 357 and 378 and are addressed to all sorts of correspondents, including his friend Gregory as well as bishops, nuns, close relatives, and magistrates. This correspondence is a fertile source for the history of the age; at the same time it presents a lively picture of an active and generous man who is always ready to intervene in practical questions and to defend his diocese or his flock, but who is also amicable, tolerant, and understanding.

His friendship with Gregory of Nazianzus commends both men to us. Gregory was within a few months of Basil's age. He too studied in Caesarea, and then in Alexandria and Athens. He became a priest in 361 to assist his father, who was bishop of Nazianzus. For the rest of his life he was caught up in a constant oscillation between two poles; he would court solitude, only to let himself be torn from it in order to help his father or his friend Basil, archbishop of Caesarea, or to help the orthodox faithful of Constantinople, who were in danger after his dear Basil's death. Each time he returned as soon as he could to the solitary life that alone suited him. While he worked closely with his friend and was dedicated to defending the same ideas, he was of a quite different temperament.

His output, too, parallels that of Basil, though some of it strikes a tone that is more particularly his own. In the first place—a fact highly characteristic of the man—this cultivated lover of solitude was one of the few Christian authors to write poetry; the gap between Christianity and Greek letters was steadily closing. The subjects of his poems are ethical and religious. He also wrote epitaphs and epigrams. There is even a poem *On His Own Life*, and a shorter one *On the Sufferings of His Soul*; the expression of personal feeling no longer seemed out of place beside theology. In the fifty-odd speeches of Gregory's that have survived we also find occasional pieces, theological pieces, invectives (aimed at Julian), and eulogies (e.g., that on Athanasius, in 373). But this last category includes highly personal pieces, such as the eulogy for Caesarius (his brother), and above all the one for Basil in 379, in which the friend's emotion lends a confidential tone to the words of praise and the author's admiration for the man he is honoring takes on a poignant quality. Here too, then, the expression of personal feeling enters Christian literature. This is obviously an exceptional case, but the same tendencies may be found throughout Gregory's works. Accustomed to meditation, Gregory seems always to consult his personal experience—or his imagination—when he writes. Even his arguments have a personal coloring. Finally, we have a collection of his letters, as we do of Basil's (there are almost 250 of them, mainly dating from the end of his life). Their elegance and their very brevity are intrinsic to the art of the "lettered" man. Knowing this, the reader may be surprised that he was called "Gregory the Theologian"—a name evoking the solidity of his doctrine in the five *Theological Orations* delivered during his tenure as archbishop of Constantinople. His literary persona, in fact, was more original than his theology, and it may be that the former ensured acceptance of the latter.

Basil's brother Gregory of Nyssa, ten years younger than Basil, was raised by him and schooled in the same ideas. He too wrote a *Eulogy of Basil*, as well as a *Eulogy of Macrina*, their sister. A fervid theologian, he was a better philosopher than his two elders, as we can see from his treatises (such as the *Great Catechism*), his many speeches, and his letters. But he was also a lesser writer, and thus less important in the perspective of Greek literature.

In that perspective another Christian, a virtual contemporary of the three men I have been discussing (he was a few years younger than Gregory of Nyssa), has an important place—Saint John Chrysostom. With him, Christian preaching joined forces with the tradition of Greek learning, before the latter was snuffed out. He was born in 345 in Antioch, and he too received a solid classical education: he studied under Libanius and at first planned to make his career as an orator. This early training was to bear fruit in later years. Then John was baptized. His inclination drew him to solitude and asceticism; against his teachers' wishes he spent six years as an anchorite, and we shall find his taste for the monastic life expressed in his work. Returning to Antioch, he assumed pastoral duties, and for sixteen years was continually speaking, preaching, and pleading the cause of virtue. In 397 he was called, against his wishes, to the bishopric of Constantinople; and there everything went badly for him. He quarreled with the powerful eunuch Eutropius, then with the empress Eudoxia. He was unseated, banished, recalled, then abducted from his church in 404 and sent into exile. Transferred in 407 from the Armenian border to the east coast of the Black Sea, he died en route. This man who had held the crowds of Antioch and Constantinople in sway with his words met his end in the throes of oppression.

For John Chrysostom was above all a preacher. Treatises and letters of his have survived, but the most important part of his work is made up of homilies. Even his treatises are scarcely distinguishable from homilies; they are not scholarly works of theology but moral exhortations. This is true of his treatises *On the Priesthood* and *On Celibacy*, as well as of the other short works on Christian celibacy entitled *On Suspect Cohabitations* and *How to Practice Virginity*. The titles are sufficient indication that John was dedicated not only to sexual purity but to the ideal of ascetic and monastic life he had himself practiced in his youth, which at that time was not yet organized by orders and convents, each with its own strict rules.

It was naturally in his homilies that his gift for preaching found its fullest expression. They represent almost twenty years of ministry (even in Constantinople he preached twice a week). They show John to be a stern, acute critic of the vices rampant all around him. He criticized the love of pleasure, the practice of usury, the luxury in which the rich lived, and their hard-heartedness—no wonder he bothered the powerful classes in Constantinople. He knew too how to stand firm in the face of power and speak with great authority, as he did in his sermons *On the Statues,* delivered in a dark hour for the people of Antioch when they were trembling in anticipation of the emperor's judgment.[6] But John's tone is usually milder. He had a deep faith in God's goodness and love for mankind. Like Saint Paul, whom he particularly admired, he extolled pity, forgiveness, and gentleness. In his eyes, the preacher's task was to cure men's ills—and in caring for a sick man one does not resort to anger or brutal treatment: "If indeed it were a matter of punishment and our task were that of a judge, indignation would be *required*; but if we renounce this role for that of the doctor or healer, we must exhort and beg our patients, and if necessary even grasp their knees in supplication to win our ends" (*On Suspect Cohabitations* 1). Thus speech, whose power and efficacy know no limits, should also take on the qualities of understanding and penetration.

This is as much as to say that John recognized oratory as a precious means of action. He enriched it by drawing on all the rhetorical devices he had learned as a young man. Quotations from Scripture abound in his work, but we also find echoes and reminders of many classical Greek authors—Plato, Aeschylus, Homer, Demosthenes. His sentences, like those of Demosthenes, alternate between urgent haste and periodic fullness. His images are drawn from the Bible, but also from the poets of the Periclean age, or from his own experience. All of these resources are combined, caught up in a single flow of language, and attached to the service of a single cause. If John, like Dio, was "golden-mouthed," it was because he had disengaged himself from sectarian quarrels and had assimilated the heritage of pagan culture. It was also because, in the spirit of that culture, he tried to speak directly to men in order to improve their lives.

---

6. During a tax riot in 387, the Antiochenes threw stones at the statues of the emperors and dragged them from their bases. There was fear that all the citizens would be punished, but the emperor was prevailed upon to pardon most of them.—Trans.

With John Chrysostom we see Greek culture incorporated into a newly ascendant Christianity. It would distort the picture, however, to pass over the final effort, likewise made in the fourth century, to defend pagan values. To conclude my account of paganism—and of Greek literature—I shall describe this last upsurge, which took place under the aegis of the emperor Julian.

VIII · THE LAST FLARE OF PAGANISM

As young men, Basil the Great and Gregory of Nazianzus studied under pagan teachers of rhetoric, Himerius and Libanius. Hellenism in its traditional form was still alive and, indeed, enjoyed a last blaze of glory in the course of the fourth century. Those responsible were three professors and an emperor: Himerius, Libanius, Themistius—and Julian. They make up a fairly homogeneous group. The three professors, who loosely represent the three great cities of Athens, Antioch, and Constantinople, were very close in age. Julian was younger; he was born in 331, fifteen or twenty years later than the other three, and died earlier, killed in the course of a military retreat in 363. He was a patron to the three teachers: he summoned Himerius to Constantinople (and Himerius agreed to quit Athens for as long as Julian should live); he offered high office to Themistius, though without success; and he maintained a close friendship with Libanius. Libanius and Themistius were, moreover, "official" orators, in fairly close touch with the emperors, who could offer political advice or propose models for the rulers of the age; they were orators in the full sense of the word as it had been used in the Greek city-states.

Himerius remained a more marginal figure. He was primarily a Sophist who practiced his art in Athens, had a taste for poetry, and stubbornly carried on the traditional genre of the fictitious lawcourt speech. Twenty-four of his speeches have been preserved, representing less than a third of his work; but they are not of a quality to make us mourn the loss of the rest—except insofar as Himerius is a source for the life of his own day and for the earlier Greek poets, whom he quotes freely.

Libanius was less fettered by scholarly traditions. He was born in Antioch, where he ultimately settled down to teach, after having taught for a time in Constantinople and in Nicomedia. This great professor, bred on classical literature, could see beyond the limited craft of the man of letters. To be sure, he left technical works resembling those of Himerius; but in the tradition of the Second Sophistic he also knew how to involve himself in public affairs—how to speak out, give testimony, admonish, demand, and advise. Orators feel responsible for their cities, just as bishops do; and we have several speeches on the subject of his city, Antioch. Libanius's interests even extended beyond his city: faithful to the traditions of Hellenism and paganism, he put his hopes in Julian, who wanted to reaffirm their values. Several of his works are devoted to Julian, including the *Monody on Julian* and the *Epitaph on Julian*, which mourns the emperor's death and, with it, the end of the dream the two men had shared. Libanius's correspondence, including over

1600 letters, reflects the tireless activity of a man who was universally acclaimed but who saw that the studies and ideas he prized most highly were slowly dying.

Themistius had a still more direct link to political power and ideas. A native of Bithynia, he first taught in Constantinople, newly created the capital by Constantine in 330. He was close to the emperors and enjoyed good relations with them. He devoted speeches, official addresses, and encomiums to them—to Constantine as early as 347, and then to Jovian, Valens, and Theodosius. He even served as tutor to Theodosius's son, the future emperor Arcadius. So Julian was not his special hope or even, perhaps, his favorite pupil. Instead, what comes to the forefront in his speeches is a general theory of the good king, who lets himself be guided by philosophy. Here we recognize an ancient ideal, introduced by the Greeks of the fourth century B.C. Themistius refurbished it somewhat, by adapting it to the context of the empire and by further emphasizing certain values and ideas; thus he speaks readily of clemency, tolerance, and gentleness, or of the imitation of God. But in calling for a good monarch of this kind, to be molded by pagan thought alone, he was obviously reviving and building on ideas from the past. Likewise, in contrast to many Sophists of the period preceding his own, he refused to accept the divorce between oratory and philosophy; this rhetorician produced commentaries on Plato and Aristotle. Finally, Themistius was imbued with ancient oratory; this Bithynian defended Atticism. Like his two contemporaries he was faithful to the Greek tradition, which seemed threatened and which he wanted to revive at all costs.

The efforts of all three of these men (especially Libanius) played a part in the development of the emperor Julian's ideas; but the ideal of a Hellenic renaissance that animated Julian had deeper roots, a more religious emphasis, and a more militant cast. Moreover, his political position obviously gave it added weight.

Julian was the son of one of the emperor Constantine's brothers. Five years old when Constantine died, he narrowly escaped the death that overtook many of his family, whose existence troubled the heirs to the throne (his father and brother, an uncle, and several of his cousins were murdered at that time). As a result, Julian was raised far from the seats of power, in solitude; but the Scythian eunuch Mardonius, who was his pedagogue, filled his childhood with a love of Greek literature. This first introduction to Hellenism, which he thoroughly absorbed and made his own, was later rounded out by a more advanced course of instruction; Julian obtained permission to pursue his studies, which kept him removed from politics. He was a pupil of the rhetoricians and studied under Libanius (or, at least, read copies of his lectures) in Nicomedia before moving on to Athens, the old capital of Greek letters. At the same time, Julian became acquainted with Neoplatonism and its taste for mysteries and initiations, which the students of Iamblichus were promulgating. Thus the Hellenic heritage was being revived in both its forms—one literary and rational, the other transformed by the mystical leanings of the age.

Under this double influence, Julian found all he needed to meet his spiritual needs in the renascent pagan tradition. He renounced the Christian faith in which he had been raised, and from then on opposed it with all his might. As fortune would have it, in 355 Julian was recalled from Athens, given the title of Caesar,[7] and sent to Gaul, where his victories led to his being proclaimed emperor by the troops. He was destined to reign only two years, from 361 to 363. But this brief and brilliant career allowed him to express his convictions in word and deed.

Julian was violently attacked by the Christians as an apostate and as a persecutor of Christians. Yet he was above all an idealist, and his own tastes inclined him to tolerance. He wrote a treatise *Against the Christians* (of which we can form a fairly good idea, thanks to the responses it provoked). He complained of the absurdities to be found in the Bible and of the injustice and harshness of the Jewish God. He also seems to have had a horror of the intransigence shown by the Christians of his day, who had mired themselves in theological disputes and totally rejected the humanistic ideal developed by the Greeks. He clearly hoped that Greek beliefs, including Greek respect for political life, could restore the rightful glory of the empire.

On the other hand, the paganism he embraced had all the mystical warmth the age seemed to foster. His surviving oration *On the Sun King*, a kind of meditation, both pious and ecstatic, expresses his philosophy. He sings the praises of the Sun, which corresponds to the Good from which it emanates, as in Plato, but here takes on a mysterious power to protect and unify the world. The Sun "imparts to the whole visible universe a certain share of intelligible beauty." It "watches over the whole of the human race," and Julian prays to it as monotheists pray to their God: "May he grant me a virtuous life, a more perfect wisdom, a divine intelligence. May I depart from this life in complete serenity, at the hour chosen by destiny. May I then ascend to him and abide with him forever." Yet he offers equally fervent worship to other gods; thus we have his oration *On the Mother of the Gods*, written in a single night in a burst of devotion. Julian succeeded in finding a religious and philosophical meaning in the pagan myths. By combining the Cybele and Attis cults and the gods of the classical pantheon in a lofty syncretism, and by infusing the whole with the mysticism of his own day, Julian sought to give paganism the kind of fervor the Christians seemed to have made their own—a fervor true paganism had never known.

Julian's religious ardor was crowned by an austere and rather fierce sense of moral duty, which is conveyed more or less directly in his various writings and letters. It may be wrong to look for signs of it in his earliest orations, occasional works in which he does not always say what he thinks—such as the

7. In this period the title of *caesar* was given to members of the imperial family who were granted administrative authority over designated portions of the empire.—Trans.

encomiums on Constantius and Eusebia, or the little piece *On Kingship*, which is another encomium on Constantius. Some are much more sincere, like the letter *To the Senate and People of Athens*, issued in 361 as a manifesto and a passionate self-justification. Sometimes he adopts a more direct tone, as in the short satiric work called the *Misopōgon* or "Beard Hater." This too is a self-justification, but with nothing official about it, written in the aftermath of his bitter disappointment at Antioch in 362–63. Julian had hoped to establish a great cult of the sun god Apollo in that city; but his festival was a disaster, the temple was destroyed by fire, and the emperor, with his awkward figure and his beard, was made a figure of fun. In the *Misopōgon* he lashes out in his turn at the effeminate Syrians and their pleasure-filled life; he prefers the rustic virtue of the Celts. Resigning himself to unpopularity, he cites his acts of generosity and reproves the Antiochenes for their ingratitude.

An excitable and passionate man, Julian reveals himself as directly in this text as Jean-Jacques Rousseau could have done. But he also reveals a particular moral ideal, which is latent in his other works and only here finds more overt expression. This moral ideal demands justice, truth, and a disdain for pleasures. But of a sovereign it also demands virtues proper to his station. The sovereign should "do good to men" insofar as that is humanly possible. Libanius and Themistius said the same thing, but Julian is still more insistent, and the idea takes on a personal coloring, for in speaking of himself he affirms that this is what he has really tried to do at all times. How should one "do good"? Julian expounds this idea in terms of *philanthrōpia* ("love of men"), gentleness, and moderation. And he comes back to these values again and again. He speaks of them in some of his letters, and in his treatises; his references to them are doubtless the most genuine element of the encomiums composed in his youth, which, with respect to the persons they are supposed to describe, surely lack sincerity. He speaks of the same values in his satire *The Caesars*, a sizing-up of the various emperors in which *philanthrōpia* is often a criterion—and which gives the palm to the pagan philosopher-emperor, Marcus Aurelius.

This praise of gentleness may seem surprising, coming from a man who made himself known for persecutions. As a matter of fact, Julian had begun by issuing edicts of tolerance in favor of the pagans. But he came too late: the Christians could not bring themselves to relinquish the advantages they had won, and their stubborn opposition provoked his. Even the leniency he recommended to his administrators was often intended as a form of competition with the Christians. Lines were drawn; battle was joined; and Julian lost.

Of all the debates that filled the fourth century, the most baffling may be the one I have just discussed, which set Hellenism and Christianity against one another. Hellenism was anything but a religion; it was by no means synonymous with paganism. Indeed, if the defenders of paganism were swept from the scene with Julian, leaving the empire Christian from top to bottom, Hellenism could not vanish from the eastern empire, whose language was Greek. But it seems worthwhile to consider, in conclusion, the reasons for the confusion.

The reasons are of two kinds. The first are rooted in the history of the age. Clearly, neither the Christians nor the pagans had any intention of dissociating culture and religion; they could hardly have imagined such a thing was possible. The Christians, in many cases, represented a new social stratum. They were rejecting an entire tradition, whose literary works were full of the gods and legends of paganism. And if, after several centuries, the doctors of the Church were willing to look to Greek art for means to serve their faith, these very borrowings fueled their polemic against paganism. It was the same with the pagans. Without a doubt, they too were yielding to external influences; they even created a pagan form of mysticism; but, seeing their values threatened along with their religion, they equated the two. At the same time it cannot be denied that amidst political difficulties, geographic dispersion, and changing conditions and problems, Greek culture was becoming impoverished and lacked the fertility of earlier ages. This made it easier to identify it with the pagan religion, which it did not seem destined to outlive. Not until the Renaissance did Hellenism as a culture make its reappearance, in the very bosom of Christianity.

For us, in the modern age, this first group of reasons is augmented by a distorting effect of perspective. If Hellenism seems to have died with paganism, it is partly because both disappeared together when liberty disappeared from the Byzantine—as from the western—empire. Political liberty was supplanted by autocracy; philosophic and religious liberty was supplanted by the authority of the Church. And the two powers were linked, for the emperor was the head of the Church: the same ranks that had produced the martyrs now produced great administrators.

The lifeblood of Hellenism had been inquiry and debate, political struggles and struggles over ideas, discoveries, effort, criticism, and hope—all in search of the best possible life. Already under Alexander, and then under Roman rule, Hellenism had lost much of its vitality. The clear and living spring of its endlessly renewed questioning was cut off with the independence of the city-states, and of Greece itself: Hellenism could live only on liberty. It had managed to survive by taking an eager interest in the history of this new world that still resembled the old, or in the ideas, ethical or philosophical, that seemed still rooted in the old world. But the quality of historical writing deteriorated along with political liberty; and the process of intellectual renewal could not withstand the loss of religious liberty. Hence the impression that Hellenism disappeared with the triumph of Christianity—when in fact its disappearance was merely sealed by the loss of this last form of liberty.

More accurately, Hellenism did not disappear but fell into a long sleep. It was still alive, though dormant, in Byzantine Greece; it reappeared outside Greece during the Renaissance; and it reappeared in Greece after that country's liberation from the Turks. It is alive today. And I would like to think that my *Short History*, by bearing witness to this spiritual adventure of the past, might in some way foster its extension into the future.

Chronological Tables

The following tables combine information of several kinds (dates of birth and death, dates of works), much of it imprecise in nature. There is often considerable uncertainty about the exact dates to be associated with ancient authors, and some of these dates are objects of scholarly debate. Those I indicate here are thus simply approximate guidelines.

Events	Epic and Didactic Poetry
1500–1200: The Achaean age	
1180: Traditional date of the sack of Troy	
1200–1000: Dorian invasions	
Eighth Century 750–600: Age of colonization	Homer
Seventh Century	Hesiod
Sixth Century 594: Solon's reforms in Athens	
561–528: Pisistratus tyrant of Athens	
510: End of tyranny at Athens	

Lyric Poetry	*Philosophy*

Archilochus, Tyrtaeus, Semonides,
  Callinus

Alcman, Terpander

Mimnermus   Thales

Solon, Sappho, Alcaeus

                                                   Anaximander, Anaximenes

                                                   Xenophanes, Pythagoras

Theognis, Anacreon

                                                   Heraclitus

Simonides

                                                   Parmenides

525: Birth of Aeschylus
         (d. 455)

518: Birth of Pindar
         (d. 438)

Events	Drama
	499: Birth of Sophocles (d. 406–405)
490–480: Persian Wars; Greek victories at Marathon and Salamis	ca. 480: Birth of Euripides (d. 406–405)
477: Creation of Delian League; Athens assumes hegemony	472: Aeschylus, *Persians* (oldest extant Greek tragedy)
460: Pericles' faction takes the lead in Athens	
	458: Aeschylus, *Oresteia*
	ca. 445: Birth of Aristophanes (last work: 388)
443: Foundation of Thurii	442: Sophocles, *Antigone*
	438: Euripides, *Alcestis* (oldest extant tragedy by Euripides)
431: Beginning of Peloponnesian War (Athens and her allies versus Sparta and her allies)	431: Euripides, *Medea*
429: Plague at Athens; death of Pericles	428: Euripides, *Hippolytus*
	425–422: Aristophanes, *Archarnians, Knights, Clouds, Wasps* (in order of production)
421: Peace of Nicias between Athens and Sparta (soon broken)	

History	Philosophy
Birth of Herodotus (d. 425)	
	ca. 490: Birth of Protagoras (d. ca. 420)
	Empedocles
	ca. 470: Birth of Socrates
ca. 460: Birth of Thucydides	ca. 460: Birth of Democritus and Hippocrates
	Anaxagoras
	Protagoras drafts laws for Thurii
Thucydides begins his history of the war	
	427: Gorgias's embassy to Athens
424: Thucydides exiled	

Events	Drama
415–13: Sicilian Expedition	414: Aristophanes, *Birds*
	412: Euripides, *Helen*
411: Oligarchic coup at Athens	
	410: Euripides, *The Phoenician Women*
	409: Sophocles, *Philoctetes*
	408: Euripides, *Orestes*
	406–405: Deaths of Euripides and Sophocles; Aristophanes, *Frogs*
404: End of Peloponnesian War; defeat of Athens	
403: Oligarchy of the Thirty at Athens; its overthrow	
401: Xenophon's departure for Asia Minor with the "Ten Thousand"	401: Sophocles, *Oedipus at Colonus* (staged posthumously)

History	Philosophy

Point at which Thucydides'
history ends

Beginnings of Oratory

403: Lysias, *Against Eratosthenes*

Events	Drama	Oratory
399: Death of Socrates		399: Andocides, *On the Mysteries*
	392: Aristophanes, *Assembly of Women*	
	388: Aristophanes, *Plutus*	
377: Constitution of the Second Athenian League		
371: End of Spartan hegemony		
362: End of Theban hegemony		
360: Accession of Philip of Macedonia		
		355–354: Demosthenes enters political life
		349: Demosthenes, *Olynthiacs*
	342: Birth of Menander	
		341: Demosthenes, *On the Chersonese, Third Philippic*

Other Prose	_Philosophy_
	ca. 398: First dialogues of Plato (b. 427)
393: Isocrates (b. 346) opens his school	
ca. 390: Xenophon settles at Scillus	
	387: Plato opens the Academy
380: Isocrates, _Panegyricus_	
	367: Plato's second trip to Sicily
ca. 355: Death of Xenophon; Isocrates, _Areopagiticus_	
	347: Death of Plato
	342: Aristotle named tutor to Alexander

Events	Drama	Oratory
338: Philip's victory at Chaeronea		
334–323: Alexander's Asian campaign		330: Demosthenes, *De Corona*
323: Death of Alexander		322: Death of Demosthenes

Other Prose	*Philosophy*

338: Death of Isocrates

322: Death of Aristotle

Events	Latin Literature	Drama
		316: Menander, *Dyskolos*
		293–92(?): Death of Menander
285–246: Ptolemy II Philadelphus king of Egypt		
264–241: First Punic War between Rome and Carthage		
247–222: Ptolemy III Euergetes king of Egypt	Naevius	
200–197: First war between Rome and Macedonia	Ennius, Plautus, Cato	

Poetry	History	Philosophy
		Theophrastus succeeds Aristotle as head of the Lyceum
	Historians of Alexander	306: Epicurus opens his school
	Duris of Samos	301: Zeno opens his school in Athens
290–285: Callimachus settles in Alexandria		
		282: Cleanthes arrives in Athens
275: Theocritus, *Idyll* 16; Aratus invited to Macedonia		270: Death of Epicurus
		262: Death of Zeno
	ca 250: Death of Timaeus	
	246: Eratosthenes named librarian at Alexandria	
244: Last dated poem by Callimachus		
ca. 250–240: Apollonius, *Argonautica*		
		ca. 205: Death of Chrysippus (Old Stoa)
	ca. 200 (?): Birth of Polybius (d. aged 82)	

Events	Latin Literature	Drama
196: Flamininus proclaims the independence of Greece		
148: Macedonia becomes a Roman province		
	106–43: Cicero	
	100–44: Caesar	
	86–34: Sallust	
82–79: Dictatorship of Sulla	70–19: Virgil	
59: Caesar elected consul	A.D. 59–17: Livy	
44: Death of Caesar		
29: Accession of Augustus		

Poetry	History	Philosophy
	185–112: Panaetius	
167: Polybius in Rome		
	156: Carneades' embassy to Rome	
146: Polybius returns to Greece	135–51: Poseidonius	
ca. 90: Birth of Diodorus		
Between 60 and 55: Birth of Dionysius of Halicarnassus		
36: Last event referred to in Diodorus's *History*	39: Philo of Alexandria's embassy to Rome	

Events	Latin Literature	Poets
29 B.C.–A.D. 68: Rule of the Julio-Claudians	Ovid, Phaedrus	
	Seneca (4 B.C.[?]–65 A.D.)	
	23–79: Pliny the Elder	
	55–120: Tacitus	
	61–112: Pliny the Younger	
69–96: Rule of the Flavians		
96–192: Rule of the Antonines:		
117–138: Reign of Hadrian		
	ca. 124: Birth of Apuleius	
161–180: Reign of Marcus Aurelius		
	Tertullian (end of 2d to beginning of 3d c.)	
312: Constantine's victory at the Milvian Bridge		Quintus of Smyrna

Prose Authors	Christian Authors

ca. 40: Birth of Dio Chrysostom
   (d. 120)

ca. 50: Birth of Plutarch (d. 120)

Epictetus

95: Birth of Arrian (d. 175)

ca. 120: Birth of Lucian
   (d. sometime after 180)

Pausanius
129–189: Aelius Aristides

                                         150?–215: Clement of Alexandria

155–235: Dio Cassius

                                         185–255: Origen

204: Birth of Plotinus (d. 274)

Iamblichus

                                         265–340: Eusebius of Caesarea

                                         295–373: Athanasius

314–393: Libanius

317–388: Themistius

Events	Latin Literature	Poets
330: Byzantium named capital of the Empire		
	ca. 340: Birth of Ammianus Marcellinus	
	St. Hilarius, St. Ambrose, St. Jerome	
	354–430: St. Augustine	
361–363: Reign of Julian		
		Nonnus of Panopolis (5th c.)

Prose Authors	Christian Authors
	330: Birth of St. Basil and St. Gregory of Nazianzus
	345: Birth of St. John Chrysostom
410–485: Proclus	

Bibliography

The present bibliography has been compiled especially for this English edition, and differs substantially from that offered by Jacqueline de Romilly. Yet I have tried to use her entries as points of departure wherever possible, retaining many of the French works cited while adding works in English for the benefit of English-speaking readers. (The few German and Italian entries are works of considerable importance.) I have also tried to apply what I take to be the author's principles of selection for the original bibliography. Thus the listings are generous, though far from comprehensive, and represent a considerable range of scholarly opinion; they also include works that are basic tools of classical scholarship, for the benefit of beginning students and readers from outside the discipline. It should be noted that not all the works cited are available in every college library; students should not let this be a source of discouragement, for in many cases there are several good alternative editions. Because of space limitations, scholarly articles and many excellent secondary works have been omitted. The serious student, however, will find extensive bibliographies in most of the general works cited below. Lesky's *History of Greek Literature* and the *Oxford Classical Dictionary* are especially thorough, though Lesky quite naturally includes a high proportion of German sources, as de Romilly did of French ones. A virtually exhaustive listing of publications (including articles) on classical topics is available for the years since 1924 in the form of an annual, *L'Année philologique: Bibliographie critique et analytique de l'antiquité gréco-latine*. Though published in Paris, it is compiled by two distinct teams of researchers, one French and one American, who are helped by individual contributors in other countries. It should be noted that this work, like many of the foreign editions and concordances listed below, can be used quite easily by students whose only modern language is English, once a few conventional abbreviations have been mastered. The student with some knowledge of Latin will have an advantage, particularly in using some of the older editions and the Oxford and Teubner texts, which have notes or *apparatus criticus* in Latin. (*L'Année philologique* had two predecessors, still available in good reference collections: Scarlat Lambrino's *Bibliographie de l'antiquité classique*, covering the years 1896–1914, and J. Marouzeau's *Dix Années de bibliographie classique*, covering 1914–24 [rev. ed. 1957].)

The four most complete, and most frequently available, collections of Greek texts are the following: the Loeb Classical Library, published by Heinemann in London and by Harvard University Press in Cambridge, Massachusetts (a series of bilingual editions with Greek and English on facing pages); the Scriptorum Classicorum Bibliotheca Oxoniensis, commonly known as the Oxford Classical Texts (OCT), published by Oxford University Press (Greek only, with *apparatus criticus*); the Collection des Universités de France, usually referred to as the Budé editions because they are issued under the auspices of the Association Guillaume Budé (bilingual texts with Greek and French on facing pages); and the Bibliotheca Scriptorum Graecorum et Romanorum Teubneriana (Greek texts only, with *apparatus criticus*), published in Leipzig by Teubner. Because the Loeb editions are particularly useful to English-speaking beginners, I have made special mention of them while omitting the parallel editions in other collections except where these are exceptional in some way. Other editions (including many published by Oxford but not in the OCT series) are listed because they are especially good, frequently cited, or furnished with helpful commentaries. Because the translations in many of the Loeb editions are somewhat old, I have included a selection of good recent translations—and some classic translations—all of which are readily available. Unless identified as translations, all editions are in the original Greek.

BASIC REFERENCE WORKS

Andrewes, Antony. *The Greeks*. London: Hutchinson; New York: Knopf, 1967. A good general introduction to the cultural context of Greek literature.

Bengtson, Hermann, and Vladimir Milojcić. *Grosser historischer Weltatlas*. 4th ed. Munich: Bayerischer Schulbuch-Verlag, 1976. The best available atlas of the classical world.

Buck, Carl D. *The Greek Dialects*. Chicago: 1928. 3d ed. University of Chicago Press, 1955.

Cambridge Ancient History. 3d ed. London: Cambridge University Press, 1970–. An important multivolume work (still far from complete), available in many libraries. Earlier complete editions are also available.

Denniston, J. D. *The Greek Particles*. 2d ed., rev. K. J. Dover. Oxford: Clarendon Press, 1954.

Encyclopaedia Britannica. 11th ed. London and New York: Encyclopaedia Britannica, 1910. The famous eleventh edition, essentially reprinted in the twelfth and thirteenth editions, is still an excellent source of information on the classical world.

Jacoby, Felix. *Die Fragmente der griechischen Historiker*. 3 vols. in 16. Vols. 1 and 2, Berlin: Weidmann, 1923. Vol 3, Leiden: Brill. All vols. reprinted by Brill. Fragments of the Greek historians.

Kessels, A. H. M., and W. J. Verdenius. *A Concise Bibliography of Greek Language and Literature*. 2d ed. Apeldoorn: Administratief Centrum, 1982.

Kitto, H. D. F. *The Greeks*. London and Baltimore: Penguin, 1954.

Lefkowitz, Mary R., and Maureen B. Fant. *Women's Life in Greece and Rome: A Source Book in Translation*. London: Duckworth; Baltimore: Johns Hopkins University Press, 1982.

Liddell, Henry George, Robert Scott, Henry S. Jones, and Roderick McKenzie. *A Greek-English Lexicon*. 9th ed. Oxford: Clarendon Press, 1940. The leading Greek-English dictionary, often cited as "Liddell & Scott" or "LSJ." It is also published in two abridged versions for students. A supplement (ed. E. A. Barber) appeared in 1968.

The Oxford Book of Greek Verse. Ed. Gilbert Murray et al. Oxford: Clarendon Press, 1930. A selection of Greek verse from Homer to the Hellenistic age. In Greek.

The Oxford Book of Greek Verse in Translation. Ed. T. F. Higham and C. M. Bowra. Oxford: Clarendon Press, 1938. English translations of the poetry included in the *Oxford Book of Greek Verse*.

The Oxford Classical Dictionary. 2d ed. Ed. N. G. L. Hammond and H. H. Scullard. Oxford: Clarendon Press, 1970. A concise, reliable reference work, readily available.

The Oxford Companion to Classical Literature. Ed. Sir Paul Harvey. Oxford: Clarendon Press, 1937. Reprinted with corrections, 1966. Reprinted in paperback, 1984.

Pauly, August Friedrich von, and Georg Wissowa, eds. *Paulys Realencyclopaedie der classischen Altertumswissenschaft*. 24 vols. in 31. Stuttgart: J. B. Metzler, 1894–1963. Abridged and rev. as *Der Kleine Pauly: Lexikon der Antike*. 5 vols. Stuttgart: A. Druckenmüller, 1964–75. The unabridged edition, usually referred to as "Pauly-Wissowa," is the most exhaustive reference work on the classical world. The latest edition of *Der Kleine Pauly* ("Little Pauly") includes more recent bibliography.

Smyth, Herbert Weir. *Greek Grammar*. Rev. Gordon M. Messing. Cambridge, Mass.: Harvard University Press, 1956. First published in 1918, this is still the best reference grammar of ancient Greek in English.

West, Martin L. *Greek Metre*. Oxford: Clarendon Press; New York: Oxford University Press, 1982.

GENERAL CRITICAL STUDIES

As De Romilly notes in her bibliography, some of the most important and interesting works of classical scholarship are those whose scope would exclude them from a chapter-by-chapter listing. A limited selection of these is accordingly given here.

Adkins, Arthur W. H. *From the Many to the One: A Study of Personality and Views of Human Nature in the Context of Ancient Greek Society, Values, and Beliefs*. London: Constable, 1970.

————. *Merit and Responsibility: A Study in Greek Values*. Oxford: Clarendon Press, 1960.

Dodds, Eric R. *The Greeks and the Irrational*. Berkeley: University of California Press, 1964.

Guthrie, W. K. C. *The Greek Philosophers from Thales to Aristotle*. London: Methuen, 1950. Reprinted 1967.

————. *A History of Greek Philosophy*. 6 vols. Cambridge: Cambridge University Press, 1962–81. From the Presocratics through Aristotle.

Jaeger, Werner W. *Paideia: The Ideals of Greek Culture*. 3 vols. Trans. Gilbert Highet. 2d ed. London and New York: Oxford University Press, 1945. From the second German edition of 1936.

Lesky, Albin. *A History of Greek Literature*. Trans. James Willis and Cornelis de Heer. London: Methuen; New York: Crowell, 1966. From the second German edition of 1963. A third German edition appeared in 1971.

Marrou, Henri-Irénée. *Histoire de l'éducation dans l'antiquité*. 5th ed. Paris: Seuil, 1960.

Onians, R. B. *The Origins of European Thought about the Body, the Mind, the Soul, the World, Time, and Fate*. Cambridge: Cambridge University Press, 1954. Reprint, New York: Arno, 1973.

Sandys, Sir John Edwin. *A History of Classical Scholarship*. 3 vols. 3d ed. 1908–21. Reprint, New York: Hafner, 1958.

Snell, Bruno. *The Discovery of the Mind: The Greek Origins of European Thought*. Trans. T. G. Rosenmeyer. 1953. Reprint, New York: Harper & Row, 1960. From the first German edition of 1946; the most recent German edition is the fourth (Göttingen, 1975).

CHAPTER 1

Greek Editions and Translations

There are Loeb editions of all the works attributed to Homer: the *Iliad* (2 vols., 1924), the *Odyssey* (2 vols., 1919), and the Homeric Hymns (bound with the poems of Hesiod and fragments of the epic cycle, 1914). The Budé edition of the *Odyssey* (1955–59) contains a sprightly French translation by Victor Bérard; but some sections are printed in an idiosyncratic order.

Allen, Thomas W., W. R. Halliday, and E. E. Sikes, eds. *The Homeric Hymns*. 2d ed. Oxford: Clarendon Press, 1936. Reprint, Amsterdam: A. M. Hakkert, 1963.

Ameis, Carl Friedrich, Carl Hentze, and Paul Cauer, eds. *Homers Ilias*. 2 vols. in 8. Stuttgart: Teubner, 1905–32. Reprint, Amsterdam: A. M. Hakkert, 1965.

––––––. *Homers Odysee*. 2 vols. in 4. Leipzig: Teubner, 1908–20. Reprint, Amsterdam: A. M. Hakkert, 1964.

Boer, Charles, trans. *The Homeric Hymns*. 2d ed. Irving, Texas: Spring Publications, 1979. Daring but engaging modern translation.

Lattimore, Richmond, trans. *The Iliad of Homer*. Chicago: University of Chicago Press, 1951. By far the best modern English *Iliad*.

––––––, trans. *The Odyssey of Homer*. New York: Harper & Row, 1967.

Lawrence, Thomas Edward [T. E. Shaw], trans. *The Odyssey of Homer*. London and New York: Oxford University Press, 1932. A somewhat quirky but vigorous prose *Odyssey*.

Leaf, Walter, ed. Homer, *Iliad*. 2d ed. London: Macmillan, 1900–1902.

Richardson, Nicholas J., ed. *The Homeric Hymn to Demeter*. Oxford: Clarendon Press, 1974.

Sargent, Thelma, trans. *The Homeric Hymns: A Verse Translation*. New York: Norton, 1975.

Stanford, W. B., ed. Homer, *Odyssey*. 2d ed. New York: St. Martin's Press, 1961–62.

Lexicons, Concordances and Grammars

Chantraine, Pierre. *Grammaire homérique*. 2 vols. Paris: Klincksieck. Vol. 1, 1942, rev. 1958. Vol. 2, 1953.

Cunliffe, Richard John. *A Lexicon of the Homeric Dialect*. 1924. Reprint, Norman, Okla.: University of Oklahoma Press, 1963.

Dunbar, Henry. *A Complete Concordance to the Odyssey of Homer*. Rev. Benedetto Marzullo. 2 vols. Hildesheim: Georg Olms, 1962.

Monro, David B. *A Grammar of the Homeric Dialect*. Oxford: Clarendon Press, 1882.

Prendergast, Guy Lushington. *A Complete Concordance to the Iliad of Homer*. Rev. Benedetto Marzullo. Hildesheim: Georg Olms, 1962.

Critical Studies

Bespaloff, Rachel. *On the Iliad*. Trans. Mary McCarthy. 1947. Reprint, Princeton, N.J.: Princeton University Press, 1970. Bollingen Series no. 10.

Bowra, C. M. *Heroic Poetry*. London, 1952. Reprint, New York: St. Martin's Press, 1961.

Carpenter, Rhys. *Folktale, Fiction, and Saga in the Homeric Epics*. Berkeley: University of California Press, 1946.

Finley, Moses I. *The World of Odysseus*. 3d ed. New York: Viking Press, 1978.

Griffin, Jasper. *Homer on Life and Death*. Oxford: Clarendon Press, 1980.

Kirk, Geoffrey S. *The Songs of Homer*. Cambridge: Cambridge University Press, 1962. Abridged as *Homer and the Epic*. Cambridge University Press, 1965.

Lord, Albert B. *The Singer of Tales*. Cambridge, Mass.: Harvard University Press, 1960. Reprint, New York: Atheneum, 1965.

Mazon, Paul. *Introduction à l'Iliade*. Paris: Collection des Universités de France, 1942.

Nilsson, Martin P. *Homer and Mycenae*. London: Methuen, 1933.

Page, Denys L. *History and the Homeric Iliad*. Berkeley: University of California Press, 1959.

————. *The Homeric Odyssey*. Oxford: Clarendon Press, 1955.

Parry, Milman. *The Making of Homeric Verse: The Collected Papers of Milman Parry*. Ed. Adam Parry. Oxford: Clarendon Press, 1971.

Redfield, James M. *Nature and Culture in the Iliad: The Tragedy of Hector*. Chicago: University of Chicago Press, 1975.

Schadewaldt, Wolfgang. *Von Homers Welt und Werk*. 1944. 4th ed. Stuttgart: Koehler, 1965.

Wace, A. J. B., and F. H. Stubbings. *A Companion to Homer*. London: Macmillan; New York: St. Martin's Press, 1962. This work, designed primarily for those reading Homer in Greek for the first time (but useful to those reading him in translation), was planned and partially written in the 1930s; important research of the 1950s is included, however.

Webster, T. B. L., *From Mycenae to Homer*. London: Methuen, 1958.

Whitman, Cedric H. *Homer and the Heroic Tradition*. Cambridge, Mass.: Harvard University Press, 1958. Draws speculative but suggestive comparisons between the poetry of Homer and the pottery of the Geometric age.

Willcock, Malcolm. *A Companion to the Iliad, Based on the Translation by Richmond Lattimore*. Chicago: University of Chicago Press, 1976.

CHAPTER 2
Greek Editions and Translations

The works of Hesiod are bound with the Homeric Hymns in a single Loeb volume (1914). Because of twentieth-century discoveries on papyrus, it is important to use relatively recent editions of the lyric poets. The Loeb is being completely reedited by David A. Campbell (the first volume, dated 1982, is available); the old edition of J. M. Edmonds (*Elegy and Iambus*, 2 vols., 1931, and *Lyra Graeca*, 3 vols., 1922–27) contains an unreliable translation. There is also a Loeb edition of Pindar (1915). The standard edition of the Presocratics is that of Hermann Diels and Walther Kranz (see below), commonly cited as "Diels-Kranz." Because the extant remains are so fragmentary, it is important to use a good commentary in conjunction with any edition or translation. Two excellent commentaries are: Geoffrey S. Kirk and J. E. Raven (see below), and Barnes (see below, under "Critical Studies").

Bergk, Theodor, ed. Poetae Lyrici Graeci. 3 vols. Leipzig: Teubner, 1914–15. Includes some anonymous and folk lyrics not found in most collections.

Campbell, David A., ed. *Greek Lyric Poetry: A Selection of Early Greek Lyric, Elegiac, and Iambic Poetry*. New York: St. Martin's Press; London: Macmillan, 1967.

Diehl, Ernst, ed. *Anthologia Lyrica Graeca*. 3d ed. Leipzig: Teubner, 1949.

Diels, Hermann, and Walther Kranz, eds. *Die Fragmente der Vorsokratiker*. 3 vols. 10th ed. Berlin: Weidmann, 1960–61. Standard edition of the Presocratics.

Fagles, Robert, trans. *Bacchylides: Complete Poems*. New Haven, Conn.: Yale University Press, 1961. Reprint, Westport, Conn.: Greenwood Press, 1976.

Farnell, Lewis R., ed. and trans. *The Works of Pindar*. 3 vols. London: Macmillan, 1930–32. Reprint, Amsterdam: A. M. Hakkert, 1961.

Freeman, Kathleen. *Ancilla to the Presocratic Philosophers: A Complete Translation of the Fragments in Diels, Fragmente der Vorsokratiker*. Cambridge, Mass.: Harvard University Press, 1948. This translation is not quite complete, and less than reliable.

Jebb, Sir Richard C., ed. *Bacchylides: The Poems and Fragments*. Cambridge: Cambridge University Press, 1905.

Kirk, Geoffrey S., and J. E. Raven, eds. *The Presocratic Philosophers: A Critical History with a Selection of Texts*. Cambridge: Cambridge University Press, 1957.

Lattimore, Richmond, trans. *Greek Lyrics*. 2d ed. Chicago: University of Chicago Press, 1960. Contains some Pindar and Bacchylides, with a selection of shorter lyrics.

———, trans. Hesiod, *Works and Days, Theogony, and Shield of Heracles*. Ann Arbor: University of Michigan Press, 1959.

———, trans. *The Odes of Pindar*. 2d ed. Chicago: University of Chicago Press, 1976.

Lobel, Edgar, and Denys L. Page, eds. *Poetarum Lesbiorum Fragmenta*. 3d ed. Oxford: Clarendon Press, 1968. Fragments of the poets of Lesbos (Sappho and Alcaeus).

Maehler, Herwig, and Bruno Snell, eds. Bacchylides, *Carmina cum Fragmentis*. Leipzig: Teubner, 1970.

———, eds. Pindar, *Carmina cum Fragmentis*. 2 vols. 5th ed. Leipzig: Teubner, 1971–75.

Nisetich, Frank J., trans. *Pindar's Victory Songs*. Baltimore: John Hopkins University Press, 1980.

Page, Denys L., ed. *Poetae Melici Graeci*. Oxford: Clarendon Press, 1962. Includes Alcman, Stesichorus, Ibycus, Anacreon, Simonides, Corinna, and anonymous popular lyrics.

———, ed. *Supplementum Lyricis Graecis*. Oxford: Clarendon Press, 1974. Recently discovered fragments of the lyric poets.

Turyn, Alexander, ed. *Pindari Carmina cum Fragmentis*. 1948. Reprint, Oxford: Blackwell, 1952.

Voigt, Eva-Maria, ed. *Sappho et Alcaeus*. Amsterdam: Polak & van Gennep, 1971.

West, Martin L., ed. Hesiod, *Theogony*. Oxford: Clarendon Press, 1966.

————, ed. Hesiod, *Works and Days*. Oxford: Clarendon Press, 1978.

————, ed. *Iambi et Elegi Graeci*. 2 vols. Oxford: Clarendon Press, 1971–72. Iambic and elegiac poets.

Lexicons and Concordances

Minton, William W. *Concordance to the Hesiodic Corpus*. Leiden: Brill, 1976.

Paulson, Johann. *Index Hesiodeus*. Lund, 1890. Reprint, Hildesheim: Georg Olms, 1962.

Slater, William J. *Lexicon to Pindar*. Berlin: de Gruyter, 1969.

Critical Studies

Barnes, Jonathan. *The Presocratic Philosophers*. 2 vols. Rev. ed. London and Boston, Mass.: Routledge & Kegan Paul, 1982.

Bowra, C. M. *Greek Lyric Poetry from Alcman to Simonides*. 2d ed. Oxford: Clarendon Press, 1961.

————. *Pindar*. Oxford: Clarendon Press, 1964.

Burn, A. R. *The Lyric Age of Greece*. New York: St. Martin's Press, 1960.

Burnett, Anne Pippin. *Three Archaic Poets: Archilochus, Alcaeus, Sappho*. Cambridge, Mass.: Harvard University Press, 1983.

Carrière, Jean. *Théognis de Mégare*. Paris: Bordas, 1948.

Finley, John H. *Pindar and Aeschylus*. Cambridge, Mass.: Harvard University Press, 1955.

Fondation Hardt pour l'étude de l'antiquité classique. *Entretiens sur l'antiquité classique*. Vol. 7, *Hésiode et son influence*. Vandoeuvres-Genève, 1962.

Fränkel, Hermann. *Early Greek Poetry and Philosophy*. Trans. Moses Hadas and James Willis. New York and London: Harcourt Brace Jovanovich, 1975. Includes a discussion of Homer.

Freeman, Kathleen. *The Work and Life of Solon, with a Translation of His Poems*. Cardiff: University of Wales Press Board, 1926. Reprint, New York: Arno, 1976.

Guthrie, W. K. C. *Orpheus and Greek Religion*. 2d ed. 1952. Reprint, New York: Norton, 1967.

Jaeger, Werner W. *The Theology of the Early Greek Philosophers*. Trans. Edward S. Robinson. Oxford: Clarendon Press, 1947. Reprint, New York: Oxford University Press, 1968.

Kirkwood, Gordon M. *Early Greek Monody: The History of a Poetic Type*. Ithaca, N.Y.: Cornell University Press, 1974.

Lefkowitz, Mary R. *Lives of the Greek Poets*. Baltimore: Johns Hopkins University Press, 1981. Interesting to read in conjunction with Rankin's study (below) for the contrast between the two approaches.

————. *The Victory Ode: An Introduction*. Park Ridge, N.J.: Noyes Press, 1976. Some knowledge of Greek is necessary for a full understanding of this excellent study.

Linforth, Ivan M. *Solon the Athenian*. Berkeley: University of California Press, 1919. Reprinted 1971.

Norwood, Gilbert. *Pindar*. Berkeley: University of California Press, 1945.

Page, Denys L. *Sappho and Alcaeus*. Oxford: Clarendon Press, 1955.

Rankin, H. D. *Archilochus of Paros*. Park Ridge, N.J.: Noyes Press, 1977.

Solmsen, Friedrich. *Hesiod and Aeschylus*. Ithaca, N.Y.: Cornell University Press, 1949.

Vernant, Jean-Pierre. *Mythe et pensée chez les Grecs*. 2d ed. Paris: Maspero, 1966. Pages 19–47 are a discussion of Hesiod's myth of the races of man; a much-discussed article.

Wilamowitz-Moellendorff, Ulrich von. *Pindaros*. Berlin: Weidmann, 1922. In German.

Woodhouse, William J. *Solon the Liberator*. London: Oxford University Press, 1938. Reprint, New York: Octagon Books, 1965.

CHAPTER 3

Greek Editions and Translations

There are Loeb editions for both Herodotus (4 vols., rev. ed. 1938) and Aeschylus (2 vols., 1922; vol. 2 reedited with additional fragments, 1957). The article on Herodotus in Pauly-Wissowa is especially recommended.

Broadhead, H. D., ed. Aeschylus, *Persians*. Cambridge: Cambridge University Press, 1960.

Denniston, John, and Denys L. Page, eds. Aeschylus, *Agamemnon*. Oxford: Clarendon Press, 1957.

Fagles, Robert, trans. Aeschylus, *Oresteia*. New York: Viking, 1975. Reprint, with revisions. Harmondsworth and New York: Penguin, 1979.

Fraenkel, Eduard, ed. Aeschylus, *Agamemnon*. 3 vols. Oxford: Clarendon Press, 1950.

Grene, David, and Richmond Lattimore, eds. *The Complete Greek Tragedies*. Vol. 1, *Aeschylus*. Chicago: University of Chicago Press, 1959. Good modern translations. Also printed in two volumes as *Aeschylus* 1 and 2 in the Phoenix paperback edition.

Griffith, Mark, ed. Aeschylus, *Prometheus Bound*. Cambridge: Cambridge University Press, 1983.

How, W. W., and J. A. Wells. *A Commentary on Herodotus*. 2 vols. Oxford: Clarendon Press, 1912. Reprint, with corrections, 1928.

Hude, Karl, ed. *Herodoti Historiae*. 3d ed. Oxford: Clarendon Press, 1957–58.

MacNiece, Louis, trans. *The Agamemnon of Aeschylus*. London: Faber & Faber, 1936. Reprinted in *Ten Greek Plays*, ed. L. R. Lind. Boston: Houghton Mifflin, 1957.

Nauck, August, ed. *Tragicorum Graecorum Fragmenta*. Teubner, 1889. Reprint, with supplement by B. Snell, Hildesheim: Georg Olms, 1964. Collected fragments of the tragedians.

Rawlinson, George, trans. Herodotus, *History of the Greek and Persian War*. 1858. Reprint, New York: Random House, 1964. There are other editions of this classic translation, some abridged, some with slightly different titles.

Rose, Herbert J. *A Commentary on the Surviving Plays of Aeschylus*. 2 vols. Amsterdam: Noord-Hollandsche Uitg. Mij., 1957–58.

Lexicons and Concordances

Italie, Gabriel. *Index Aeschyleus*. Leiden: Brill, 1955.

Powell, J. Enoch. *A Lexicon to Herodotus*. Cambridge: Cambridge University Press, 1938. Reprint, Hildesheim: Georg Olms, 1960.

Critical Studies

Arnott, Peter D. *An Introduction to the Greek Theatre*. London: Macmillan, 1959. Reprint, Bloomington: Indiana University Press, 1963. Good general introduction.

Fornara, Charles W. *Herodotus: An Interpretative Essay*. Oxford: Clarendon Press, 1971.

Hartog, François. *Le Miroir d'Hérodote: Essai sur la représentation de l'autre*. Paris: Gallimard, 1980.

Hunter, Virginia J. *Past and Process in Herodotus and Thucydides*. Princeton: Princeton University Press, 1982.

Immerwahr, H. R. *Form and Thought in Herodotus*. Cleveland: Western Reserve Press for the American Philological Association, 1966.

Kitto, H. D. F. *Form and Meaning in Drama*. London: Methuen, 1956. Reprint, New York: Barnes & Noble, 1960.

——. *Greek Tragedy*. London: Methuen, 1939. Reprinted 1968. Also reprinted in New York by Barnes & Noble, 1961.

Lebeck, Anne. *The Oresteia: A Study in Language and Structure*. Washington, D.C.: Center for Hellenic Studies. Distributed by Harvard University Press, 1971. Outstanding study of Aeschylus's imagery.

Lesky, Albin. *Greek Tragedy*. Trans. H. A. Frankfort. London: Benn; New York: Barnes & Noble, 1965.

Méautis, Georges. *Eschyle et la trilogie*. Paris: Grasset, 1936.

Murray, Gilbert. *Aeschylus, the Creator of Tragedy*. Oxford: Clarendon Press, 1940.

Myres, J. L. *Herodotus, Father of History*. Oxford: Clarendon Press, 1953.

Pickard-Cambridge, A. W. *The Dramatic Festivals of Athens*. 1953. 2d ed. Oxford: Clarendon Press, 1968. A knowledge of Greek is necessary for a full understanding of this important work.

Romilly, Jacqueline de. *La Crainte et l'angoisse dans le théâtre d'Eschyle*. Paris: Les Belles Lettres, 1958.

——. *Time in Greek Tragedy*. Ithaca, N.Y.: Cornell University Press, 1968.

——. *La Tragédie grecque*. Paris: Presses Universitaires de France, 1970.

Selincourt, Aubrey de. *The World of Herodotus*. Boston: Little, Brown, 1963.

Taplin, Oliver. *The Stagecraft of Aeschylus*. Oxford: Clarendon Press, 1977.

Thomson, George D. *Aeschylus and Athens: A Study in the Social Origins of Drama*. 2d ed. London: Lawrence & Wishart, 1946. Reprint, New York: International Publishers, 1950.

Vernant, Jean-Pierre, and Pierre Vidal-Naquet. *Mythe et tragédie en Grèce ancienne*. Paris: Maspero, 1972.

Vickers, Brian. *Towards Greek Tragedy*. London: Longman, 1973. Reprinted 1979. Vol. 1 of his *Comparative Tragedy* (incomplete).

CHAPTER 4

Greek Editions and Translations

There are Loeb editions for Sophocles (2 vols., 1912), Euripides (4 vols., 1912), and
Aristophanes (3 vols., 1924). As in many of the older Loebs, the translations are
somewhat old-fashioned, and although that of Aristophanes, by Benjamin Bickley
Rogers (3 vols., 1924), is a classic, it also tones down the obscenity which is a prominent feature of the original. The Penguin Classics translations, by David Barrett and
Alan H. Sommerstein (3 vols.), are the most reliable complete set. The best Greek text
of Aristophanes now available is the Budé edition of Victor Coulon (listed below).

Aristophanes. *Acharnians.* Ed. and trans. W. J. M. Starkie. London: Macmillan,
     1909. Starkie's ingenious translations require considerable familiarity with
     Shakespearean comic diction.

_____. *Clouds.* Ed. Kenneth J. Dover. Oxford: Clarendon Press, 1968.

_____. *Clouds.* Ed. and trans. W. J. M. Starkie. London, 1911. Reprint, Amster-
     dam: A. M. Hakkert, 1966.

_____. *Ecclesiazusae.* Ed. R. G. Ussher. Oxford: Clarendon Press, 1973.

_____. *Frogs.* Trans. Richmond Lattimore. Ann Arbor: University of Michigan
     Press, 1962.

_____. *Frogs.* Ed. W. B. Stanford. 2d ed. London: Macmillan; New York: St. Mar-
     tin's Press, 1963.

_____. *Knights.* Ed. Robert A. Neil. Cambridge: Cambridge University Press, 1901.

_____. *Wasps.* Ed. Douglas M. MacDowell. Oxford: Clarendon Press, 1971.

Euripides. *Alcestis.* Ed. A. M. Dale. Oxford: Clarendon Press, 1954.

_____. *Bacchae.* Ed. E. R. Dodds. 2d ed. Oxford: Clarendon Press, 1960.

_____. *Electra.* Ed. J. D. Denniston. Oxford: Clarendon Press, 1939. Reprinted
     1960.

_____. *Helen.* Ed. A. M. Dale. Oxford: Clarendon Press, 1967. Reprint, Bristol:
     Bristol Classical Press, 1981.

_____. *Heracles.* Ed. Godfrey W. Bond. Oxford: Clarendon Press; New York: Ox-
     ford University Press, 1981.

_____. *Hippolytus.* Ed. W. S. Barrett. Oxford: Clarendon Press, 1964.

_____. *Medea.* Ed. Denys L. Page. Oxford: Clarendon Press, 1938. Reprinted with
     corrections 1961.

Fitts, Dudley, trans. *Aristophanes: Four Comedies.* New York: Harcourt, Brace &
     World, 1962. Includes *Birds, Frogs, Lysistrata,* and *Thesmophoriazusae.*

Grene, David, and Richmond Lattimore, eds. *The Complete Greek Tragedies.* Vol. 2,
     Sophocles. Vols. 3 & 4, *Euripides.* Chicago: University of Chicago Press, 1959.
     Good modern translations. Also printed in seven volumes (*Sophocles* 1 and 2
     and *Euripides* 1, 2, 3, 4, and 5) in the Phoenix paperback edition.

Kock, Theodor. *Comicorum Atticorum Fragmenta.* 3 vols. Leipzig: Teubner, 1880–
     88. A standard edition of fragments of the comic poets.

Sophocles. *The Fragments of Sophocles.* Ed. Alfred C. Pearson. 1917. Reprint, Am-
     sterdam: A. M. Hakkert, 1963.

_____. *The Papyrus Fragments of Sophocles.* Ed. Richard Carden. Berlin and New
     York: De Gruyter, 1979.

_____. *The Plays of Sophocles: Commentaries.* Ed. Jan C. Kamerbeek. 7 vols. Lei-
     den: Brill, 1953–80.

_____. *Sophocles: The Plays and Fragments*. Ed. Sir Richard Jebb. 7 vols. Cambridge: Cambridge University Press, 1893–1900. There exist later editions, revised by other hands, for some of the plays.

_____. *The Three Theban Plays: Antigone, Oedipus the King, Oedipus at Colonus*. Trans. Robert Fagles. New York: Viking, 1982. Reprint, Harmondsworth and New York: Penguin, 1984.

Lexicons and Concordances

Allen, James T., and Gabriel Italie. *A Concordance to Euripides*. Berkeley: University of California Press, 1954.

Dunbar, Henry. *A Complete Concordance to the Comedies and Fragments of Aristophanes*. 1883. 2d ed., rev. Benedetto Marzullo. Hildesheim: Georg Olms, 1973.

Ellendt, Frederick T. *Lexicon Sophocleum*. Berlin: Borntraeger, 1872. 2d ed. Hildesheim: Georg Olms, 1965. Abridged and translated as *A Lexicon to Sophocles* (translator not named). Oxford: D. A. Talboys, 1841. Reprint, Hildesheim: Georg Olms, 1958.

Todd, O. J. *Index Aristophaneus*. Cambridge, Mass.: Harvard University Press, 1932.

Critical Studies

Bowra, C. M. *Sophoclean Tragedy*. Oxford: Clarendon Press, 1944.

Burnett, Anne Pippin. *Catastrophe Survived: Euripides' Plays of Mixed Reversal*. Oxford: Clarendon Press, 1971.

Dover, K. J. *Aristophanic Comedy*. Berkeley: University of California Press, 1972.

Ehrenberg, Victor. *The People of Aristophanes*. Oxford, 1943. 3d ed., New York: Schocken, 1962. Reprint, New York: Barnes & Noble, 1974.

_____. *Sophocles and Pericles*. Oxford: Blackwell, 1954.

Fondation Hardt pour l'étude de l'antiquité classique. *Entretiens sur l'antiquité classique*. Vol. 6, *Euripide*. Vandoeuvres-Genève, 1960.

Grube, G. M. A. *The Drama of Euripides*. London, 1941. Corrected reprint, New York: Barnes & Noble, 1961.

Kirkwood, Gordon M. *A Study of Sophoclean Drama*. Ithaca, N.Y.: Cornell University Press, 1958. Reprint, New York: Johnson Reprint Corp., 1967.

Knox, Bernard M. W. *The Heroic Temper: Studies in Sophoclean Tragedy*. Berkeley: University of California Press, 1964.

_____. *Oedipus at Thebes*. New Haven: Yale University Press, 1957.

Murray, Gilbert. *Aristophanes*. Oxford: Clarendon Press, 1933.

Norwood, Gilbert. *Greek Comedy*. London: Methuen, 1931. Reprint, New York: Hill & Wang, 1963.

Reinhardt, Karl. *Sophocles*. Trans. Hazel Harvey and David Harvey. New York: Barnes & Noble, 1979. From the third German edition of 1947.

Romilly, Jacqueline de. *L'Evolution du pathétique d'Eschyle à Euripide*. Paris: Presses Universitaires de France, 1961.

Ronnet, Gilberte. *Sophocle, poète tragique*. Paris: Boccard, 1969.

Sandbach, F. H. *The Comic Theatre of Greece and Rome*. New York: Norton, 1977.

Strohm, Hans. *Euripides*. Munich: Beck, 1957. In German.

Webster, T. B. L. *An Introduction to Sophocles*. Oxford: Clarendon Press, 1936.

_____. *The Tragedies of Euripides*. London: Methuen, 1967.

Whitman, Cedric H. *Aristophanes and the Comic Hero*. Cambridge, Mass.: Harvard University Press for Oberlin College, 1964. Martin Classical Lectures, 9.

_____. *Sophocles: A Study of Heroic Humanism*. Cambridge, Mass.: Harvard University Press, 1951.

Winnington-Ingram, Reginald P. *Sophocles: An Interpretation*. Cambridge and New York: Cambridge University Press, 1980.

Zuntz, Gunther. *The Political Plays of Euripides*. Manchester, Eng.: Manchester University Press, 1955. Corrected reprint, 1963. On the *Heracleidae* and the *Suppliants*.

CHAPTER 5

Greek Editions and Translations

There exist Loeb editions of some Hippocratic works (4 vols., 1923–31), but the only complete edition of the Hippocratic corpus is that of Littré (listed below). The *Corpus Medicorum Graecorum*, a comprehensive edition of ancient Greek writings on medicine (begun by Teubner in 1908), is still being edited and published in Berlin by Akademie-Verlag; the Greek texts are accompanied by German, French, or English translations, depending on the nationality of the editor.

Fragments of the Sophists are arranged alphabetically by author's name in Diels-Kranz, *Fragmente der Vorsokratiker*; see entry under chapter 2.

The Budé edition of Thucydides is that of Jacqueline de Romilly herself, in collaboration with Raymond Weil and Louis Bodin (5 vols. in 6, 1955–72). There is also a Loeb edition of Thucydides (4 vols., rev. ed., 1956).

Crawley, Richard, trans. Thucydides, *The History of the Peloponnesian War*. London, 1874. Reprint, New York: Modern Library, 1951. Still available in a paperback edition.

Gernet, Louis, ed. and trans. Antiphon, *Discours, suivis des fragments d'Antiphon le Sophiste*. Paris: Les Belles Lettres, 1954. Greek text with French translation.

Gomme, Arnold W., Antony Andrewes, and K. J. Dover. *A Historical Commentary on Thucydides*. 5 vols. Oxford: Clarendon Press, 1959–81.

Hobbes, Thomas, trans. Thucydides, *The Peloponnesian War*. Ed. David Grene. Ann Arbor: University of Michigan Press, 1959. Also ed. Richard Schlatter. New Brunswick, N.J.: Rutgers University Press, 1975. A classic translation, perhaps more elegant than the original but preserving both its periodic style and austere tone.

Jones, Henry Stuart, ed. *Thucydidis Historiae*. 2 vols. 2d ed., rev. J. Enoch Powell. Oxford: Clarendon Press, 1942.

Littré, E., ed. and trans. *Oeuvres complètes d'Hippocrate*. 10 vols. Paris: J. B. Baillère, 1839–61. Greek text with French translation.

Lloyd, G. E. R., ed. *Hippocratic Writings*. Trans. J. Chadwick, W. N. Mann, et al. 1950. Reprinted, with additional material, Harmondsworth and New York: Penguin, 1978.

Lonie, Iain M. *The Hippocratic Treatises "On Generation," "On the Nature of the Child," "Diseases IV." A Commentary*. Berlin and N.Y.: De Gruyter, 1981.

Marchant, Edgar C., ed. Thucydides, *History*. Book 2, 1891; Book 6, 1897; Book 7, 1893. London and New York: Macmillan, Macmillan's Classics Series for Colleges and Schools.

Critical Studies

Cornford, Francis M. *Thucydides Mythistoricus*. 1907. Reprint, London: Routledge & Kegan Paul, 1965. Also reprinted in New York: Greenwood, 1969.

Dupréel, Eugène. *Les sophistes: Protagoras, Gorgias, Prodicus, Hippias*. Neuchâtel: Editions du Griffon, 1949.

Edelstein, L. *Ancient Medicine*. Baltimore: Johns Hopkins University Press, 1967.

Finley, John H. *Thucydides*. Cambridge, Mass.: Harvard University Press, 1942.

Guthrie, W. K. C. *The Sophists*. Cambridge: Cambridge University Press, 1971.

Hunter, Virginia J. *Past and Process in Herodotus and Thucydides*. Princeton: Princeton University Press, 1982.

———. *Thucydides, the Artful Reporter*. Toronto: A. M. Hakkert, 1973.

Joly, Robert. *Le Niveau de la science hippocratique*. Paris: Les Belles Lettres, 1966.

Jones, W. H. S. *Philosophy and Medicine in Ancient Greece*. Baltimore: Johns Hopkins University Press, 1946.

Kagan, Donald. *The Archidamian War*. Ithaca, N.Y.: Cornell University Press, 1974.

———. *The Outbreak of the Peloponnesian War*. Ithaca, N.Y.: Cornell University Press, 1969.

———. *The Peace of Nicias and the Sicilian Expedition*. Ithaca, N.Y.: Cornell University Press, 1981. This and the two previous works are parts of an ongoing study of Thucydides that takes the speeches more seriously as historical documents than do most critics.

Romilly, Jacqueline de. *Histoire et raison chez Thucydide*. Paris: Les Belles Lettres, 1956.

———. *Thucydides and Athenian Imperialism*. Trans. Philip Thody. Oxford: Blackwell, 1963.

Westlake, Henry D. *Individuals in Thucydides*. Cambridge: Cambridge University Press, 1968.

CHAPTER 6
Greek Editions and Translations

There are Loeb editions for Aeschines (1919), Demosthenes (7 vols., 1926–49), Isaeus (1927), and Lysias (1930), as well as a collection of the *Minor Attic Orators* (2 vols., 1941–54), including Andocides, Antiphon, Demades, Dinarchus, Hyperides, and Lycurgus.

Goodwin, William W., ed. Demosthenes, *Against Midias*. Cambridge: Cambridge University Press, 1906.

———, ed. Demosthenes, *On the Crown*. Cambridge: Cambridge University Press, 1901.

MacDowell, Douglas M., ed. Andocides, *On the Mysteries*. Oxford: Clarendon Press, 1962.

———, ed. and trans. Gorgias, *Encomium of Helen*. Bristol: Bristol Classical Press, 1982.

Pickard-Cambridge, A. W., trans. *The Public Orations of Demosthenes*. Oxford: Clarendon Press, 1912. Reprint, New York: Dutton, 1963.

Sandys, Sir John Edwin, ed. *The First Philippic and the Olynthiacs of Demosthenes*. London 1897. Reprints, New York: St. Martin's Press, 1955; New York: Arno, 1979.

———, ed. Demosthenes, *On the Peace, Second Philippic, On the Chersonesus, Third Philippic*. London: Macmillan, 1900. Rev. eds., 1913, 1953. Reprint, 1st ed., N.Y.: Arno, 1979.

———, and Paley, F. A., eds. Demosthenes, *Select Private Orations*. 2 vols. in one. 3d ed. 1898. Reprint, New York: Arno, 1979.

Saunders, A. N. W., trans. *Greek Political Oratory*. Harmondsworth and New York: Penguin, 1970. Includes speeches of Lysias, Andocides, and Demosthenes.

———, trans. *Demosthenes and Aeschines*. Harmondsworth and New York: Penguin, 1975. Includes *On the Embassy, On the Crown, Against Ctesiphon*.

Weil, Henri, ed. *Les Plaidoyers politiques de Démosthène*. Paris, 1883–86. Reprint, Hildesheim: Georg Olms, 1974. De Romilly notes: "There is still much to be learned from this remarkable edition."

Wyse, William, ed. *The Speches of Isaeus*. Cambridge: Cambridge University Press, 1904. Reprints, Hildesheim: Georg Olms, 1967; New York: Arno, 1979.

Concordances

Forman, Lewis L. *Index Andocideus, Lycurgeus, Dinarcheus*. Oxford: Clarendon Press, 1897. Reprint, Amsterdam: A. M. Hakkert, 1962. Also reprinted with Preuss, *Index Aeschineus*, New York: Arno, 1979.

Holmes, David Hull. *Index Lysiacus*. Bonn: F. Cohen, 1895.

Preuss, Siegmund. *Index Aeschineus*. Leipzig: Teubner, 1896. Reprinted with Forman, *Index Andocideus, Lycurgeus, Dinarcheus*, New York: Arno, 1979.

———. *Index Demosthenicus*. Leipzig: Teubner, 1892.

Critical Studies

Blass, Friedrich W. *Die attische Beredsamkeit*. 3 vols. 2d ed. Leipzig: Teubner, 1887–98.

Dover, Kenneth J. *Lysias and the Corpus Lysiacum*. Berkeley: University of California Press, 1968.

Due, Bodil. *Antiphon: A Study in Argumentation*. Copenhagen: Museum Tusculanum, 1980.

Durrbach, Felix. *L'Orateur Lycurgue*. Paris: E. Thorin, 1889.

Jaeger, Werner. *Demosthenes: The Origin and Growth of his Policy*. Trans. Edward S. Robinson. Berkeley: University of California Press, 1938. Reprint, New York: Octagon Books, 1963.

Jebb, Sir Richard. *The Attic Orators from Antiphon to Isaeus*. 2 vols. London: Macmillan, 1876. Reprinted 1962.

Kennedy, George. *The Art of Persuasion in Greece*. Princeton: Princeton University Press, 1963.

Pearson, Lionel. *The Art of Demosthenes*. Meisenheim am Glan: A. Hain, 1976. Reprint, Chico, California: Scholars Press, 1981.

Pickard-Cambridge, A. W. *Demosthenes and the Last Days of Greek Freedom, 384–322 B.C.* New York: Putnam, 1914. Reprint, New York: AMS Press, 1978.

Ronnet, Gilberte. *Etude sur le style de Démosthène dans les discours politiques*. Paris: Boccard, 1951.

Schaefer, Arnold. *Demosthenes und seine Zeit*. Leipzig: Teubner, 1856–58. Reprint, Hildesheim: Georg Olms, 1966.

CHAPTER 7

Greek Editions and Translations

There are Loeb editions for both Isocrates (3 vols., 1928–45) and Xenophon (7 vols., 1914–25); Pseudo-Xenophon, *The Constitution of the Athenians*, is added to vol. 7 in a 1968 edition.

Forster, Edward S., ed. Isocrates, *Cyprian Orations: Evagoras, Ad Nicoclem, Nicocles aut Cyprii*. Oxford 1912. Reprint, New York: Arno, 1979.

Marchant, Edgar C., ed. Xenophon, *Hellenica*. Oxford 1906. Reprint, New York: Arno Press, 1979.

Sandys, Sir John Edwin, ed. Isocrates, *Ad Demonicum et Panegyricus*. London 1872. Reprint, New York: Arno, 1979.

Saunders, A. N. W., trans. *Greek Political Oratory*. Harmondsworth and New York: Penguin, 1970. Includes Isocrates' *Panegyricus* and *Philip*.

Tredennick, Hugh, trans. Xenophon, *Memoirs of Socrates and The Symposium*. Harmondsworth and New York: Penguin, 1970.

Warner, Rex, trans. Xenophon, *A History of My Times [Hellenica]*. 1966. Reprint, Harmondsworth and New York: Penguin, 1978.

Concordance

Preuss, Siegmund. *Index Isocrateus*. Leipzig: Teubner, 1904.

Critical Studies

Cloché, Paul. *Isocrate et son temps*. Paris: Les Belles Lettres, 1963.

Delebecque, Edouard. *Essai sur la vie de Xénophon*. Paris: Klincksieck, 1957.

Henry, William Patrick. *Greek Historical Writing*. Chicago: Argonaut, 1967.

Higgins, William E. *Xenophon the Athenian*. Albany: State University of New York Press, 1977.

Luccioni, Jean. *Les Idées politiques et sociales de Xénophon*. Paris: Les Belles Lettres, 1947.

_____. *Xénophon et le socratisme*. Paris: Presses Universitaires de France, 1953.

Mathieu, Georges. *Les Idées politiques d'Isocrate*. 1925. Reprint, Paris: Les Belles Lettres, 1966.

Strauss, Leo. *On Tyranny: An Interpretation of Xenophon's "Hiero."* Rev. ed. New York: Free Press of Glencoe, 1963.

_____. *Xenophon's Socratic Discourse: An Interpretation of the Oeconomicus*. Ithaca, N.Y.: Cornell University Press, 1970.

CHAPTER 8
Greek Editions and Translations

There are twelve Loeb volumes (1914–35) devoted to Plato and twenty-three (1926–70, one still forthcoming) devoted to Aristotle. The OCT edition of Plato, often cited, is that of John Burnet (5 vols., 1899–1906).

Adam, James, ed. Plato, *Republic*. 2 vols. Cambridge: Cambridge University Press, 1902. Reprinted 1938. 2d ed. 1963.

————, and Adam, A. M., eds. Plato, *Protagoras*, 2d ed. 1905. Reprint, Cambridge: Cambridge University Press, 1962.

Cope, Edward M., and J. E. Sandys, eds. Aristotle, *Rhetoric*. Cambridge: Cambridge University Press, 1877.

Dodds, E. R., ed. Plato, *Gorgias*. Oxford: Clarendon Press, 1959.

Dover, K. J., ed. Plato, *Symposium*. Cambridge: Cambridge University Press, 1980.

Else, Gerald F., trans. Aristotle, *Poetics*. Ann Arbor: University of Michigan Press, 1967.

Hackforth, Reginald, trans. and comm. Plato, *Phaedo*. Cambridge, Cambridge University Press, 1955. Reprinted 1972.

————, trans. Plato, *Phaedrus*. Cambridge: Cambridge University Press, 1952.

————, trans. and comm. Plato, *Philebus*. Cambridge: Cambridge University Press, 1945. Reprinted 1972.

Hamilton, Edith, and Huntington Cairns, eds. *The Collected Dialogues of Plato* [in English translation]. New York: Pantheon, 1961.

Jowett, Benjamin, and Lewis Campbell, eds. Plato, *Republic*. 3 vols. 1894. Reprint of vol. 2 only (Essays), New York: Arno, 1973. It should be noted that Jowett's translations of Plato (and of Aristotle's *Politics*), though elegant, are inaccurate.

Lucas, D. W., ed. Aristotle, *Poetics*. Oxford: Clarendon Press, 1968.

McKeon, Richard P., ed. *The Basic Works of Aristotle* [in English translation]. New York: Random House, 1941. Includes the most important treatises. Translations are reprinted from the complete edition of Ross (see below).

Newman, W. L., ed. Aristotle, *Politics*. 4 vols. Oxford: Clarendon Press, 1887–1903.

Ross, William David, ed. Aristotle, *De Anima*. Oxford: Clarendon Press, 1961.

————, ed. Aristotle, *Fragmenta Selecta*. Oxford: Clarendon Press, 1958. A translation of these *Select Fragments*, also by Ross, was published by Oxford in 1952.

————, ed. and trans. Aristotle, *Metaphysics*. Oxford: Clarendon Press, 1929.

————, ed. Aristotle, *Physics*. Oxford: Clarendon Press, 1936.

————, ed. *The Works of Aristotle Translated into English*. 12 vols. Oxford: Clarendon Press, 1908–52. Reprint, Princeton: Princeton University Press, 1984.

Taylor, Alfred Edward. *A Commentary on Plato's Timaeus*. Oxford: Clarendon Press, 1928. Based on Burnet's OCT edition.

Weil, Raymond. *L'Archéologie de Platon*. Paris: Klincksieck, 1959. A commentary, in French, on book 3 of the *Laws*.

Concordances

Bonitz, Hermann. *Index Aristotelicus*. 1870. Reprints, Berlin: Akademie-Verlag, 1955; Graz: Akademische Druck-u. Verlagsanstalt, 1955.

Brandwood, Leonard. *A Word Index to Plato*. Leeds: W. S. Maney, 1976.

Critical Studies

Adkins, Arthur W. H. *Merit and Responsibility: A Study in Greek Values*. Oxford: Clarendon Press, 1960.

Allan, D. J. *The Philosophy of Aristotle*. London and New York: Oxford University Press, 1957.

Crombie, I. M. *An Examination of Plato's Doctrines*. 2 vols. New York: Humanities Press, 1962–63.

Field, Guy Cromwell. *The Philosophy of Plato*. 1949. 2d ed. London and New York: Oxford University Press, 1969.

———. *Plato and His Contemporaries*. London: Methuen; New York: Dutton, 1930. Reprint, New York: Haskell House, 1975.

Fondation Hardt pour l'étude de l'antiquité classique. *Entretiens sur l'antiquité classique*. Vol. 11, *La "Politique" d'Aristote*. Vandoeuvres-Genève, 1965.

Friedlaender, Paul. *Plato*. 3 vols. Trans. Hans Meyerhoff. Vols. 1 & 2, New York: Pantheon Books for the Bollingen Foundation, 1958–64. Vol. 3, Princeton: Princeton University Press for the Bollingen Foundation, 1969. Bollingen Series, 59.1–3. From the 2d German edition of 1954–60.

Goldschmidt, Victor. *Les Dialogues de Platon: Structure et méthode dialectique*. Paris: Presses Universitaires de France, 1947. De Romilly calls this "a remarkable, though somewhat difficult work."

Gould, John. *The Development of Plato's Ethics*. Cambridge: Cambridge University Press, 1955.

Hardie, William Francis Ross. *Aristotle's Ethical Theory*. 1968. 2d ed. Oxford: Clarendon Press, 1980.

———. *A Study in Plato*. Oxford: Clarendon Press, 1936.

Irwin, Terence H. *Plato's Moral Theory: The Early and Middle Dialogues*. Oxford: Clarendon Press, 1977.

Jaeger, Werner W. *Aristotle: Fundamentals of the History of His Development*. Translated, with author's corrections, by Richard Robinson. Oxford: Clarendon Press, 1934. Originally published in German in 1923.

Jones, John. *On Aristotle and Greek Tragedy*. London and New York: Oxford University Press, 1962.

Joseph, J. W. B. *Knowledge and the Good in Plato's Republic*. London: Oxford University Press, 1948.

Laborderie, J. *Le Dialogue platonicien de la maturité*. Paris: Les Belles Lettres, 1978.

Levinson, R. B. *In Defense of Plato*. Cambridge, Mass.: Harvard University Press, 1953.

Lloyd, G. E. R. *Aristotle*. Cambridge: Cambridge University Press, 1968.

Ross, William David. *Aristotle*. 1923. 5th ed. London: Methuen, 1949. Reprinted 1964. Also reprinted in New York: Barnes & Noble, 1964.

———. *Plato's Theory of Ideas*. Oxford: Clarendon Press, 1951. Reprint, Westport, Conn.: Greenwood, 1976.

Shorey, Paul. *What Plato Said*. Chicago: Univerity of Chicago Press, 1934. A résumé of Plato's works.

Solmsen, Friedrich. *Plato's Theology*. Ithaca, N.Y.: Cornell Univeirsty Press, 1942.

Taylor, Alfred Edward. *The Mind of Plato*. 1922. Reprint, Ann Arbor: University of Michigan Press, 1960. The 1922 edition was entitled *Plato*.

———. *Plato, the Man and His Work*. London: Methuen, 1926.

CHAPTER 9
Greek Editions and Translations

In editions and studies of Menander and Callimachus, be sure to pay attention to dates of publication, as there have been (and continue to be) new discoveries on papyrus. The most recent Loeb edition of Menander is that of W. G. Arnott (three volumes projected, one in print, 1979–); the most recent OCT edition is that of Sandbach (1972). New fragments of Callimachus are to be found in the 1958 Loeb edition (by C. Trypanis), now bound with Musaeus's *Hero and Leander* (1974); the old Loeb Callimachus (1921, revised 1955) is bound with works of Aratus and Lycophron. The 1939 Budé edition, by Emile Cahen, of Callimachus is a completely revised version, with new fragments, of Cahen's 1922 edition; the most recent (5th) edition, based on that of 1939, was issued in 1961.

Other Hellenistic authors in Loeb editions include Apollodorus (2 vols., 1921), Apollonius Rhodius (1912), the bucolic poets Theocritus, Bion, and Moschus (1 vol.; rev. ed. 1928), Euclid (in *Greek Mathematical Works*, 2 vols, 1939–41), Polybius (6 vols., 1922–27), and Theophrastus (*Enquiry into Plants*, 2 vols., 1916; *Characters*, 1929). There is also a combined edition of the Palatine and Planudean Anthologies (5 vols., 1916). The most recent edition of Polybius is the Budé, not yet complete (ed. Paul Pédech et al., 1961–).

Arnim, Hans F. von. *Stoicorum Veterum Fragmenta*. 4 vols. Leipzig: Teubner, 1903–24. Reprint, Stuttgart: Teubner, 1968. Fragments of Zeno, Chrysippus, and Cleanthes; the fourth volume is a concordance.

Bailey, Cyril, ed. and trans. *Epicurus: The Extant Remains*. Oxford: Clarendon Press, 1926. Reprints, Hildesheim: Georg Olms, 1970; Westport, Conn.: Hyperion Press, 1979.

Cahen, Emile, ed. and trans. *Callimaque*. 5th ed. Paris: Les Belles Lettres, 1961. Greek text with French translation.

_____. *Les Hymnes de Callimaque, commentaire explicatif et critique*. Paris: Boccard, 1930. A companion volume to *Callimaque et son oeuvre poétique* (see below, under Critical Studies).

Casson, Lionel, ed. and trans. *The Plays of Menander*. New York: New York University Press, 1971.

Cunningham, Ian Campbell, ed. Herondas, *Mimiambi*. Oxford: Clarendon Press, 1971.

Davenport, Guy, trans. *The Mimes of Herondas*. San Francisco: Grey Fox Press, 1981.

Edelstein, Ludwig, and I. G. Kidd, eds. *Posidonius*. Cambridge: Cambridge University Press, 1972–. Text in Greek and Latin; preface and introduction in English. Edition incomplete; one volume in print.

Fränkel, Hermann. *Noten zu den Argonautika des Apollonios*. Munich: Beck, 1968. Commentary in German on the *Argonautica*.

_____, ed. Apollonius Rhodius, *Argonautica*. Oxford: Clarendon Press, 1961. Reprinted with corrections, 1964.

Gillies, Marshall M., ed. Apollonius Rhodius, *Argonautica Book III*. Cambridge: Cambridge University Press, 1928. Reprint, New York: Arno, 1979.

Gomme, Arnold W., and F. H. Sandbach. *Menander: A Commentary*. Oxford: Clarendon Press, 1973.

Gow, A. W. F., ed. *Bucolici Graeci*. Oxford: Clarendon Press, 1952. Texts of Theocritus, Bion, and Moschus.

―――, trans. *The Greek Bucolic Poets*. Cambridge: Cambridge University Press, 1953. English translation of the texts found in *Bucolici Graeci*.

―――, ed. and trans. *Theocritus*. 2 vols. Cambridge: Cambridge University Press, 1950.

―――, and A. F. Scholfield, eds. and trans. Nicander of Colophon, *Poems and Poetical Fragments*. Cambridge: Cambridge University Press, 1953.

Grilli, Alberto, ed. Diogenes of Oenoanda, *Fragments*. Milan: Cisalpino, 1960.

Handley, E. W., ed. Menander, *Dyskolos*. Cambridge, Mass.: Harvard University Press, 1965.

Headlam, Walter, and A. D. Knox, eds. *Herodas: The Mimes and Fragments*. Cambridge: Cambridge University Press, 1922. Reprint, New York: Arno, 1979.

Heath, T. L., trans. Apollonius of Perga, *Treatise on Conic Sections*. Cambridge: Cambridge University Press, 1896. Reprint, Cambridge, Eng.: W. Heffer, 1961.

―――, trans. *The Thirteen Books of Euclid's Elements*. 3 vols. Cambridge: Cambridge University Press, 1908.

―――, trans. *The Works of Archimedes*. Cambridge: Cambridge University Press, 1912. Reprint, New York: Dover Books, n.d.

Koerte, Alfred. *Menandri Quae Supersunt*. 2 vols. 2d ed. Leipzig: Teubner, 1957–59.

Lloyd-Jones, Hugh, and Peter Parsons. *Supplementum Hellenisticum*. Berlin and New York: De Gruyter, 1983. A supplement to Powell, *Collectanea Alexandrina* (see below).

Maas, Ernst, ed. Aratus, *Phaenomena*. Berlin: Weidmann, 1893.

Martin, Jean, ed. Aratus, *Phaenomena*. Florence: La Nuova Italia, 1956.

Pearson, A. C., ed. *The Fragments of Zeno and Cleanthes*. London, 1891. Reprint, New York: Arno, 1973.

Pfeiffer, Rudolf, ed. *Callimachus*. Oxford: Clarendon Press, 1949–53. Reprint, New York: Arno, 1979.

Post, Levi Arnold, trans. *Menander: Three Plays*. London: Routledge & Kegan Paul; New York: Dutton, 1929. Includes *The Samian Woman*, *The Arbitrators*, and *The Shorn Girl*.

Powell, John Undershell. *Collectanea Alexandrina*. 1925. Reprint, Oxford: Clarendon Press, 1970. Fragments of Greek poets of the Alexandrian school who worked between 323 and 146 B.C.

Puccioni, Giulio, ed. *Herodae Mimiambi*. Florence: La Nuvoa Italia, 1950.

Rieu, E. V., trans. Apollonius Rhodius, *The Voyage of Argo [Argonautica]*. Harmondsworth and Baltimore: Penguin, 1959.

Sandbach, F. F., ed. *Menandri Reliquiae Selectae*. Oxford: Clarendon Press, 1972.

Scott-Kilvert, Ian, trans. *The Rise of the Roman Empire [Polybius's Histories*, abridged.] Harmondsworth, Eng. and Baltimore: Penguin, 1980.

Shuckburgh, Evelyn, trans. *The Histories of Polybius*. 2 vols. 1889. Reprint, Bloomington: Indiana University Press, 1962.

Turner, E. G., trans. Menander, *The Samian Woman*. London: Athlone, 1972.

Usener, Hermann K. *Epicurea*. 1887. Reprint, Rome: Bretschneider, 1963.

Vian, Francis, ed. and trans. Apollonius Rhodius, *Argonautiques*. 3 vols. Paris: Les Belles Lettres, 1974–81. Best available Greek edition; translation in French.

_____, ed. and trans. Quintus of Smyrna, *La Suite d'Homère [Posthomerica]*. 3 vols. Paris: Les Belles Lettres, 1963–69. Best available Greek edition; translation in French.

Walbank, Frank W. *A Historical Commentary on Polybius*. 3 vols. Oxford: Clarendon Press, 1957–79.

Wehrli, Fritz. *Die Schule des Aristoteles*. 10 vols. 2d ed. Basel: B. Schwabe, 1967–69. Text, with commentary in German, of the Peripatetics.

Williams, Frederick, ed. Callimachus, *Hymn to Apollo*. Oxford: Clarendon Press; New York: Oxford University Press, 1978.

Critical Studies

Cahen, Emile. *Callimaque et son oeuvre poétique*. Paris: Boccard, 1929.

Couat, Auguste. *Alexandrian Poetry under the First Three Ptolemies, 324–222 B.C.* Trans. James Loeb. New York: Putnam, 1931. Originally published in French, 1882.

Dillon, John M. *The Middle Platonists: A Study of Platonism, 80 B.C. to A.D. 200*. London: Duckworth, 1977.

Festugière, André-Marie. *Epicurus and His Gods*. Trans. C. W. Chilton. Oxford: Blackwell, 1955.

Fondation Hardt pour l'étude de l'antiquité classique. *Entretiens sur l'antiquité classique*. Vol. 16, *Ménandre*. Vandoeuvres-Genève, 1970.

Fritz, Kurt von. *The Theory of the Mixed Constitution in Antiquity*. New York: Columbia University Press, 1954.

Koerte, Alfred. *Hellenistic Poetry*. Trans. Jacob Hammer and Moses Hadas. New York: Columbia University Press, 1929.

Laffranque, Marie. *Poseidonios d'Apamée*. Paris: Presses Universitaires de France, 1964.

Long, A. A. *Hellenistic Philosophy*. New York: Scribner, 1974.

Méautis, Georges. *Le Crépuscule d'Athènes et Ménandre*. Paris: Hachette, 1954.

Meillier, Claude. *Callimaque et son temps*. Lille: Université de Lille III, 1979.

Murray, Gilbert. *The Stoic Philosophy*. London: Watts & Co., 1915.

Onians, John. *Art and Thought in the Hellenistic Age: The Greek World View, 350–50 B.C.* London: Thames & Hudson, 1979.

Peters, F. E. *The Harvest of Hellenism*. New York: Simon & Schuster, 1970.

Pfeiffer, Rudolf. *Kallimachosstudien*. Munich: M. Hueber, 1922. De Romilly calls this work "very important."

Pohlenz, Max. *Die Stoa*. 1948–49. 2 vols. 4th ed. Göttingen: Vandenhoeck & Ruprecht, 1970–72. De Romilly calls this "an essential work."

Préaux, Claire, *Le Monde hellénistique*. 2 vols. Paris: Presses Universitaires de France, 1978.

Rist, John M., ed. *The Stoics*. Berkeley: University of California Press, 1978.

Robin, Léon. *La Morale antique*. Paris: Felix Alcan, 1938.

Sambursky, Samuel. *The Physical World of Late Antiquity*. London: Routledge & Kegan Paul: New York: Basic Books, 1962. An account of how thinkers from Aristotle to the sixth century after Christ understood the workings of the physical world. Many translations of key passages are incorporated into the text.

Tarn, W. W., and G. T. Griffith. *Hellenistic Civilization*. 3d ed. London: Arnold, 1952.

Walbank, Frank W. *Polybius*. Berkeley: University of California Press, 1972.

Webster, T. B. L. *Hellenistic Poetry and Art*. London: Methuen, 1964.

———. *An Introduction to Menander*. Manchester: Manchester University Press; New York: Barnes & Noble, 1974.

———. *Studies in Later Greek Comedy*. 2d ed. Manchester: Manchester University Press; New York: Barnes & Noble, 1970.

———. *Studies in Menander*. 2d ed. Manchester: Manchester University Press, 1960.

Will, Edouard. *Histoire politique de monde hellénistique*. 2 vols. Nancy: Presses Universitaires de Nancy, 1966–67.

CHAPTER 10

Greek Editions and Translations

Authors of the Roman period for whom Loeb editions exist include: Achilles Tatius (1917, revised 1969), Aeneas Tacticus (= "the Tactitian," 1923), Alciphron (1949), Appian (4 vols., 1912–31), Aristides (1973– , one volume in print), Arrian (2 vols., reedited 1976–84), Athenaeus (7 vols., 1927–41), Basil (4 vols., 1926–34), Clement of Alexandria (1919), Dio Cassius (9 vols., 1914–27), Dio Chrysostom (5 vols., 1932–51), Diodorus Siculus (12 vols., 1933–67), Diogenes Laertius (2 vols., 1925, revised 1938), Dionysius of Halicarnassus (7 vols. of *Roman Antiquities*, 1937–50, and 2 of *Critical Essays*, one in print, 1974), Epictetus (2 vols., 1925–28), Eusebius (2 vols., 1926–32), Galen (*On the Natural Faculties*, 1916), Herodian (2 vols., 1969), Josephus (9 vols., 1926–65), Julian (3 vols., 1913–23), Libanius (3 vols. projected, 2 in print, 1969–), "Longinus" (*On the Sublime*, bound with Aristotle's *Poetics*, rev. 1932), Longus (bound with Parthenius, 1916), Lucian (8 vols., 1913–67), Marcus Aurelius (1916, rev. 1930), Nonnus (3 vols., 1940), Pausanias (5 vols., 1918–35), Philo of Alexandria (10 vols., 1929–62), Philostratus (bound with Alciphron, 1949), Plotinus (7 vols. projected, 1966– ; 5 to be in print by fall 1984), Ptolemy (bound with Manetho, 1940), Quintus of Smyrna (1913), Sextus Empiricus (4 vols., 1933–49), and Strabo (8 vols., 1917–32).

1940), Quintus of Smyrna (1913), Sextus Empiricus (4 vols., 1933–49), and Strabo (8 vols., 1917–32).

There are also Loeb editions of Plutarch's *Lives* (11 vols., 1914–26) and *Moralia* (16 vols., 1927–76). The Budé edition of the *Lives* (*Vies*, ed. R. Flacelière et al., 1957–83) is now the best available. Recent English translations of Plutarch's *Lives* (by Rex Warner and Ian Scott-Kilvert) are available in four paperback volumes from Penguin Classics; there are also numerous editions of a classic translation attributed to Dryden. De Romilly notes the outstanding article on Plutarch in Pauly-Wissowa.

Burton, Anne. *Diodorus Siculus, Book 1: A Commentary*. Leiden: Brill, 1972.

Dorsch, T. S., trans. "Longinus," *On the Sublime*. In *Classical Literary Criticism*. Baltimore: Penguin, 1965.

Farquharson, Arthur S. L., ed. and trans. Marcus Aurelius Antoninus, *Meditations*. 2 vols. Oxford: Clarendon Press, 1944. Reprinted 1968.

Fowler, H. W., and F. G. Fowler, trans. *The Works of Lucian of Samosata, Complete, with Exceptions Specified in the Preface*. Oxford: Clarendon Press, 1905. Reprinted 1949.

Jacobitz, Karl G. Lucian, *Opera*. 3 vols. Leipzig: Teubner, 1887. Volume 3 contains a detailed index to Lucian's works.

Macleod, M. D. *Luciani Opera*. 3 vols. Oxford: Clarendon Press, 1972–80.

Migne, Jacques Paul. *Patrologiae Cursus Completus, Series Graeca*. 161 vols. in 166. Paris: Migne, 1857–66. Complete edition of the Greek Church Fathers. There are two indexes, by Ferdinand Cavallera (1912) and Theodore Hopfner (1928–45).

Schenkl, Heinrich, ed. Epictetus, *Dissertationes*, Stuttgart: Teubner, 1916. Reprinted 1965.

Warner, Rex, trans. Plutarch, *Moral Essays*. Harmondsworth and Baltimore: Penguin, 1971. Selections from the *Moralia*.

Critical Studies

Anderson, Graham. *Lucian: Theme and Variation in the Second Sophistic*. Leiden: Brill, 1976.

———. *Studies in Lucian's Comic Fiction*. Leiden: Brill, 1976. Continuation of the preceding entry.

Athanassiadi-Fowler, Polymnia. *Julian and Hellenism: An Intellectual Biography*. Oxford: Clarendon Press, 1981.

Babut, Daniel. *Plutarque et le stoicisme*. Paris: Presses Universitaires de France, 1969.

Barrow, Reginald. *Plutarch and His Times*. Bloomington: Indiana University Press, 1967.

Bidez, Joseph. *La Vie de l'empereur Julien*. 2d ed. Paris: Les Belles Lettres, 1965.

Bompaire, Jacques. *Lucien écrivain: Imitation et création*. Paris: Boccard, 1958.

Boulanger, André. *Aelius Aristide et la sophistique dans la province d'Asie au IIe siècle de notre ère*. 1923. Reprint, Paris: Boccard, 1968.

Bowersock, Glen Warren. *Greek Sophists in the Roman Empire*. Oxford: Clarendon Press, 1969.

———. *Julian the Apostate*. London: Duckworth, 1978.

Braun, René, and Richer, Jean, eds. *L'Empereur Julien*. 2 vols. Paris: Les Belles Lettres, 1978–81.

Bréhier, Emile. *La Philosophie de Plotin*. 1928. 2d ed. Paris: Vrin, 1961.

Caster, Marcel. *Lucien et la pensée religieuse de son temps*. Paris: Les Belles Lettres, 1937.

Festugière, André-Marie. *Antioche paienne et chrétienne*. Paris: Boccard, 1959.

———. *La Révélation d'Hermès Trismégiste*. 4 vols. Paris: J. Gabalda, 1949–54.

Fondation Hardt pour l'étude de l'antiquité classique. *Entretiens sur l'antiquité classique*. Vol. 5; *Les Sources de Plotin*. Vandoeuvres-Genève, 1960.

Germain, Gabriel. *Epictète et la spiritualité stoicienne*. Paris: Seuil, 1964.

Hadot, Pierre. *Plotin, ou la simplicité du regard*. Paris: Plon, 1963.

Jónes, Christopher P. *Plutarch and Rome*. Oxford: Clarendon Press, 1971.

———. *The Roman World of Dio Chrysostom*. Cambridge, Mass.: Harvard University Press, 1978.

Lévèque, Pierre. *Aurea Catena Homeri: Une étude sur l'allégorie grecque*. Paris: Les Belles Lettres, 1959.

Millar, Fergus. *A Study of Cassius Dio*. Oxford: Clarendon Press, 1964.

Momigliano, Arnaldo. *The Conflict between Paganism and Christianity in the Fourth Century*. Oxford: Clarendon Press, 1963.

———. *The Development of Greek Biography*. Cambridge, Mass.: Harvard University Press, 1971.

Perry, Ben Edwin. *The Ancient Romances: A Literary-Historical Account of Their Origins*. Berkeley: University of California Press, 1967.

Petit, Paul. *Les Etudiants de Libanius*. Paris: Nouvelles Editions Latines, 1956.

Puech, Aimé. *Historie de la littérature grecque chrétienne depuis les origines jusqu'à la fin du IVe siècle*. 3 vols. Paris: Les Belles Lettres, 1928–30.

Reardon, Bryan P. *Courants littéraires grecs des IIe et IIIe siècles aprés J.-C.* Paris: Les Belles Lettres, 1971.

Renan, Ernest. *Marc Aurèle et la fin du monde antique*. 6th ed. Paris: Calmann Lévy, 1891. Vol. 7 of his *Histoire des origines du christianisme*, 7 vols., 1888–91.

Rohde, Erwin. *Der Griechische Roman und seine Vorläufer*. 1876. 3d ed. Leipzig: Breitkopf & Härtel, 1914.

Russell, Donald Andrew. *Plutarch*. New York: Scribner, 1973.

Sanctis, Gaetano de. *Studi de storia della storiografia greca*. Florence: La Nuova Italia, 1951.

Schwartz, Eduard. *Griechische Geschichtschreiber*. Leipzig: Koehler & Amelang, 1959.

Schwartz, Jacques. *Biographie de Lucien de Samosate*. Brussels: Latomus, 1965.

Trouillard, Jean. *La Procession plotinienne*. Paris: Presses Universitaires de France, 1955.

———. *La Purification plotinienne*. Paris: Presses Universitaires de France, 1955.

Whittaker, Thomas. *The Neo-Platonists*. 2d ed. Cambridge: Cambridge University Press, 1918. Reprint, Hildesheim: Georg Olms, 1961.

Index

References in italics are to passages devoted exclusively or primarily to the subject indicated.